Slaver

OXFORD NEW HISTORIES OF PHILOSOPHY

Oxford New Histories of Philosophy provides essential resources for those aiming to
diversify the content of their philosophy courses, revisit traditional narratives about
the history of philosophy, or better understand the richness of philosophy's past.
Examining previously neglected or understudied philosophical figures, movements,
and traditions, the series includes both innovative new scholarship and
new primary sources.
*

Published in the series

Mexican Philosophy in the 20th Century: Essential Readings
Edited by Carlos Alberto Sánchez and Robert Eli Sanchez, Jr.

Sophie de Grouchy's Letters on Sympathy: *A Critical Engagement with Adam Smith's*
The Theory of Moral Sentiments
Edited by Sandrine Bergès and Eric Schliesser. Translated by Sandrine Bergès

Margaret Cavendish: Essential Writings
Edited by David Cunning

Women Philosophers of Seventeenth-Century England: Selected Correspondence
Edited by Jacqueline Broad

The Correspondence of Catharine Macaulay
Edited by Karen Green

Mary Shepherd's Essays on the Perception of an External Universe
Edited by Antonia Lolordo

Women Philosophers of Eighteenth-Century England: Selected Correspondence
Edited by Jacqueline Broad

*Frances Power Cobbe: Essential Writings of a Nineteenth-Century
Feminist Philosopher*
Edited by Alison Stone

*Korean Women Philosophers and the Ideal of a Female Sage: Essential Writings
of Im Yungjidang and Gang Jeongildang*
Edited and Translated by Philip J. Ivanhoe and Hwa Yeong Wang

Louise Dupin's Work on Women: *Selections*
Edited and Translated by Angela Hunter and Rebecca Wilkin

Edith Landmann-Kalischer: Essays on Art, Aesthetics, and Value
Edited by Samantha Matherne. Translated by Daniel O. Dahlstrom

*Mary Ann Shadd Cary: Essential Writings of a Nineteenth Century
Black Radical Feminist*
Edited by Nneka D. Dennie

Slavery and Race: Philosophical Debates in the Eighteenth-Century
Julia Jorati

Slavery and Race

*Philosophical Debates in
the Eighteenth Century*

JULIA JORATI

OXFORD
UNIVERSITY PRESS

Oxford University Press is a department of the University of Oxford. It furthers
the University's objective of excellence in research, scholarship, and education
by publishing worldwide. Oxford is a registered trade mark of Oxford University
Press in the UK and certain other countries.

Published in the United States of America by Oxford University Press
198 Madison Avenue, New York, NY 10016, United States of America.

Library of Congress Cataloging-in-Publication Data
Names: Jorati, Julia, author.
Title: Slavery and race : philosophical debates in the
eighteenth century / Julia Jorati.
Description: New York, NY : Oxford University Press, [2024] |
Series: Oxford new histories of philosophy |
Includes bibliographical references and index.
Identifiers: LCCN 2023033834 (print) | LCCN 2023033835 (ebook) |
ISBN 9780197659243 (paperback) | ISBN 9780197659236 (hardback) |
ISBN 9780197659267 (epub)
Subjects: LCSH: Slavery—Philosophy—History—18th century. |
Race—Philosophy—History—18th century.
Classification: LCC HT867.J673 2024 (print) | LCC HT867 (ebook) |
DDC 306.3/6209033—dc23/eng/20230905
LC record available at https://lccn.loc.gov/2023033834
LC ebook record available at https://lccn.loc.gov/2023033835

DOI: 10.1093/oso/9780197659236.001.0001

Contents

Series Editors' Foreword

Oxford New Histories of Philosophy (ONHP) speaks to a new climate in philosophy.

There is a growing awareness that philosophy's past is richer and more diverse than previously understood. It has become clear that canonical figures are best studied in a broad context. More exciting still is the recognition that our philosophical heritage contains long-forgotten innovative ideas, movements, and thinkers. Sometimes these thinkers warrant serious study in their own right; sometimes their importance resides in the conversations they helped reframe or problems they devised; often their philosophical proposals force us to rethink long-held assumptions about a period or genre; and frequently they cast well-known philosophical discussions in a fresh light.

There is also a mounting sense among philosophers that our discipline benefits from a diversity of perspectives and a commitment to inclusiveness. In a time when questions about justice, inequality, dignity, education, discrimination, and climate (to name a few) are especially vivid, it is appropriate to mine historical texts for insights that can shift conversations and reframe solutions. Given that philosophy's very long history contains astute discussions of a vast array of topics, the time is right to cast a broad historical net.

Lastly, there is increasing interest among philosophy instructors in speaking to the diversity and concerns of their students. Although historical discussions and texts can serve as a powerful means of doing so, finding the necessary time and tools to excavate long-buried historical materials is challenging.

Oxford New Histories of Philosophy is designed to address all these needs. It contains new editions and translations of significant historical texts. These primary materials make available, often for the first time, ideas and works by women, people of color, and movements in philosophy's past that were groundbreaking in their day, but left out of traditional accounts. Informative introductions help instructors and students navigate the new material. Alongside its primary texts, ONHP also publishes monographs and collections of essays that offer philosophically subtle analyses of understudied topics, movements, and figures. In combining primary materials and astute philosophical analyses, ONHP makes it easier for philosophers, historians, and instructors to include in their courses and research exciting new materials drawn from philosophy's past.

ONHP's range is wide, both historically and culturally. The series includes, for example, the writings of African American philosophers, twentieth-century Mexican philosophers, early modern and late medieval women, Islamic and Jewish authors, and non-western thinkers. It excavates and analyses problems and ideas that were prominent in their day, but forgotten by later historians. And it serves as a significant aid to philosophers in teaching and researching this material.

As we expand the range of philosophical voices, it is important to acknowledge one voice responsible for this series. Eileen O'Neill was a series editor until her death, December 1, 2017. She was instrumental in motivating and conceptualizing ONHP. Her brilliant scholarship, advocacy, and generosity made all the difference to the efforts that this series is meant to represent. She will be deeply missed, as a scholar and a friend.

We are proud to contribute to philosophy's present and to a richer understanding of its past.

Christia Mercer and Melvin Rogers
Series Editors

Acknowledgments

There are many individuals and institutions without whom this book would not have come into existence. First, I am deeply indebted to my teachers—particularly Michael Della Rocca and Bernd Ludwig, who taught me how to be a scholar of early modern philosophy and who were astoundingly generous and supportive. Next, I could not have written this book without my wonderful partner Hadi Jorati, who always cheers me on (and up!), and who put up not only with my distractedness but with ridiculously large piles of books in our living room. I also owe gratitude to my parents Elisabeth and Reinhard von Bodelschwingh, who funded my education and supported all my career choices wholeheartedly, even when these choices led me far away from them.

A fellowship at the Centre for Advanced Studies in the Humanities "Human Abilities" in Berlin enabled me to start writing this book in early 2021, during a Covid-19 lockdown. I thank the directors of this project—Dominik Perler and Barbara Vetter—for hosting me and for creating many opportunities to interact with the other fellows, despite the pandemic restrictions. Without this fellowship and the wonderful scholarly community at the Centre, I probably would not have tackled this book project. I am also thankful to the other fellows, the Centre's staff, the participants in Dominik's colloquium, and Dominik and Barbara themselves, who gave invaluable feedback when I presented early drafts of various chapters.

Moreover, I am profoundly grateful to Julie Walsh and Jeffrey McDonough, who organized a manuscript workshop for portions of this book and portions of my project about slavery and race in seventeenth-century philosophy. This workshop, which was held at Harvard University in April 2022 and generously funded by Harvard's Provostial Fund, was incredibly helpful and improved this book in numerous ways. In addition to Julie and Jeff, I thank everyone who participated in the workshop: Colin Chamberlain, Aaron Garrett, John Harfouch, Aminah Hasan-Birdwell, Rafeeq Hasan, Dwight Lewis, Alison McIntyre, Alison Peterman, Susanne Sreedhar, and Ken Winkler.

I have presented portions of this project to many different audiences, and I thank everyone who listened, asked questions, or made suggestions. These people include the participants in the workshop "Teleology, Mechanism and the Mind-Body Problem between Leibniz and Kant," the New York City Workshop in Early Modern Philosophy, the Royal Institute of Philosophy Lecture Series at Keele University, the University of Cape Town Philosophy Seminar, the Virtual Early Modern Philosophy Workshop, the Atlantic Canada Seminar in Early Modern Philosophy, the University of California, San Diego History of Philosophy Roundtable, the symposium "Slavery in Early Modern Philosophy" at the University of Toronto, and the Society for Early Modern Philosophy at Yale University. My discussions with all these fabulous scholars helped me organize my thoughts and gain a deeper understanding of the material.

Many people were kind enough to read portions of my manuscript and give me valuable feedback: Patrick Connolly, Adam Dahl, John Harpham, Rafeeq Hasan, Lauren Kopajtic, Dwight Lewis, Antonia LoLordo, Huaping Lu-Adler, Johan Olsthoorn, Hope Sample, Stephan Schmid, Hasana Sharp, Justin Smith, Susanne Sreedhar, Julie Walsh, Ken Winkler, and two anonymous referees for Oxford University Press. Bex Staneslow read the entire manuscript and made countless stylistic improvements; this editing work was generously funded by the University of Massachusetts Healy Endowment Grant. I also thank Christia Mercer and Melvin Rogers—the series editors—as well as OUP editor Peter Ohlin; they were enormously supportive and helped me solve several difficult problems.

Last, I owe gratitude to individuals and institutions who helped me discover and access primary and secondary literature. Aminah Hasan-Birdwell introduced me to several important primary authors and texts with whom I was unfamiliar; Pauline Kleingeld gave me access to transcriptions of some of Kant's lectures that I was unable to find elsewhere. The W. E. B. Du Bois Library at UMass helped me procure many obscure texts and—like the library of the Freie Universität in Berlin—enabled me to access print materials even during Covid lockdowns.

Introduction

Afro-British abolitionist and formerly enslaved man Quobna Ottobah Cugoano tells us in his 1787 book that some proponents of slavery believe that "the stealing, kidnapping, enslaving, persecuting or killing a black man, is . . . less criminal, than the same evil treatment of [some] other man of another complexion" (1999: 34). He reports that this double standard, though clearly unjustifiable, is widely accepted. Elsewhere in the book, Cugoano describes the attitudes he often encounters as a free Black man in England as follows:

> it cannot but be very discouraging to a man of my complexion . . . to meet with the evil aspersions of some men, who say . . . [t]hat an African is not entitled to any competent degree of knowledge, or capable of imbibing any sentiments of probity; and that nature designed him for some inferior link in the chain, fitted only to be a slave. (1999: 11–12)

In short, Cugoano tells us that some of his White contemporaries view Black people as naturally inferior in intellect and moral character, which in turn they use to defend transatlantic slavery. They also believe that Black people lack at least some of the moral rights that White people have and are fit only for slavery. Other Black authors in the eighteenth century describe their experiences of racism in very similar ways. Take, for instance, Absalom Jones and Richard Allen, two prominent African American theologians and leaders of the free Black community in Philadelphia who—like Cugoano— were formerly enslaved. In a 1794 pamphlet, they report that White people "stigmatize us as men, whose baseness is incurable, and who may therefore be held in a state of servitude, that a merciful man would not doom a beast to" (1794: 23).[1]

---

[1] We will discuss Cugoano, Jones, and Allen in more detail in chapters 1–2, and we will also examine several other descriptions of racist attitudes.

Slavery and Race. Julia Jorati, Oxford University Press. © Oxford University Press 2024.
DOI: 10.1093/oso/9780197659236.003.0001

These eloquent descriptions of racist attitudes are a perfect starting point for an exploration of connections between slavery and race in the eighteenth century—which is precisely what my books aims to do. More specifically, this book aims to investigate the philosophical ideas, theories, and arguments that occur in eighteenth-century debates about slavery, with a particular focus on the role that race plays in these debates. We will see that while some authors theorize about slavery without mentioning race explicitly, the racist attitudes that Cugoano, Jones, and Allen describe are central to large portions of these debates. Many defenders of the transatlantic slave trade employ the idea that Black people are naturally suited for slavery, and many opponents of slavery refute it. Some authors, along similar lines, attempt to defend slavery by contending that Black people are better off in slavery due to their allegedly inferior capacities or due to the purportedly terrible living conditions in Africa. Some proponents of slavery endorse the moral double standard that Cugoano describes: they view Black people as having an inferior moral status—as subpersons. We will also see, however, that these racist attitudes are not limited to proslavery authors. Many opponents of slavery share at least some of these attitudes.

By investigating the role that race plays in eighteenth-century debates about slavery, this book aims to serve as a resource for scholars, instructors, and students of philosophy. Most of the primary sources that this book explores are rarely taught or studied in philosophy departments. This unfortunate neglect has a variety of causes. One cause is that many of us are simply unfamiliar with these sources, in part because there is a dearth of literature about this material written specifically for scholars and students of philosophy. Even though scholars in other disciplines have published more extensively about these debates, they do not typically focus on the aspects that are most significant philosophically and often use methodologies that are unfamiliar to historians of philosophy. My book is written specifically for scholars, instructors, and students of philosophy and neighboring disciplines who are interested in this material and are looking to gain a better understanding of the relevant debates. I aim to introduce readers to many philosophically important texts about slavery from the eighteenth century, explore some interpretive questions about these texts, and point readers to further resources. I hope to illustrate that early modern discussions about slavery and its connections to race are an important part of the history of philosophy and deserve far more attention in our research and teaching.

I.1. Thematic Focus

This book is regrettably narrow in some respects and ludicrously broad in others. It is narrow because it is not about the history of slavery in general; it concentrates on one small aspect of this history: philosophical ideas, theories, and arguments about the moral permissibility of slavery and its relation to race. Early modern debates about slavery have many other important aspects that this book will ignore almost entirely. For instance, there are extensive discussions of legal, economic, and scriptural reasons for and against transatlantic slavery. Even within my focus area, I had to make many difficult choices about which authors and texts to include because there are simply too many. In one respect, then, the book's project is narrow. Yet it is extremely broad in other ways: it covers a huge number of texts written in English, French, Latin, and German in several European countries and parts of North America across an entire century, by authors of many different backgrounds. We will examine texts from a great variety of genres, including treatises, essays, dialogues, letters, sermons, poems, novels, plays, autobiographies, book reviews, pamphlets, petitions, and legal texts. Casting such a wide net will allow us to investigate a far larger range of perspectives and hence a greater breadth of philosophical ideas about slavery. I hope that the book strikes a balance between breadth and depth that allows readers to see the big picture and makes it easy to dive more deeply into specific aspects of the debate on their own.

Our whirlwind tour of eighteenth-century debates will take us to North America (chapter 1), Scotland (chapter 2), England (chapter 3), France (chapter 4), and Germany and the Netherlands (chapter 5). The tour could easily be expanded to include other stops. Unfortunately, space constraints, my linguistic limitations, and the types of primary texts that I was able to access forced me to limit myself to these six locations. By organizing my book geographically, I do not mean to suggest that these debates were self-contained. We will see, in fact, that the authors from these six locations were often familiar with each other's works and sometimes knew each other personally. Antislavery networks in Britain, America, and France were particularly closely connected. The reason I decided to separate the debates geographically is simply that other ways of organizing the material seemed even less helpful. Moreover, the political, social, legal, theological, and economic contexts—and to some extent the intellectual or philosophical contexts—in these places are different, which is sometimes relevant for un-derstanding the argumentation.

Two other limitations of my project are important to mention here. First, I am writing this book as a White woman who grew up in Germany. I have gained some awareness of the legacy of racial slavery since immigrating to the United States, but there is still a lot that I do not understand, and I do not have firsthand experience of the ways in which racism affects people of color. This perspective has inevitably shaped my book in many respects. In addition, I am limited methodologically by my academic training, which is mainly in the history of early modern philosophy and so-called analytic philosophy. While I have some background in religious studies and litera-ture as well, I have no formal training in history, philosophy of race, African American studies, political science, or many other relevant fields. I have tried to fill some of these gaps, but many remain.

A potential worry about the book's thematic focus is that it might be problematic to concentrate on philosophical ideas and arguments about slavery and race, for at least three reasons. One reason is that it may be wrong—and perhaps naive—to think that arguments, or philosophical ideas more generally, had a major impact on transatlantic slavery or its abolition. Arguably, philosophical ideas about slavery and race were not the reasons why Europeans started the transatlantic slave trade; rather, these ideas were developed after the fact, to defend an existing institution that was enormously lucrative. As Ibram X. Kendi argues, racist ideas are simply "the public relations arm" of racist institutions (2016: 509); they do not bring these institutions into existence. Likewise, the reason that trans-atlantic slavery was eventually abolished is arguably not that people were suddenly convinced by philosophical arguments against slavery. Rather, it was presumably due to political and economic factors. A related reason to worry about the book's focus is that instead of exploring ideas and theories about slavery and race, it may seem far more important to examine sys-temic racism—for instance, by investigating the legal frameworks behind transatlantic slavery—as well as the experiences and material conditions of enslaved people. A third and final reason to worry about the book's focus is that it may seem morally wrong to take the arguments for and against slavery seriously, since this may seem to suggest that the moral permis-sibility of slavery is genuinely up for debate. Or, at least, it may seem in-sensitive to dissect these arguments dispassionately as if they were mere theoretical curiosities.

These are serious worries; let me briefly respond. First, my book is not meant to suggest that philosophical ideas had important effects on transatlantic slavery or its abolition. Indeed, I do not aim to address the question of what caused the beginning, growth, and decline of transatlantic slavery. While that is an excellent question, I am interested in a completely different question: how did people in the eighteenth century theorize about slavery, and what role did race play in these theories? This question is important even if these theories had little or no direct impact on the transatlantic slave trade. After all, understanding the history of racist ideas is necessary—though not sufficient—for understanding racism more generally. The eighteenth century is particularly important for this history because many aspects of modern racial and racist thinking originated in this period.[2]

Investigating eighteenth-century ideas about slavery and race is also important for gaining a more accurate understanding of early modern philosophy. These ideas are historically important in their own right, and they are also intimately connected to other central philosophical debates. Indeed, many early modern theories about topics other than slavery—such as property rights, self-ownership, liberty, gender, war, human nature, and so on—are shaped by their authors' attitudes toward slavery and race.

Moreover, even if these ideas did not have large-scale effects on the transatlantic slave trade, they did have tangible effects on the lives of Black people in the early modern period. We already encountered testimony by Cugoano, Jones, and Allen about the negative impact that the racist attitudes of their contemporaries have had on them. Cugoano reports, for instance, how discouraging it is to be viewed and treated as inferior on a daily basis. He also notes later in his book that racist attitudes can make Black people physically unsafe: "the European seafaring people in general, who trade to foreign parts, have such a prejudice against Black People, that they use them more like asses than men, so that a Black Man is scarcely ever safe among them" (1999: 106). Other Black authors in the eighteenth century—along with some White authors—describe racism and its effects in very similar ways, as we will see in this book. These authors found it important to reflect on the nature of racist ideas and they attempted to fight slavery and racism through philosophical

---

[2] I am, of course, not the first to examine the history of racist ideas with a focus on the early modern period; other authors who have done this include Charles Mills (1997; 2005; 2006; 2014), Ibram X. Kendi (2016), and John Harfouch (2018).

argumentation. Whether these attempts were successful or not, they deserve a place in the history of philosophy.

Regarding the worry that it is morally wrong to take the arguments for and against slavery seriously, I think it matters how and why one examines these arguments. As historians of philosophy, we often investigate historical debates about a certain philosophical question in order to make progress on finding the correct answer to this question. For instance, we may study early modern discussions of the mind-body problem in order to come closer to solving this problem. Yet this is not what I aim to do in this book. It is not my goal to determine whether there is anything wrong with slavery and racist ideas, because there obviously is. Rather, I investigate these arguments simply because I find it important to understand how early modern authors thought about slavery and race. This is in part because as a historian of philosophy I want to understand central aspects of historical worldviews and their interconnections and in part because early modern ideas about slavery and race have shaped racial thinking ever since. I will try not to lose sight of the horrors of transatlantic slavery while discussing these ideas, and I will foreground texts by Black authors wherever possible.

I.2. Background and Terminology for Discussing Slavery

Before embarking on our tour of eighteenth-century debates about slavery, it will be helpful to survey the historical and theoretical background to these debates and clarify some important terminology. Let us start with the term 'slavery' itself, which can mean a variety of different things. Early modern authors sometimes use this term and corresponding terms in other languages in extremely broad ways—not only for the type of colonial chattel slavery that we associate with it today, but also for many other forms of subordination. These include not just various types of unfree labor, such as serfdom and other forms of feudalism, but also the subjection of citizens to a tyrannical monarch, the subjection of women to their husbands, the subjection of human reason to the passions, and the subjection of human souls to sin. Some authors draw careful distinctions between different kinds of unfree labor, for instance by distinguishing between slaves and servants, or slavery and servitude, while others place a broad range of subordination relations into one category. Accordingly, we find many different definitions of slavery in early modern texts. For example, some definitions insist that slavery must be involuntary on the part of the enslaved person, or that it must constitute a permanent and absolute subordination, or that it must be hereditary, or that the subordinated person must have the same legal status as chattel. Other definitions do not include these necessary conditions. Some authors use the term 'slavery' for any form of despotic rule, that is, for any type of rule that is exercised for the sake of the ruler's interests, using the ruled as mere instruments for the ruler's ends. This is how Aristotle defined despotic rule, and the rule of masters over their slaves is his central example. Despotic rule differs from what is typically called paternal rule, which is practiced for the sake of the ruled, and from good political rule, which is practiced for the common interest. Despotic rule benefits the ruled at best accidentally (Aristotle, *Politics* iii.6, 1984: 2029–30). This Aristotelian definition explains why early modern texts often use the term 'slavery' for the subordination of citizens to a despotic monarch and for the subordination of women to a tyrannical husband.

To navigate this conceptual maze, I find it most useful to treat 'slavery' as a cluster concept. In other words, instead of trying to find a definition that captures all and only the types of subordination that are relevant to this project, I will specify a paradigmatic type of slavery and then examine forms of subordination that bear a sufficient resemblance to this paradigm. The paradigm that is most relevant to this project is, of course, racial chattel slavery, and more specifically, the enslavement of Black people in European colonies in the United States and elsewhere in the New World in the eighteenth century.[3] I will typically refer to this type of slavery as 'transatlantic slavery'.[4] While transatlantic slavery in the eighteenth century was not completely uniform, this paradigm is specific enough to serve as a useful guide. Many of the texts we will examine in this book discuss this type of slavery directly. Yet I also include some texts that discuss broader or slightly different forms of subordination, since such discussions can be helpful for understanding early modern attitudes toward transatlantic slavery. Wherever relevant and possible, I will specify how a particular author defines slavery, or which forms of subordination the author examines.

---

[3] This is not the only form of slavery that was practiced in European colonies. For instance, colonists also enslaved American Indians. Yet my main focus will be on the enslavement of Black people.

[4] Some scholars use the terms 'African slavery' or 'Black slavery', but I avoid these terms because they can also refer to slavery practices within Africa.

There are a few theoretical frameworks that are particularly important for early modern debates about slavery. Authors who defend transatlantic slavery often claim that it is an instance of one or more forms of slavery that are traditionally viewed as licit. Before examining these traditional justifications, let us briefly note a few other common proslavery strategies. The White English poet Anna Seward (1742–1809) is a helpful source of several such strategies. In a letter to the White English abolitionist Josiah Wedgwood—written in February 1788, only a few months after Cugoano published his antislavery book—Seward admits that she used to oppose abolition but that the arguments contained in Wedgwood's previous letter changed her mind.[5] What is most interesting for our purposes is her detailed description of her earlier proslavery views and the reasons why she held them. This description includes a long list of common eighteenth-century defenses of slavery. For her, interestingly, these defenses did not amount to full moral justifications, since she viewed transatlantic slavery as unjust but necessary, and abolitionist efforts as "fruitless and dangerous, though just and humane" ([1788] 1811: 30). Other authors, however, took these types of defenses to be providing moral justifications for slavery.

One of Seward's past reasons for viewing transatlantic slavery as a necessary evil was economic: "the purchase, employment, and strict discipline of the negroes [is] absolutely necessary to maintain [England's] empire, and our commerce, in the Indies" (1811: 29). Thus, she used to oppose abolition in part because she worried that it would have devastating economic consequences for England. Economic considerations played a massive role in eighteenth-century debates about slavery—as one would expect, since transatlantic slavery constituted a large segment of the economies of Britain, France, the Netherlands, and the United States.[6] As we will see in this book, some antislavery authors argued that economic considerations are irrelevant because abolition is morally required regardless of its costs. Yet many antislavery authors used a different strategy, insisting that abolition would not have devastating economic effects. Some—including most famously Adam

---

[5] I was unable to determine whether Wedgwood's letter to Seward has come down to us. Wedgwood was a prominent abolitionist, one of whose main contributions to abolitionism was the well-known antislavery medallion "Am I Not a Man and a Brother?" Incidentally, Wedgwood's daughter Susannah, whose married name was Darwin, was the mother of the famous biologist Charles Darwin.

[6] For more on the role of economic considerations in proslavery thought, see Drescher 1986.

Smith—even argued that abolition would have positive economic effects for Europe.[7]

Seward additionally tells Wedgwood that her initial horror at reports about the cruel treatment of colonial slaves was offset by arguments that "negroes . . . [are] of a nature so sordid and insensible, as to render necessary a considerable degree of severity" (1811: 29) and that their temper is "treacherous, ungrateful, and bloody" (1811: 30). She also claims to have heard about cases in which masters who treated their slaves humanely were brutally killed by these slaves, which in her mind supported the claim that severity is necessary (1811: 29–30). In addition, proslavery acquaintances assured her that many reports about the cruelty of masters and overseers are either false or at least "infinitely exaggerated" (1811: 29). This has to be the case, she reasoned, since it would be contrary to the economic self-interest of slaveowners to treat their valuable human property so barbarously (1811: 29). And finally, she believed that "in some countries, the subjection of beings, that form the latest link in the chain descending from human to brute animality, was an evil inevitable" (1811: 30). This last consideration is a version of natural slavery, which is among the traditional justifications that we will examine in more detail soon. Natural slavery is the doctrine that it is permissible to enslave individuals or groups who are naturally inferior in specific ways. Seward, like Cugoano, connects this doctrine with the idea of a Great Chain of Being, or a hierarchical ordering of all created things, in which Black people were often thought to occupy a lower rank than White people.

At least two other common defenses of transatlantic slavery are missing from Seward's list. One is the claim that transatlantic slavery is justified because it saves countless souls. After all, according to this justification, many enslaved Black people convert to Christianity, and they would not have converted if they or their ancestors had remained in Africa. Another common defense is that the situation in Africa is so horrific that forcing Africans to live in "civilized" countries—even in slavery—benefits them. Some proslavery authors even go so far as to say that Black people are happier in colonial slavery than they would be in Africa.[8] These defenses are paternalist arguments, since they view it as permissible to force people into ways of life that are allegedly in their best interest.

---

[7] Unfortunately, while these economic debates are important, I will not be able to examine them in detail in this book.

[8] Eliphalet Pearson, whom we will discuss in chapter 1, endorses both these arguments (Parsons and Pearson 1773: 24–31).

Many defenders of transatlantic slavery invoke reasons like the ones just seen, and many opponents of slavery counter these types of arguments. However, authors on both sides of the debate frequently appeal to broader theoretical frameworks as well. These frameworks are general theories about what—if anything—can make it morally permissible to enslave a human being. The two most important sources of such theoretical frameworks are Christian theology and natural law ethics. These two frameworks overlap, but there are some purported theological justifications for slavery that draw directly on the Bible, rather than on natural law. The idea behind these justifications is that if the Bible commands or permits the enslavement of certain individuals or groups, then it is justified.

Natural law ethics has its roots in antiquity and developed many different branches during its long history. One idea that unites the various branches is a commitment to moral principles that are grounded in human nature. These principles are the 'natural laws' or the 'laws of nature.' In the Christian natural law tradition, these laws are part of God's plan for creation, but we can know them without reference to special divine revelation, simply through reasoning and examining human nature (Murphy 2019: §1.4). In other words, natural lawyers hold that we can deduce the moral laws that apply to human beings from an accurate understanding of human nature.

Proponents of natural law ethics can take surprisingly different positions on slavery. We can distinguish two broad branches of this tradition. According to one branch, a study of human nature reveals significant differences among individuals that make it natural for some human beings to be free and for others to be enslaved. This branch views human beings as naturally unequal. The other branch denies that there are significant natural differences and insists that it is the natural state of all human beings to be free and equal. Consequently, they argue, no human being is a slave by nature. In the eighteenth century, proponents of this second branch of natural law often argue that all humans possess certain natural rights, such as the right to life and liberty.

The natural law doctrine that all human beings are naturally free and equal, or have certain natural rights, has powerful potential for the abolitionist cause.[9] Many of the antislavery authors whom we will encounter in this book use this doctrine to argue against the moral permissibility of transatlantic slavery. It is important to note, however, that not all natural law theorists in

---

[9] For some of the features that make this doctrine particularly useful for the abolitionist cause, see Mills 1998: 174.

this period view this doctrine as applying to literally everyone. As Charles Mills convincingly argues, many authors implicitly restrict full moral personhood, and hence full natural rights, to Europeans or White people—or more specifically, to White men. According to Mills, these authors use a racist framework in which "non-Europeans are generally seen not as persons but as 'savages' and 'barbarians'" (Mills 2005: 171). In short, some natural lawyers do not appear to view these principles as truly universal. As we will see, several antislavery authors criticize their contemporaries for implicitly restricting these rights to White people. They argue that in order to be consistent, White people who claim to champion these rights must extend them to everyone. If Mills's interpretation is correct, this is an example of how moral principles from originally racist frameworks can be appropriated for antiracist projects.

It is also important to note that a commitment to the natural equality or natural liberty of all human beings is compatible with the doctrine that there are morally permissible forms of slavery. Most natural lawyers in this branch of the tradition hold that human conventions, circumstances, and actions can in principle justify enslavement. For instance, it is common to argue that people can licitly lose (or forfeit) their natural right to liberty through specific actions and circumstances, or that they can voluntarily give it up, selling (or alienating) it. While nature makes humans free and equal, specific circumstances and actions can make them unfree and unequal.

Figure I.1 captures the theoretical frameworks that are most important for eighteenth-century debates about slavery. Going from left to right, the first branching represents three major types of alleged justifications for slavery: the idea that enslavement can be justified by specific circumstances or actions, the idea that it can be justified by natural characteristics of the individuals or groups who are to be enslaved, and the idea that it can be justified through God, that is, through divine permission or divine intentions. I will refer to the first branch as 'circumstantial slavery' and the second as 'natural slavery.'

Circumstantial slavery has several subtypes, which are unified by the basic idea that specific actions or circumstances—rather than natural characteristics—justify slavery. It views slavery as resulting from bad luck or bad choices and as something that can in principle affect anyone. The most common types of circumstantial slavery are presented in the figure: (a) voluntary slavery, or the doctrine that individuals can sell themselves into slavery, typically because they are destitute, (b) slavery through parental sale, or the doctrine that parents have the right to sell their children into slavery,

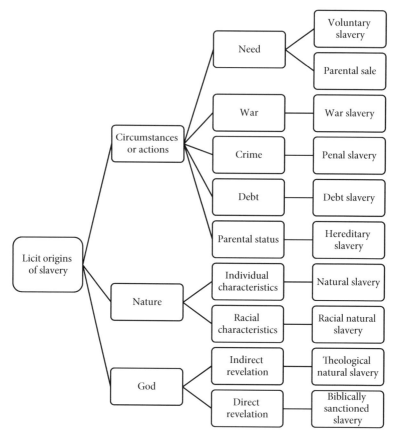

Figure I.1 Theories about the Licit Origins of Slavery

for instance when they have no other way to support their children, (c) war slavery, or the doctrine that it is permissible to enslave captured enemy soldiers in a war in lieu of killing them, (d) penal slavery, or the doctrine that it is permissible to enslave criminals as a just punishment for their crimes, (e) debt slavery, or the doctrine that it is permissible to enslave a debtor who cannot pay off their debt in another way, and finally (f) hereditary slavery, or the doctrine that children born to enslaved parents are automatically enslaved as well.[10] Practically everyone until the mid-eighteenth century

---

[10] Hereditary slavery is a type of circumstantial slavery because it is based not on the natural characteristics of the child, but simply on the circumstances into which the child is born. Some authors subsume this type under one of the other types, most commonly under debt slavery. The idea is that if the parents are enslaved and hence do not own resources to raise their children, these children

accepted at least one type of circumstantial slavery.[11] Yet some types started becoming controversial in the late seventeenth century, and beginning in the mid-eighteenth century, there were authors who rejected all types. We will see examples of such rejections in this book.

Some proslavery authors attempted to justify transatlantic slavery by arguing that it is a licit instance of at least one type of circumstantial slavery. The two most common such defenses are that the enslaved Black people purchased by European traders in West Africa were originally enslaved as prisoners of war in inter-African conflicts or as penal slaves.[12] That would make transatlantic slavery licit, in this theoretical framework, because it was traditionally thought that the rightful owner of an enslaved person has the right to sell this person to someone else. Some authors even claim that transatlantic slavery saves the lives of the people it enslaves since in the absence of European buyers, African governments would execute their prisoners and war captives.[13] There are also proslavery writers who claim that some transatlantic slaves were sold into slavery by their parents.[14] Proponents of these justifications typically also accept hereditary slavery and hence contend that the descendants of licit slaves automatically have the same status as their parents. In response to these arguments, antislavery authors have two options: they can reject the moral legitimacy of the various forms of circumstantial slavery, or they can argue that transatlantic slavery is not an instance of them. We will see many examples of both strategies in this book.

Natural slavery, as mentioned earlier, is the doctrine that some human beings possess natural characteristics—which could be physiological or mental—that mark them out for slavery. According to this doctrine, it is fitting or permissible to enslave people who possess these characteristics, independently of anything they have done and independently of their

depend on the master for sustenance during infancy. This means that they are indebted to the master and must work to pay off this debt once they are old enough.

[11] The only exceptions of which I am aware are some proponents of natural slavery who reject circumstantial slavery categorically because they hold that only natural slaves ought to be enslaved (e.g., Felden 1664: 3). I am not aware of any authors before the mid-eighteenth century who categorically reject both natural and circumstantial slavery.

[12] See, for instance, Bosman 1705: 364; Thompson 1772: 25–26; Long 1774: 388–89 and 394–95; Romans 1776: 108; Turnbull 1786: 11. For a helpful discussion of the role of war slavery in debates about the legitimacy of transatlantic slavery, see Glover 2017.

[13] See, for instance, Turnbull 1786: 10–11; Snelgrave 1734: 160–61; Beckford 1788: 60; Long 1774: 389; Parsons and Pearson 1773: 30–31.

[14] See, for instance, Long 1774: 388. We will see several other instances of this argument later, particularly in chapter 4.

circumstances. The idea goes back at least to Aristotle, who argues that there are human beings who lack the cognitive abilities required for life as a free person and who are therefore natural slaves, while others are natural masters (*Politics* i.5, 1984: 1990–91; i.13, 1984: 1999). He even claims that at least some "barbarian" nations are generally natural slaves and that this makes it permissible to wage war against these nations and enslave them (*Politics* i.2, 1984: 1987; i.7, 1984: 1992). While Aristotle's notion of "barbarians" is arguably not racial in a modern sense, there are many clear instances of racialized versions of the doctrine of natural slavery in the early modern period. Most relevantly, some early modern authors argued that all Black people—or all Black people from certain ethnic groups—are natural slaves because they possess racial traits that mark them out for slavery. One example is the White proslavery author Bernard Romans, who writes in 1776 that Black people are naturally inferior to White people (1776: 105) and that they are a "naturally subjected species of mankind" (1776: 107). This was also a common way to defend slavery in nineteenth-century antebellum America.[15] I will refer to this combination of natural slavery and racist ideas—or the doctrine that some racialized groups are natural slaves—as 'racial natural slavery.'

Racial natural slavery is enormously important for this book because it is the most direct way to employ race as a justification for enslavement. We have already seen references to this idea in Cugoano and Seward, and less directly in Jones and Allen. Nearly all the authors in this book discuss some version of racial natural slavery. It is one of the central aims of my book to show that this doctrine played a crucial role in eighteenth-century debates about slavery.

The observation that racial natural slavery is an important component of early modern proslavery discourse is far from new. Charles Mills, for instance, argues that the doctrine of racial natural slavery played an important role in modern racism (2021: 488–89), including Kant's racism (2014: 146). Indeed, there are some early modern authors who make this

---

[15] One of the most explicit versions occurs in the infamous 1861 Cornerstone Speech by Alexander H. Stephens, a White American politician and vice president of the Confederacy. Stephens claimed that the cornerstone of the Confederate States was "the great truth, that the negro is not equal to the white man; that slavery—subordination to the superior race—is his natural and normal condition" (1866: 721). Later, he contends that American slavery is in accordance with the natural law because "Subordination is [the negro's] place. He, by nature . . . is fitted for that condition which he occupies in our system" (1866: 722–23). See also George Frederick Holmes, who devotes an entire essay to this topic and discusses Aristotle's formulation of the doctrine in depth (Holmes 1850). For more proslavery arguments from the nineteenth century that rely on racial natural slavery, see Elliott 1860. For a discussion of these arguments, see Monoson 2011; Campbell 1974.

point—including Cugoano, as already seen. A particularly explicit example is the White New Jersey Quaker David Cooper, who writes in a 1772 pamphlet that the custom of enslaving Black people "casts the most indelible odium on the whole people, occasioning some from hence to infer that they are a different race, formed by the Creator for brutal services" (1772: 8). Cooper here contends—like several other early modern authors, as we will see in this book—that transatlantic slavery gave rise to racist attitudes and in particular to the racist idea that Black people are intended for slavery by God. He goes on to say that practically every proponent of transatlantic slavery adopted this doctrine, ridiculous and misguided as it is, since it is impossible to jus-tify the institution without it: "However extravagant such a supposition may appear, it is the only rational one that can fully justify the practice, and give peace of mind to a slave-keeper; . . . and I am fully persuaded there is few to be found who justifies the practice but is more or less tinctured with this opinion" (1772: 8). About fifteen years later, the White English abolitionist Thomas Clarkson makes a similar point. He states that when proponents of transatlantic slavery encounter refutations of their other attempts to justify the institution, they unfailingly resort to racial natural slavery, that is, to the idea "that the Africans are an inferiour link of the chain of nature, and are made for slavery" (*Essay* 3.7/3.8, 2010: 176). This suggests that eighteenth-century proponents of slavery routinely relied on racial natural slavery.[16]

The bottom branch of Figure I.1 comprises defenses of slavery that present the institution as authorized by God. Proponents of this strategy typically claim either that the Bible explicitly authorizes slavery or that we can infer this authorization from the characteristics that God has given to specific individuals or groups.[17] I categorize the former as an authorization through direct revelation and the latter as an authorization through indirect revela-tion. The idea that God authorized one group of human beings to enslave another group by giving this second group natural characteristics that mark them out for slavery is a theological version of natural slavery. Many versions of natural slavery are theological in a broad sense, since many proponents of

---

[16] Along similar lines, the White New England merchant Josiah Quincy Jr. reports in his 1773 journal that many people he encountered during his trip to the American South used racial natural slavery to defend the institution of slavery: "The Africans are said to be inferior in point of sense and understanding, sentiment and feeling, to the Europeans and other white nations. Hence the one infer a right to enslave the other" (Quincy 1915: 463).

[17] Some authors claim that we can infer this authorization from the mere fact that God has not stepped in to stop transatlantic slavery; Jonathan Edwards Jr., whom we will examine in chapter 1, refutes this type of argument explicitly (1791: 22).

natural slavery are Christians who view the natural law as part of God's plan. Yet I will reserve the label 'theological natural slavery' for something more specific. After all, it seems important to distinguish between authors who hold that certain natural characteristics directly justify someone's enslavement and authors who hold that such characteristics justify enslavement only indirectly, by constituting evidence of divine authorization.[18] Only the latter counts as theological natural slavery in my sense.

One proponent of theological natural slavery is the White Massachusetts judge and politician John Saffin (1626–1710). In a 1701 pamphlet, Saffin explicitly rejects the doctrine that all human beings are naturally free and equal (1997: 821), as well as the doctrine that Christians ought to love and respect all human beings equally (1997: 824). Instead, he argues, inequality and subordination are ordained by God. The doctrine that all human beings "have equal right to Liberty, and all outward comforts of this life," he contends, "seems to invert the Order that God hath set in the World" (1997: 821). After all, God has clearly ordained some human beings "to be born Slaves, and so to remain during their lives" (1997: 821). Saffin does not base this on any explicit Bible passage. Rather, he appears to base this claim on a general theory of divine providence as well as the biblical command to accept one's station in life (1997: 822). He does not state that all and only Black people are born to be slaves. Nevertheless, it is clear that he views his theory as applying most straightforwardly, or perhaps exclusively, to Black people. After all, he rejects the idea that Black people deserve the same "love, kindness, and . . . respect" as "the best of men" (1997: 824). Moreover, he ends his text with a short poem titled "The Negroes Character," which argues that the situation of enslaved Black people is not at all parallel to the situation of the biblical Joseph—who was enslaved unjustly—because Black people are innately "Cowardly and cruel," as well as "Libidinous, Deceitful, False and Rude" (1997: 825). Thus, Saffin appears to believe that transatlantic slavery is justified because God has ordained inequality and has marked out Black people as deserving of, and born for, slavery through their allegedly natural characteristics.

This book will not discuss alleged biblical justifications for transatlantic slavery in great depth. However, two such justifications will come up a few times: the curse of Ham and the curse of Cain. Let me say a few words about

---

[18] One reason why this distinction matters is that proponents of the latter type of theory do not need to claim that the characteristics in question have any direct or intrinsic moral relevance. Indeed, they can claim that characteristics that are morally neutral when considered in themselves—such as skin color—are a sign of God's intentions and thus have only an indirect or extrinsic moral relevance.

these two justifications, starting with the theory that the enslavement of modern Africans is licit because they descend from the biblical Ham, who was cursed to slavery. On this theory, modern humans descend from Noah's three sons Shem, Ham (sometimes spelled 'Cham'), and Japheth. More specifically, it was common to claim that Asians descend from Shem, Africans from Ham, and Europeans from Japheth.[19] According to Genesis, while Noah was drunk and sleeping, Ham saw him naked and told his brothers, who covered their father without looking at him (Genesis 9: 21–23).[20] As punishment for Ham's indiscretion, Noah cursed Ham's son Canaan to be a slave to Japheth and Shem, though some early modern authors claim that it was Ham himself and all his descendants who were cursed in this way. This switch often appears to be based on circular reasoning: since Africans were thought to descend from Ham's son Kush, rather than from Canaan, interpreters concluded that the curse could not have been limited to Canaan and his posterity (Goldenberg 2005: 177, 101). Some authors additionally claim that Black complexion was part of the punishment for Ham's posterity. A somewhat less common theory traces slavery and Blackness back even further, to Adam's son Cain.[21] According to Genesis, Cain killed his brother Abel and as punishment was cursed to wander the earth (Genesis 4:11–12). God marked Cain in an unspecified way in order to prevent other people from killing him (Genesis 4:15). Some later interpreters claim that Cain's mark is Black skin and that his punishment was slavery. In both biblical theories, slavery is a divinely sanctioned condition for an entire lineage of people: God ordains—or at least authorizes—the enslavement of all descendants of the original subject of the curse. The idea is that if modern Africans are descendants of these original subjects, Europeans can licitly enslave them based simply on their ancestry.

Let us take a quick look at a proponent of the curse of Ham theory from the eighteenth century: White British slave trader Gilbert Francklyn (1733–1799). In his 1789 *Answer to the Rev. Mr. Clarkson's Essay*, he examines the curse in Genesis 9 and argues that it clearly applies not just to Canaan but to all of Ham's sons—including Kush, who, according to Francklyn, was Black and the ancestor of modern Africans (letter 2, 1789: 31–32, 38). Thus, he contends, the Bible clearly asserts "that a considerable part of mankind were,

---

[19] This idea is based on Genesis 10.

[20] The history of interpretations of this story is complex and fascinating; for book-length treatments, see Haynes 2002; Whitford 2009; Goldenberg 2005; 2017.

[21] For an in-depth discussion of the history of this theory, see Goldenberg 2005: 178–82.

from the earliest ages, destined to live in a state of slavery to the other part; [and] that a part of those, so destined, were descended from a black ancestor" (1789: 34). This is obviously a form of biblically sanctioned slavery.

I.3. Background and Terminology for Discussing Race and Racism

Another important preliminary question concerns the meanings of the terms 'race' and 'racism.' The term 'race' was sometimes used in the early modern period, but it had several different meanings—for instance, it can mean 'lineage,' such as in the context of discussing a royal family. To make things even more complicated, early modern authors often used terms like 'species,' 'type,' or 'kind' to refer to what might be the concept of race, or they used terms like 'Black,' 'White,' 'Negro,' 'mulatto,' 'Moor,' or 'Ethiopian'—or terms like 'nation,' 'Guinean,' 'African,' 'English,' and 'European'—to refer to what appear to be racial categories. In short, the early modern terminology is extremely confusing, and we need independent criteria to determine whether a particular author is discussing race. The latter also applies to the term 'racism': this term was not coined until the late nineteenth or early twentieth century, which means that it does not occur at all in the primary texts we will examine here. Yet, as already seen, some early modern authors describe or theorize about prejudices against Black people—like Cugoano, Jones, and Allen—and some authors express attitudes that we would categorize as racist if someone expressed them today. Thus, while the term 'racism' did not exist, racism itself appears to have existed.

It is, however, controversial whether the terms 'race' and 'racism' can—or should—be applied to any discussions of human diversity in the early modern period and, if so, how. There is a danger of being anachronistic, that is, of applying these terms in a way that blurs crucial differences between the ways in which early modern authors conceived of human diversity and the ways in which we do today. For instance, one might suspect that the present-day concept is so intertwined with ideas from evolutionary biology that it would be misleading to use the same term for early modern views. Or one might consider it as linked inextricably to so-called scientific racism, which is typically thought to originate in the late eighteenth century. Accordingly, some scholars argue that modern racism originated during the time of the American Revolution (Fields and Fields 2012: 121); others suggest that Kant was the originator of modern racism.[22] If that is correct, it could be misleading to apply these concepts to any early modern theory prior to the late eighteenth century.

While there is a genuine danger of anachronism, there is also the opposite danger: obscuring important patterns and continuities between early modern ideas and later ideas. These patterns and continuities are crucial for the project of this book, and, more generally, they are important for anyone studying the history of race and racism. There are clearly important connections between the attitudes that Cugoano experienced and the racist attitudes that Black people experienced in the nineteenth and twentieth centuries and still experience today. Moreover, there are important continuities between the attitudes that Cugoano describes and the attitudes described in texts from the early eighteenth century and even the late seventeenth century.[23] Of course, there are also discontinuities. But whether we find specific continuities more relevant than specific discontinuities depends at least in part on our theoretical interests. What matters most for projects like mine are continuities with respect to the types of attitudes described by Cugoano.

A common justification for the thesis that one cannot find genuine instances of racial thinking or racism until the late eighteenth century is the assumption that such instances would have to be based on a well-developed theory of race. That assumption is mistaken. As Charles Mills points out—building on arguments by Audrey Smedley (1993) and David Stannard (1992)—"a concept can be in formation in popular consciousness long before its developed critical articulation by intellectuals" (Mills 2006: 223). And that appears to be the case for the concept 'race': it started out as a folk concept and was only theorized in systematic ways much later (Smedley 1993: 25). Even a rudimentary folk concept of race is sufficient for the formation of racist ideas. In other words, racist ideas can develop even in the absence of systematic theories of race. Since my book aims to investigate the ways in which racial or racist thinking shaped eighteenth-century debates about slavery, it is not a problem if most of the authors I examine did not endorse systematic theories of race. It is sufficient if they operated with a folk concept that is continuous in significant ways with our concept.

---

[22] Mills discusses the history of the latter attribution in depth (2014: 130–31).
[23] I explore the role of race and racism in seventeenth-century debates about slavery in Jorati, forthcoming.

Based on these considerations, it makes sense for the purposes of this project to understand race and racism—like slavery—as cluster concepts. Instead of starting with a set of necessary and sufficient conditions for racism or racial thinking, I will start with a paradigmatic example. The paradigm that is most relevant to my purposes are attitudes like the ones described by Cugoano in the passages I quoted earlier. The most central attitude is the belief that Black people are naturally inferior to White people and that due to this natural inferiority, Black people do not merit equal treatment, or have a lower moral status. This kind of racist attitude sometimes takes the form of racial natural slavery, but sometimes it does not. Indeed, we will encounter authors whose views are paradigmatically racist but who argue against transatlantic slavery.[24]

Many instances of my paradigm also fall under the definitions of racism proposed by some scholars of race. For instance, Charles Mills defines racism as "a normative system . . . that makes whiteness a prerequisite for full personhood and generally . . . limits nonwhites to 'subperson' status" (2005: 170). In a more recent paper, Mills proposes a broader definition, according to which racism consists of the following three beliefs: "(1) that the human race is subdivided into discrete 'races'; (2) that these races are hierarchically arranged; and (3) that this hierarchy is grounded in particular racially differentiated traits and tendencies," adding that possible grounds for racist hierarchies include "the cognitive, the characterological, the aesthetic, the physical, and the spiritual" (Mills 2014: 127–28). Somewhat similarly, George Fredrickson proposes that we understand racism as originating "from a mind-set that regards 'them' as different from 'us' in ways that are permanent and unbridgeable. This sense of difference provides a motive or rationale for using our power advantage to treat the ethnoracial Other in ways that we would regard as cruel or unjust if applied to members of our own group" (2015: 9). These definitions are helpful and capture nearly all the attitudes on which I want to focus. Nevertheless, I prefer not to use these definitions to delimit my project because I also want to examine attitudes that share only some features of my paradigm and that may not be covered by these definitions.

---

[24] This is only one of several important historical paradigms of racism. I do not mean to suggest that it is the only one, or even the most important one; it is simply the one that is most relevant to my project. Moreover, I focus on forms of racism that specifically target Black people, though there are, of course, also forms of racism that target other racialized groups.

What I will do when examining various historical statements about human diversity is to ask how close these statements are to the paradigm. This method will not always yield clear answers to the question of whether a specific conception of human diversity is racist. There will be some conceptions that resemble the paradigm in every way, others that are completely different, and yet others that are somewhere in the middle. However, encountering some vagueness in projects of this type is unsurprising. Race and racism are enormously messy concepts today, and their historical roots are even messier. This is not ultimately problematic for my project since it is not my goal to sort historical theories or authors neatly into the categories 'racist' and 'nonracist.' Rather, I simply aim to understand the extent to which eighteenth-century debates about slavery employed ideas that are continuous with, and contributed to, later instances of racist thinking. We should not expect this to be all-or-nothing.

Because of how important the term 'natural' is in my paradigmatic example of racism, I will say a few more words about it. The clearest case of a natural trait, in the relevant sense, is a trait that is innate or inborn. In other words, natural traits are not acquired during one's lifetime—for instance as a result of certain experiences, choices, or even cultural and environmental factors. If my skin turns red due to sun exposure, for example, this new skin color is not a natural trait of mine. Likewise, if I am afraid of clowns because I once had a negative experience at a circus, this fear is not natural. In contrast, an innate fear of spiders or an inborn tendency to have pale skin would count as natural in the sense that interests us here. Natural traits in the relevant sense are furthermore at least semipermanent, or not easily changeable. However, they need not be essential. A belief in natural differences among individuals or racial groups is compatible with the theory that all human beings belong to the same biological species or share the same essence. As a result, paradigmatically racist attitudes need not postulate an essential difference between Black and White people.

Even though this book is not about theories of race, it will be helpful to briefly mention some of the theoretical frameworks that eighteenth-century authors used when they theorized about race.[25] One major question for early modern authors concerned the origin of racial differences. The most commonly accepted theory was what we today call 'monogenesis'

---

[25] For much more extensive discussions of early modern theories of race, see Curran 2011; Smith 2015; Harfouch 2018; Garrett 2006.

or 'monogenism', which is simply the doctrine that all racial groups have common ancestors and were not originally distinct. Many early modern proponents of this doctrine argue that racial differences developed as a result of environmental factors, such as climate, diet, and geography. They typically hold that these environmental factors resulted in different physiological traits. Some also argue that they resulted in different character traits—sometimes described as 'national character'—and different mental capacities. Moreover, proponents of this theory usually claim that once racial groups have become differentiated, the relevant traits become hereditary and are hence natural traits. This divergence into racial groups is sometimes viewed as the result of the degeneration of groups who live in unfavorable environments, the evolution or advancement of groups who live in particularly favorable environments, or simply an adjustment to various environments that constitutes neither a deterioration nor an improvement of original human traits. For some proponents of this type of environmental account, the resulting differences are reversible: if people from one racial group live in a foreign environment for a sufficiently long time, they gradually acquire the characteristics that other people in that foreign environment possess. Other proponents view these differences as completely irreversible, and yet others hold that it would take a significant number of generations to undo these differences. There are also monogenists who reject this type of environmental theory altogether, for instance by claiming that God intervened at some point in human history to change the characteristics of specific groups.

Some early modern authors rejected monogenesis and instead claimed that different racial groups have completely separate origins. This doctrine is called 'polygenesis' or 'polygenism.' Because many early modern intellectuals considered this doctrine to be incompatible with the biblical account of creation, it was enormously controversial. Yet some authors defended it explicitly—we will see in chapter 4 that Voltaire is an example of this—while others flirted with it but did not embrace it fully. Polygenism allows for particularly extreme forms of racism that categorize some racial groups as literally subhuman and essentially inferior. It is important to note, however, that polygenism is not a necessary condition for racism as we are understanding it in this book. After all, monogenists can—and often do—embrace the attitudes that we are treating as paradigmatically racist here. They can claim, after all, that some racial groups are inferior to other groups in ways that are permanent or semipermanent.

It is worth noting that while very few published authors in the eighteenth century claim that Black people are literally subhuman, many antislavery authors ascribe this belief to their opponents. For instance, the White English novelist Charlotte Smith includes a character in her 1792 novel *Desmond* who defends slavery by endorsing the subhuman status of Black people and a version of racial natural slavery. This character, who is a member of Parliament and owns land in the West Indies, claims that "negroes . . . are not fit to be treated otherwise than as slaves, for they have not the same senses and feelings as we have. . . . They have no understanding to qualify them for any rank in society above slaves; and, indeed, are not to be called men—they are monkies" (1792, vol. 3: 162*).[26] An earlier and even more explicit example occurs in the anonymous 1773 pamphlet *Personal Slavery Established*, which appears to be a parody of Robert Nisbet's 1773 proslavery tract *Slavery not Forbidden by Scripture*. The anonymous author of the parody proposes to "subdivide the Africans into five *classes*, arranging them in the order as they approach nearest to reason, as 1st, Negroes, 2d, Ourang Outangs, 3d, Apes, 4th, Baboons, and 5th, Monkeys" (Anonymous 1977: 253). In both examples, the authors appear to be pointing to the absurdity of holding that Black people are subhuman, but at the same time, they appear to be ascribing this opinion to at least some proponents of slavery. How common this opinion was among proponents of slavery is somewhat unclear since it was not frequently defended in print.

With this background information in tow, we can now commence our tour of eighteenth-century debates about slavery and race, starting in North America. Some of the authors we will meet along the way will be familiar to nearly all readers—for instance, Thomas Jefferson, David Hume, Mary Wollstonecraft, Voltaire, and Immanuel Kant. Others will almost certainly be unfamiliar, but I hope that after finishing the book, many readers will want to deepen their acquaintance with some authors of the latter type.

---

[26] This edition's page numbers are irregular; there are two pages numbered '162,' the second of which has an asterisk, and it occurs two pages after page 168.

1

North American Debates about Slavery and Race

The first stop on our tour of eighteenth-century debates about slavery is North America—or more precisely, the British colonies in North America that later become the United States and the early American republic.[1] Several factors make the North American debate particularly interesting. First, and perhaps most obviously, most authors who participated in this debate were personally familiar with—and, in some cases, personally affected by—racial slavery. Some of them were currently or formerly enslaved, others current or former slaveowners. Even those who were in neither category lived in a society that was increasingly dependent on slave labor: in some southern colonies, enslaved people outnumbered free people, and there was a sizable population of enslaved people even in New England until the late eighteenth century. Second, White people in North America often portrayed themselves as champions of liberty. Some of them came to America in search of religious and political freedom, and, starting in the 1770s, colonials fought to liberate themselves from what they described as the tyranny of the British Crown. They claimed to value liberty so much that they were prepared to die for it. After independence, many White Americans proudly viewed their nation as an ideally free society, exemplifying the political theories of European philosophers who placed liberty at the center of their systems. It would be astounding not to find lively debates about slavery in a society that claimed to value liberty so much and at the same time practiced racial slavery on such a large scale. Third, North America was home to intense religious fervor. As a result, many people claimed to be firmly committed to theological doctrines that are difficult to square with racial slavery, such as the doctrine that all human beings are brethren or that one should love one's neighbor as oneself.[2]

---

[1] For the sake of simplicity, I will use 'North America' as shorthand.

[2] Charles Mills argues that "Christianity's ostensible universalism has never constituted more than a weak, easily overcome barrier against racism" (2005: 186). Even so, many antislavery writers invoke universalist Christian doctrines in their attempts to change their readers' minds. How successful this

Slavery and Race. Julia Jorati, Oxford University Press. © Oxford University Press 2024.
DOI: 10.1093/oso/9780197659236.003.0002

The central aim of this chapter is, quite simply, to introduce readers to some of the most remarkable texts about slavery in eighteenth-century North America, which historians of philosophy have so far ignored almost completely. We will concentrate mainly on antislavery texts, though we will encounter a few important proslavery texts along the way as well. I hope to illustrate that these texts are philosophically sophisticated, important to the history of race and racism, and that they ought to be read, studied, and taught by philosophers much more widely. While I will not be able to devote nearly as much attention to these texts as they deserve, I hope to whet my readers' appetites enough to motivate them to take a closer look themselves.

North American antislavery texts often borrow ideas from European philosophers.[3] Part of what is interesting is how they use widely accepted philosophical doctrines to craft arguments against transatlantic slavery, applying existing theories to a new context. This is an excellent example of applied ethics, and in many cases of what we would today call public philosophy, since these texts often target very broad audiences. Many of these authors find vivid and persuasive ways to show that general principles which their audience members already accept entail that racial slavery is wrong. Thus, some of these texts are noteworthy for the new ways in which they employ theories and ideas from European philosophy. Other texts do something even more original by explicitly analyzing race, racial bias, and the effects of enslavement.[4] The unparalleled context in which these authors write prompts them to philosophize about new subject matters. This is one respect in which the texts discussed in this chapter differ from most contemporaneous texts by authors residing in Europe, who were typically far less aware of the racial dynamics in America.

Our whirlwind tour of North American debates about slavery will reveal several important things.[5] First, we will see that some authors were acutely

strategy was is unclear, but it is clear that these religious ideas play an important role in eighteenth-century debates about slavery.

[3] A large proportion of texts draws, at least implicitly, on the natural law tradition. The European philosophers who appear to have influenced American antislavery writings most directly and most deeply include John Locke, Algernon Sidney, Francis Hutcheson, and Montesquieu. Hugo Grotius's and Samuel Pufendorf's philosophies also had a palpable influence on these debates. We will discuss Hutcheson in chapter 2 and Montesquieu in chapter 4. For the other authors, see Jorati, forthcoming.

[4] We will encounter these theoretical innovations in sections 1.4–1.5.

[5] I expect that these things will be surprising to many scholars and students of philosophy. People in other disciplines—such as American history, African American studies, and American literature—may find these things less surprising, since they are more familiar with these texts.

aware of racism and its effects, and they analyzed both with astonishing subtlety. They knew that racism played a major role in defenses of slavery and believed that modern racism was in part a cause and in part an effect of transatlantic slavery. When I started researching early modern antislavery writings from North America, this was one of the things that astonished me the most. At the same time, we will see that some antislavery authors explicitly endorse certain forms of racial bias. While arguing for equal rights and against racial slavery, some of these writers oppose miscegenation or defend the intellectual or cultural superiority of White people.[6] Only some argue for complete equality. Relatedly, we will see that racial natural slavery is almost always in the background of these discussions, and often in the foreground. Finally, we will see that the American Founders cannot get off the hook as easily as sometimes thought for their tolerance, or even outright support, of slavery.[7] Transatlantic slavery was far from universally accepted in their day; there was a well-organized antislavery movement in America quite some time before the Constitution was drafted. Indeed, members of the Constitutional Convention were lobbied extensively by antislavery activists and had access to a wealth of eloquent and philosophically sophisticated antislavery writings.[8]

The eighteenth century was a tumultuous time for North America, and antislavery debates reflect this. The two most important upheavals were the American Revolution and the subsequent founding of the United States. The Revolution impacted North American slavery in multiple ways. Many enslaved people were able to flee in the chaos of the war or gain freedom by agreeing to fight for the loyalists. This significantly increased the free Black population in America, and it also impacted the ways in which Americans

---

[6] A particularly striking example of someone who argues against slavery while holding that Black people are intellectually and morally inferior is the White Virginia physician and jurist Arthur Lee (1740–1792). Lee criticizes Adam Smith for unfairly portraying White American colonists as monsters and enslaved Black people as heroes. (Lee is referring to a passage from Smith's 1759 book *Theory of Moral Sentiments* 5.2.9, 1976: 206–7.) Against Smith, he contends that Black people are "the most detestable and vile [race] that ever the earth produced" (1764: 30). He describes them as barbarous, stubborn, vicious, and unintelligent (1764: 11–15), noting that these traits might be innate or the results of a lack of culture (1764: 38). On the other hand, Lee argues for the abolition of slavery, both because of its injustice and because of its negative effects on both masters and enslaved people (1764: 37–45; see also his 1767 "Address on Slavery," in Nash 1990: 91–96).

[7] Ta-Nehisi Coates makes this point as well (2012a).

[8] This is common knowledge among scholars who study early antislavery movements in America. However, historians of early modern philosophy are not always aware of it. The same is true for the general public in America, which in my experience—based on my discussions with undergraduate and graduate students—assumes that practically nobody criticized slavery in America until the nineteenth century and that the Founders can hence get off the hook quite easily.

thought about slavery. The attitude toward slavery of American colonists had already started changing before the Revolution: as we will see, there was a marked increase of antislavery sentiments in the decade or two leading up to American independence. While there had already been an antislavery movement in the first half of the eighteenth century and even to some extent in the late seventeenth century, it is around the middle of the eighteenth century that this movement truly came into its own.[9] A veritable flood of anti-slavery texts were published in North America during this time. One reason for this may be that the political and moral ideals invoked by many American colonists in this period made the injustice of transatlantic slavery particularly blatant. As W. E. B. Du Bois put it, "the new philosophy of 'Freedom' and the 'Rights of man,' which formed the corner-stone of the Revolution, made even the dullest realize that, at the very least, the slave-trade and a struggle for 'liberty' were not consistent" (2007: 30).[10] Or, to view this history through a materialist lens, there may have been economic and political factors that prompted more people in North America to oppose slavery.[11] In any case, calls for abolition increased significantly around this time. Most states in what is today the Northeast of the United States abolished slavery soon after American independence: Vermont in 1777, New Hampshire and Massachusetts (which then included Maine) in 1783, Connecticut and Rhode Island one year later, and Pennsylvania and New York gradually, starting in 1780 and 1799 respectively.

Even though there were many influential opponents of slavery in the Revolutionary Era, their abolitionist ideas ultimately did not make their way into the Declaration of Independence or the US Constitution. This was in part due to the opposition of some southern states that depended on slave labor to a large extent. Yet, as some historians argue, there were likely other factors that prevented northerners from insisting that the United States not

---

[9] We will examine very few texts from the first half of the eighteenth century in this chapter; one particularly important text from that period is Hepburn 1715. For the seventeenth-century debate, see Jorati, forthcoming.

[10] David Brion Davis refers to "a remarkable convergence of cultural and intellectual developments which . . . undercut traditional rationalizations for slavery" around the time when the American Revolution started (1999: 48; see also Nash 1990: 3–23). Even some eighteenth-century authors viewed things in this way. For instance, the White Massachusetts politician Samuel Dexter writes in 1795, "About the time of the Stamp Act [i.e. 1765], what before were only slight scruples in the minds of conscientious persons became serious doubts, and, with a considerable number, ripened into a firm persuasion, that the slave trade was malum in se [that is, bad in itself]" (1795: 2).

[11] Du Bois explains that one of the reasons was "the economic failure of slavery in the Middle and Eastern colonies" (2007: 30).

tolerate slavery in any of its territories (Nash 1990: 25–55). Economic and social factors—including the invention of the cotton gin in 1793—were presumably also key reasons why the antislavery movement in America became weaker toward the end of the eighteenth century (Kendi 2016: 127 and 131; Kolchin 2003: 86–88).

Because so many important texts about slavery were composed in eighteenth-century North America, this chapter would feel disjointed if we examined each separately in chronological order. Thus, I have structured the chapter around a few common themes, grouping together texts that make related points. This will make it easier to see the connections between these texts and to analyze the philosophical arguments they contain. In addition, it serves as an introduction to some central types of antislavery arguments which recur in European debates, as we will see in later chapters. I chose five broad themes that are particularly relevant to my project: (a) the doctrine that all human beings have equal natural rights, (b) the Golden Rule, that is, the principle that we ought to treat everyone else the way we would demand to be treated if we were in their place, (c) the doctrine that all human beings have the same souls, (d) the doctrine that all human beings have the same mental capacities, and (e) racial bias and its role in proslavery sentiments. Each section of this chapter examines one of these five themes. Some authors make notable contributions to multiple themes and hence appear in more than one section.

1.1. Equal Natural Rights

One major strategy in North American antislavery writings is the argument that all human beings have the same natural rights and that this makes the forcible enslavement of innocent human beings morally wrong. The popularity of this strategy is unsurprising since the equality of natural rights is widely accepted among early modern philosophers, who often present it as the main reason to reject natural slavery. As we saw in the introduction, this is a standard way for proponents of natural law ethics to argue that nobody is a slave by nature. The basic idea is that if all humans have the same natural rights—and particularly if these rights include a right to liberty or a right to equal treatment—then one cannot justify slavery based on racial differences or differences in natural human capacities. We can think of this argument as follows:

1. Racial differences and differences in natural capacities are irrelevant for determining a human being's natural rights.
2. If the doctrine of natural slavery is correct, then racial differences or differences in natural capacities are relevant for determining a human being's natural rights.
3. Therefore, the doctrine of natural slavery is incorrect.

The first premise of this argument is a direct consequence of the principle that all human beings have the same natural rights. Premise 2, in turn, appears to be an accurate statement about the doctrine of natural slavery. According to this doctrine, as we saw in the introduction, human beings with superior capacities have the natural right to enslave those with inferior capacities, and the latter therefore lack the natural right to liberty. Or, according to the racial version of natural slavery, entire racial groups are destined for slavery and lack the natural right to liberty. The argument's second premise is hence true by definition. Combined with the popularity of the doctrine of equal natural rights, this makes the argument enormously promising. Of course, there is evidence that many early modern philosophers implicitly restrict natural rights to White Europeans, and some even do so explicitly.[12] This means that the first premise does not state a platitude; it insists that these popular principles must be applied more broadly than they often are.

Many early modern authors accept the doctrine of equal natural rights not just for philosophical but for theological reasons: Christian theology teaches that God created all human beings equal, in God's image. Each human soul—regardless of the person's race, place of birth, gender, or social position—is capable of salvation and has the same status under God. Commonly cited biblical evidence for this equality includes Romans 2:11, which states that "there is no respect of persons with God"—that is, God judges each person impartially, according to their deeds—as well as Acts 17:26, which states that God has "made of one blood all nations of men." Antislavery authors in this period often combine theological and philosophical considerations freely.

In the North American context, the doctrine of equal rights becomes a particularly potent weapon in the abolitionist arsenal during the Revolutionary Era due to the centrality of this doctrine in arguments for American independence and subsequently in the self-conception of the newly founded United

---

[12] See Mills 1997. I explore evidence that this was the case for seventeenth-century natural law theorists in Jorati, forthcoming.

States. Thus, many antislavery writers highlight the hypocrisy of those who argue passionately for the importance of liberty while subjecting innocent people to the most horrific bondage. As Abigail Adams reflects in a letter to her husband John, it is "a most iniquitous scheme . . . to fight ourselves for what we are daily robbing and plundering from those who have as good a right to freedom as we have" (September 24, 1774, 1876: 41–42).

In the current section, we will take a look at some particularly noteworthy examples of authors who invoke equal natural rights to argue against slavery. These authors do not typically argue for the doctrine of equal rights, nor do they typically theorize in depth about these rights. What makes their discussions of equal rights philosophically interesting is the way in which they apply commonly accepted doctrines to a specific context: racial slavery in America. These applications also shed light on the history of racism. We will start with authors who invoke racial equality or equal rights to criticize transatlantic slavery and then turn to authors who address the hypocrisy of White Americans during the Revolutionary Era.

1.1.1. Racial Equality

One of the many antislavery authors who appeal to equal natural rights is James Otis (1725–1783), a White lawyer and political activist from Massachusetts. In his 1764 treatise *The Rights of the British Colonies Asserted and Proved*, Otis argues against racial justifications for slavery by noting that all men—"white or black"—are born free. Then he ridicules those who justify slavery on racial grounds:

> No better reasons can be given, for enslaving those of any color than such as baron Montesquieu has humorously given. . . . Does it follow that tis right to enslave a man because he is black? Will short curl'd hair like wool, instead of christian hair, as tis called by those, whose hearts are as hard as the nether millstone, help the argument? Can any logical inference in favour of slavery, be drawn from a flat nose, a long or short face. Nothing better can be said in favor of a trade that is the most shocking violation of the law of nature. (2015: 140)

Like Montesquieu—whom we will examine in chapter 4—Otis here describes racial justifications for slavery as preposterous and at the same time as the best strategy available to those who defend transatlantic slavery. Hence, the transatlantic slave trade is indefensible; there is no justification for denying Black people the natural right to liberty. Physical traits such as skin color, hair texture, and nose shape are obviously irrelevant for natural rights.

After the Declaration of Independence had been composed and circulated, many antislavery authors appealed to this document to argue against slavery and for racial equality. One of the first antislavery writers to do so was Lemuel Haynes (1753–1833), a biracial Calvinist minister who lived in Massachusetts, Connecticut, and Vermont.[13] Haynes begins his tract *Liberty Further Extended: Or Free Thoughts on the Illegality of Slave-keeping*— probably composed in 1776—with the famous passage about self-evident truths from the Declaration of Independence.[14] He then uses the ideals described in this passage to argue for his main thesis, namely, "That an *African*, or, in other terms, *that a Negro may Justly Challenge, and has an undeniable right to his Liberty: Consequently, the practise of Slave-keeping, which so much abounds in this Land is illicit*" (1990: 19). All human beings clearly have the same moral rights, he states, since they are all of the same species (1990: 19).[15] It is ridiculous to think that differences in skin color could result in different natural rights. As he asks sarcastically, "Because a man is not of the same color with his Neighbour, shall he Be Deprived of those things that Distinguish him from Beasts of the field?" (1990: 20; spelling modernized).

In a particularly interesting passage, Haynes asks his opponents why according to them White people—and more specifically White English people—have different natural rights than Black people. Did the Englishman receive these special privileges "in his original constitution? or By Some Subsequent grant? Or Does he Boast of some higher Descent that gives him this pre-eminence?" (1990: 20; spelling modernized). Clearly not, Haynes responds. There is no basis for the claim that White people have more extensive natural rights than Black people. There simply are no differences in descent or nature between these two groups, or at least none that could justify a difference in natural rights. Nor, he adds, is there any reason to think God granted White people special rights at some point in history. Haynes

---

[13] Haynes's biography is fascinating: he is the son of a Black man and a White woman about whom we know very little. His parents abandoned him when he was an infant, and he was raised by a White family in Massachusetts as an indentured servant (Bogin 1983: 85–86; Newman 1990: xi; MacLam 1990: xix–xx; Jeffers 2017: 133–36). For more on Haynes's life and thought, see Saillant 2003.

[14] This text appears to have been intended for publication, though the only extant manuscript is unfinished (Bogin 1983: 89–90).

[15] Like many others, Haynes justifies the claim about the sameness of species by referring to Acts 17:26, which states that God made all nations "of one Blood."

then turns to the question of whether Black people may have forfeited their natural rights. He acknowledges that people who behave criminally or immorally sometimes forfeit their right to liberty because they are no longer fit for society. Yet, he continues, this type of explanation cannot possibly apply to Black Africans generally; it applies at most to some individuals. It is clearly not true that every single African has forfeited their right to liberty through a crime or through immoral behavior (1990: 20). This argument is interesting in part because it confirms that Haynes is specifically addressing racial justifications for slavery: he is responding to people who claim that all Africans, or all Black people, deserve to be slaves. And to argue against this, he refutes each of the ways in which such a general claim about a group might be justified: through differences in natural capacities and in descent, through special divine favors, or through rights forfeiture. This argument by elimination is designed to show that there is simply no basis whatsoever for the claim that all Black people deserve to be slaves.

James Forten (1766–1841), a free Black Philadelphia businessman, argues in a similar way in an 1800 letter to George Thacher (or, as Forten spells the name, Thatcher), a member of Congress from Massachusetts: "Though our faces are black, yet we are men; and though many of us cannot write, yet we all have the feelings and passions of men, and are as anxious to enjoy the birth-right of the human race as those who from our ignorance draw an argument against our Petition" (in Porter 1995: 333).[16] This passage goes beyond the familiar argument that Black and White people are equally human and hence have the same natural rights; it also stresses that all human beings have the same passions, and particularly, the same love of liberty. Forten asks Thacher later in this letter to "Judge what must be our feelings, to find ourselves treated as a species of property, and levelled with the brute creation" (in Porter 1995: 333).[17]

A final author who is important for examining the ways in which Americans used the doctrine of equal natural rights to assess the permissibility of slavery is Thomas Jefferson, the White slaveholder and Founding Father from Virginia who became president of the United States at the

---

[16] The petition to which Forten is referring is the 1799 petition to the US president and Congress signed by Absalom Jones and many other free Black Philadelphians (in Porter 1995: 330–32). Thacher had supported the petition, and Forten composed his letter to thank him for his support (McClish 2007: 304).

[17] Discussions about the equality of passions as well as the love of liberty will play a central role in chapters 2 and 3, when we discuss Scottish and English debates about slavery. Forten's appeals to the passions are reminiscent of the eighteenth-century Scottish tradition (McClish 2007).

beginning of the nineteenth century. Jefferson's writings are vivid illustrations of the fraught relation between the ideals of the American Revolution and racial slavery.[18] He claims to be committed to universal natural rights, most famously in the Declaration of Independence, of which he was the primary author.[19] He sometimes even claims that these rights are incompatible with racial slavery. At the same time, he personally owned large numbers of enslaved people until the end of his life and held extremely racist beliefs about the natural capacities of Black people.[20] These racist beliefs, which Jefferson expresses most explicitly in his 1785 *Notes on the State of Virginia*, had an enormous impact on American racism.[21] It is surely also relevant that, as a politician with extensive power, he did not make abolition a priority. These facts, in addition to the large role he played in shaping American laws and institutions, make Jefferson's writings important for present purposes.

One place in which Jefferson claims that transatlantic slavery violates the natural rights of Black people is a draft of the Declaration of Independence. This draft accuses the British king of waging "cruel war against human nature itself, violating it's most sacred rights of life and liberty in the persons of a distant people who never offended him, captivating & carrying them into slavery in another hemisphere, or to incur miserable death in their transportation thither" (1984: 22). On the most straightforward reading, this passage states that Africans, like all human beings, have the right to life and liberty, and that transatlantic slavery is wrong because it violates these rights. As Jefferson explains in his 1821 autobiography, this passage—which he describes as "reprobating the enslaving [of] the inhabitants of Africa"—was

[18] For in-depth discussions, see Kendi 2016: 104–59; Andrews 2001; Jordan 1968: 429–81.

[19] Incidentally, there is evidence that Jefferson took these natural rights to be known not through reason but through our moral sense. For instance, he explains in a letter to John Manners, dated June 12, 1817, that "the evidence of . . . our right to life, liberty, the use of our faculties, the pursuit of happiness, is not left to the feeble and sophistical investigations of reason but is impressed on the sense of every man" (2014: 432–33). Likewise, he writes to Peter Carr on August 10, 1787, that "Man . . . was endowed with a sense of right & wrong. . . . This sense . . . is the true foundation of morality" (1984: 901).

[20] Some historians argue that Jefferson was unable to free his slaves because of his debts and that there is no basis for concluding that he was unwilling to free them (e.g., Countryman 2012: 70–71). However, this cannot be the full explanation—among other things because Jefferson also advised others, who were not in debt, against freeing their slaves, claiming that it would be a betrayal of their country (letter to Edward Coles, August 25, 1814, 1984: 1346).

[21] The famous African American abolitionist David Walker writes in his 1829 *Appeal . . . to the Coloured Citizens of the World* that one of Jefferson's racist claims "has in truth injured us more, and has been as great a barrier to our emancipation as any thing that has ever been advanced against us" (Article 2, 2011: 31); he adds that Jefferson's racist claims "have sunk deep into the hearts of millions of the whites, and never will be removed this side of eternity" (2011: 32). He devotes large portions of his *Appeal* to discussing and refuting Jefferson's statements. For a general discussion of the reception of Jefferson's racist claims, see Jordan 1968: 440–45.

removed in the final draft of the Declaration, "in complaisance to South Carolina and Georgia" (1984: 18). Taken at face value, this suggests that Jefferson was firmly committed to universal or transracial natural rights and saw clearly that transatlantic slavery violated these rights. Portions of his 1785 work *Notes on the State of Virginia* give a similar impression. After describing the negative effects of the institution of slavery on free and enslaved people in America, he asks rhetorically, "with what execration should the stateman be loaded, who permitting one half of the citizens thus to trample on the rights of the other, transforms those into despots, and these into enemies, destroys the morals of the one part, and the amor patriæ of the other" (Query 18, 1984: 288).[22] A few sentences later, he adds that God cannot possibly side with White Americans on this issue, who should therefore fear their creator's wrath (1984: 289). He then expresses the hope that everyone will soon come to realize that slavery is wrong and prepare "for a total emancipation" (1984: 289). Here again, Jefferson appears to express a firm commitment to transracial natural rights and an opposition to transatlantic slavery.[23]

However, there are reasons not to take Jefferson's claims about the universality of natural rights and his opposition to slavery at face value. These reasons include the fact that he only freed a very small proportion of his own slaves and did not advocate abolition as fervently as a genuine commitment to these ideals would require. Thus, if he truly believed that transatlantic slavery violated natural rights, he was unwilling to act in ways that are consistent with this belief. This means that he was, at the very least, far less concerned about the violation of the rights of Black than of White people: he was willing to risk everything to rectify the violation of White natural rights during the American Revolution and unwilling to risk anything to rectify the far more blatant violation of Black natural rights.

This discrepancy is likely due to Jefferson's appallingly racist attitudes, which he expressed openly. In *Notes on the State of Virginia*, for instance, he hypothesizes that "the blacks, whether originally a distinct race, or made distinct by time and circumstances, are inferior to the Whites in the

---

[22] Ta-Nehisi Coates describes the long passage in which Jefferson discusses the negative effects of slavery on both masters and enslaved people as "just beautiful, beautiful writing reflecting a clarity of thought and understanding that I have rarely encountered in Jefferson's contemporaries" (2012b).

[23] In his Sixth Annual Message to Congress in 1806, Jefferson also expresses relief that Congress will soon be permitted by the constitution "to withdraw the citizens of the United States from all further participation in those violations of human rights which have been so long continued on the unoffending inhabitants of Africa" (1984: 528). See Kolchin for a helpful discussion of changes in Jefferson's attitude toward slavery during his lifetime (2003: 88–89). For a book-length discussion, see Wiencek 2012.

endowments both of body and mind," though he also acknowledges that his evidence for this hypothesis is insufficient (Query 14, 1984: 270). A few pages earlier, he makes a stronger claim: there is proof that the "inferiority [of Black people] is not the effect merely of their condition of life" (Query 14, 1984: 267). This proof comprises the alleged fact that mixed-race people are physically and mentally superior to unmixed Black people, whereas Black people who live in the same conditions as White people do not show signs of improvement.[24] He also claims that, based on his own experiences, Black people are "in reason much inferior" to Whites and incapable of producing art or literature (Query 14, 1984: 266). In response to potential counterexamples like Phillis Wheatley and Ignatius Sancho, he disparages their literary achievements. Wheatley, he writes, was not a genuine poet and "The compositions published under her name are below the dignity of criticism" (Query 14, 1984: 267). Likewise, he describes Sancho's writings as inferior to the prose of White authors and as "always substituting sentiment for demonstration" (Query 14, 1984: 267). For good measure, he also raises doubts about their authenticity.[25] Of course, Jefferson's belief in intellectual differences is logically compatible with a commitment to moral equality. He says so explicitly, for instance in a letter to Henri Gregoire from February 25, 1809: "whatever be [Black people's] degree of talent it is no measure of their rights" (1984: 1202). Nevertheless, even if Jefferson believed that Black and White people have the same moral rights, he clearly also believed in White supremacy. This presumably explains why he was not as committed to the abolitionist cause as he ought to have been, given his moral principles.

[24] Jefferson provides another purported proof, namely that among ancient Roman slaves—whom he describes as White—there were many artists and scientists, whereas there are none among transatlantic slaves. Since Roman slaves were treated worse than American slaves are, he claims, this shows that the mental inferiority of Black people is natural rather than due to environmental factors (Query 14, 1984: 268). In a letter to Chastellux from June 7, 1785, he seems more optimistic that environmental changes can gradually remedy the purported inferiority: "I believe the Indian, then, to be, in body and mind, equal to the white man. I have supposed the black man, in his present state, might not be so; but it would be hazardous to affirm, that, equally cultivated for a few generations, he would not become so" (1984: 801).

[25] Jefferson says something similar about the almanacs published by Benjamin Banneker, a Black surveyor and mathematician whom we will discuss later: "we know [Banneker] had spherical trigonometry enough to make almanacs, but not without the suspicion of aid from Ellicot, who was his neighbor & friend, & never missed an opportunity of puffing him. I have a long letter from Banneker, which shews him to have had a mind of very common stature indeed" (letter to Joel Barlow, October 8, 1809, 2004: 588–89). In the same letter, Jefferson dismisses a book chronicling exceptional achievements of Black people by claiming that these reports are largely unauthenticated and sometimes about men of color with some "degree of mixture" (2004: 588). As Winthrop Jordan aptly puts it, it is clear that in this respect Jefferson did not have "a happily receptive scientific mind patiently awaiting appropriate evidence" (1968: 454); Jefferson dismissed any evidence that was incompatible with his belief in the intellectual inferiority of Black people.

1.1.2. American Hypocrisy

Many antislavery authors in the Revolutionary Era level accusations of hypocrisy against White Americans—such as Jefferson—who enslave their fellow human beings while claiming to be champions of liberty and universal natural rights.[26] Several Black opponents of slavery make use of this argumentative strategy. One example is Caesar Sarter, a formerly enslaved Black man who published a short antislavery text titled *Essay on Slavery* in 1774.[27] Addressing proponents of slavery, he writes dryly, "I need not point out the absurdity of your exertions for liberty, while you have slaves in your houses" (1990: 170 / 1977: 340). Several petitions by enslaved and free Black men employ a similar rhetoric, for instance, a 1773 petition by four enslaved Black Bostonians: Peter Bestes, Sambo Freeman, Felix Holbrook, and Chester Joie. This petition advocates a policy that would allow enslaved people to work for wages one day a week and eventually purchase their own freedom. The authors start by expressing their approval of the recent efforts of Massachusetts legislators to free themselves from slavery, that is, from their subjection to the British Crown. Then—with what appears to be a note of sarcasm—they add, "We expect great things from men who have made such a noble stand against the designs of their fellow-men to enslave them" (Nash 1990: 173 / Aptheker 1979: 7). With this and their subsequent proposal for providing enslaved people a path to freedom, they subtly point out that the very principles that American politicians invoke to criticize British rule undermine transatlantic slavery.

In January 1777, formerly enslaved Prince Hall (1735–1807) and seven other Black men in Massachusetts whose names are unknown composed another noteworthy petition.[28] The petitioners echo language from the recently composed Declaration of Independence by referencing the universal and inalienable right to liberty.[29] Based on this right, the authors note, slavery is clearly "in violation of Laws of Nature and of Nations" (in Bruns 1977: 428–29; spelling modernized). Toward the end of the petition, they

---

[26] One of the first was the White minister Nathaniel Appleton (1767: 19 / Bruns 1977: 136). Appleton may even have been the first to raise this point (Rosenthal 1973: 74–75). Many later antislavery writers follow suit. For instance, Thomas Paine makes this point in his 1775 "Letter to the Pennsylvania Journal" (in Basker 2012: 64).

[27] For more information about Sarter, see Cameron 2014: 41–44.

[28] For more about Prince Hall and his other philosophical writings, see Levecq 2008: 164–78.

[29] A petition by nineteen enslaved people in New Hampshire from November 1779 spells out the argument from God-given universal rights more extensively, though without echoing the Declaration of Independence as clearly (in Bruns 1977: 452–53).

express astonishment about the fact "that it has never been considered that every principle from which America has acted in the course of their unhappy difficulties with Great Britain pleads stronger than a thousand arguments in favour of your petitioners" (Bruns 1977: 429; spelling modernized). Taking an even more direct approach, they then point out the inconsistency of White Americans who act "the part which they condemn and oppose in others" (Bruns 1977: 429; spelling modernized).

Prime and Prince,[30] two enslaved Black men who submitted a petition to the General Assembly of the State of Connecticut in 1779, use a similar strategy. They raise the hypocrisy argument while also invoking theological reasons for the equality of all human beings, asking "whether it is consistent with the present Claims, of the united States, to hold so many Thousands, of the Race of Adam, our Common Father, in perpetual Slavery" (in Nash 1990: 175 / Aptheker 1979: 11). They also reject racial natural slavery: having reflected on their rights and obligations, they state, "we . . . can never be convinced that we were made to be Slaves" (Nash 1990: 175 / Aptheker 1979: 11).

The enslaved Black poet and prose writer Jupiter Hammon (1711–ca. 1806), who lived in New York, makes a similar point in his *Address to the Negroes in the State of New York* when looking back at the Revolutionary War in 1787:

> That liberty is a great thing we may know from our own feelings, and we may likewise judge so from the conduct of the white-people, in the late war. How much money has been spent, and how many lives has been lost, to defend their liberty. I must say that I have hoped that God would open their eyes, when they were so much engaged for liberty, to think of the state of the poor blacks, and to pity us. (1787: 12–13)

Hammon chose to make this point somewhat indirectly, but the idea is nevertheless clear: White revolutionaries should have fought not only for their own freedom but also for the freedom of enslaved Black people, whose situation was far worse than a subjection to the British Crown. Like other authors, Hammon draws a direct connection between the political liberty for which

---

[30] The petition is signed by Prime and Prince, "in Behalf of themselves and other Petitioners" (Nash 1990: 176 / Aptheker 1979: 12). The document does not state the authors' full names; they merely identify themselves as "prime a Negro man servant to Mr. Vam A. Sturge of Fairfield" and "Prince a Negro man servant of Capt. Stephen Jenings of Fairfield" (Nash 1990: 176 / Aptheker 1979: 12).

the revolutionaries fought and the freedom from slavery to which Black Americans are entitled.

Another author who raises the hypocrisy point is Black poet Phillis Wheatley (c. 1753–1784), one of the best known authors discussed in this chapter.[31] She was also a celebrity during her lifetime, both in America and Europe, and her achievements as a poet were often cited as evidence against the intellectual inferiority of Black people.[32] Wheatley was born somewhere in West Africa and sold into slavery as a young child.[33] She was purchased by a merchant in Boston and remained enslaved until 1773, when she was manumitted upon publishing a book of poetry. In her poems, particularly the ones she composed while enslaved, her statements about slavery are quite guarded—as one might expect, given her circumstances. Yet she keeps returning to the topic of liberty and her abduction from Africa, making her stance quite clear.[34]

One of her most relevant poems is "To the Right Honourable WILLIAM, Earl of DARTMOUTH, His Majesty's Principal Secretary of State for North-America, & co.," composed in 1772 and published in 1773. This poem is addressed to the British statesman William Legge. The first two stanzas praise America's freedom from "wanton *Tyranny*" (2001: 39–40). The speaker turns to her biography in the next stanza, explaining that her appreciation for freedom is partially due to the fact that she was kidnapped in her native Africa and sold into slavery. She vividly describes the "pangs excruciating" that her parents must have felt when she was taken from them, as well as the cruelty and heartlessness of her kidnappers (2001: 40). The stanza ends with the lines, "Such, such is my case. And can I then but pray / Others may never feel tyrannic sway?" (2001: 40).[35] This poem draws a direct parallel between the political tyranny from which America is attempting to free itself and the slavery to which Wheatley and many other Black people are subjected in America: the speaker notes that she wants America to be free

[31] For a helpful overview of Wheatley's life, work, and ideas, as well as a compelling argument for her importance for the history of philosophy, see Garrett 2023.

[32] See, for instance, Crawford 1784: 5–7 and Clarkson, *Essay* 3.7/3.8 ([1786/1788] 2010: 180–81). For a helpful overview, see Carretta 2001. It is of course relevant that Wheatley was not just Black, but a Black woman, which in the eyes of her contemporaries makes her accomplishments even more noteworthy.

[33] Wheatley's birth name is unknown, as is her exact place of birth. Her slave name derives from the name of the slave ship on which she arrived—the *Phillis*—and her master's last name, Wheatley. After she married John Peters in 1778, she used his last name.

[34] For a discussion of Wheatley's place in the Black abolitionist tradition, see Cameron 2014: 29–41.

[35] There are two other variants of this poem, which use slightly different wording to make what I take to be the same point; see 2001: 128–31.

from tyranny because of her firsthand knowledge of the horrors of transatlantic slavery. Someone who understands how horrible slavery is cannot but want to counter tyranny in all its forms. And this clearly works in the opposite direction as well: those who fight political tyranny, if they are consistent, must oppose transatlantic slavery. Thus, this poem seems to contain a subtle version of the hypocrisy argument.

Wheatley criticizes this hypocrisy far more explicitly after she becomes free. One particularly helpful text is a 1774 letter to Samson Occom, a Presbyterian minister and member of the Mohegan nation. Occom was a longtime friend of Wheatley's and of the Wheatley family, that is, the family who used to enslave her and with whom she still lived at the time.[36] In her letter—subsequently published in several newspapers in New England—Wheatley thanks Occom for a previous letter that unfortunately does not survive, but in which he evidently argued for the equal rights of Black people.[37] She writes, "I . . . am greatly satisfied with your Reasons respecting the Negroes, and think highly reasonable what you offer in Vindication of their natural Rights" (2001: 152). Later in this letter, she claims that God has given every human being a "Love of Freedom" (2001: 153). The most relevant portion of this letter is its last two sentences, in which Wheatley expresses the hypocrisy point. Those who are involved in the slave trade, she states, are acting absurdly, since their "Words and Actions are so diametrically opposite" (2001: 153). She ends by noting sarcastically, "How well the Cry for Liberty, and the reverse Disposition for the Exercise of oppressive Power over others agree,—I humbly think it does not require the Penetration of a Philosopher to determine" (2001: 153). In other words, the hypocrisy of White Americans who support transatlantic slavery could hardly be more obvious.[38]

---

[36] Occom also supported a proposal by Samuel Hopkins to send Wheatley to Africa as a missionary. Occom refers to this plan in the postscript of a letter to Susannah Wheatley from March 5, 1771: "what harm woud it be to Send Phillis to her Native Country as a Female Preacher to her kindred, you know Quaker Women are alow'd to preach, and why not others in an Extraordinary Case" (Occom 2006: 97). Phillis Wheatley politely declined this proposal, explaining that it was too dangerous and that she did not speak any African languages (letter to John Thornton, October 30, 1774, 1966: 211).

[37] For more information, see Occom 2006: 97 n. 67; 2006: 5.

[38] Four years later, during the Revolutionary War, she makes a related point in the poem "On the Death of General Wooster." In this poem, the speaker imagines the dying general's prayer in which he asks God to grant the Patriots victory. Toward the end of his prayer, he worries that it would be presumptuous for Americans to expect support from God, "While yet (O deed ungenerous!) they disgrace / And hold in bondage Afric's blameless race" (2001: 93).

One antislavery pamphlet, published anonymously in 1783 by the White New Jersey Quaker David Cooper (1725–1795), makes the hypocritical attitudes of Americans its main focus.[39] This is clear even from its title: *A Serious Address to the Rulers of America, On the Inconsistency of their Conduct Respecting Slavery: Forming a Contrast between the Encroachments of England on American Liberty and American Injustice in Tolerating Slavery.* Cooper cleverly juxtaposes the grievances of White Americans with the injustice of slavery by splitting portions of his text into two columns. In the left column, he describes the ways in which England has treated its American colonies and quotes from several important texts such as the Declaration of Independence. In the right column, he describes the condition of enslaved Black people and argues that the principles invoked in the left column directly undermine the legitimacy of transatlantic slavery.[40] At one point, for instance, he quotes a passage from the 1774 "Address to the People of Great Britain" in the left column—a passage in which American revolutionaries insist that they have the same freedom as their "fellow-subjects in Britain." Cooper's corresponding entry in the right column reads, "Does this reasoning apply more forcibly in favour of a white skin than a black one?" (1783: 12 / Nash 1990: 122). Similarly, next to the famous lines from the Declaration of Independence declaring all men to be created equal and to have equal inalienable rights, he quips,

> If these solemn *truths* . . . are *self-evident*: unless we can shew that the African race are not *men*, words can hardly express the amazement which naturally arises on reflecting, that the very people who make these pompous declarations are slave-holders, and, by their legislative, tell us, that these blessings were only meant to be the *rights* of *white men*, not of *all men*. (1783: 14 / Nash 1990: 123–24)

In short, Cooper bluntly accuses the Founders of implicitly restricting the supposedly universal inalienable rights to White people, or as denying that Black people are human.[41]

---

[39] George Washington owned a copy of this pamphlet; see Bruns 1977: 476 for an image of the cover page of Washington's copy.

[40] Unfortunately, Bruns does not reproduce this two-column format (1977: 475–86), which makes his edition highly confusing. Nash reproduces it, however (Nash 1990: 117–31).

[41] White Virginia law professor St. George Tucker makes a similar point in 1796. After lamenting the hypocrisy of Americans, he notes that these inconsistencies arise from a "partial system of morality which confines rights and injuries, to particular complexions" (1796: 10)—that is, a racist system of morality that gives only White people moral rights.

These accusations of hypocrisy do not end after the Revolutionary War or even with the ratification of the US Constitution. Indeed, one of the most brilliant instances of this accusation occurs in Benjamin Banneker's 1791 letter to Thomas Jefferson, which was published one year later.[42] Banneker (1731–1806), a free Black man born in Maryland, was a surveyor and mathematician who also wrote poetry and published almanacs. In his letter, which accompanied one of his almanacs, Banneker first tries to convince Jefferson to help eradicate the many prevalent prejudices against Black people (August 19, 1791, Basker 2012: 129–30 / Jefferson 1986: 49). Next, he argues that "it is the indispensible duty of those, who maintain for themselves the rights of human nature, . . . to extend their power and influence to the relief of every part of the human race" (Basker 2012: 130 / Jefferson 1986: 50). Getting even more direct, he then points out that if Jefferson and other White revolutionaries are sincere in their claims about natural rights, they simply must do what they can to free enslaved Black people from "the unjustifiable cruelty and barbarism of men" (Basker 2012: 130 / Jefferson 1986: 50). Later, he asks Jefferson to think back to the Revolutionary Era and remember the sentiments he expressed so eloquently in the Declaration of Independence (Basker 2012: 131 / Jefferson 1986: 51). In this context, Banneker levels the most direct accusation of hypocrisy against Jefferson, which deserves to be quoted at length:

> This [i.e., the Revolutionary Era], Sir, was a time when you clearly saw into the injustice of a state of slavery, and in which you had just apprehensions of the horrors of its condition. . . . [B]ut, Sir, how pitiable is it to reflect, that although you were so fully convinced of the benevolence of the Father of Mankind, and of his equal and impartial distribution of these rights and privileges, which he hath conferred upon them, that you should at the same time counteract his mercies, in detaining by fraud and violence so numerous a part of my brethren, under groaning captivity and cruel oppression, that you should at the same time be found guilty of that most criminal act, which you professedly detested in others, with respect to yourselves. (Basker 2012: 131 / Jefferson 1986: 51)

---

[42] For a helpful discussion of this letter and its context, see Andrews 2001.

Banneker is splendidly direct in this passage: he accuses Jefferson not only of a "pitiable" inconsistency but also of fraud, violence, oppression, and of being guilty of a "most criminal act."[43]

Antislavery poetry often invokes the idea of equal natural rights as well and criticizes the hypocrisy of Americans. One excellent example is a poem titled *The American in Algiers, or the Patriot of Seventy-Six in Captivity*, published in 1797 by an anonymous author who identifies as a "sable bard," that is, a Black poet (1797: 21). Addressing those who fought in the Revolutionary War, or White Americans generally, this poem asks:

> Where are the rights you once so fondly taught?
> Or where the liberty for which you fought?
> You say all men were first created free,
> Whence then the right t' usurp their liberty?
> Hath not the African as good a right,
> Deriv'd from nature to enslave the white?
> As whites to say the hue our climate gave,
> Our rights shall forfeit and ourselves enslave?
>
> (1797: 26 / Basker 2012: 174)

What is particularly interesting about this poem is that it not only invokes equal rights and criticizes hypocrisy, but it also points out how ridiculous it is to claim that Black skin—which is simply a product of climate—results directly in the forfeiture of rights. Within the natural law framework that views all human beings as naturally and inalienably free, the only way to lose one's right to liberty is to forfeit it through some action, such as a crime. Yet it would be absurd to claim that simply being Black is a way of forfeiting one's natural liberty. Thus, this poem implies, the idea of natural liberty is inconsistent with racial slavery.

1.2. The Golden Rule and Imaginary Role Reversal

In addition to doctrines about equal natural rights, many North American antislavery texts invoke the Golden Rule, the moral principle that we ought to treat others the way we would want to be treated if the positions were

---

[43] I briefly discuss Jefferson's response to this letter at the end of this chapter.

reversed. This principle has great intuitive appeal and receives additional support from the Bible, which explicitly commands it.[44] We can view the Golden Rule as a cousin of the doctrine of equal natural rights. After all, the rule states that if we claim a certain right for ourselves or demand that others treat us in a certain way, we need to accord the same right to other people. We cannot consistently assert that a certain behavior is wrong when directed at us but permissible when directed at others in the same circumstances. Thus, this rule presupposes that all human beings are entitled to the same treatment in the same circumstances.

The Golden Rule is a powerful tool for antislavery writers because American slaveholders ought to find it difficult to view their behavior as consistent with this rule. It is hard to claim truthfully that if you were an enslaved Black person in America, you would not demand to be freed. Some early modern authors attempt to reconcile the Golden Rule with slavery by arguing that this rule only requires slaveholders to treat enslaved people humanely, since that is what slaveholders would demand if they were enslaved.[45] However, it seems clear that the Golden Rule should apply not only to someone's treatment while in slavery but also to slavery itself. If slaveholders ask themselves what they would demand if they had been enslaved illicitly, the honest answer is surely that they would demand to be set free, not merely to be treated humanely while remaining in slavery.[46] Thus, the idea behind Golden Rule arguments against slavery is the following:

1. If American slaveholders were in the position of their slaves, they would demand to be freed.
2. Everyone should treat others the way they would demand to be treated if they were in the others' position.
3. Therefore, American slaveholders should free their slaves.

Some antislavery writers combine this appeal to the Golden Rule with graphic descriptions of the brutality of the slave trade, the cruelty of

---

[44] According to the New Testament, Jesus commands the Golden Rule both in the Sermon on the Mount (Matthew 7:12) and the Sermon on the Plain (Luke 6:31). A closely related Christian principle is loving one's neighbor as oneself (e.g., Luke 10:27 and Galatians 5:14). Both principles occur frequently in antislavery texts.

[45] One author who argues this way is Raimundo Hormoza, a Spanish Jesuit who lived in England and published a proslavery work under the pen name "Raymond Harris" (*Scriptural Researches* 3.23–24, 1788: 73–74).

[46] Elhanan Winchester (1751–1797), a White preacher and theologian, argues this explicitly in a 1774 sermon (Basker 2012: 58 / Bruns 1977: 363).

masters and overseers, and the plight of enslaved people more generally. These descriptions make it even more difficult for slaveholders to maintain that their actions are consistent with the Golden Rule. Other writers go farther yet and ask their White readers to imagine in vivid detail how they would feel if they were kidnapped from their homes, separated from their loved ones, crammed into a ship, taken to a faraway country, and then forced to perform backbreaking tasks for heartless masters. In what follows, we will explore some representative examples of this imaginary role reversal and other antislavery arguments based on the Golden Rule. Like the arguments discussed in the previous section, these arguments are philosophically valuable mainly because they apply a widely accepted moral principle in new and resourceful ways to transatlantic slavery.

One author who employs an imaginary role reversal is Caesar Sarter, whom we already encountered earlier. In his 1774 *Essay on Slavery*, he describes several very specific scenarios that he asks his readers to imagine—for instance, being separated from their "tender and beloved offspring, whom, not an hour before, perhaps, they were fondling in their arms and in whom they were promising themselves much future happiness" (1990: 168 / 1977: 338). Another scenario involves getting kidnapped and transported across the ocean together with one's loved ones and then being sold separately at a slave auction, never to see them again (1990: 169 / 1977: 339).[47]

White Connecticut theologian and pastor Jonathan Edwards Jr. (1745–1801), son of the even more prominent Jonathan Edwards Sr.,[48] discusses the Golden Rule in particular detail in his sermon *The Injustice and Impolicy of the Slave Trade, and of the Slavery of the Africans* (1791). He starts his sermon by quoting Matthew 7:12, one of the New Testament passages commanding the Golden Rule. He then clarifies the rule's meaning in a helpful way: it does not require us to do whatever we would wish in the other person's circumstances, but only what we would *reasonably* wish in those circumstances (1791: 3). This Bible passage is especially suitable for an antislavery sermon, he claims, because the Golden Rule "is particularly useful to direct our conduct toward inferiours, and those whom we have in our power" (1791: 4). He does not explain why it is particularly useful for this

---

[47] Other authors who use versions of this strategy include Benjamin Rush (1773b: 50–52); Levi Hart (1775: 18–19 / Bruns 1977: 346–47); Lemuel Haynes ([1776] 1990: 22); the anonymous author of *Essay on Negro Slavery, No. 1*, published in 1788 under the apparent pseudonym "Othello" (in Basker 2012: 108); and Samuel Hopkins in his 1776 *Dialogue* (1852: 573 and 583).

[48] Jonathan Edwards Sr. did not share his son's antislavery views; see Minkema 2002.

purpose, but his idea might be that we need to be especially circumspect in our behavior toward those over whom we have authority, since they lack the power to defend themselves against unjust treatment. Next, Edwards applies the Golden Rule to slavery, making the familiar point that slavery is clearly incompatible with this rule and that skin color is irrelevant (1791: 4). In this context, he uses a notable argument: differences in skin color form a continuous spectrum, with the inhabitants of Germany on one end and those of Guinea on the other end. Thus, one reason why Black complexion cannot be a justification for enslavement is that there is clearly no sharp line between Black and White (1791: 4).[49]

One author even provides an explanation of why—despite the intuitiveness of the Golden Rule—so many White people in America cannot see the wrongness of slavery. This is the anonymous author of the pamphlet *Tyrannical Libertymen: A Discourse upon Negro Slavery in the United States*, published in New Hampshire in 1795, who argues that "we ourselves [i.e., White Americans] are too secure to *imagine* the case our own; otherwise we might appeal to [the Golden Rule]" (1795: 5). The suggestion appears to be that White Americans take their freedom from personal slavery for granted and have a hard time putting themselves into the shoes of enslaved people. The author then implores his readers to try harder to apply the Golden Rule and to ask themselves "with what feeling should *we* stand forth for sale, be slaves, be called *that species of property*; we, who denied our parent country the right of taxing us, and edged our swords to maintain our liberty, or to die!" (1795: 5–6).

The idea of role reversal is also present in early modern fiction. One excellent example is the 1794 play *Slaves in Algiers; or, A Struggle for Freedom* by White British-American novelist Susanna Haswell Rowson (1762–1824), most famous for her novel *Charlotte Temple*. In the play, Rowson appears to use a particularly elaborate version of the role reversal strategy: she illustrates the wrongness of slavery by describing the plight of a few fictional White Americans who become enslaved in Algiers. Interpreters disagree about whether this play is meant as a criticism of transatlantic slavery.[50] It is

---

[49] The Scottish author James Ramsay makes a similar point (1784: 7), but not nearly as explicitly as Edwards. English author Thomas Clarkson uses this argument more explicitly (*Essay* 3.8/3.9 [1786/1788], 2010: 189–90). This point is similar to a reason often cited against the reality of race today: alleged racial differences like skin color come in degrees and thus cannot yield sharply delineated racial groups (see Zack 2002: 88).

[50] See Oldfield 2013: 152–54; Dillon 2004; Montgomery 1994.

difficult, however, not to read it that way—especially since Rowson explicitly criticizes the transatlantic slave trade elsewhere.[51] Moreover, several other writers in this period invoke the enslavement of White Americans on the Barbary Coast in order to argue against transatlantic slavery. It was a popular argumentative strategy.[52]

Rowson's play describes many different aspects of the plight of enslaved White and North African people on the Barbary Coast. Several of the characters make claims suggesting that slavery is generally unjustifiable and worse than death (1794: 60, 68).[53] Moreover, when the White slaves gain freedom at the end of the play and overpower the governor of Algiers, one of the Americans assures him, "we neither mean to enslave your person, or put a period to your existence—we are freemen, and while we assert the rights of men, we dare not infringe the privileges of a fellow-creature" (1794: 70). In this way, the White American claims that it would be wrong to enslave an African man, even though this man has wronged him in the most hor-rific ways. Another White American—Rebecca—adds that "By the Christian law, no man should be a slave; it is a word so abject, that, but to speak it dyes the cheek with crimson. . . . [L]et us not throw on another's neck, the chains we scorn to wear" (1794: 70). These quotations make it clear that the play illustrates not just the wrongness of enslaving White people on the Barbary Coast, but the wrongness of slavery in general. Rowson's choice to focus on the suffering of White slaves in Algiers, rather than of Black people in America, is presumably meant to help White Americans understand the wrongness of slavery by imagining themselves enslaved.

A few years later, White American jurist and playwright Royall Tyler (1757–1826) uses a very similar plot device to argue against slavery. His widely read 1797 two-volume novel *The Algerine Captive* is the fictional au-tobiography of a White American man who is captured and enslaved on the Barbary Coast while working as a surgeon on a slave ship. Shortly after his capture, one of the enslaved Black people from the slave ship secretly brings him food. The narrator is very touched and amazed that "one of those men,

---

[51] See Rowson 1788: 1–8 / Basker 2012: 116–18. I will discuss this text in section 1.3.

[52] Examples include Hopkins's 1776 *Dialogue* (1852: 573 / Basker 2012: 72) and the anonymous poem *The American in Algiers, or the Patriot of Seventy-Six in Captivity* (1797). For a helpful discus-sion and further examples, see Montgomery 1994.

[53] Rowson also makes some fascinating points about gender equality throughout her play. To men-tion just one: a female North African character states that she learned from an enslaved American woman that "woman was never formed to be the abject slave of man. Nature made us equal with them, and gave us the power to render ourselves superior" (1794: 9).

whom we are taught to vilify as beneath the human species, . . . brings me sustenance, perhaps at the risk of his life" (1802: 212). He then vows that if he ever regains freedom, he will dedicate the remainder of his life to the abolitionist cause in America (1802: 213). Living for just a few hours as a slave and observing the courage and generosity of a Black person leads this narrator to finally grasp the humanity of Black people and thereby understand the injustice of transatlantic slavery. The novel is presumably intended to help White American readers arrive at the same insight by sympathizing with the narrator and his plight.

1.3. Souls, Salvation, and Slavery

Another central theme in many North American antislavery texts is the claim that Black and White people possess the same souls. Let us call this 'the same-souls strategy.' Antislavery authors use this strategy in a variety of ways. Sometimes, it is simply a way to make the metaphysical point that Black people are human beings with human souls, rather than subhuman animals. While this claim is descriptive, it has obvious normative implications: human beings have a special status that comes with special rights and privileges, which in turn are commonly held to make it illicit to enslave a human being who has not forfeited their special rights and privileges. Antislavery writers do not always spell out these implications, but they are clearly implied: the reason why the sameness of souls is relevant for the antislavery cause is precisely that it undercuts one common attempt to justify the enslavement of Black people, namely, something akin to racial natural slavery. Here is one way to spell out this strategy:

1. Black people have human souls.
2. Whoever has a human soul has natural right X.[54]
3. Transatlantic slavery violates natural right X.
4. Therefore, transatlantic slavery violates the natural rights of Black people.

In many texts, the same-souls strategy has a theological dimension: Black people have immortal souls, which makes them capable of salvation and

---

[54] For many authors, the most relevant natural right is the right to liberty, but other possibilities include the right to pursue happiness and the right to own property.

precious to God.[55] This means that White Christians are obligated to treat Black people as brethren, which antislavery authors typically view as incompatible with slavery. Yet there are also authors who think that the sameness of souls is compatible with slavery; it primarily gives Christian slaveholders an obligation to Christianize their slaves and treat them humanely, but not necessarily to free them. One example is the prominent White Puritan theologian and slaveowner Cotton Mather (1663–1728). In his 1706 *The Negro Christianized*, he argues that skin color is irrelevant for salvation, and that the linguistic and practical abilities of Black people clearly prove that they have rational souls, even if they seem barbarous and unintelligent (1706: 23–25). Yet, in this text as well as in his 1710 *Theopolis Americana*, Mather argues merely for the duty to treat enslaved people humanely and to Christianize them (1706: 2–22; 1710: 21–23). Thus, he appears to view the sameness of souls as compatible with slavery.

Some of the authors whom we will encounter in this section use an intriguing metaphor to describe the sameness of souls: they describe Black people as having white souls—or, in some cases, as having souls that can become white, typically through baptism or salvation. What exactly they mean by this metaphor is not always clear. In some cases, 'white' and 'black' appear to symbolize moral goodness and sinfulness, respectively. There are also texts that use these color terms to symbolize 'Christian' and 'non-Christian.'[56] However, some authors appear to racialize souls in a more direct way when they refer to the souls of Black people as white or potentially white: even though they presumably do not think that souls can literally be colored, they hold that the souls of Black people are, or can become, like the souls of White people, or "White" souls, which these authors appear to view as the ideal kind of human soul. This would be the mental analogue of a theory of racial difference that states that all human skin is naturally White but that it can become Black through exposure to hot climates. On such views, Whiteness is the norm and the ideal for human beings, and asserting racial equality hence means asserting that Black people are in some sense White.

---

[55] Benjamin Rush spells out this theological justification for equality nicely. Addressing clergymen, he says, "Ye who estimate the worth of your fellow creatures by their Immortality, and therefore must look upon all mankind as equal,—let your zeal keep pace with your opportunities to put a stop to slavery" (1773a: 26). Samuel Hopkins makes a similar point in a 1776 antislavery sermon: "can we who are set to watch for Souls, and who ought to Estimate the worth of our fellow creatures by their immortality, See multitudes turned into beasts by Slavery and hold our peace?" (2002: 86).

[56] As we saw in section 1.1, James Otis contrasts the hair of Black people with "christian hair" (2015: 140). He does this sarcastically, but in doing so he parodies authors who identify 'Christian' with 'White.'

Phillis Wheatley uses the same-souls strategy in her poem "On Being Brought from AFRICA to AMERICA," published in 1773, but probably composed in 1768. In this poem, the speaker reflects on what she represents as the spiritual benefits of her enslavement: it removed her from a "*Pagan* land" and allowed her to become a Christian. Interestingly, this short poem ends with a reflection on racial bias and equality: "Some view our sable race with scornful eye, / 'Their colour is a diabolic die.' / Remember, *Christians*, *Negroes*, black as *Cain*, / May be refin'd, and join th' angelic train" (2001: 13). In other words, Black people are capable of salvation, or of being good Christians. Blackness is not inextricably linked with paganism. And this realization, the poem contends, ought to lead White Christians to stop viewing Black people with such contempt.

Other eighteenth-century poets and novelists in America take a similar approach. One example is White poet Jane Dunlap (fl. 1765–1771). The first stanza of her 1771 poem "The Ethiopians Shall Stretch out their Hands to God, or a Call to the Ethiopians" encourages the "Poor Negroes" to flee,[57] adding that regardless of their color they will be welcomed by Christ, who died for their redemption (Basker 2012: 49). The second stanza then uses 'black' and 'white' to refer not to skin color, but to a state of sinfulness and righteousness of the soul, respectively: "And though your souls made black with sin, / The Lord can make them white; / And cloath'd in his pure righteousness, / They'l shine transparent bright" (Basker 2012: 49). What matters, in other words, is not complexion but rather the state of one's soul. Susanna Rowson uses the same strategy in her 1788 work *The Inquisitor; or, Invisible Rambler* and plays with the connotations of 'black' and 'white.' After describing the horrendous suffering and death of an—apparently fictional— Black man kidnapped in Africa and enslaved in Barbados, she asks: "Had not that poor negro a soul? Yes—and in futurity it shall appear white and spotless at the throne of Grace, to confound the man who called himself a Christian, and yet betrayed a fellow-creature into bondage" (1788: 8–9 / Basker 2012: 118).[58]

---

[57] It is not entirely clear whether the poem tells Black people to flee from slavery—as Basker appears to interpret it (Basker 2012: 49)—or whether it merely refers to an escape from paganism or sinfulness.

[58] It is worth noting that Rowson appears to be opposed to all forms of slavery, since she states that the word 'slave' "should never be used between man and man" (1788: 3 / Basker 2012: 116). As we saw in the previous section, her 1794 play *Slaves in Algiers* contains further evidence of her antislavery stance.

Another poem taking this approach was composed in 1794 by White abolitionist David Humphrey (1752–1818). In this poem, which is titled "A Poem on Industry Addressed to the Citizens of the United States of America," one stanza starts with an unflattering description of the physiological features of Black people and then asks, "Yet has not God infus'd immortal pow'rs, / The same their organs and their souls as ours? / Are they not made to ruminate the sky? / Or must they perish like the beasts that die? / Perish the thought, which men's high worth impairs, / Sons of Omnipotence and Glory's Heirs!" (Basker 2012: 166). This poem insists that, despite physical differences, Black people have the same souls as White people, which means that they are immortal and have the same special status as other human beings. In the next two stanzas, the poem then expresses the hope that all enslaved Black people will soon be freed (Basker 2012: 166).

We find a particularly explicit use of the same-souls strategy in Andrew Eliot's 1774 work *Twenty Sermons*. Eliot (1718–1778), a White Calvinist minister in Boston, argues that we ought to treat all human beings as brethren since each human being, no matter what their situation may be, has a rational, immaterial soul (1774: 48–49). He adds that even those in inferior situations probably have "as large a share of understanding," but even if they do not, that is no excuse for despising or abusing them (1774: 49). All that matters is that they have a rational and immortal soul. Eliot then applies this idea explicitly to enslaved Black people: "The meanest slave hath a soul as good by nature as your's, and possibly by grace it is better. A dark complection may cover a fair and beautiful mind" (1774: 50). Like Mather, Dunlap, and Rowson, he makes the point about the sameness of souls by claiming that the souls of Black people can be white or "fair."

1.4. Natural Capacities, Equality, and Slavery

As just seen—most explicitly in Eliot's sermon—the same-souls strategy is largely independent of the question of whether Black and White people have the same mental capacities. Its point can simply be that differences in natural capacities are morally irrelevant; all that matters is whether the individual has a human soul. Combined with the idea that anyone with a human soul has moral rights that, unless forfeited or alienated, are incompatible with slavery, this is one way to counter racial natural slavery.

Many antislavery texts take a different route, however: they argue that Black and White people have not only the same kind of soul but also the same mental capacities. Let us call this 'the same-capacities strategy.' This approach is significant in part because of the prominent role that alleged differences in mental capacities play in many racist theories of human diversity as well as in many defenses of racial slavery. Some antislavery texts make the general claim that there are no natural differences in mental capacities along racial lines. Other texts focus on the sameness of specific capacities that are presented as particularly relevant for the question of whether slavery is wrong, such as the capacity to make free choices or the capacity to be in charge of one's own life.

We can view the same-souls strategy and the same-capacities strategy as attacking two different premises of the following argument for the claim that Black people are natural slaves:

1. Any human being who naturally lacks mental capacity X, or who naturally has X to a sufficiently low degree, is a natural slave.
2. Black people naturally lack mental capacity X, or naturally have X to a sufficiently low degree.
3. Therefore, Black people are natural slaves.

Antislavery authors who employ the same-souls strategy typically reject premise 1, which is a normative claim: these authors deny that inferior mental capacities make enslavement licit or fitting. Instead, they argue that no one who has a human soul is a natural slave, regardless of their natural capacities. Some, but not all, of these authors accept a version of premise 2; they agree with proponents of slavery who describe Black people as mentally inferior. In contrast, antislavery authors who use the same-capacities strategy reject premise 2, which is a descriptive claim. They deny that there are relevant differences in natural capacities. Sometimes, these authors acknowledge that there are some differences, but they argue that these differences are acquired and changeable, rather than natural: they contend that these differences can be explained through differences in education and other environmental factors. Many of them point out that it is unsurprising for someone who has been enslaved for a long time to seem mentally inferior. This often takes the form of what I call the 'effects-of-slavery strategy,' which argues that the allegedly inferior capacities of Black people in America are merely an effect of enslavement and hence cannot be used to justify slavery.

In what follows, we will examine some examples of the same-capacities strategy and the effects-of-slavery strategy. We will also investigate a troubling aspect of the latter: some antislavery authors hold that long-term enslavement makes enslaved people unfit for liberty and that as a result it would be imprudent and dangerous to emancipate all enslaved people immediately.

1.4.1. The Sameness of Capacities

As mentioned earlier, some authors argue for the general claim that the capacities of White and Black people are the same, while others focus on one specific capacity. The White Quaker John Hepburn (fl. 1664–1715), a former indentured servant in New Jersey, takes the latter approach. In doing so, he apparently wants to pinpoint what it is about human beings that makes it wrong to treat them in the way in which one treats domestic animals. The capacity on which Hepburn focuses is freedom of the will, and he uses theological premises to argue that it is wrong to enslave individuals who have free wills. What is particularly noteworthy about his argument is that he frames it as an argument against paternalism: if someone has a free will, then it is wrong to force them to do something against their will, even if the action is in their best interest. This is the very first argument of his 1715 tract *The American Defence of the Christian Golden Rule, or An Essay to Prove the Unlawfulness of Making Slaves of Men.*[59]

Let us look at Hepburn's free will argument in more detail. His tract starts with a moral principle, namely the principle that the more closely human beings conform to God's attributes, the more just they are. This principle is a good starting point since many Christians accept it: they view God as omnibenevolent and hence as an ideally just agent and a model for human behavior. Humans ought to imitate divine justice as much as they can. Hepburn then considers what it would mean to imitate God's justice. He observes that God, who has given us the capacity to make good and bad choices, allows us to make our own choices, even if we choose badly. God does not compel us to do what is right, even though he easily could. Hepburn infers that we ought

[59] Hepburn apparently composed this text in 1713–14 (Carey 2012: 123). For a helpful in-depth discussion of this fascinating text, see Carey 2012: 123–35.

to do the same; we ought to allow our fellow humans to make free choices, even if they choose badly. Applying this to slavery, he concludes,

> we ought not to force and compel our fellow creatures, the Negroes, [into slavery], Nay, not although we judge it for them a better way of living; For when we force their will, this is a manifest Robbery of that noble Gift their bountiful Creator hath given them, and is a right down Contradiction to the aforesaid Attributes of God, and consequently an Anti-Christian Practice. (1715: 1 / Basker 2012: 15)

This passage appears to contain two separate, though related, arguments. In addition to the argument that is based on our obligation to imitate divine justice, or conform to God's attributes, it also contains an argument that is based on the claim that freedom of the will—and more specifically, the freedom to choose one's own way of life—is a gift from God, which it is wrong to take away. I understand these two arguments as follows:

Free Will Argument 1
1. It is wrong to do something that contradicts God's attributes.
2. Not allowing human beings to make free choices contradicts God's attributes.
3. Forcing people into slavery is an instance of not allowing human beings to make free choices.
4. Forcing people into slavery contradicts God's attributes (from 2, 3).
5. Therefore, it is wrong to force people into slavery (from 1, 4).

Free Will Argument 2
1. It is wrong to take away something that is a noble gift from God.
2. The freedom to choose one's way of life is a noble gift from God.
3. Thus, it is wrong to take away someone's freedom to choose their way of life (from 1, 2).
4. Forcing people into slavery takes away their freedom to choose their way of life.
5. Therefore, it is wrong to force people into slavery (from 3, 4).

The first argument is quite straightforward, and we have already discussed its main idea. Premise 1 is supposed to be a moral principle with strong theological support. Premise 2, in turn, is based on the observation that God does not force human beings to do things against their will—even things that are good for them—but instead respects their free will and allows them to make their own choices. Of course, Hepburn might view some level of interference with free choices, such as the imprisonment of dangerous criminals, as permissible. Hence, premise 2 might be implicitly restricted to specific types of cases, such as cases in which this person is innocent and is not making choices that violate anybody else's rights. With the relevant restrictions in place, premises 1–2 are quite persuasive within the Christian context. Premise 3 is also hard to reject, because enslaving someone obviously prevents this person from choosing a way of life, as well as from making many other choices. The second argument is similarly straightforward. Premise 4 is obviously true, which means that proponents of slavery need to reject premises 1 or 2, both of which are quite plausible.

These two theological arguments against paternalism are noteworthy in part because they do not depend on a rejection of the proslavery claim that slavery is in the best interest of Black people. These arguments hence allow authors to grant this claim for the sake of argument, which can be an effective strategy. Perhaps for this reason, several later antislavery writers adopt versions of Hepburn's free will arguments.[60] The proslavery claim that slavery benefits Black people is, of course, closely connected to the doctrine of natural slavery: as we saw in the introduction, many proponents of the doctrine argue that slavery is in the best interest of natural slaves, whose inferior capacities make it impossible for them to live good lives outside of slavery. Hepburn's arguments leave that contention unchallenged and insist instead that, even if that were true, it would not justify slavery.

Another author who argues for the sameness of specific capacities is White New Jersey tailor John Woolman (1720–1772), one of the most famous Quaker antislavery activists in this period. His work *Some Considerations on the Keeping of Negroes*—published in two parts in 1754 and 1762, respectively[61]—contains an astonishingly insightful analysis of racial bias,

---

[60] We find the first argument, for instance, in Elihu Coleman's 1733 tract *A Testimony Against that Anti-Christian Practice of Making Slaves of Men* (in Bruns 1977: 41). Lemuel Haynes makes a similar argument in his 1776 *Liberty Further Extended*: "Liberty is a Jewel which was handed Down to man from the cabinet of heaven.... And as it proceed[s] from the Supreme Legislator of the universe, so it is he which hath a sole right to take away; therefore, he that would take away a man's Liberty assumes a prerogative that Belongs to another" (1990: 18, spelling modernized).

[61] Woolman apparently composed the first part of this tract in 1746, but held off publication because of its controversial content (Crosby 2013: 6). For more on Woolman, see Carey 2012: 182–90.

which we will examine later. What is relevant for the present discussion is the way he employs the same-capacities strategy, concentrating on the capacity to be in charge of one's own life, which he sometimes glosses as a fitness for liberty or as the ability to use one's freedom well. This capacity is different from freedom of the will in a few important ways. Freedom of the will can be understood, as we saw in Hepburn, as the capacity to choose good or bad actions, or the capacity to choose a way of life for oneself, whether it is good or bad. Woolman, in contrast, is concerned with the capacity to make good choices for one's own life, where 'good' primarily appears to mean 'prudent.' Thus, the capacity in question is something akin to practical wisdom or prudence. This capacity is relevant for natural slavery. According to many proponents of natural slavery, if someone lacks prudence, or is unable to live a good life as a free person, it is fitting and justifiable for them to be enslaved by someone who has this capacity.

Woolman raises two objections to the argument that enslaving Black people is permissible because they are unfit for liberty. On the one hand, he denies that they are generally incapable of being in charge of their own life, even if some are. This means that proponents of racial slavery are at the very least guilty of overgeneralizing, and hence of enslaving many people who are fit for liberty. On the other hand, he repudiates the general principle that it is permissible to enslave anyone who lacks this capacity. Thus, he rejects both premises of the racial natural slavery argument that I laid out at the beginning of the current section.

Let us look more closely at Woolman's argument, starting with his rejection of the claim that Black people are generally unfit for liberty, or unable to live good lives outside of slavery. At one point, he acknowledges that there are some human beings who need guardians because their abilities are "inferior to the affairs which relate to their convenient subsistence," that is, who cannot provide for themselves. He notes that he knows of some White people who are in this situation. Presumably, he is referring to individuals with what we would today describe as intellectual disabilities. Yet, he adds, "where equal care is taken in all parts of education, I do not apprehend cases of this kind are likely to occur more frequently amongst one sort of people than another" (part 2, 1818: 193 / 1971: 213). In other words, there is no reason to think that this inability to live independently is naturally more common among Black than among White people, let alone that all Black people are naturally in this situation. If it is more common among Black people, he implies in this passage, this is likely due to a lack of education, rather than to differences in natural capacities. This fits well with Woolman's usage of the effects-of-slavery strategy, which we will examine later.

Woolman also cites more direct evidence against the alleged natural inferiority of Black people. For instance, he claims that "Some negroes in these parts, who have had an agreeable education, have manifested a brightness of understanding equal to many of us," and then quotes a passage from Willem Bosman's 1704 *New and Accurate Description of the Coast of Guinea* about the outstanding arithmetical abilities of African merchants (Woolman 1818: 207 / 1971: 224; see Bosman, Letter 18, 1705: 352). Later, Woolman states that many of the children born in America to enslaved Black parents "appear as likely to make a right use of freedom as other people" (1818: 220 / 1971: 235).[62] One reason why he restricts this claim to children born in America might be that he, like many of his contemporaries, holds that the climate and cultures of Africa are not conducive to human flourishing. As a result, he might believe that growing up in Africa makes it less likely that one can use one's freedom correctly. Yet the main reason appears to be Woolman's concession that some of the enslaved people brought to America might be licit penal slaves: "Negroes may be imported who, for the cruelty to their countrymen, and the evil disposition of their minds, may be unfit for liberty" (part 2, 1818: 193–94 / 1971: 213).[63] To sidestep this complication, he focuses primarily on children born to enslaved people in America, to whom this alleged justification for enslavement clearly does not apply. There is no justification for enslaving these individuals, since they are clearly as fit for liberty as White people. Or, as he puts it, they are "innocent men, capable to manage for themselves," who therefore "were not intended to be slaves" (1818: 207 / 1971: 224). In short, even if it is justifiable to enslave those who are unfit for liberty, this clearly does not justify hereditary chattel slavery as practiced in America. If enslaved people can provide for themselves and are innocent, their enslavement can be justified neither through natural nor through circumstantial slavery.

So far we have examined Woolman's argument against the descriptive claim that Black people are generally unfit for liberty, or unable to live freely.

---

[62] He makes a similar point one page earlier: some enslaved people born in America are "capable and likely to manage well for themselves" and their "understandings and behaviour are as good as common among other people" (1818: 219 / 1971: 234).

[63] He is quick to add that White slaveholders rarely know whether the people they are enslaving have committed any crimes, let alone what crimes exactly and whether there were extenuating circumstances. Thus, he cautions against making hasty judgments about someone's unfitness for freedom.

Interestingly, he also argues against the normative claim that an unfitness for liberty justifies enslavement. One intriguing, though not entirely explicit, instance of this argument occurs in a passage already mentioned, in which Woolman points out that there are some people who cannot live independently. After claiming that he knows of some White people who are in this situation and are lovingly cared for, he states, "I believe there are such amongst negroes; and that some people in whose hands they are, keep them with no view of outward profit . . . but account them persons who have need of guardians; and, as such, take care of them" (part 2, 1818: 193 / 1971: 213). While his main point is that this condition does not naturally occur more frequently among Black than among White people, he appears to make another point here—namely, that the right thing to do with respect to such individuals is not to enslave them, but rather to take care of them. In short, he appears to suggest that while such individuals need to be ruled by others, the appropriate kind of rule is paternal, rather than despotic.[64] Incidentally, Woolman describes the benevolent or paternal way of taking care of Black people who are unable to manage for themselves in a very telling way: their guardians "do not consider them as black men, who, as such, ought to serve white men" (1818: 193 / 1971: 213). What he is saying here is that these guardians do not subscribe to racial natural slavery, according to which being Black means being a natural slave.

Woolman levels two additional arguments against the claim that it is legitimate to enslave people whose abilities are inferior. One is an argument from divine providence. When considering the differences between brute animals and human beings, he states, it is obvious that God intends some animals to serve human beings.[65] Yet, he continues, it is equally clear that God does not intend humans to serve other humans. Even though some humans are weaker in body or mind than others, they can typically find good ways to support themselves. Indeed, "while each is at liberty, the latter [that is, those with weaker bodies or minds] may be as happy, and live as comfortably, as the former [that is, those with stronger bodies or minds]" (part 2,

---

[64] As we saw in the introduction, this is an Aristotelian distinction that was widely used in the early modern period. Slave masters rule enslaved people despotically, that is, use them merely as instruments for their own ends. This type of rule benefits enslaved people at best accidentally, since despotic rule does not aim at the good of the ruled. Paternal rule, in contrast, is practiced for the sake of the ruled (Aristotle, *Politics* iii.6, 1984: 2029–30).

[65] It is noteworthy that he describes such animals as meant to serve humans "in moderation, so far as relates to the right use of things" (1818: 205 / 1971: 222). This suggests that Woolman, like other Quakers, worries about the maltreatment of animals.

1818: 205 / 1971: 222). In contrast, the enslavement of those with inferior abilities by those with superior abilities is detrimental for both parties. After all, this kind of subordination is practically guaranteed to make slaveholders treat the enslaved with cruelty, forcing them to work far too hard and thus causing immense misery (1818: 205 / 1971: 222).[66] Likewise, this subordination is bad for slaveholders, who lack meaningful work—a condition which is bound to make them unhealthy and unhappy (1818: 206 / 1971: 223). Since slavery has such enormous negative effects on both masters and enslaved people, Woolman concludes that the theological version of natural slavery cannot be correct: God does not intend humans with superior abilities to enslave those with inferior abilities.[67]

Woolman's other argument does not rely on divine providence, but merely on claims about human nature and "right reason." It is an intriguing argument against paternalism that focuses on the capacities of masters rather than slaves. The basic idea is that human beings cannot be trusted with absolute power over others, which means that nobody is fit to be a master. Humans lack the wisdom and goodness that would be needed to justify slavery paternalistically; we are too "liable to err" and too "biassed by narrow self-love" to rule enslaved people in a way that could be beneficial for them (part 2, 1818: 203 / 1971: 221).[68] Even if some people have the purest intentions, becoming slave masters will "vitiate their minds, and make them more unfit for government" (1818: 204 / 1971: 221).[69] For this reason, being enslaved by a human master, that is, being "subject to the uncontrolable will of man, liable to err," is not advantageous for any human being; it is, rather, "most painful and afflicting" (1818: 203 / 1971: 221). Thus, paternalist arguments for slavery fail for the simple reason that nobody is better off enslaved than free, which in turn is due to the fact that no human being is fit to be a master of others.

---

[66] Interestingly, Woolman also discusses invisible infirmities that make it impossible or painful for enslaved people to perform certain tasks. Slaveholders, however, are likely to "disbelieve what [these slaves] say, and grievously afflict them" as punishment for disobedience (1818: 205 / 1971: 223).

[67] This argument is similar to Francis Hutcheson's teleological argument against natural slavery, which we will examine in chapter 2 and with which Woolman may have been familiar.

[68] This argument is somewhat similar to another one of Francis Hutcheson's arguments, though Hutcheson's version is epistemic: he argues that we cannot know whether any given person has the wisdom and goodness that is required for being a fitting ruler (*System* 2.5.3, 1755, 1: 302–3; see my discussion in chapter 2).

[69] Samuel Hopkins makes a similar point in his 1776 *Dialogue*: very few people "are fit to be masters; to have the sovereign dominion over a number of their fellow-men, being his property, and wholly at his disposal, who must abide his sentence and orders, however unreasonable, without any possibility of relief" (1852: 579).

A final text that argues for the sameness of specific capacities is the fascinating *Forensic Dispute on the Legality of Enslaving the Africans* by Theodore Parsons (1752–1779) and Eliphalet Pearson (1752–1826). Parsons and Pearson were two White students at Harvard College, and the *Forensic Dispute* is the written version of a public debate between these two men that was held at the Harvard commencement in 1773.[70] The question for this debate was "Whether the slavery, to which Africans are in this province, by the permission of law, subjected, be agrable to the law of nature" (1773: 3–4). Because the opposing sides are simply labeled "A" and "B" in the published version of this dispute, it is not entirely clear which side was taken by which author. Indeed, it is not entirely clear whether this dispute expresses their actual opinions or merely represents their best effort to argue for a side that they were assigned.[71] According to Peter Galison (2019: 355), the antislavery disputant "A" is Parsons, and the proslavery disputant "B" is Pearson.[72] My discussion will assume that this is correct.

The portion of this dispute that is most relevant for present purposes is somewhat reminiscent of Woolman's discussion; it concerns specific capacities that someone would need to have in order to be a natural master or a natural slave. Pearson argues that one adult is a natural slave to another when their natural capacities are analogous to a young child's and a parent's capacities, respectively (1773: 14 / Bruns 1977: 282).[73] Parsons responds by accepting this principle but providing two reasons why it does not justify transatlantic slavery. First, he expresses doubts that any two adults differ so radically in their "ability for the proper direction of conduct" that they are analogous to parent and child (1773: 21 / Bruns 1977: 284). He also argues that in order for slavery to be natural and completely parallel to the parent-child case, natural masters would need to have the same "principle of affection" and the same natural concern for the welfare of the enslaved as parents naturally have toward their children (1773: 20 / Bruns 1977: 284). Parsons then challenges Pearson to show him adults who fit this description, implying

---

[70] For helpful background and analysis, see Galison 2019. Galison and Henry Louis Gates directed a short film titled *No More, America* in 2017 that includes a reenactment of the forensic dispute.

[71] The footnotes in the published version suggest that whoever prepared this dispute for publication favored the antislavery side, since the footnotes all appear to support that side.

[72] Some interpreters endorse the inverse attribution, for example, Rosenthal 1973.

[73] Pearson's claim is disjunctive: there have to be either differences in natural capacities or in "the means of improvement, or in disposition properly to employ such means" (1773: 14 / Bruns 1977: 282). The last two disjuncts are unimportant for present purposes because Parsons's response focuses on the first disjunct, which is also most relevant for us.

that there are none. In short, the specific capacities that would make people natural slaves and natural masters are nowhere to be found.

Parsons adds a second objection to the parent-child analogy: even if there are some natural slaves and natural masters among adult human beings, it is clearly false that Black people are generally in the former category and White people in the latter. A comparison between Black and White people simply does not yield the kinds of differences in natural capacities that, according to Pearson, justify enslavement. Parsons adds sarcastically, "I suppose you will hardly imagine the darkness of a man's skin incapacitates him for the direction of his conduct, and authorises his neighbours, who may have the good fortune of a complexion a shade or two lighter, to exercise authority over him" (1773: 21 / Bruns 1977: 284). He also ridicules the possibility that the principle of subordination might have to do with hair: if that were the case, then anyone whose hair is not perfectly straight had better be on guard (1773: 21–22 / Bruns 1977: 284). With even more snark, he jokes that if anybody tries to justify the subordination of Africans on the basis of differences in nasal shape, "I can't but think this circumstance against them, for if a man is to be led and governed by the nose, it may well be questioned, whether a nose of a different figure would not be better adapted to the purpose" (1773: 22 / Bruns 1977: 284–85). The point of these questionable jokes is that the only genuine differences between Black and White people concern superficial bodily features, which are clearly irrelevant to the issue of natural subordination.

Let us now turn to an author who, instead of focusing on specific capacities, defends the general claim that Black people have the same natural capacities as White people: Anthony Benezet (1713–1784), one of the most influential and prolific North American antislavery writers of the eighteenth century. Benezet, a White Quaker who was born in France and immigrated to Philadelphia in 1731, made his living as a schoolteacher. He founded a school for Quaker girls as well as a school for Black children, and he additionally taught Black adults at his house (Crosby 2013: 3). Some of his students—Black and White—became outspoken abolitionists themselves.[74] In his antislavery writings, Benezet's main strategy is empirical and encyclopedic. He collects and presents many firsthand reports about Africa, Africans, and the transatlantic slave trade by European authors; a large portion of his publications consist of direct quotations from such reports together with his

[74] These students include William Dillwyn and Absalom Jones, both of whom we will discuss later.

own comments and analyses. In other words, his role is in part that of a syn-thesizer and disseminator of information from other sources.[75]

One major goal of Benezet's antislavery tracts is to show that there are no significant racial differences in natural capacities. As he puts it in his 1762 tract *A Short Account of that Part of Africa Inhabited by the Negroes*—which one interpreter describes as a "user's manual for antislavery activists" (Crosby 2013: 84)—he aims to prove that "the *Negroes* are generally a sensible, hu-mane, and sociable people, and that their capacity is as good and as capable of improvement as that of the whites" (2013: 30).[76] Toward the end of this text, he claims that his discussion has shown that "Negroes . . . have the same ra-tional powers, the same natural affections, and are as susceptible of pain and grief as [whites]" (2013: 75). This is helpfully specific: he defends the same-ness of both rational and affective capacities. In his 1783 *Short Observations on Slavery*, he supports his claims about equal capacities through his own experience as a teacher of Black children and adults: he reports that he has found among his Black students "as great variety of talents, equally capable of improvement as among a like number of whites" (2013: 233).

1.4.2. The Effects-of-Slavery Strategy

We can now turn to the effects-of-slavery strategy, that is, to the argument that the alleged inferiority of Black people in America is merely an effect of their en-slavement and hence cannot be used to justify slavery. Some authors concentrate on the purported intellectual inferiority of Black people, whereas others concen-trate on an alleged inferiority in moral character or virtue. There are also versions of the effects-of-slavery strategy that cover both forms of alleged inferiority. This argumentative strategy is a staple of American antislavery discourse,[77] and it can be very effective. However, as we will see later, it can also be used as an ex-cuse to delay the abolition of slavery, and it runs the danger of dehumanizing and othering enslaved people by describing them as intellectually or morally degraded.[78]

[75] For a helpful discussion of Benezet, see Carey 2012: 211–13.

[76] He reuses this passage almost verbatim in his 1767 text *A Caution and Warning to Great Britain and Her Colonies* (2013: 93).

[77] We will encounter a similar argument when discussing Rousseau in chapter 4. Woolman's usage of this strategy, which we are about to discuss, predates Rousseau's, who uses it in *The Social Contract* (1762). For a brief discussion of this strategy, see Jordan 1968: 281–82.

[78] For a helpful present-day discussion of the effects of oppression on the moral characters of the oppressed, as well as of the dangers of acknowledging such effects, see Tessman 2005.

One author who uses this strategy is John Woolman, whom we already encountered earlier. He notes in part 1 of *Some Considerations on the Keeping of Negroes* (published in 1754) that it is common for White people to believe that Black people are inferior to them by nature. To counter this belief, he asks his readers to suppose "that our [i.e., White people's] ancestors and we had been exposed to constant servitude, . . . that we had been destitute of the help of reading and good company; . . . [that we] had generally been treated as a contemptible, ignorant part of mankind" (part 1, 1818: 180 / 1971: 202). If that had been the case, he asks, would White people not have precisely the same characteristics that are observed among enslaved Black people in America? (part 1, 1818: 180–81 / 1971: 202). His point is clear: Black people only seem inferior because of the inhumane circumstances in which they and their ancestors have been forced to live. Woolman then goes on to speculate about the negative psychological and moral effects of enslavement on the enslaved, claiming that these mechanisms explain most of the "great disparity which some make between us and them" (part 1, 1818: 181 / 1971: 202).

In response to the allegation that enslaved Black people are slothful, Woolman argues in his posthumously published *Journal* that this too is simply a natural result of slavery, which removes all incentives for being industrious. After all, "free men, whose minds were properly on their business, [find] a satisfaction in improving, cultivating, and providing for their families" (ch. 4, 1818: 51 / 1971: 61). In contrast, these inducements are absent in enslaved people, who are "labouring to support others who claim them as their property, and expecting nothing but slavery during life" (ch. 4, 1818: 51 / 1971: 61).[79] In short, he argues that the characteristics invoked by defenders of slavery to justify enslavement are actually effects of enslavement. Far from making enslavement morally permissible, these characteristics are among the reasons why enslavement is wrong, since they are among the horrendous effects that enslavement has on the enslaved. Life in slavery is detrimental to human flourishing.

Anthony Benezet is also among the authors who employ the effects-of-slavery strategy. For instance, he argues in *A Short Account*,

Though the natural capacity of many [enslaved Black people] be ever so good, yet they have no inducement or opportunity of exerting it to any

[79] This argument is somewhat reminiscent of Adam Smith's economic argument against slave labor in his 1776 *Wealth of Nations* (3.2.9, 1986: 488–89). Smith makes a similar point in his *Lectures of Jurisprudence* in 1762–63 (1978: 185).

advantage, which naturally tends to depress their minds and sink their spirits into habits of idleness and sloth, which they would in all likelihood have been free from had they stood upon an equal footing with the white people. (2013: 67–68)

He adds that he knows of Black people—both free and enslaved—who exhibit the sagacity that one would expect from White people in the same circumstances, which supports his claim that there are no general differences in natural capacities. He also points out that the living conditions of emancipated Black people in America are far from conducive to intellectual achievement: they have "but little more opportunity of knowledge and improvement than when in slavery" because they typically lack opportunities for interacting with educated White people (2013: 68).[80] Presumably, considerations like these led Benezet to devote his life to teaching.

William Dillwyn (1743–1824), a White Quaker and former student at Benezet's school in Philadelphia who later moved to England, uses the effects-of-slavery strategy in a similar way in his 1773 pamphlet *Brief Observations on Slavery, and the Expediency of Its Abolition*. As he eloquently puts it, "Every thing that debases the mind, unfits it for society; and this is a distinguishing characteristick of Slavery, which naturally suppresses every generous expansion of the mind" (1773: 7 / Bruns 1977: 273). Later in this text, in response to the claim that some enslaved people are better off living in slavery because they are "unfit for liberty," Dillwyn acknowledges that this can happen, adding that "nothing [is] so likely to occasion it, as a long continuance in the situation they have been in" (1773: 11 / Bruns 1977: 275). In genuine instances of this, he claims, it is permissible for slaveholders to keep these individuals enslaved (1773: 11 / Bruns 1977: 275).[81] Yet his point appears to be once again that this condition results from enslavement and hence cannot be the original justification for it.

Theodore Parsons also uses the effects-of-slavery strategy in his contribution to the 1773 *Forensic Dispute on the Legality of Enslaving the Africans*.[82] At first, he sets aside the inhumane conditions in which enslaved people are forced to live in American colonies in order to examine the effects of their

---

[80] Benezet repeats this and the two foregoing points almost verbatim in his 1771 *Some Historical Account of Guinea*, ch. 14, 2013: 179–80.

[81] Benezet makes a similar point in his 1762 *Short Account* (2013: 66–67).

[82] His description of the effects of slavery is somewhat reminiscent of Francis Hutcheson's explanation for why slavery makes humans so miserable (*System* 2.5.2, 1755, 1: 300; see my discussion in chapter 2).

awareness of their absolute and permanent subjection. Because every human being has an innate sense of liberty, such an awareness

> must necessarily mar the happiness of every gratification, effectually chill the sense of pleasure, and stop every natural source of felicity. A keen excruciating sense of liberty forever lost must still predominate, till, the spirit broken by the fatigue of incessant distress, they sink into a state of lifeless insensibility. (1773: 41 / Bruns 1977: 289)

In other words, slavery has atrocious effects even on those who are enslaved by comparatively benevolent masters. By its very nature, slavery breaks the spirits of the enslaved and makes their lives miserable. Freedom is a necessary condition for happiness. This means that no matter how bad the conditions in Africa may be, it cannot possibly be true that free Africans are less happy than transatlantic slaves. And if one takes into consideration the inhumane conditions in which transatlantic slaves are forced to live, Parsons adds, what is surprising is not that they appear inferior but rather that "there are any of the least appearances of sensibility remaining in them" (1773: 42 / Bruns 1977: 289). Given that life in slavery has these effects, Parsons notes, it is astonishing that his fellow White people have the audacity to "tax them [i.e., Black slaves] with natural stupidity; and make the very thing that our unnatural treatment has occasioned the ground of our justification" (1773: 41 / Bruns 1977: 289). This is a particularly explicit and forceful version of the effects-of-slavery strategy, which we can reconstruct as follows:

1. Black people appear intellectually inferior merely as a result of their enslavement.
2. If someone appears intellectually inferior merely as a result of their enslavement, this apparent intellectual inferiority cannot justify their enslavement.
3. Therefore, the apparent intellectual inferiority of Black people cannot justify their enslavement.

This is an argument against racial natural slavery and, more specifically, against the doctrine that the alleged intellectual inferiority of Black people justifies their enslavement. Proponents of that doctrine would, presumably, reject premise 1 and insist on a natural inferiority. To support this premise, antislavery writers can do at least two things: they can explain why exactly slavery has these psychological effects, and they can cite empirical evidence to support the claim that free Black people lack these characteristics. Parsons concentrates mainly on the former, but as already seen, other writers supply the latter.

One author who invokes the abilities of free Black people in Africa to strengthen the effects-of-slavery strategy is Benjamin Rush (1746–1813)—a White professor of chemistry and medicine in Pennsylvania, a member of the Second Continental Congress, and a signatory of the Declaration of Independence. In his influential 1773 tract *An Address to the Inhabitants of the British Settlements*, he turns to the capacities of Black people on the very first page, pointing out that travel reports refute claims about the natural inferiority of Africans: "they are equal to the Europeans, when we allow for the diversity of temper and genius which is occasioned by climate" (1773a: 2). The proviso suggests that while Rush rejects natural or innate differences, he believes in differences that result from climate. In his follow-up tract *Vindication of the Address, to the Inhabitants of the British Settlements*—published in the same year[83]—he additionally acknowledges differences resulting from political and cultural factors in Africa (1773b: 24–28).[84]

Rush argues that environmental influences also need to be taken into consideration when judging the capacities of enslaved Black people in America—most importantly, the influence of slavery itself. In this context, Rush uses the effects-of-slavery strategy:

> Slavery is so foreign to the human mind, that the moral faculties, as well as those of the understanding are debased, and rendered torpid by it. All the vices which are charged upon the Negroes in the southern colonies and the West-Indies, such as Idleness, Treachery, Theft, and the like, are the genuine offspring of slavery, and serve as an argument to prove that they were not intended for it. (1773a: 2)

---

[83] *Vindication* is a refutation and response to Nisbet 1773, which in turn is a response to Rush's *Address*. Intriguingly, Rush also argues that bias in favor of one's own culture can skew one's judgments about other cultures: we often judge the practices of other cultures to be vicious or foolish, even though there are analogous practices in our own culture (1773b: 30–32).

[84] He also argues that even if there were natural intellectual differences, that would not justify enslavement. He asks rhetorically, "Would it avail a man to plead in a Court of Justice that he defrauded his Neighbour, because he was inferior to him in Genius or Knowledge?" (1773b: 33). His point here appears to be that all human beings clearly have the same moral rights, independently of their intellectual capacities. Thus, he rejects both premises of the racial natural slavery argument.

One thing that is notable about this passage is that it foregrounds moral traits and mentions intellectual traits only in passing.[85] But what I find even more intriguing is the final clause of this quotation, which draws a connection to natural slavery: the fact that slavery has such detrimental effects on the minds and characters of Black people proves that they are not natural slaves. The background assumption is presumably that if something is natural for you, it cannot be utterly bad for you.[86] Or, more precisely, when a certain way of life completely corrupts your intellect and moral character, it cannot be the way of life for which you are intended. We can reconstruct this argument as follows:

1. The state of slavery corrupts the moral and intellectual faculties of Black people.
2. No state that corrupts a person's moral and intellectual faculties is the intended or natural state for that person.
3. Therefore, the state of slavery is not the intended or natural state for Black people.

This is quite a strong argument against racial natural slavery. Proponents would presumably reject the first premise. The second premise is quite difficult for someone with a teleological or providential worldview to deny, and proponents of natural slavery typically embrace this kind of worldview, since they understand natural slavery in teleological or providential ways.

Lemuel Haynes employs the effects-of-slavery strategy as well. In his 1776 *Liberty Further Extended*, he argues that enslaved Black people are "stiled the ignorant part of the world" because enslavement is incompatible with the cultivation of human genius (1990: 27). If Black people were provided with the same advantages as Whites, the alleged differences might disappear completely. In his address on the twenty-fifth anniversary of American independence in 1801, titled *The Nature and Importance of True Republicanism*, Haynes spells out the effects of slavery on enslaved Black people in America in a remarkable way, invoking what appears to be internalized oppression or

---

[85] Like some of the other authors whom we have already discussed, Rush holds that slavery has detrimental effects on the moral faculties of masters as well as slaves: free people in the West Indies are "exposed to Vice from every Quarter, and . . . breathe nothing but the polluted Atmosphere of Slavery" (1773b: 13). That kind of atmosphere corrupts everyone's moral character.

[86] As we saw earlier, Woolman makes a similar argument: since slavery is bad for slaves and masters, it is clear that God does not intend human beings to enslave each other (*Some Considerations* part 2, 1818: 205–6 / 1971: 222).

internalized racism: "being subjected to slavery, . . . they have been taught to view themselves as a rank of beings far below others, which has suppressed, in a degree, every principle of manhood, and so they become despised, ignorant, and licentious" (1990: 82). This text is among the earliest of which I am aware that explicitly discuss the effects of slavery, and racial oppression more generally, on the self-conception of the oppressed.[87] Haynes's description is similar to what W. E. B. Du Bois later describes as double consciousness.

There are also authors who argue that only a portion of the alleged inferiority of Black people is an effect of slavery. One particularly clear example is Thomas Jefferson. As we saw earlier in this chapter, he argues in his 1785 *Notes on the State of Virginia* that Black people are intellectually and physically inferior to White people by nature, rather than merely as a result of their circumstances (Query 14, 1984: 266–68). In other words, he does not think that Black people are inferior merely as a result of their enslavement. Yet he also argues in the same text that there is no natural inferiority with respect to virtue or moral character: there are as many instances of "benevolence, gratitude, and unshaken fidelity" among enslaved Black people as among free Whites (Query 14, 1984: 269). Any apparent differences in moral character are merely the effects of slavery, he claims. In particular, the alleged disposition for stealing among Black people must be ascribed to their circumstances rather than "to any depravity of the moral sense" (Query 14, 1984: 269). It makes perfect sense, Jefferson explains, that enslaved people have less respect for laws of property than free people, since these laws are made exclusively in favor of the latter. The root of the problem, then, is that these laws of property are unjust and arbitrary, "founded in force, and not in conscience," because they are not reciprocal (Query 14, 1984: 269).[88] There is simply no good reason for an enslaved person to respect this type of law. In fact, Jefferson asks White slaveholders to consider "whether the slave may not as justifiably take a little from one, who has taken all from him, as he may slay one who would slay him" (Query 14, 1984: 269).

Let us examine one final text about the effects of slavery: a remarkable 1794 pamphlet by Absalom Jones (1746–1818) and Richard Allen (1760–1831), two African American clergymen and leaders of the free Black community in Philadelphia. In 1787, they cofounded the Free African Society in

---

[87] The only earlier author of which I am aware who discusses internalized racism is the Scottish antislavery writer James Dunbar (1780: 389), whom we will discuss in chapter 2.

[88] This point is reminiscent of some of Levi Hart's claims in *Some Thoughts on the Subject of Freeing the Negroes* (ca. 1775; see particularly Bruns 1977: 371), which we will examine later.

Philadelphia, a nondenominational mutual aid society. Both men were formerly enslaved and gained freedom during the Revolution. Jones founded a Black church shortly after composing the pamphlet, and he would later become the first Black person in the United States to be ordained as an Episcopal priest. He was also a former student in Benezet's school. Allen founded the African Methodist Episcopal Church in 1794 and would later become the first bishop of this church. Their 1794 pamphlet is titled *A Narrative of the Proceedings of the Black People, During the Late Awful Calamity in Philadelphia, in the Year 1793*.[89] For our purposes, the two most relevant sections of this tract are "Address to those who keep Slaves, and Approve of the Practice" (1794: 23–26)—which contains arguments against slavery and for equality—and "To the People of Colour" (1794: 26–27), which contains advice for free and enslaved Black people in America. Both sections address the effects of slavery. These discussions make multiple points that we have not encountered before, perhaps as a consequence of the authors' firsthand experience of slavery and their intimate familiarity with the oppression faced by free Black people in the United States.

Jones and Allen start the section "Address to those who keep Slaves, and Approve of the Practice" by arguing against a version of the racial natural slavery argument. In the authors' words, they are refuting the argument that "our [i.e., Black people's] . . . baseness is incurable, and [that we] may therefore be held in a state of servitude, that a merciful man would not doom a beast to" (1794: 23). Or, as they put it later, they are rebutting White people who "plead our incapacity for freedom . . . as a sufficient cause for keeping us under the grievous yoke" (1794: 25). In response to this argument, Jones and Allen use the effects-of-slavery strategy, albeit slightly differently than the authors discussed so far. First, they point out how unreasonable it is for White people to expect "a superior good conduct" from enslaved Black people, especially while White people are doing whatever they can "to prevent our rising from the state of barbarism [that] you represent us to be in" (1794: 23).

---

[89] The "Late Awful Calamity" referenced in this title was a deadly yellow fever epidemic (Countryman 2012: 89–91). The first part of the pamphlet describes the ways in which Jones and Allen, together with other free Black people in Philadelphia, organized care for the sick and burials for the dead, at an enormous personal risk (1794: 3–23). The authors defend themselves against the charge that they took advantage of the epidemic to enrich themselves—a charge which, they explain, could not be further from the truth. They also describe how the burden of caring for the sick and burying the dead fell largely on poor Black Philadelphians, while White people often refused to help (1794: 10). Moreover, they discuss the emotional toll of this work as well as some of the most heartbreaking situations they encountered (1794: 18–20). Their description of the yellow fever epidemic is extremely touching to read, especially in the midst of the Covid-19 pandemic.

This is a remarkable claim. Jones and Allen are not only saying that the racial natural slavery argument gets things backward by justifying enslavement through something that is in fact an effect of enslavement. They also appear to be saying—even though the wording is somewhat ambiguous—that White people intentionally keep Black people in "barbarism" in order to be able to continue enslaving them. In other words, the horrendous effects of slavery on the minds of the enslaved are not unintended side-effects; they are intentional.[90] From today's standpoint, it may seem obvious that systems of oppression, such as racial slavery, have built-in mechanisms that ensure the continued subordination of the oppressed. It may also seem obvious that slaveholders typically kept their slaves uneducated in order to be able to continue enslaving them. Yet only very few authors in this period make these points.[91]

Later in the same section, Jones and Allen accuse White defenders of slavery of being "wilfully blind and extremely partial" in failing to acknowledge that the traits that allegedly justify slavery are mere effects of slavery (1794: 24). After all, it is obvious that freedom and slavery affect the human mind in opposite ways (1794: 24). While slavery debases the mind and leads to bad behavior, freedom fosters intellectual and moral virtues. The accusation of willful ignorance might confirm my earlier suggestion: the authors are accusing proponents of racial natural slavery not of inadvertently interpreting the effects of slavery as natural traits, but rather of something much more sinister. These defenders of slavery know, at least on some level, that slavery causes these traits and thus that their justification for slavery is a sham. Yet they pretend not to know this, or push that knowledge aside, in order to keep Black people enslaved.

To strengthen the point that the traits invoked by White people to justify slavery are mere effects of slavery, Jones and Allen argue that if their White oppressors were forced to live in abject slavery, these oppressors would exhibit the same traits that enslaved Black people exhibit. With a pinch of sarcasm, they speculate that the only difference might be a higher degree of "keen resentment and revenge" in these White slaves (1794: 23–24). In other

---

[90] Jones and Allen later restate this point, but the restatement is even more ambiguous: White people use Black people's alleged incapacity for freedom as a justification for slavery "because you [i.e., whites] have reduced us to the unhappy condition our colour is in" (1794: 25).

[91] One other author who makes this point, as we will see in chapter 3, is Olaudah Equiano (*Narrative* ch. 5, 2003: 111).

words, if White people were enslaved, they would, if anything, behave less virtuously than Black people.

Jones and Allen also propose an experiment to White defenders of slavery: try cultivating the minds of some Black children "with the same care, and let them have the same prospect in view, as to living in the world, as you would wish your own children" (1794: 24). This experiment would prove once and for all that there is no inferiority in the natural mental capacities of Black people and that the apparent differences are due to differences in circumstances. The reference in this passage to a "prospect . . . as to living in the world" is intriguing. As I understand them, the authors are stating that it is crucial for children to have optimism about their own futures, or to believe that they can live a good life. This stands in stark contrast with children who are raised in the hopelessness of American chattel slavery—as Jones and Allen were—with almost no prospect of ever gaining freedom or leading happy lives.[92] The proposed experiment involves children because, according to the authors, it is difficult to completely undo the damage that slavery has caused in someone's mind. Thus, it is unreasonable for White people to expect perfect conduct even from recently freed Black people. "It is in our posterity enjoying the same privileges with your own, that you ought to look for better things" (1794: 24).[93]

The next section of the pamphlet—titled "To the People of Colour"—is notable in part because it addresses free and enslaved Black people; it is one of a very small number of eighteenth-century texts in which a Black author specifically speaks to a Black audience.[94] Jones and Allen's advice for enslaved people, based on their own experience as slaves, is to find ways not to get discouraged and to seek comfort in religion (1794: 26). Their advice for free Black people is particularly relevant for our purposes because it mentions

---

[92] Later in this pamphlet, the two authors describe their former enslavement quite vividly as a state of "darkness and perplexity" as well as desperation, with only occasional flickers of hope (1794: 26).

[93] This point is similar to a point made by several early modern advocates of women's rights: men should not expect women in their present state to be as accomplished, intelligent, or virtuous as men, since they have not benefited from the same educational and societal privileges. Yet future generations of women, if they are raised with the same opportunities, will be men's equals in all these respects. Some early modern feminists even propose experiments very much like the experiment that Jones and Allen propose. One example is Émilie Du Châtelet (preface to *Fable of the Bees* [1735], 2009: 48–49).

[94] Another example of such a text is Jupiter Hammon's 1787 *Address to the Negroes in the State of New York*; yet another is the shortened version of Ottobah Cugoano's *Thoughts and Sentiments*, whose subtitle specifies that it is "*Addressed to the Sons of Africa, by a Native.*" We will discuss Cugoano in chapter 3.

racial natural slavery once more. After advising free Black people to show gratitude toward White people, Jones and Allen stress that the free Black community can do a lot to help their enslaved brethren. In particular, free Black people need to be extremely careful not to confirm stereotypes that can be used to defend racial slavery:

> if we are lazy and idle, the enemies of freedom plead it as a cause why we ought not to be free, and say we are better in a state of servitude, and that giving us liberty would be an injury to us, and by such conduct we strengthen the bands of oppression, and keep many in bondage who are more worthy than ourselves. (1794: 27)[95]

In short, the authors argue that the free Black community bears a colossal responsibility. Their conduct is scrutinized by White people who are likely to see any instances of bad behavior as a confirmation of their racist beliefs and as an excuse for continuing to enslave Black people. More specifically, White defenders of slavery are likely to claim that the bad behavior of emancipated slaves demonstrates that Black people are natural slaves and better off in slavery.[96] This claim would, of course, be unjustified. As already seen, Jones and Allen argue that this behavior is merely a manifestation of the effects of slavery rather than of natural traits. Moreover, we might add, some bad behavior occurs in any group of people, and the White person's judgment that free Black people are "lazy and idle" to a higher degree than Whites is itself suspect. This judgment is likely to be influenced by various biases and the higher level of scrutiny to which free Black people are subjected. Jones and Allen do not call out the unfairness of this situation in this text. They merely advise members of the free Black community to try not to give any further ammunition to defenders of racial natural slavery.

---

[95] This passage is very similar to Jupiter Hammon's advice to free Black people from his 1787 *Address*, which I will quote later in this chapter (1787: 18–19).

[96] Jones and Allen's strategy here might be what Kendi calls "uplift suasion," which is the suggestion that Black Americans can uplift themselves by improving their behavior and thus undermining racist justifications for slavery (2016: 124). Kendi argues that this strategy is racist: it is based on the racist idea that Black people's behavior is at least in part to blame for the existence and persistence of racism; the strategy buys into the notion that Black people are inferior (2016: 124–25). He also argues that history has proved this strategy to be ineffective and that we must hence abandon it (2016: 505).

1.4.3. The Alleged Dangers of Emancipation

A crucial aspect of eighteenth-century debates about slavery is the question of, not just whether, but how to abolish the institution. There were many different proposals—the details of which need not concern us here—ranging from an immediate emancipation of all enslaved people and the payment of reparations to plans for transporting emancipated slaves to Africa. One facet of these discussions is important for our purposes in this section because it has to do with the capacities of enslaved Black people. Many White authors, including some antislavery and many proslavery writers, express the worry that freeing all enslaved people immediately would be dangerous to White people in America and possibly also detrimental for freed slaves. These authors typically justify such worries by claiming that at least some enslaved Black people are unable to lead good, law-abiding, productive lives as free people, either due to an allegedly natural inferiority or due to the effects that slavery has had on their intellects and moral characters. In other words, these authors hold that some or all enslaved Black people lack the capacities that are required for freedom. Defenders of transatlantic slavery often invoke this as a reason not to abolish slavery. We find this type of proslavery argument as early as 1701, in John Saffin's *Brief and Candid Answer*, in which he warns that former slaves would be "a plague to this Country" unless they are expatriated or placed under a strict authority (1997: 822). In contrast, antislavery authors often propose measures to mitigate the alleged dangers of emancipation; some propose settling formerly enslaved Black people far away from White people or preparing them for liberty before emancipating them.

We have already encountered an instance of this type of worry: William Dillwyn's argument that some enslaved people, as a result of their enslavement, are unfit for liberty and need to be kept in slavery. Benjamin Rush also worries that immediate emancipation could have disastrous effects and as a result favors a gradual abolition of slavery. Like Dillwyn, he believes that some enslaved people are unfit for freedom—not due to a natural inferiority, but rather due to the corrupting effects of slavery and, in some cases, due to old age (1773a: 19–20; similarly 1773b: 10). Thus, he proposes that American colonies should stop importing slaves immediately and then abolish slavery gradually by educating enslaved children and placing time limits on their service (1773a: 20). Those who are unfit for freedom should remain in slavery, "for the good of society" (1773a: 20).

His worry appears to be not just that these individuals cannot live fruitful lives outside of slavery but also that their corrupted moral faculties would make them a danger to society. This nicely illustrates that the effects-of-slavery strategy is two-edged, since it can be used to legitimize some forms of slavery: the horrendous effects that slavery allegedly has on the intellects and characters of the enslaved can be used to justify their continued enslavement. According to this line of thought, Black people are not naturally unfit for liberty, but many are unfit for liberty as a result of having been forced to live in slavery for too long. This makes the effects-of-slavery strategy extremely problematic.[97]

At least one enslaved Black man appears to share this worry: Jupiter Hammon, whom we already encountered earlier, writes in 1787 that "many of us, who are grown up slaves, and have always had masters to take care of us, should hardly know how to take care of ourselves; and it may be more for our own comfort to remain as we are" (1787: 12). He even adds that he himself does "not wish to be free" (1787: 12). Nevertheless, he argues that liberty is extremely valuable and that it would be wonderful if younger enslaved Black people were able to gain freedom (1787: 12). Hammon does not make a concrete proposal for ending slavery, but it sounds as if he agrees with Dillwyn and Rush in at least one respect: emancipation would have negative consequences for people who have been enslaved so long that it would be extremely difficult for them to adjust to liberty. His advice for enslaved Black Americans is to try not to think about their enslavement because it will not do them any good, and instead to focus on freeing themselves from their "bondage to sin and Satan" (1787: 18).[98] His advice for free Black people in America—which is quite similar to the advice that Jones and Allen provide some seven years later—shows that he disagrees with the claim that all Black people are unfit for liberty. He cautions that if free Black Americans are idle or behave badly, they will prevent their enslaved brethren from gaining freedom. After all, he explains,

[97] Kendi argues that this strategy is racist because it portrays Black people as inferior, and it suggests that there is something wrong with Black people (2016: 98). For Kendi, this is sufficient for racism since he does not view racism as requiring a commitment to natural differences.

[98] Earlier in the same text, he argues that "whether it is right, and lawful, in the sight of God, for them to make slaves of us or not, I am certain that while we are slaves, it is our duty to obey our masters," unless the masters command us to sin (1787: 7). All this, of course, is compatible with the belief that transatlantic slavery is a horrendous wrong and ought to be abolished. We should not read too much into the fact that he does not say so explicitly; as an enslaved man, he had strong prudential reasons not to state things like that publicly.

> One great reason that is given by some for not freeing us, I understand is, that we should not know how to take care of ourselves, and should take to bad courses. That we should be lazy and idle, and get drunk and steal. Now all those of you, who follow any bad courses, and who do not take care to get an honest living by your labour and industry, are doing more to prevent our being free, than any body else. (1787: 18–19)

The first thing that strikes modern ears about this passage is the unfairness of blaming free Black people for the continuation of American slavery. Yet the passage also indicates that Hammon was far more staunchly opposed to slavery than the remainder of this text suggests and that he was strongly in favor of emancipation. After all, he clearly thinks it would be terrible if slavery in America continued to exist, and he urges his audience to do what they can to end it. Moreover, Hammon's advice entails that he views arguments against emancipation based on its alleged negative effects as—at least sometimes—mistaken. Formerly enslaved people are in principle capable of living honest and productive lives outside of slavery, and Hammon hopes to encourage them to do so. Thus, while he claims earlier in this text that it is better for some enslaved people to remain in slavery because they would struggle to adjust to freedom, he clearly thinks that this must not be used as an excuse to delay abolition.

Absalom Jones also appears to agree, to some extent, with the argument that an immediate emancipation would be detrimental to some enslaved people due to the psychological toll of slavery. In a 1799 petition to the US president and Congress, signed by Jones and seventy-three other free Black Philadelphians, he eloquently argues that slavery is incompatible with America's founding documents as well as with the Golden Rule and human dignity. He adds, however, "We do not ask for an immediate emancipation of all, knowing that the degraded state of many, and their want [i.e., lack] of education, would greatly disqualify for such a change" (in Porter 1995: 331 / Lubert et al. 2016: 51). Instead, he asks the US government to "prepare the way for the oppressed to go free," which presumably means enacting legislation that would gradually abolish slavery (in Porter 1995: 331 / Lubert et al. 2016: 51). James Forten, who was a signatory of Jones's petition, explains in 1800 that the petition "has in view the diffusion of knowledge among the African race, by unfettering their thoughts, and giving full scope to the energy of their minds" (in Porter 1995: 333). This suggests that the petitioners—or at least some of them—wanted Congress to create educational opportunities for enslaved Black people in order to remove potential obstacles to their emancipation.[99]

Levi Hart (1738–1808), a White Calvinist pastor in Connecticut, provides a contrasting assessment of the alleged dangers of emancipation in his treatise *Some Thoughts on the Subject of Freeing the Negroes* (ca. 1775). First, he employs the effects-of-slavery strategy: "there is no apparent want [i.e., lack] of capacity in the Negroes in general to conduct their own affairs & provide for themselves, but what is the natural consequence of the Servile state they are in, & the treatment they receive" (in Bruns 1977: 370–71). These natural consequences, he continues, include "break[ing] the spirits & benumb[ing] the powers of the human mind" (Bruns 1977: 371). He then addresses the contention that Black people would be a danger to society once they are emancipated. Rush, as we saw earlier, endorses this contention: he believes that some enslaved people should not be freed because their characters and minds have become so corrupted that they would be dangerous to society. Hart disagrees. Against the claim that liberated Black people will behave much more viciously than they allegedly behave in slavery (Bruns 1977: 370), he contends that quite the opposite would be the case. Emancipated people will after all "be members of the community, & have a common interest with others in the support of good order & preservation of private property"— neither of which is the case for someone living in slavery (Bruns 1977: 371).

This is a notable point.[100] Hart appears to be adding a new dimension to the effects-of-slavery strategy here. Because enslaved people are not allowed to own property and are excluded from the community, they lack many of the incentives that prompt free people to obey civil and moral laws.[101] There is little reason for enslaved people to respect the rules of a community that completely ostracizes them. This is yet another way in which the allegedly

---

[99] Fascinating excerpts of debates in the House of Representatives in early January 1800, in response to Jones's petition, are included in Lubert et al. 2016: 52–55. During this debate, a representative from South Carolina ridiculed the petition's reliance on the "new-fangled French philosophy of liberty and equality" (2016: 52–53); a representative from Georgia asked rhetorically whether Congress would really want "these people [i.e., Black people] turned out in the United States to ravage, murder, and commit every species of crime" (2016: 54).

[100] Benezet makes a similar point, in passing, in a letter to John Fothergill from April 28, 1773: he argues that when slavery gets abolished, it would be dangerous to all concerned to create a separate society for freed Black people. Instead, he argues, emancipated people should "be mixed amongst the whites & by giving them a property amongst us, make them parties & interested in our welfare & security" (Bruns 1977: 268).

[101] As we saw earlier, Jefferson makes a similar point about property laws (Query 14, 1984: 269).

immoral behavior of enslaved people is an effect of slavery—and, indeed, an effect that would disappear as soon as they are emancipated and fully integrated into the community.

Hart also describes another reason for the allegedly immoral behavior of enslaved people: they have every reason to retaliate against their masters, for instance by secretly taking their masters' property. After all, they "feel a sense of Injury in the loss of their liberty, & view themselves as entitled to a reward from their masters for their service" (Bruns 1977: 371). Since it is clear that their masters will not give them what they deserve, it makes perfect sense for them to use any means of retaliation that are available to them. This incentive would also vanish with emancipation (Bruns 1977: 371). Hence, Hart concludes, there is no reason to fear that emancipated people would be dangerous to society, especially if—as he advocates—each enslaved person is freed gradually, by first staying with their master for a few additional years[102] and then being assigned to an overseer who plays a role akin to a social worker or parole officer and helps them transition into full freedom (Bruns 1977: 372–73).

Thomas Jefferson, in contrast, agrees with Rush that Black people who were raised in slavery are typically unfit for liberty. Slavery, he explains bluntly in a letter to the White abolitionist Edward Coles, has rendered enslaved Black people "as incapable as children of taking care of themselves" and turned them into "pests in society by their idleness, and the depredations to which this leads them" (August 25, 1814, 1984: 1345). According to Edward Bancroft, Jefferson made a similar claim at a dinner party in France in the 1780s, which Bancroft attended. At this dinner, Jefferson apparently mentioned the case of a slaveowner in Virginia who had freed his slaves and tried to employ them as wage workers on his plantation instead. This plantation owner allegedly discovered that slavery had made his former slaves "incapable of Self Government, or at least that no regard for futurity could operate on their minds with sufficient Force to engage them to any thing like constant industry or even so much of it as would provide them with food and Cloathing," and that "the most sensible of them" wanted to return to slavery (letter from Bancroft to Jefferson, September 16, 1788, in Jefferson 1956: 607). In response to Bancroft's request for more information about this

---

[102] More specifically, Hart proposes that enslaved people between the ages of twenty-five and fifty remain with their masters for an additional one to three years. Those over fifty ought to stay with their masters permanently, Hart suggests, presumably because they are too old to support themselves and are owed support in old age. Those under twenty-five are supposed to stay with their masters until they reach the age of twenty-five (Bruns 1977: 372).

anecdote, Jefferson states that "as far as I can judge from the experiments which have been made, to give liberty to, or rather, to abandon persons whose habits have been formed in slavery is like abandoning children" (January 26, 1789, 1958: 492). He adds an additional anecdote about Quakers in Virginia who freed their slaves but nevertheless had to continue supervising them very closely and "even to whip them" in order to make them work. Slavery, Jefferson explains, naturally turns people into thieves who cannot "conceive that property is founded in any thing but force" (1958: 492). Thus, he proposes a plan for gradual emancipation and even announces that he will try it out on his own plantation (1958: 492)—a plan that he never executes.

Jefferson also voices other worries about abolition, such as fears about miscegenation and the belief that it is impossible for Black and White people to live together peacefully.[103] In his 1785 *Notes on the State of Virginia*, he lists a whole range of reasons why any attempt to integrate emancipated Black people into American society would be disastrous:

> Deep rooted prejudices entertained by the whites; ten thousand recollections, by the blacks, of the injuries they have sustained; new provocations; the real distinctions which nature has made; and many other circumstances, will divide us into parties, and produce convulsions which will probably never end but in the extermination of one or the other race. (Query 14, 1984: 264)

This is quite a bleak prediction. The first two reasons that Jefferson lists are at least somewhat plausible: it seems reasonable to worry that the racist attitudes of White Americans and the awareness among Black Americans of the horrendous injustice of slavery would make it harder to form a harmonious society. Yet Jefferson mentions real natural differences as another reason. As he puts it later in the same text, the "unfortunate difference of colour, and perhaps of faculty, is a powerful obstacle to the emancipation of these people" (1984: 270). What he has in mind are in part natural differences in intellectual capacities and in part physiological differences, which he claims make White people more beautiful (1984: 264). It is in this context that Jefferson expresses worries about miscegenation:[104] if physical beauty

---

[103] We will see later that Jonathan Edwards Jr. shares these two worries.

[104] It is worth noting that Jefferson denounces miscegenation while also practicing it: as we know today, he fathered several children with Sally Hemings, a Black woman enslaved by Jefferson.

is important "in the propagation of our horses, dogs, and other domestic animals; why not in that of man?" (1984: 265). The only way to safeguard the "dignity and beauty" of human nature, he contends, and to prevent "staining the blood" of White Americans, is to remove emancipated Black people "beyond the reach of mixture" (1984: 270).[105] Anyone who understands natural history, he adds, will excuse the need "to keep those in the department of man as distinct as nature has formed them" (1984: 270).

Another author who is relevant in this context is Benjamin Franklin (1706–1790), the well-known White writer, scientist, and politician, who served on the committee to draft the Declaration of Independence and was a delegate to the Constitutional Convention. Franklin's attitude toward slavery appears to have changed over time; he was a slaveowner when he was younger but later started advocating abolition and became president of the Pennsylvania Society for Promoting the Abolition of Slavery in 1787. In a rare public statement about slavery—a short address delivered in 1789 in his capacity as president of the abolitionist society—he discusses the effects of slavery on the enslaved. This passage is not strictly speaking an instance of the effects-of-slavery strategy because Franklin does not describe these effects to argue that slavery is wrong, nor to refute racial natural slavery. Rather, he invokes them as evidence that "freedom may often prove a misfortune to [a former slave], and prejudicial to society" (2005: 431). In short, he agrees with many of his contemporaries that slavery can render enslaved people unfit for society and that this makes emancipation difficult. Yet, unlike Rush and Dillwyn, Franklin does not propose keeping such individuals enslaved. Instead, he argues—like Hart—that this is a reason to provide various types of support to the newly emancipated, in order to qualify them "for the exercise and enjoyment of civil liberty, to promote in them the habits of industry, to furnish them with employments, . . . and to procure their children an education" (2005: 431). He seems hopeful that well-designed support mechanisms can avert the negative effects of emancipation on the enslaved and on society as a whole about which many of his contemporaries are worried. Indeed, he seems optimistic that emancipated Black people can be fully integrated into American society.

---

[105] Jefferson did not change his mind about this, writing about thirty years later that the "amalgamation [of Black people] with the other color produces a degradation to which no lover of this country, no lover of excellence in the human character can innocently consent" (letter to Edward Coles, August 25, 1814, 1984: 1345). In the same letter, he states that the best way to abolish slavery is to do so gradually by freeing enslaved people born after a specific date, educate them, and then expatriate them.

The passage in which Franklin describes the effects of slavery on the enslaved is worth quoting at length. He first describes slavery as "an atrocious debasement of human nature" and then elaborates on this claim as follows:

> The unhappy man, who has long been treated as a brute animal, too frequently sinks beneath the common standard of the human species. The galling chains, that bind his body, do also fetter his intellectual faculties, and impair the social affections of his heart. Accustomed to move like a mere machine, by the will of a master, reflection is suspended; he has not the power of choice; and reason and conscience have but little influence over his conduct, because he is chiefly governed by the passion of fear. He is poor and friendless; perhaps worn out by extreme labour, age, and disease. (2005: 430–31)

Some aspects of this passage are similar to descriptions of the effects of slavery that we have already encountered. Other aspects are new, for instance, the effects of living in constant fear, the consequences of not being allowed to think or choose for oneself, and the physical and social toll of enslavement.

Franklin appears to have changed his mind about racial equality over time. To see this, it is helpful to juxtapose his 1789 abolitionist address with his 1751 *Observations Concerning the Increase of Mankind, Peopling of Countries, Etc.* In the latter text, Franklin criticizes slavery in American colonies not for its effects on the enslaved, but for its effects on free White people and society as a whole. The text shows clearly that Franklin held racist beliefs. After arguing that the institution of slavery makes free White people lazy, feeble, and arrogant (2005: 326), Franklin laments the fact that the earth contains such a small number of White people, expressing the wish that "their Numbers were increased" (2005: 329).[106] This leads him to claim that American settlers should not "darken" their new abode by importing Black people. After all, these settlers "have so fair an Opportunity, by excluding all Blacks and Tawneys, of increasing the lovely White and Red" (2005: 329). He ends this discussion by acknowledging that he is "perhaps . . . partial to the Complexion of my Country," but that this partiality is only natural (2005: 329). Hence, he simultaneously admits and defends his own bias.

---

[106] According to him, the English and the Saxons are practically the only White people on earth, whereas "*Spaniards, Italians, French, Russians, . . . Swedes,*" and Germans except for Saxons, "are generally of what we call a swarthy Complexion" (2005: 329).

Jonathan Edwards Jr. also addresses the argument that enslaved people need to be kept in slavery because emancipated Black people would be dangerous to society. In *The Injustice and Impolicy of the Slave Trade*, he responds that the worry is unjustified with respect to northern states, where the number of enslaved people is so low that immediate emancipation would not be dangerous at all (1791: 33). He even presents empirical evidence: Massachusetts freed all enslaved people at once, and the negative consequences predicted by proslavery authors did not materialize (1791: 34). In contrast, Edwards claims, there is indeed reason to worry about negative consequences of immediate abolition in southern states in which a large proportion of the population is enslaved. However, this is no justification for delaying emancipation. He proposes one measure for mitigating the dangers of abolition: appointing Black overseers who enforce good behavior among formerly enslaved people (1791: 34). This measure, he notes, would be much more effective than employing White overseers for this purpose (1791: 34–35). Even more intriguingly, Edwards argues that even if the dangers of emancipation cannot be mitigated and there is a significant risk that emancipated people will attack their former masters or stage a coup, this is not an acceptable justification to delay abolition. After all, that justification "rests on the same ground, as the apology of the robber, who murders the man whom he has robbed" (1791: 35). A robber does not have the right to kill the person they have robbed in order to prevent this person from retaliating or calling the police. Likewise, slaveholders do not have the right to keep people enslaved in order to prevent them from retaliating (1791: 35). In this respect, Edwards goes quite a bit farther than many of the other authors considered so far: he argues that slavery must be abolished immediately, even if White slaveholders risk death or injury by freeing their slaves. It is morally wrong to continue an oppressive and horrendously unjust practice even when abandoning this practice has horrendous consequences for oneself.

The anonymous author of *Tyrannical Libertymen* (1795) also discusses potential difficulties associated with emancipation in a way that is reminiscent of Franklin. This text portrays the situation as a dilemma: keeping enslaved people in bondage is morally wrong, but freeing them is difficult because "It will require money, and labour, and wisdom, and vigilance" (1795: 8). After all, the text explains, simply emancipating enslaved people is dangerous for society; freed slaves are likely to commit crimes out of ignorance, wantonness, hunger, or a desire for revenge (1795: 8). The anonymous author then elaborates on the ways in which enslavement makes the enslaved unfit for freedom: "they have been habituated, not to reason, but obey; their wills have been crushed; they are scarce conscious of the power of willing; and, what is worse, they are not taught the duties that arise from social relations, nor disciplined in good morals" (1795: 8). This description is noteworthy because it focuses, more than other descriptions of the effects of slavery seen so far, on the will and on moral education.

Like Franklin and Edwards, the anonymous author denies that the difficulties of emancipation justify delaying the abolition of slavery. Indeed, this author suggests that those who make this excuse do not care sufficiently about the injustice of slavery. Americans—with all their resources and idealistic attitude—can solve these problems if they really want to (1795: 8–9). The text then proposes a solution: enslaved people are to be liberated from slavery immediately but placed in a temporary guardianship until they are ready to live independently.[107] In the author's words,

> If they are not fit for freedom, they must be fitted. They must be considered, for a time, as in a state of minority. It must be a state of dependence and discipline, not servitude. They must therefore be taken away from their masters, and, by direction of the magistrate, put under temporary guardians, governours, and instructors, to be educated, to be made acquainted with their rights and duties, and some honest method of acquiring a livelihood; to be prepared for citizenship. (1795: 9)

The idea behind this proposal is that it will take some time and effort for the formerly enslaved to become capable of being fully free. This is no excuse to delay the abolition of slavery, since people cannot become fit for freedom while enslaved. After all, slavery has the opposite effect. Thus, according to this proposal, White Americans need to manumit all enslaved people immediately and treat them like children who temporarily require guardians, or like formerly incarcerated people who require parole officers, until they develop the capacities that are required for independent living.

The suggestion that formerly enslaved people need to be treated like children until they learn how to be free—and, one might add, until they are no longer considered a danger to society—is problematic in obvious ways, among other things because of its resemblance to paternalist proslavery arguments that liken Black people to children. Still, the proposal in this text is

---

[107] The author adds later, "I do not know, but *some* should be returned to Africa" (1795: 9).

clearly better than Rush's and Dillwyn's, since the anonymous author argues against the notion that it is justifiable to keep individuals in slavery if they are unfit for liberty.[108] Thus, the anonymous author realizes, unlike some other writers, that given the horrendous effects of slavery on the enslaved, this institution must be abolished immediately. Moreover, the author realizes that it would be wrong to force emancipated people to stay with their former masters for a certain time, as Hart had proposed. The author even acknowledges that masters have obligations toward former slaves, admonishing masters who refuse to bear the costs associated with the proposed solution: "wretch! how long have you revelled upon the fruit of [your slave's] labours, ungratefully; and do you ask, . . . how he shall be supported through the painful residue of a devoted life? Give him food from your own table; and beg him to pray for your avaricious soul" (1795: 9). For these reasons, this text seems closer to today's moral sensibilities than many antislavery texts from this period.

1.4.4. Explicit Rejections of Natural Slavery

Many of the authors we have encountered so far in this section argue against racial natural slavery by insisting that there are no racial differences in the relevant capacities. Some antislavery texts address natural slavery more explicitly. One of these texts is a sermon by Samuel Hopkins (1721–1803), a White Calvinist pastor in Rhode Island and one of the most philosophically sophisticated antislavery writers in eighteenth-century America. This sermon is noteworthy because it directly responds to Aristotle's version of natural slavery. It was probably composed in 1776 and focuses on Isaiah 1:15, which contains the phrase "Your hands are full of blood." Hopkins aims to show that this phrase applies to America: the entire country has blood on its hands for the countless deaths and sufferings caused by transatlantic slavery (2002: 66).

Hopkins's main response to natural slavery takes the form of a historical comparison. According to Aristotle, he notes, "the nations of Greece and some other countries, being naturally Superior in genius, have a natural Right to Empire, and . . . the Rest of mankind being naturally Stupid

---

[108] In this way, the proposal is similar to Woolman's claim that if someone cannot live independently, they ought to be governed paternally by a guardian, rather than despotically by a master.

are destined to Slavery" (2002: 89; spelling modernized). Hopkins points out that we know, in hindsight, that Aristotle was wrong: the Greeks are not naturally superior to those whom Aristotle called 'barbarians.' This is clear because in the modern era, the roles are almost reversed: the Greeks have sunk extremely low, and many "barbarian" nations are now highly accomplished and respected (2002: 89). His example of the latter are the inhabitants of Britain, who in antiquity were as savage as modern American Indians and whom the Romans considered "a Stupid crew fit for nothing but beasts of burden" (2002: 90).[109]

The lesson from this historical comparison is this: since the Romans and the Greeks were wrong in their judgments about their own natural superiority and the natural inferiority of others, eighteenth-century Europeans and Americans are probably also wrong to claim that they are naturally superior to Africans (2002: 89). After all, "We have now the same opinion of the Negroes that the Greeks and Romans had of the neighbouring nations, and we treat them in the same unnatural manner" (2002: 89; spelling modernized). Nations that are presently "savage" and enslaved may soon become free and eminent, and nations that are presently free and eminent might soon sink into servitude (2002: 89). In short, this comparison shows that there is no such thing as natural stupidity among human nations; there are only waxing and waning fortunes. Hence, the doctrine of natural slavery is wrong, at least when applied to entire nations or racial groups.[110]

Hopkins argues elsewhere—in his 1776 *Dialogue, Concerning the Slavery of the Africans*—that there is at least one domain in which enslaved Black people are intellectually superior to their White masters. This superiority is due to their perspectives and experience, rather than natural differences in mental capacities. The relevant domain is knowledge about the injustice of slavery: "[Black slaves] have a thousand times more discerning and sensibility in this case than their masters, or most others." After all, "they think much of it almost every day, though they are obliged to keep it to themselves" (1852: 569). In other words, enslaved people are experts at analyzing injustice. This is connected to Hopkins's claim, which we will examine later, that slaveowners ought not trust their own judgments about how good or bad their slaves' situation is.

---

[109] We will see other instances of this argument in chapters 2 and 3.
[110] Hopkins also uses the effects-of-slavery strategy in this sermon, but he borrows it from Parsons almost entirely verbatim (2002: 78).

Jonathan Edwards Jr. also argues explicitly against the doctrine of natural slavery in *The Injustice and Impolicy of the Slave Trade*, though, unlike
Hopkins, he does not mention Aristotle. One thing that is particularly important about his discussion is the way he disambiguates the claim that "some
men are intended by nature to be slaves" (1791: 22). According to Edwards,
this claim can be interpreted in three different ways, and all three versions
are false. I will briefly describe the three versions and Edwards's arguments
against each of them. The second one is most relevant for present purposes,
though the other two are worth mentioning as well.

The first possible interpretation of natural slavery that Edwards considers
is "that the author of nature has given some men a licence, to enslave others"
(1791: 22). He rejects this option by pointing out that there is no evidence
for it. Earlier in this tract, he refutes alleged biblical evidence for the claim
that God gave White people permission to enslave Black people, for instance, through the curse of Ham (1791: 13–15).[111] His point regarding natural slavery appears to be that since these alleged scriptural justifications fail,
there is no evidence that the enslavement of Africans is divinely sanctioned.

This leads Edwards to consider a second possible interpretation: "God hath
made some [people] of capacities inferior to others, and that the last have a
right to enslave the first" (1791: 22). This option is racial natural slavery: the
right to enslave Black people stems not from an explicit divine permission,
but rather from the inferiority of their natural—or God-given—capacities.
Edwards's argument against this version of natural slavery takes the form of a
reductio ad absurdum: if inferior natural abilities justify enslavement, "some
of the citizens of every country, have a right to enslave other citizens of the
same country" (1791: 22). Even more absurdly, this would also mean that
"some have a right to enslave their own brothers and sisters" (1791: 22). The
point here appears to be that there is a diversity in natural abilities everywhere, and it would be preposterous to claim that it is permissible to enslave
fellow citizens or family members on this basis. But if the latter is preposterous, it is also preposterous for White Americans to enslave Black people
on the basis of the latter's alleged inferiority.

It is worth noting that Edwards does not deny in this passage that Black
people have inferior capacities; he merely argues that such an inferiority does

---

[111] His main argument is a very standard one: only Ham's son Canaan and his posterity was cursed,
and Africans are not descended from Canaan, though they are descended from Ham (1791: 14–15).
For more on the curse of Ham, see the introduction.

not justify enslavement. This in turn suggests that, despite his arguments against slavery and for equal rights, he harbors some racial prejudices. This impression is confirmed in the appendix of this text. There Edwards claims that societies in which enslaved people outnumber free people are inherently unstable. Sooner or later, the former will either drive out their enslavers or attain the same status and intermix with them (1791: 35). This means, he continues, that there are only two options for the southern United States and the West Indies: White people can compensate Black people for the injustice of slavery either by integrating them into society or by abandoning their states and leaving the land and all their possessions to formerly enslaved Black people (1791: 36). Of these options, he continues, the latter is clearly preferable because the prospect of intermixing, and of giving all inhabitants of America darker skins, is "inconceivably more mortifying, than the loss of all their real estates" (1791: 37). This is clearly racist. And while Edwards does not explicitly ascribe inferior natural capacities to Black people, it is likely that this belief is in the background.

Returning to Edwards's arguments against natural slavery, he considers a third and last interpretation of the doctrine: "God in his providence suffers some men to be enslaved, and . . . this proves, that from the beginning he intended they should be enslaved, and made them with this intention" (1791: 22). In other words, God tolerates the enslavement of Africans, which shows that this is part of God's plan. To undermine this version of the doctrine, Edwards uses a reductio ad absurdum again. He argues that the same line of thinking would justify murder, since God tolerates some instances of murder (1791: 22). The idea appears to be that we cannot infer anything about God's intentions from observations about what God tolerates. Hence, all three versions of the natural slavery doctrine fail to justify racial slavery.

1.5. The Nature, Origins, and Effects of Racial Bias

Several North American antislavery texts analyze racial bias with an enormous amount of sophistication. This should be unsurprising: people living in eighteenth-century North America had ample occasion to reflect on racism and its various manifestations. Free and enslaved Black people in particular, who were at the receiving end of this bias, had many opportunities to reflect on its nature and effects. Thus, it makes perfect sense that we find sophisticated analyses of racism in such a context. These reflections on racism are among the most innovative and important aspects of North American anti-slavery writings.

Early modern analyses of racial bias are directly related to natural slavery. After all, the type of bias that many of these authors describe and on which I will focus here is the belief that Black people are natural slaves. This typically takes the form of the belief that the natural capacities of Black people are inferior to those of Whites, and that this makes it permissible and fitting for White people to enslave Black people. This is a paradigmatically racist belief, on the conception of racism that I adopted in this book.

We will examine authors who provide several different, though mutually compatible, explanations of the origins of racial bias. One explanation is connected to the effects-of-slavery strategy: White people mistakenly believe that the characteristics that slavery causes in the enslaved are natural or innate characteristics of all Black people. In this way, racial slavery gives rise to racial bias by causing characteristics that people are likely to attribute to race, rather than to the state of slavery. And, as already seen, these characteristics are often used to justify racial slavery. Another explanation is even more straightforward: racial slavery can give rise to racial bias, not by causing specific characteristics in enslaved people, but simply by leading people to associate Blackness with slavery and thus with a degrading and undignified status. White people who have only ever seen Black people in a state of abject slavery may start believing that this low condition is somehow natural or fitting for them. This is a second way in which racial slavery creates biased beliefs that can then be used to justify racial slavery. We will also see a few additional accounts of the origins of racial bias as well as astute analyses of the nature and effects of such bias.

1.5.1. John Woolman

One of the first writers to provide a deep and insightful analysis of racial bias in the North American context is John Woolman, whose account appears to have influenced later writers. Some of his analysis is in part 1 of his tract *Some Considerations on the Keeping of Negroes*, which was composed in 1746 and published in 1754, and some in part 2, which was published in 1762.

Regarding the nature or content of racial bias, Woolman notes that many White people mistakenly view Black people as "froward, perverse, and worse, by nature," which leads these White people to treat Black people in unchristian—that is, immoral or unjust—ways (part 1, 1818: 180 / 1971: 202). In part 2, Woolman connects racial bias to natural slavery: in the minds of White people, "the idea of slavery [has become] connected with the black colour, and liberty with the white" (1818: 208 / 1971: 225). This association causes White people to be far less disturbed by the enslavement of a Black person than they would be by the enslavement of a White person (1818: 207 / 1971: 224–25), presumably because they view the former as natural or fitting. Once such a false belief has become firmly rooted in a person's mind, Woolman continues, it is extremely difficult to deracinate it; these beliefs can become almost entirely impervious to reason and contrary evidence (1818: 208 / 1971: 225). This explains how people who are not at all troubled by racial slavery are simultaneously able to believe that all men are God's children and equally accountable to God (1818: 208 / 1971: 225). Racial bias allows people to tolerate or even engage in practices that directly contradict their theological and moral beliefs without feeling any cognitive dissonance. And sometimes, as Woolman explains later, bias causes us to rationalize indefensible behavior. For instance, the biases of slaveholders may make them come up with excuses for refusing to free their slaves (1818: 221 / 1971: 235).

Woolman spells out the affective effects of this bias in very perceptive ways. For instance, he notes that we react much more wrathfully when we encounter disrespect in someone whom we judge to be inferior to us than in someone whom we judge to be superior (1818: 204 / 1971: 221). Conversely, when someone treats us kindly or generously, we react with much more gratitude when we consider this person superior to us than when we consider them inferior (1818: 209 / 1971: 226). This means that anyone who believes that some group of people is naturally inferior is unable to judge the behavior of members of this group fairly (1818: 204 / 1971: 221). Moreover, those who are biased are likely to treat the people against whom they are biased with cruelty and disregard, especially if the former have wide-ranging power over the latter, as in the case of slavery. Woolman elaborates,

> he whose will is a law to others, and can enforce obedience by punishment; he whose wants are supplied without feeling any obligation to make equal returns to his benefactor, his irregular appetites find an open field for motion and he is in danger of growing hard, and inattentive to their convenience who labour for his support; and so loses that disposition, in which alone men are fit to govern. (1818: 204 / 1971: 221–22)

What Woolman says here relates to his claim—which we discussed earlier—
that no human being is fit to have absolute power over others, since such
power corrupts us. We can now see how bias contributes to this corruption: if
you believe that someone is inferior to you, you are less likely to feel grateful
for the services they render to you, and hence you will not feel obligated to
reciprocate. Instead, you will probably start feeling entitled to these services,
and you will become indifferent toward this person's suffering.

Let us turn to the mechanisms that cause racial bias. Woolman identifies
three different, though related, mechanisms. The first is connected to
Woolman's point about the corrupting influence of power. Having absolute
power over other human beings, according to him, not only makes you cruel
and callous, but it also gives you mistaken beliefs about your natural superiority over them. This mechanism has a very strong effect on White children who grow up in slave-owning households. All children who grow up in
luxury and leisure tend to develop bad habits, Woolman claims, but the pres-
ence of slaves increases the negative effects of such a privileged upbringing:

> if children are not only educated in the way of so great temptation, but have
> also the opportunity of lording it over their fellow-creatures, and being
> masters of men in their childhood, how can we hope otherwise than that
> their tender minds will be possessed with thoughts too high for them?
> (Part 1, 1818: 184–85 / 1971: 205–6)

The idea seems to be that someone who from a very early age has almost
absolute power over other human beings is practically guaranteed to start
thinking of this subordination as natural. This mechanism is particularly
strong in children, but, as seen earlier, Woolman appears to hold that it also
operates in adults. In this way, racial bias is not only a reason why White
people are able to practice or tolerate slaveholding without moral qualms. It
also results from the practice of slaveholding. Slavery and racism are mutually reinforcing.

The second mechanism that Woolman describes is somewhat similar,
since it is also about our natural tendency to infer a natural inferiority
from a contingent and unnatural subordination. Yet this second mechanism applies not just to those who have extensive power over others but
also to those who merely observe this type of subordination. Woolman
explains: "Placing on men the ignominious title SLAVE, dressing them in
uncomely garments, keeping them in servile labour, in which they are

often dirty, tends gradually to fix a notion in the mind, that they are a sort of people below us in nature" (part 2, 1818: 204 / 1971: 221). This, like the first mechanism, means that racial bias is in part an effect of racial slavery. White people in a society that systematically enslaves Black people not only start associating Blackness with slavery; they also start viewing Black people as naturally inferior, simply because they constantly see them in the lowest and least dignified of circumstances. The human mind turns a contingent social inferiority into a natural inferiority. If a certain group is consistently treated with contempt, observers are likely to start believing that members of this group possess some natural trait that warrants this contempt.

Woolman explains the second mechanism in a slightly different way in part 1 of *Some Considerations*. Bias against Black people arises, he contends, when White people focus too much on the "outward circumstances" of Black people and too little on the fact that all human beings are brethren (part 1, 1818: 178 / 1971: 200). As a result of this focus, the minds of White people are "apt to be filled with fond notions of superiority" (part 1, 1818: 178–79 / 1971: 200). The idea is, once again, that human beings are quick to make inferences about the natural inferiority of other groups on the basis of the circumstances in which they observe that group.

A version of this mechanism can also operate at the societal level, and this can make it extremely difficult for individuals to counter racial bias. Woolman expresses this idea quite poetically at the beginning of part 2: "Where unrighteousness is justified from one age to another, it is like dark matter gathering into clouds over us" (1818: 192 / 1971: 212). These clouds make it hard for us to see things clearly, and they become stronger over time if left undisturbed. He applies this idea to the slave trade. Because this trade has been going on for a very long time, most White people have become so accustomed to it that they are not able to see its injustice clearly; they view it as natural and justified and cannot think about it in a rational, unbiased way. Unfortunately, this also means that those who do see the injustice may be afraid to speak up because their society is so strongly in favor of the practice and unwilling to question it: "We . . . may feel a desire, from a love of equity, to speak on the occasion; yet, where error is so strong, that it may not be spoken against, without some prospect of inconvenience to the speaker, this difficulty is likely to operate on our weakness, and quench the good desires in us" (1818: 192 / 1971: 212). Because objections are silenced, the bias is likely to get even stronger.

Woolman mentions a third and final mechanism that gives rise to racial bias: self-love. People who value themselves too much are likely to err when weighing their own needs and interests against those of others: "When self-love presides in our minds, our opinions are biassed in our own favour" (part 1, 1818: 181 / 1971: 202). This is always a problem, but it is particularly problematic in people who have extensive power over others—which is why Woolman warns, as already seen, that "so long as men are biassed by narrow self love, so long an absolute power over other men is unfit for them" (part 2, 1818: 203 / 1971: 221). In addition to the reasons already seen, absolute power over others corrupts our minds—especially if we are already prone to self-love—because those under our absolute rule "have no voice to plead their own cause" (part 1, 1818: 181 / 1971: 203). When you ignore the needs or interests of your equals, they call you out and remind you that they matter as much as you do. But when you ignore the needs and interests of absolute subordinates, they have no recourse. Over time, Woolman argues, not being called out for your selfish behavior will lodge these selfish tendencies even more firmly in your mind, until "by long custom, the mind becomes reconciled with it, and the judgment itself infected" (part 1, 1818: 181 / 1971: 203). The idea seems to be that an unreflective tendency to put yourself first can, in this way, turn into an explicit judgment. You will become fully convinced that your own interests are of immense importance and that the needs and interests of your subordinates do not matter. Presumably, this mechanism works with respect to individual masters and their slaves, as well as with respect to entire groups in a society, such as White people in eighteenth-century North America, who have enormous power, and Black people, who do not. Accordingly, self-love might explain not only why individual masters discount the interests of their slaves but also why White people as a group systematically discount the interests of Black people.

Woolman describes an additional way in which self-love can explain racial bias. This way is connected to the wretched conditions in which enslaved Black people are forced to live. Only people who "live in the spirit of true charity" are able to exhibit sympathy and friendship toward someone in such a wretched state; selfish people, in contrast, will only befriend someone who has power or wealth (part 2, 1818: 209 / 1971: 226).[112] This might be in part because selfish people are only nice to others when they think they can get

---

[112] Woolman mentions something else that stands in the way of friendships between Black and White people: "the disgrace arising from an open friendship with a person of so vile a stock, in the common esteem, would naturally tend to hinder it" (part 2, 1818: 209 / 1971: 226).

something in return, but Woolman also appears to believe that there is a natural tendency in human beings to sympathize less with someone in low circumstances (part 2, 1818: 209 / 1971: 226). To become a virtuous person, he notes, we need to cultivate our love for others, regardless of their situation, and counteract this natural tendency.

1.5.2. Anthony Benezet, Levi Hart, and Lemuel Haynes

Anthony Benezet knew Woolman and his arguments well—he even helped Woolman to publish *Some Considerations* (Crosby 2013: 6). Thus, it is not surprising that Benezet's analysis of racial bias echoes Woolman's, restating and building on many aspects of his fellow Quaker's theory. Since Benezet's versions are often more straightforward and since he goes beyond Woolman in a few important ways, let us take a quick look at how he discusses the workings of racial bias.

Like Woolman, Benezet argues that constantly seeing Black people in slavery and in miserable conditions tends to make White people believe in their own superiority and view Black people "as an ignorant and contemptible part of mankind" (*A Short Account* [1762], 2013: 67).[113] He puts this particularly well in chapter 1 of his 1771 tract *Some Historical Account of Guinea*:

> When the Negroes are considered barely in their present abject state of slavery, broken-spirited and dejected, . . . we [i.e., White people] shall be naturally induced to look upon them as incapable of improvement, destitute, miserable, and insensible of the benefits of life; and that our permitting them to live among us, even on the most oppressive terms, is to them a favor. (2013: 119)

According to this passage, the biases that naturally arise from racial slavery include not only a general belief in the inferiority of Black people but also the belief that the shortcomings of their capacities are permanent, and perhaps essential. These biases also include the notion that Black people are better off in slavery and unable to appreciate the things—such as liberty, presumably—that White people value the most. This is one way in which Benezet goes beyond Woolman's analysis.

---

[113] Benezet repeats this almost verbatim in *Some Historical Account of Guinea*, ch. 14, 2013: 179.

Benezet mentions another dimension of racial bias, following Woolman: the practice of slavery makes masters both cruel and indifferent to the plight of enslaved people (*Some Historical Account of Guinea*, ch. 7, 2013: 151). This insensitivity to the suffering of the enslaved is particularly strong in people who grow up seeing unrestrained oppression on a daily basis and in whose society slavery is widespread (*Short Observations*, 2013: 229). He connects this to the belief in inferiority: White slaveholders will start believing that Black people are naturally inferior, to the point that they will view and treat them "as beasts of burden, pretending to doubt, and some of them even presuming to deny the efficacy of the death of Christ extended to them" (2013: 151). In other words, this mechanism can dehumanize Black people so much that they get placed on the same level as farm animals and no longer count as fully human even in theological contexts. This is a stronger and more explicit claim than we find in Woolman.

Last, Benezet follows Woolman in describing something like self-love as contributing to the formation of racial bias. In his 1783 *Short Observations on Slavery*, he explains the "vulgar prejudice" that Black people have inferior capacities as "founded on the pride or ignorance of their lordly masters, who have kept their slaves at such a distance as to be unable to form a right judgment of them" (2013: 233). The idea appears to be twofold. First, human beings enjoy feeling pride, that is, thinking of themselves as better than others. I take this to be closely related to Woolman's notion of self-love. Second, human beings find it much easier to disregard the interests of others and to put their own interests first when they keep these others at a distance. Benezet could be referring to a physical distance here, in which case the thought would be that the suffering of enslaved people happens largely out of the sight of White slaveowners. It is more likely, however, that he is referring to a metaphorical distance, such as an imagined natural difference. If that is correct, Benezet's point is that viewing Black people as different and inferior by nature prevents White people from judging them fairly. Their moral judgments are skewed by their belief that Black people are completely different in nature from White people.

Several other authors argue, like Benezet, that human pride is one of the factors that give rise to racial bias. For instance, Levi Hart states in his 1775 *Some Thoughts on the Subject of Freeing the Negroes* that "national pride" leads White people to believe that Black people naturally have inferior intellectual powers. Yet, he adds, "this ungenerous self-applauding preference, doth not appear to be supported by fact, when proper allowance is

supposed for the difference of education & condition" (in Bruns 1977: 371).
This passage is interesting because it invokes not personal but national
or perhaps racial pride: English people, or White people, enjoy thinking
of themselves as better than others, and this leads them to believe in the
natural inferiority of Black people. Lemuel Haynes provides a slightly different explanation in his 1776 *Liberty Further Extended*: English people
believe themselves naturally superior to Black people in part because
human beings "have an insatiable thirst after Superiority one over another"
(1990: 20).

1.5.3. David Cooper, Samuel Hopkins, and Caesar Sarter

David Cooper—whom we already encountered earlier and who, as a fellow
New Jersey Quaker, presumably knew Woolman as well—discusses racial
bias in his 1772 tract *A Mite Cast into the Treasury* in a way that is quite reminiscent of Woolman. One thing that is noteworthy about Cooper's discussion
is how central racial bias is to his tract: he brings it up at the very beginning
and uses it to frame the entire text. Something else that sets him apart from
the writers discussed so far is how explicitly he connects racial bias to natural
slavery. He also makes the intriguing claim that racist beliefs, albeit absurd,
are the only possible way to justify American slavery and soothe the conscience of slaveowners, and these beliefs are hence endorsed by practically all
defenders of slavery (1772: 8 / Bruns 1977: 186). For these reasons, Cooper's
discussion is well worth examining.

Cooper begins the introduction of his tract by stating that prejudice has
such a power over human minds that it enables us to accept even the most
extreme and glaringly absurd propositions. This, he continues, explains the
bizarre claims that defenders of slavery make about Black people (1772: iii /
Bruns 1977: 185). Cooper analyzes the origins of these prejudices much like
Woolman and Benezet, though with a more explicit connection to natural
slavery:

> The low contempt with which they [i.e., Black people] are generally treated
> by the whites, lead children from the first dawn of reason, to consider
> people with a black skin, on a footing with domestic animals, formed to
> serve and obey, whom they may kick, beat, and treat as they please, without
> their having any right to complain. (1772: iii / Bruns 1977: 185)

Thus, according to Cooper, the content of this racial prejudice is that Black people have the same status as animals, lack moral rights, and are natural slaves, that is, intended for slavery by God or nature. He makes a similar point later in the same text: the slave trade "casts the most indelible odium on [Black] people, occasioning some from hence to infer that they are a different race, formed by the Creator for brutal services, to drudge for us with their brethren of the stalls" (1772: 8 / Bruns 1977: 186). The connection to natural slavery is again obvious. Both passages show that according to Cooper, racial prejudice arises when White people—particularly during childhood—constantly see Black people mistreated and disrespected. And once these prejudices are lodged in someone's mind, he contends, it is almost impossible to remove them or to recognize that skin color has nothing to do with moral rights (1772: iii–iv / Bruns 1977: 185).

Samuel Hopkins links racial bias to natural slavery in a way similar to Cooper. In his 1776 *Dialogue Concerning the Slavery of the Africans*, Hopkins's spokesperson asks why White people fail to react to the enslavement of thousands of Black children in the way they would react to the enslavement of thousands of White children. He answers his own question in a passage that is worth reproducing in full:

> The reason is obvious. It is because they are negroes, and fit for nothing but slaves, and we have been used to look upon them in a mean, contemptible light, and our education has filled us with strong prejudices against them, and led us to consider them, not as our brethren, or in any degree on a level with us, but as quite another species of animals, made only to serve us and our children, and as happy in bondage as in any other state. (1852: 73)

This passage combines a lot of the ideas we have already encountered in other authors, including the claim that racial bias comprises the belief that Black people are natural slaves. One important aspect of this passage is that it lists both habit and education as the source of this prejudice. In other words, racist beliefs do not merely form in response to racist practices; they are also explicitly taught. Hopkins makes a similar claim in a sermon, probably written in 1776, where he states that White people are taught to consider Black people "such a miserable Stupid Savage people that they were not capable of being oppressed[,] being fit for nothing but Slaves" (2002: 89).

Hopkins also makes a series of fascinating epistemological points about bias in his *Dialogue*. The dialogue's spokesperson raises these points in response to his proslavery interlocutor's claim that he treats the people he enslaves extremely well and that they prefer slavery to freedom. The spokesperson retorts that due to racial bias, slaveowners are "not a proper judge" of how well they treat their slaves (1852: 578). Enslaved people and impartial bystanders can see the masters' cruelty clearly, while masters believe that they are acting with fairness and kindness. To illustrate how powerful this delusion can be, Hopkins's spokesperson notes that it even operates in the West Indies, where enslaved people are treated far worse than in northern colonies. He again contrasts an impartial observer's assessment with the master's assessment:

> They who from us have visited the West Indies, have beheld how servants are used by their masters there with a degree of horror, and pronounced them [i.e., the masters] very unreasonable and barbarous; while the master, and perhaps his other domestics, have thought they [i.e., Black slaves] were used well, being accustomed to such usage and never once reflecting that these blacks were in any sense on a level with themselves, or that they have the least right to the treatment white people may reasonably expect of one another, and being habituated to view these slaves more beneath themselves than the very beasts really are. (1852: 578)

The point here is clear: these masters believe that enslaved Black people do not have the same rights as White people and are at (or even below) the level of brute animals. As a result, these masters do not see the injustice and cruelty with which they treat their slaves. Thus, their judgment in these matters cannot be trusted; their bias prevents them from seeing things clearly.

In response to the interlocutor's claim that his slaves prefer slavery to freedom, Hopkins's spokesperson says that this is preposterous and that any amount of reflection will show this to be untrue. If slaveowners truly believe this, it is further evidence of the thickness of their bias and their inability or unwillingness to imagine their slaves' point of view or reflect on this issue rationally (1852: 579). Hopkins's spokesperson also questions whether slaveowners genuinely believe this, since if they did, they could easily test their hypothesis by offering their slaves freedom in a way that gives them a genuine, unconstrained choice (1852: 580). Surely they would choose freedom, if they are confident that they can make this choice without repercussions. The spokesperson explains why enslaved people do not typically tell their masters about their desire for freedom, even "if their master should . . . ask them whether they had a desire to be made free, many would not dare to declare their choice lest it should offend him, and instead of obtaining their freedom bring themselves into a more evil case than they were in before" (1852: 580).[114] Their situation is so precarious that they may never complain to their masters about their condition or treatment, yet it would clearly be a mistake to infer from this that they are happy.[115]

Hopkins is not the first author to argue that masters are in no position to judge the happiness of their slaves and that enslaved people are the best judges of their own suffering. Caesar Sarter makes this point a couple of years earlier, in his 1774 *Essay on Slavery*. He describes a form of what we would today call epistemic injustice: "Though many [white people] think we are happier here than there, and will not allow us the privilege of judging for ourselves, they are certainly in an error. Every man is the best judge of his own happiness and every heart best knows its own bitterness" (1990: 169–70 / 1977: 339). While Sarter does not explicitly link this point to racial bias, he is clearly describing a form of racism here. White people who contend that enslavement is in the best interest of Black people completely ignore the judgments of enslaved people, claiming to know best what is good for them.

1.5.4. Robert Pleasants and Benjamin Banneker

Before concluding our discussion of racial bias, it is fitting to mention two men who explicitly call out the racial bias of prominent American politicians. These two men are Benjamin Banneker, who does this in a letter to Thomas Jefferson, which we already examined earlier, and Robert Pleasants (1723–1801), who does this in a letter to George Washington. Pleasants was a wealthy White Quaker in Virginia who freed his slaves in 1782 and became one of the most forceful and influential antislavery activist in the South during this period (Oldfield 2013: 24–26). In his 1785 letter to Washington, he points out the hypocrisy of people like Washington, who were advocates of liberty during the American Revolution but then did not make any efforts

---

[114] Benezet says something along similar lines in *Some Historical Account of Guinea* (1771), ch. 14.1, 2013: 180.

[115] Jones and Allen make a similar point in their 1794 *Narrative*: we—that is, Black people—may sometimes appear to be content living in slavery, but that is merely because "were we to attempt to plead with our masters, it would be deemed insolence, for which cause they [i.e., slaves] appear as contented as they are in your sight" (1794: 25). Jones and Allen add that slave insurrections are conclusive evidence that enslaved people are far from happy with their condition.

to end slavery (in Bruns 1977: 508). Pleasants then invokes racial bias as a likely explanation for Washington's inaction:

> I cannot suppose from the uncommon generosity of thy conduct in other respects, that this can proceed altogether from interested motives: but rather, that it is the effect of long custom, the prejudices of Education towards a Blackskin, or that some other important concerns, may have hitherto diverted thy attention. (Bruns 1977: 509)

Here Pleasants accuses Washington and many of his White countrymen of being racially biased because of the way they were educated and because they have become accustomed to injustice toward Black people; as a result, they do not make abolition a priority. Even though he mentions distraction as another possible reason for Washington's failure to oppose slavery, this accusation is surprisingly blunt.

Banneker is even more direct in his 1791 letter to Jefferson. Toward the beginning of his letter, he describes the most common racial prejudices as follows: "we have long been looked upon with an eye of contempt; and ... we have long been considered rather as brutish than human, and scarcely capable of mental endowments" (August 19, 1791, Basker 2012: 129 / Jefferson 1986: 49). Next he asks Jefferson to do what he can to eradicate these absurd prejudices (Basker 2012: 130 / Jefferson 1986: 49). He also mentions, in passing, that the "barbarism" of slavery may have reduced some Black people to "a state of degradation," which he tells Jefferson to rectify (Basker 2012: 130 / Jefferson 1986: 50). This may be a reference to the effects-of-slavery strategy. Later in the letter, Banneker recommends the following to Jefferson and other White Americans: "wean yourselves from those narrow prejudices which you have imbibed with respect to them [i.e., Banneker's Black brethren]" (Basker 2012: 131 / Jefferson 1986: 51).

It is unfortunate, though perhaps unsurprising, that Jefferson did not take Banneker's words to heart. His reply comprises only two short paragraphs. He neither acknowledges his bias nor apologizes for his inaction. He merely states that he is glad to receive evidence, in the form of Banneker's almanac that had accompanied the letter, "that nature has given to our black brethren, talents equal to those of the other colours of men, and that the appearance of a want [i.e., lack] of them is owing merely to the degraded condition of their existence, both in Africa and America" (1986: 97–98). Moreover, Jefferson claims that he wishes "to see a good system commenced" for improving the mental and physical condition of Black people "to what it ought to be, as far as the imbecility of their present existence, and other circumstances which cannot be neglected, will admit" (1986: 98). In short, he does not take any responsibility and does not even promise to do anything to help enslaved Black people; he merely claims to wish—in the passive voice—that something will be done for them. Jefferson even appears to suggest that there is still not enough evidence that Black people have the same mental capacities as White people or that the alleged inferiority is simply an effect of slavery, though he insists that he hopes this to be the case: "No body wishes more than I do to see such proofs [of equal talents] as you exhibit" (1986: 97).[116] Thus, far from acknowledging racial bias, he appears to believe that White Americans are assessing the evidence concerning the intellectual capacities of Black people in a fully rational and impartial way, and the real problem is the lack of clear evidence.

---

[116] Jefferson writes something to the same effect in a letter to the French philosopher and mathe-matician Condorcet, composed on the same day as his reply to Banneker. In this letter, he first praises Banneker's almanac, which he forwarded to Condorcet, and then adds, "I shall be delighted to see these instances of moral eminence so multiplied as to prove that the want [i.e. lack] of talents observed in them [i.e. Black people] is merely the effect of their degraded condition, and not proceeding from any difference in the structure of the parts on which intellect depends" (1986: 99).

2

Scottish Debates about Slavery and Race

According to legal documents from 1770, David Spens—a Black man who had been brought to Scotland as a slave—argued for his own freedom as follows:

> I David Spens formerly called Black Tom late slave to Dr. David Dalrymple of Lindifferen hereby intimate to you the said Dr. Dalrymple that being formerly an heathen slave to you and of consequence then at your disposal but being now instructed in the Christian Religion I have embraced the same . . . and of consequence I am now by the Christian Religion Liberate and set at freedom from my old yoke, bondage, and slavery. (Speech by David Spens, 1770, quoted in Whyte 2006: 9–10)[1]

In this speech, Spens informs his former master, David Dalrymple, that he became legally free when converting to Christianity.[2] Later in the speech, he accuses Dalrymple of illegally exercising "tyrannical power" and acting arbitrarily and despotically toward him (Whyte 2006: 10). A legal battle between Spens and Dalrymple ensued, which ended without a formal judgment when Dalrymple died later that year, rendering Spens free (Whyte 2006: 10). However, the documents relating to *Dalrymple v. Spens* are important indications of Scottish attitudes toward slavery in the eighteenth century; they are also an extremely rare record of statements about slavery in this period by a Black Scot. All other authors whom I will discuss in this chapter are White men.[3]

---

[1] The documents of *Dalrymple v. Spens* (sometimes spelled 'Spence') (1770) are kept in the National Records of Scotland, reference CS236/D/4/3.

[2] A group of enslaved Black Christians from Virginia made a similar argument in 1723 in an anonymous letter to Bishop Edmund Gibson in London: they appeal to Gibson to "Release us out of this Cruel Bondage," stressing that they are "Baptised and brought up in the way of the Christian faith and follow the ways and Rules of the Church of England" (Hutchins and Smith 2021: 35, spelling modernized).

[3] There is at least one other record of statements about slavery by a Black Scot: documents relating to *Knight v. Wedderburn* (1778), in which Joseph Knight argues that he became free when his master brought him to Scottish soil. After an appeal, the Scottish Court of Session sided with Knight, establishing an important precedent. These documents are kept in the National Records of Scotland,

Slavery and Race. Julia Jorati, Oxford University Press. © Oxford University Press 2024.
DOI: 10.1093/oso/9780197659236.003.0003

The number of enslaved Black people in Scotland in the eighteenth century was extremely small compared to the number in England. One historian estimates that there were about seventy enslaved Black people in Scotland at the time of the *Dalrymple v. Spens* case—a tiny fraction of the enslaved Black population of England in this period, which some scholars estimate to be about fifteen thousand (Whyte 2006: 11; similarly, Cairns 2013: 151). The reason for this difference might be that very few slave ships originated in Scotland (Mullen 2022: 6). Nevertheless, Scots played a major role in the transatlantic slave trade: a large proportion of British slave ship captains and surgeons in the late eighteenth century were Scots, as were many West Indian planters (Mullen 2022: 6–7). The slave trade comprised a significant segment of the Scottish economy in the eighteenth century (Whyte 2006: 41–50).

Given Scotland's involvement in transatlantic slavery, it is perhaps unsurprising that many Scottish philosophers examine the moral permissibility of this institution. As we will see in this chapter, several of Britain's most outspoken and most influential antislavery writers were Scots. These authors include Adam Smith and John Millar—whom I will not discuss here because their arguments focus on economic features of the slave trade—as well as Francis Hutcheson, George Wallace, James Beattie, and James Ramsay. Eighteenth-century Scotland also produced some extremely blunt racist texts. These include an infamous footnote by David Hume, which we will discuss in this chapter.

2.1. Gershom Carmichael

Gershom Carmichael (1672–1729), a White professor of moral philosophy at the University of Glasgow who worked within the natural law tradition, played an important role in the history of moral philosophy in Scotland. Among other things, he had a profound impact on Francis Hutcheson, whom we will encounter later in this chapter.[4] Hutcheson, in turn, influenced many

reference CS235/K/2/2. Unfortunately, I was unable to travel to Edinburgh to access the documents from either case. One intriguing fact about *Knight v. Wedderburn* is that Henry Home, Lord Kames—a prominent Scottish philosopher—was among the judges who heard the case. Parts of the judgment are available in Dalrymple 1826: 776–80. According to the transcript, one of the judges stated at one point that "To say that [Knight] is a slave, because he is a black . . . is too hasty logic" (1826: 776). For a helpful discussion of legal debates about slavery in eighteenth-century Scotland, see Cairns 2013.

[4] For more information on Carmichael's role in the Scottish Enlightenment, see Moore and Silverthorne 2002: ix–xvi.

leading abolitionists. Carmichael's most important discussions of slavery are contained in his 1718 commentary on Samuel Pufendorf's *On the Duty of Man* and in his 1707 *Philosophical Theses*. Both texts were written in Latin. His comments on Pufendorf appear as footnotes in his edition of Pufendorf's work, which is titled *Supplements and Observations . . . Composed for the Use of Students in Universities*.[5] Some of his claims about slavery are similar to Pufendorf's, but there are also some important points of departure. For instance, Carmichael criticizes chattel slavery in stronger terms and restricts circumstantial slavery more extensively. What makes his writings on slavery particularly important for our purposes is that he explicitly connects these theoretical points to early modern slavery—specifically, to transatlantic slavery—and condemns it unequivocally.

Carmichael follows Pufendorf and other prominent natural lawyers in accepting the legitimacy of certain forms of circumstantial slavery, including penal slavery, debt slavery, and war slavery. Yet he places strict limits on these forms of slavery. One gets the impression that he views all types of slavery as highly problematic and regards it as legitimate in very few, extreme circumstances. For instance, he introduces his discussion of war slavery as follows:

> In nothing have the nations so strayed from the law of sociability than in their assessment of the right of *war* with regard to the introduction of *slavery*. It makes one wonder that the human race should so forget its dignity [*dignitas*], and willingly conspire to bring upon itself endless outrageous indignities, abuses, and afflictions. (Ch. 16, 2002: 139; translation altered)

This passage makes it clear that, according to Carmichael, war slavery is often applied unjustly. More specifically, it is often applied in a way that is incompatible with human dignity as well as with the duty to be sociable, which is the duty to "readily unite with one another and behave with due consideration not for oneself alone but also for others" (ch. 5, 2002: 49; translation altered). He later specifies five concrete limitations on the right to enslave prisoners of war (ch. 16, 2002: 139–40), which he believes are often violated.

---

[5] I will be citing both texts by section numbers as well as page numbers from the English translation by Moore and Silverthorne (Carmichael 2002). I will refer to Carmichael's commentary on Pufendorf by the short title *Supplements*. The Latin text of the *Supplements* is found in Carmichael 1718; I was unable to access a Latin edition of the 1707 *Philosophical Theses*, unfortunately.

Consequently, he holds that it only happens "very rarely" that the victorious side in a war has the right to enslave enemy combatants (ch. 16, 2002: 140).

Perhaps Carmichael's most important claim about circumstantial slavery is that, no matter what circumstances have reduced someone to the status of a slave, it is never permissible to treat a human being as one's property. This claim appears to be enormously important to Carmichael, since he restates it several times. He first makes this claim in the context of discussing restrictions on war slavery, though it applies to all forms of slavery: when someone is rightfully enslaved, "this does not mean that he has fallen from the class of persons into the class of things" (ch. 16, 2002: 140). This is a rejection of a legal tradition that categorizes enslaved people as things rather than persons because they lack the rights that are constitutive of legal personhood.[6] Carmichael explains his position as follows: "a man is never to be considered among the goods of his creditor, whatever thing or service he may owe him or a criminal may owe society. For men are not among the objects over which God has allowed the human race to enjoy dominion" (ch. 16, 2002: 140). Later, Carmichael reiterates this point by stating that "the bodies of slaves cannot be considered as merchandise" (ch. 16, 2002: 141). We can at most have a "*creditor's* right" over other human beings, never "an *owner's* right properly so called" (ch. 16, 2002: 141)—or, in other words, "a man cannot be in the *ownership* strictly, so called, of another man" (ch. 16, 2002: 142–43). Toward the end of the chapter, Carmichael refers to the practice of "*owning* slaves like cattle" as a "usurped right," that is, as impermissible (ch. 16, 2002: 144). In short, he clearly views all instances of chattel slavery as illicit; no human being can fully own another human being.[7] At most, someone can have a right to the services of another person.[8]

---

[6] Several early modern jurists claim that enslaved people are, legally speaking, things rather than persons; see for instance Gottfried Wilhelm Leibniz (*Nova Methodus* 2.15, 1667, 1923–: 6.1, 301 / 2017: 51); see also Hermann Vultejus, who argues in his 1598 commentary on Justinian's Institutes that enslaved people are human beings but not persons because they lack civil standing (*In Institutiones Juris Civilis* 1.3, 1598: 42). For an in-depth discussion of legal personhood and its history, see Kurki 2019.

[7] For a discussion of what full ownership over things consists in, see *Supplements* ch. 10, 2002: 101–2.

[8] Carmichael's rejection of human ownership appears to be a stronger version of Pufendorf's claim that "since humanity bids us never to forget that a slave is in any case a man, we should by no means treat him like other property, which we may use, abuse and destroy at our pleasure" (*Duty of Man* 2.4.5, 1991: 130). As this passage makes clear, Pufendorf also holds that human beings cannot be treated like cattle; our rights over other human beings are far more limited than the rights we might have over brute animals or inanimate objects. Nevertheless, Pufendorf appears to hold that enslaved people are the property of their masters, though they need to be treated differently from "other property." It is possible, however, that the difference between Carmichael's and Pufendorf's claim is mainly terminological. Like Carmichael, Pufendorf harshly condemns contemporary forms of slavery that

A final noteworthy aspect of Carmichael's discussion of circumstantial slavery is his comments about hereditary slavery. Here, he disagrees with two of Pufendorf's claims. One is Pufendorf's claim that when an enslaved woman gives birth to a child, the woman's master has the right to enslave this child in perpetuity. Pufendorf justifies this claim by arguing, among other things, that such children are indebted to the master for their maintenance during infancy and will never be able to pay off this debt in its entirety (*Duty of Man* 2.4.6, 1991: 131). Carmichael agrees that the children of enslaved women are indebted to the master but insists—against Pufendorf—that "a man endowed with even mediocre gifts of mind and body can pay off this debt in a much shorter time than the span of his whole life" (*Supplements* ch. 16, 2002: 143). Hence, masters have only a temporary right over the children of their slaves. An even more significant disagreement with Pufendorf concerns another justification for hereditary slavery. Pufendorf argues that because children are the products of their parents' bodies, anyone who owns the bodies of the parents also owns the children (*Duty of Man* 2.4.6, 1991: 131). This argument invokes a legal principle stating, roughly, that when someone fully owns a thing, they also own the products or proceeds (*fructus*) of that thing. Carmichael objects that "the offspring of a slave girl . . . cannot belong to the owner of the property as a product [*fructus*] of something he owns" because human beings cannot fall into the legal category of products (ch. 16, 2002: 142). This is closely related to Carmichael's earlier point that human beings cannot have the legal status of things or of property. He adds another reason why the Pufendorfian argument does not work: "since the soul, the nobler part of man, is not derived from the parents, it is fitting that it should draw the more ignoble part to itself" (ch. 16, 2002: 143). In other words, the argument fails because even if a child's body is the product of the parents, the child's soul is not. Presumably, Carmichael is here endorsing the widely accepted theological doctrine that God creates all souls directly and infuses them into the bodies of human fetuses at some stage of development. And because the soul is nobler than the body, it is ultimately the status of the soul

---

treat human beings like animals. He states, for instance: "the brutality [*immanitas*] of many nations has proceeded so far that they reckon their slaves in the number of their things [*res*], and to treat them not in the way of authority over human beings [*per imperium*], but through the force of ownership (*ex vi dominii*). They call them their own in the same sense as their beast of burden" (*Law of Nature and Nations* 6.3.7, 1749: 614).

that determines the status of the whole human being: if the soul does not be-long to anyone else, neither does the human being.[9]

Carmichael also claims that every human being is naturally free and has self-ownership, or in other words, "is naturally the owner of his own liberty or of the right of determining his own actions" (ch. 16, 2002: 141). This is rel-evant to his discussion of natural slavery. Like many others in the natural law tradition, he rejects natural slavery on the basis of the natural equality and liberty of human beings. According to him, natural equality means in part "that each man is equally a man, and consequently is subject to a moral obli-gation from which no human being can exempt him; and has certain rights belonging to him, which are valid against all men" (ch. 8, 2002: 74).[10] Thus, he views all human beings as having the same natural obligations and the same natural rights. These natural rights include the right to life, physical integrity, and liberty (ch. 9, 2002: 77–78). The natural law also requires us to worship God, promote the common good, be sociable, and pursue our self-interest without harming others (ch. 5, 2002: 47–49).

Carmichael uses these natural law doctrines in multiple ways to argue against natural slavery.[11] First, he claims that differences in natural abilities do not entail differences in rights or power over others: "with whatever gifts of mind or body a man may by nature be endowed above other men, he may not for that reason claim by his own right any power over others" (ch. 8, 2002: 74). All humans naturally possess the same rights and obligations in-dependently of their physical or mental abilities. This means that nobody is naturally a slave, since natural slaves would have different natural rights and obligations than natural masters.

Aristotle's version of the doctrine of natural slavery makes an appear-ance in this text as well, though Carmichael describes Aristotle's statements of the doctrine as so "ambiguous" that it is not worth examining whether they are compatible with natural liberty (ch. 8, 2002: 74). This ambiguity, he notes, might be evidence that Aristotle was merely "flattering the vanity of his countrymen, who imagined that nature had given them the right to rule

---

[9] This argument is similar to an argument that Gottfried Wilhelm Leibniz advances in a text from 1703, which I discuss in Jorati 2019 as well as in Jorati, forthcoming.

[10] In his 1707 *Philosophical Theses*, Carmichael expresses this idea slightly differently: It is an ab-solute duty "that *every man should respect and treat any other man as naturally equal to himself*. Such equality not only implies that each man is *equally a man* and consequently subject to a moral obliga-tion from which no one can exempt him, but also that he has certain rights belonging to him which no one has the right to violate" (§17, 2002: 365).

[11] These arguments closely follow Pufendorf's, which I explore in Jorati, forthcoming.

barbarians" (ch. 8, 2002: 74). Carmichael seems reluctant to attribute the doctrine to Aristotle unequivocally or to criticize Aristotle's version directly. Instead, he opts to criticize an early modern interpretation and defense of Aristotelian natural slavery, namely that of the seventeenth-century Dutch scholar Daniel Heinsius.

Carmichael focuses on criticizing Heinsius's claim that the natural liberty of human beings is the same as the natural liberty of wild animals (Heinsius 1618: 326). On this conception, natural liberty is compatible with natural slavery. After all, wild animals are typically considered naturally free only in the sense that, prior to specific human actions, these animals are not subordinated to anyone. However, they do not have the right to remain in their naturally free state. In fact, human beings may have a natural right to capture and subordinate wild animals. Hence, if humans are naturally free only in this sense, it could also be the case that some human beings have a natural right to enslave other human beings. Carmichael responds that it is absurd to claim that humans are naturally free only in this weak sense; when we call human beings naturally free, we do not merely mean that humans have the status of a fish or bird that has not yet been captured by anyone. Instead, the natural liberty of human beings includes the right, which animals lack, "not to be hauled away into slavery without a prior act" on one's own part (*Supplements* ch. 8, 2002: 75). In other words, natural freedom is not merely descriptive, but normative: we have a natural right or entitlement to freedom. We can only forfeit our natural right to freedom through specific actions, such as crimes. This means that nobody is naturally a slave: no human being lacks the natural right to freedom on the basis of inferior capacities.

In his 1707 work *Philosophical Theses*, Carmichael is similarly explicit about his rejection of natural slavery: he states that natural equality and liberty, when understood correctly, refute the ancient Greek doctrine that barbarians are natural slaves and Greeks natural masters (*Philosophical Theses* §17, 2002: 366). Nobody, he explains, "may claim for himself in his own right any power over others . . . merely because he is better furnished than others by nature with certain gifts of mind or body," since that would violate our absolute duty to treat all other human beings as naturally equal to ourselves (§17, 2002: 365–66). He immediately adds that "certain Christians should ask themselves whether their own minds are not possessed by a similarly outrageous opinion" (§17, 2002: 366). This is intriguing because Carmichael appears to be drawing a parallel between natural slavery in ancient Greece and defenses of transatlantic slavery. While this is not entirely clear, it strikes me as the most straightforward reading of this passage. After all, Carmichael here describes Christians who, in the early eighteenth century, accept something similar to the ancient Greek belief that "they had been made masters by nature and the barbarians their slaves" (§17, 2002: 366). To whom could he be referring, if not to Europeans who condone transatlantic slavery? If this reading is correct, Carmichael is accusing these Europeans of endorsing—though perhaps implicitly—a version of natural slavery, viewing themselves as natural masters and Africans as natural slaves.

Carmichael connects his theoretical discussions of slavery to early modern slavery more explicitly in his commentary on Pufendorf when justifying the enormous length of his footnotes about slavery.[12] His justification is that this topic is not only of theoretical interest but also of great practical import. This practical importance is due to the fact that "men who profess to be Christians" are currently practicing slavery "with a greater tyranny perhaps than it was by the ancient pagans" (*Supplements* ch. 16, 2002: 144). Moreover, he adds, these Christian slaveholders claim to be owners of their non-Christian slaves in the same way in which one might own cattle (ch. 16, 2002: 144). This practice, he proclaims, puts the name 'Christian' to shame and is "a sure sign of the death of sociability" (ch. 16, 2002: 144–45; italics removed).[13] He notes that this type of slavery is not typically found in Europe anymore but that it is practiced by Christians "in other parts of the world" (ch. 16, 2002: 145; see also ch. 16, 2002: 138). What he is referencing here is clearly transatlantic slavery. The fact that he mentions and condemns this contemporary form of slavery is noteworthy because many other European philosophers in this period discuss slavery in a purely theoretical way or merely in the context of ancient slavery. This also strengthens my claim that in *Philosophical Theses*, Carmichael accuses proponents of transatlantic slavery of relying on something very similar to natural slavery in order to justify this practice.

In conclusion, it is quite striking how directly Carmichael appears to connect his theoretical points about slavery to transatlantic slavery. It is also notable how strongly he condemns this practice. And finally, it is extremely

---

[12] His footnotes dwarf the corresponding section of Pufendorf's *Duty of Man*. In Moore and Silverthorne's translation, Carmichael's comments about the section on slavery are eight pages long—several pages longer than his comments on each of the previous two sections, which are on the rights of husbands over wives and on the rights of parents over children, respectively. In Pufendorf's *Duty of Man*, the corresponding chapters are proportioned very differently. The one about masters and slaves is by far the shortest and is just over two pages long.

[13] This is a quotation from another commentary on Pufendorf, namely that by Gottlieb Gerhard Titius (1709: 519, *Observ.* 538.3), whom Carmichael cites repeatedly.

interesting that he suggests that Christian proponents of transatlantic slavery rely on a doctrine very similar to Aristotelian natural slavery. He appears to be accusing them of holding, at least implicitly, that Blacks are inferior in their natural abilities and as a result do not have the same rights as Whites.

2.2. Francis Hutcheson

Francis Hutcheson (1694–1746), a White philosopher from Ireland who was educated in Scotland and spent much of his career in Glasgow, was a founding figure of the Scottish Enlightenment. He studied at the University of Glasgow under Gershom Carmichael and succeeded his former teacher as professor of moral philosophy after Carmichael's death in 1729. Carmichael's philosophy appears to have had a profound influence on him.[14] Today, Hutcheson is remembered mainly for his contributions to metaethics: he defended moral sentimentalism and moral sense theory while attacking moral rationalism and egoism. He argued, roughly, that what makes actions right or wrong is the way our moral sense naturally responds to these actions or their motivations, and that all humans naturally approve of, and are naturally motivated to pursue, both the general good and their own happiness.[15] Yet in addition to defending these metaethical doctrines, Hutcheson also contributed to political philosophy and applied his moral principles to controversial issues such as slavery. His discussions of slavery had an immense influence on later antislavery writers, both in Britain and in North America.[16]

One might initially suspect that the moral sense framework is not a particularly promising tool for the antislavery cause. As William Paley (1743–1805) argues in his 1785 *Principles of Moral and Political Philosophy*, it can be dangerous to rely on moral sense and allegedly natural intuitions in our moral reasoning, since we cannot distinguish them from prejudices and habits. As a result, he claims, moral sense theories tend to be conservative and defend existing opinions and practices. His example is natural slavery: Aristotle

---

[14] For instance, Hutcheson describes Carmichael as "by far the best commentator" on Pufendorf's *On the Duty of Man*, adding that Carmichael's notes "are of much more value than [Pufendorf's] text" (*Short Introduction*, 2007: 3).

[15] For a helpful overview of Hutcheson's philosophical views, see Dorsey 2021.

[16] See Carey 1998: 30–31 about Hutcheson's importance in the Philadelphia curriculum; Davis claims that Hutcheson lays the foundations for later abolitionism (1966: 406; see also Sypher 1939: 280). Abolitionists who cite Hutcheson include Benezet 2013: 100; Baldwin and Edwards, in Bruns 1977: 299–300.

considered the moral maxims of natural slavery to be self-evident, but that was just a way of justifying the prevailing prejudices and habits of his time (*Principles* 1.5, 2002: 11). Paley even speculates that the same might be going on with respect to the transatlantic slave trade: "I question whether the same maxim be not still self-evident to the company of merchants trading to the coast of Africa" (*Principles* 1.5, 2002: 11). Paley's basic idea is quite plausible: the doctrine that our fundamental moral maxims come from our moral sense can be dangerous insofar as our moral sense is influenced by habits and prejudices. If transatlantic slavery feels self-evidently wrong to some people, it may feel self-evidently right to others. However, as we will see, Hutcheson's version of moral sense theory might be able to avoid this problem. In his hands, moral sense theory becomes a surprisingly powerful tool in the anti-slavery toolbox.

Hutcheson discusses slavery most extensively in *A System of Moral Philosophy*, which he composed and circulated in the 1730s, but which was only published posthumously in 1755. I will focus mainly on this text, though we will also have occasion to examine portions of two other works: *Inquiry into the Original of our Ideas of Beauty and Virtue* (1725) and the textbook *A Short Introduction to Moral Philosophy*, which was published in Latin under the title *Philosophiae Moralis Institutio Compendiaria* in 1742 and in an English translation five years later, shortly after Hutcheson's death. He discusses slavery mainly in a theoretical way; his occasional references to transatlantic slavery are rather guarded and indirect. What he says about slavery is worth noting in part because of his influence on abolitionism and in part because he is using a different framework—that is, moral sense theory combined with natural law ethics—to assess the legitimacy of slavery. Because of this framework, his arguments against natural slavery differ from traditional natural-law-based arguments in important ways.

2.2.1. Hutcheson's Moral Philosophy

Let us start with a quick summary of the aspects of Hutcheson's moral philosophy on which he draws in his discussions of slavery. As already mentioned, Hutcheson combines moral sense theory with natural law. He holds that each human being has a moral sense; that is, each person naturally and immediately senses excellence in certain affections and in the actions to which these affections lead (*System* 1.4.4, 1755, 1: 58). He describes this moral sense as an instinct or "immediate determination to approve certain affections, and actions consequent upon them," and to disapprove of others (*System* 1.4.4, 1755, 1: 58). For example, when someone acts benevolently, we naturally approve and feel love toward the agent, which means that we naturally perceive moral goodness in this action and the corresponding motive. In contrast, when someone acts cruelly or ungratefully, we naturally disapprove and react with hatred toward the agent, which means that we perceive moral evil in these actions and motives (*Inquiry* 2, Introduction, 2008: 85).

The actions of which we approve most strongly are those that aim at universal happiness or are motivated by a desire for universal happiness (*System* 2.3.2, 1755, 1: 253–54). Yet we also see moral goodness in actions that aim at something narrower, such as, for instance, actions motivated by love toward one's family members. Such narrow or partial affections are morally good as long as they are subordinated to broader affections, that is, to the public interest or to universal happiness. When there is a conflict, public interest must be given more moral weight than private interest (*System* 2.3.2, 1755, 1: 254). Some historians of philosophy classify Hutcheson as a proto-utilitarian because, according to him, "that Action is best, which procures the greatest Happiness for the greatest Numbers; and that, worst, which, in like manner, occasions Misery" (*Inquiry* 2.3.8, 2008: 125). Yet there are some important differences between Hutcheson's ethics and classic utilitarianism. One difference is that Hutcheson is not a straightforward consequentialist: motivations and virtue play crucial roles in his ethics. For instance, a selfish motive decreases the moral goodness of an action, whereas a benevolent motive increases it (*Inquiry* 2.3.11, 2008: 129).[17]

The moral sense, by telling us what actions and motivations are right or wrong, also tells us what rights a person has. When our moral sense informs us that it would be virtuous or innocent for an agent to perform a particular action in particular circumstances, then this agent has a right to perform this action in these circumstances (*System* 2.3., 1755, 1: 253). Similarly, someone has a right to something if it would be wrong for someone else to take it away, and someone has the right to demand something from others if it would be wrong for these other people not to comply with the demand (*System* 2.3.1, 1755, 1: 253). Because the moral sense subordinates private good to public good, Hutcheson defines 'right' as follows:

---

[17] For other differences between classic utilitarianism and Hutcheson's ethics, see Haakonssen 1996: 76–77; Dorsey 2021: §2.2.

A man hath a *right* to do, possess, or demand any thing, when his acting, possessing, or obtaining from another in these circumstances tends to the good of society, or to the interest of the individual consistently with the rights of others and the general good of society, and obstructing him would have the contrary tendency. (*System* 2.3.1, 1755, 1: 253; see also 2.4.3, 1755, 1: 284)

Thus, we have the right to do what is in our interest as long as it is compatible with the general good. These rights can be perfect or imperfect. A perfect right is a right that is so important to the interests of society that it is permissible to use force to protect it (*System* 2.3.3, 1755, 1: 257; *Short Introduction* 2.2.3, 2007: 113). While even perfect rights may be abridged when the general interest requires it, Hutcheson claims that societies must hold these rights sacred, and that nobody can be happy in a society in which perfect rights are "promiscuously violated" (*System* 2.3.3, 1755, 1: 257–58). Imperfect rights, in contrast, are less important to the interests of society, though they may be equally important to God and to our conscience. These rights should not be enforced violently (*System* 2.3.3, 1755, 1: 258). The difference between perfect and imperfect rights is, however, one of degree, because importance to the interests of society comes in degrees (*Short Introduction* 2.2.3, 2007: 114; *System* 2.3.5, 1755, 1: 262).

Based on what I have already said, it makes sense that in order to determine what rights someone has, we need to look at this person's "senses and natural appetites, recommending and pursuing such things as tend to their happiness," as well as at "the general interest of society" (*Short Introduction* 2.4.2, 2007: 128). After all, the foundation of all rights is either a tendency to general happiness or a tendency to an individual's happiness "consistently with the general good" (*System* 2.4.3, 1755, 1: 284). Our moral sense tells us that whenever someone can pursue their own happiness without diminishing the happiness of others or the common good, they have a right to do so (*Short Introduction* 2.4.2, 2007: 128–29; *System* 2.4.4, 1755, 1: 285). Since any increase in an individual's happiness automatically increases the overall happiness if it does not diminish the happiness of others (*Short Introduction* 2.2.1, 2007: 110), it is also in the public interest that all natural desires be satisfied, as long as this satisfaction does not conflict with more important things (*System* 2.3.2, 1755, 1: 254). When we look at natural human appetites and the general interest of society, Hutcheson claims, we find that the perfect natural rights of human beings include a right to life, bodily integrity, chastity, reputation, liberty, and private judgment (*Short Introduction* 2.4.3, 2007: 129, *System* 2.3.3, 1755, 1: 257). He understands the right to liberty, which is particularly relevant for our purposes, as the right "of acting according to one's own judgment and inclination within the bounds of the law of nature" (*Short Introduction* 2.4.3, 2007: 129; see also *System* 2.3.3, 1755, 1: 257).

Let us now turn to the ways in which Hutcheson's moral sense theory incorporates natural law. As we have just seen, Hutcheson holds that our notions of the natural rights of human beings arise from the moral sense, which means that they arise prior to "any consideration of law and command" (*Short Introduction* 2.2.1, 2007: 111). Thus, he rejects Pufendorfian voluntarism as well as the doctrine that the fundamental ground of moral rights are laws that we know innately or through pure reason. In other words, he holds that the ultimate foundations of morality are neither laws commanded by God nor laws that we can discover through a priori reasoning. Nevertheless, there is a place for natural laws in Hutcheson's ethics. After all, he holds that we can apply reason to the verdicts of our moral sense and discover certain general rules that "declare the natural direct and necessary means of supporting the dignity of human nature and promoting the publick good" (*System* 2.3.9, 1755, 1: 269). These general rules, he says, are natural laws.

Knowing the natural laws is useful because they go beyond the direct determinations of the moral sense: they include principles that we do not directly sense to be good, but that we discover by reflecting on the kind of behavior that promotes the public good (*System* 2.3.10, 1755, 1: 271). Some of these rules are very easy for humans to discover; others are harder. Luckily, we have another way of discovering these laws: through God, a perfectly wise and benevolent being who aims at the happiness of humans and who reveals some of these laws to us (*System* 2.3.10, 1755, 1: 271–72). In fact, God's perfect wisdom and goodness give God a right of governing humans and making laws for us, since divine rule is clearly conducive to the general good, and since our moral sense approves of divine benevolence (*System* 2.3.7, 1755, 1: 267; *Short Introduction* 2.1.2, 2007: 104–5). Thus, we ought to obey God's laws not just out of fear of punishment but also because we can know these laws to be for the general good, even if we do not fully understand how (*System* 2.3.10, 1755, 1: 272).[18] The fact that God, our rightful

---

[18] For helpful discussions of the role of natural law in Hutcheson's ethics, see Gregg 2009; Haakonssen 1996: 77–79.

ruler, commands and enforces these laws makes them laws in a strict sense (*Short Introduction* 2.1.1, 2007: 104).

Hutcheson explains the connection between the moral sense and the laws of nature in a particularly helpful way in *Short Introduction*. There, he stresses that while our notion of rights comes from our moral sense,

> when we have ascended to the notion of a divine natural law, requiring whatever tends to the general good, and containing all these precepts or practical dictates of right reason, our definitions of moral qualities may be abridged by referring them to a law; and yet they will be of the same import; if we still remember that the grand aim of the law of nature is the general good of all, and of every part as far as the general interest allows it. (*Short Introduction* 2.2.1, 2007: 111)

Here, Hutcheson makes it very clear that the natural law is not the ultimate foundation of moral qualities; rather, talking in terms of natural law is a shortcut. What is ultimately relevant for moral qualities, as our moral sense informs us, is general and individual happiness—and, we may add, the motivation to do what is morally good. Yet obeying divine natural law is the best way to promote the general good, since God knows what is right and wrong much better than we do.

For Hutcheson, we can know how God wants us to behave—and thus what rights and obligations we have—not just through special divine revelation but also through careful observation of the world that God has created and the affections God has bestowed on human beings (*System* 2.4.4, 1755, 1: 285). After all, God must have created things in this way for a good reason. The rights that parents have over their children are an instructive example of this method. God's will regarding parental rule is perfectly clear if we pay careful attention to the natural affections of parents and the characteristics of children:

> The parental affection suggests the permanent obligation, on parents to preserve their children and consult their happiness to the utmost of their power. The weakly and ignorant state in which children long continue, suggests the parents right to an unlimited power of directing their actions for their safety and right education, and yet makes this power easy and safe to the children, by restraining all unnecessary severity. (*System* 3.2.1, 1755, 2: 188)

In short, the weakness of children is a clear sign that they need to be governed by someone wiser, while the natural affections of parents toward their children show that parents are meant to rule their children paternally or benevolently, rather than despotically (see also *System* 3.2.2, 1755, 2: 189–90). The same affections show that God wants parents to emancipate their children as soon as they reach the age of reason, but to continue helping and advising them (*System* 3.2.1, 1755, 2: 189). This method of deriving moral rights and obligations from natural human affections is important for Hutcheson's discussion of slavery, as we are about to see.

2.2.2. Hutcheson on Circumstantial Slavery

Hutcheson holds that slavery is legitimate in some circumstances—for instance, when someone voluntarily enters into contractual bondage because they cannot support themselves in any other way (*System* 3.3.1, 1755, 2: 199).[19] Yet people who have agreed to such an arrangement still possess considerable rights: they have a perfect right to compensation exceeding their bare maintenance, and they retain all their prior rights, except the right to their own labor (*System* 3.3.1, 1755, 2: 199–200). Moreover, it is impermissible for masters to exert their power in a way that jeopardizes the enslaved person's "safety and happiness" (*System* 3.3.1, 1755, 2: 200). Hutcheson adds that much harsher forms of slavery may sometimes be appropriate when someone has committed a crime, caused damages, or incurred debt "which they have by their gross vices made themselves incapable of discharging" (*System* 3.3.1, 1755, 2: 201). Unlike voluntary slaves, people enslaved on this basis can be sold without their consent and forced to perform hard labors for the rest of their lives. Nevertheless, even they retain all their natural rights, except the right to their own labor. Indeed, he claims, "they have a right to defend themselves by violence against any savage useless tortures" (*System* 3.3.1, 1755, 2: 201).

Like other natural lawyers, Hutcheson supports the rights of enslaved people by invoking the natural equality of all human beings. Masters need to respect these rights because it is important to remember "that all are of one blood, and naturally allied to each other, and that fortune is inconstant, that the souls and bodies of servants are of the same stuff with our own, and of a like constitution [*elementis*]" (*Short Introduction* 3.3.3, 2007: 234). Thus, he asks us to remember that all human beings are naturally the same and that this has implications for how we are obligated to treat each other.

To further motivate his claim that enslaved people retain their natural rights, Hutcheson echoes Carmichael by insisting that nothing can possibly turn a rational human being "into a piece of goods void of all right, and incapable of acquiring any, or of receiving any injury from the proprietor" (*System* 3.3.2, 1755, 2: 203). He justifies this through considerations about the general good: it would be contradictory to claim that "doing useless mischief, and creating excessive misery unnecessarily, can tend to the general good; and occasion no diminution of the happiness in the system" (*System* 3.3.2, 1755, 2: 203). In other words, giving masters absolute power, and thereby allowing them to treat enslaved people in any way they choose, clearly cannot contribute to the general good. Because enslaved people are human beings and capable of happiness and misery, their interests must always be taken into consideration. This means that they must retain most of their rights, and that their masters are morally obligated "to mercy and lenity, as toward a fellow-creature in less fortunate circumstances, who yet has the like affections, and is capable of the like virtues, and happiness or misery with himself" (*System* 3.3.6, 2: 1755, 211–12).

Hutcheson also follows Carmichael in arguing against most forms of war slavery: according to him, the enslavement of captives in a war is legitimate at most in very rare circumstances (*System* 3.3.2–5, 1755, 2: 203–9). He also argues that the children of enslaved people do not automatically inherit their parents' status: even though the parents' master has a right to be reimbursed for the expense of raising the child, this child can choose to repay this debt either by working for the master or in some other way (*System* 2.14.2, 1755, 2: 81–82). With respect to the legitimacy of selling one's child into slavery because one cannot provide for the child in any other way, Hutcheson argues that such arrangements can only ever result in a temporary and dischargeable debt-based slavery, not in a perpetual or even hereditary slavery. After all, parents do not have the right to keep their children in perpetual slavery, and they cannot transfer rights to someone else that they do not possess themselves (*System* 3.2, 1755, 2: 197–98).

At least twice in *A System of Moral Philosophy*, Hutcheson appears to reference transatlantic slavery. Both references occur in a section about the conditions under which one has an obligation to compensate others for important services that they have performed without a contract (*System* 2.14.3, 1755, 2: 79–85). First, he notes that the laws of some nations—even nations that claim to have immense respect for natural rights—exhibit an unjustifiable double standard with respect to children whose parents cannot support them. If someone provides financial support for the children of fellow citizens or fellow Christians, these nations do not give the benefactor the right to the child's labor or to any other form of repayment; their contribution has the status of a donation, even if that was not their intention (*System* 2.14.3, 1755, 2: 81). In contrast, he points out, the laws are quite different with respect to the children of foreigners and non-Christians, and indeed with respect to people whose complexion is different:

> the equally innocent children of captives in war, or of men of a different complexion, are detained as slaves for ever, with all their posterity, upon no other pretence of right than this claim upon them for their maintenance; as if such were not of our species, and had not bodies and souls of the same feelings with our own; or as if mens secular rights were founded on their religion, or on their complexions. (*System* 2.14.3, 1755, 2: 81)

This passage contains an argument against racial justifications for slavery: Hutcheson is criticizing those who believe, or act as if they believe, that only Christians and people of a certain complexion—that is, White people—have natural rights, and that it is morally permissible to enslave and disregard the interests of anyone who is not Christian or not White. Even though he does not use the terms 'Black,' 'White,' or 'African' in this passage, he is obviously referring to the enslavement of Africans by Europeans. His argument against this racial justification for slavery is simple: clearly non-Christians and people of color belong to the same species as White Christians and are equally susceptible to happiness and misery. Since, according to Hutcheson's moral philosophy, anyone who is equally susceptible to happiness and misery has equal natural rights, skin color and religious affiliation are completely irrelevant for determining natural rights. Thus, racial justifications of slavery fail.

The second reference to transatlantic slavery occurs a few pages later, still in the context of common excuses for imposing perpetual slavery on foreigners. One such excuse, Hutcheson notes, is "that in some barbarous nations, unless the captives were bought for slaves they would all be murthered" (*System* 2.14.3, 1755, 2: 84). He is clearly referring to a common argument in defense of the transatlantic slave trade here. This is the argument that Africans would execute their war captives if they were unable to sell them to Europeans, which means that European slave traders save the lives of the people they enslave.[20] That Hutcheson is referring to transatlantic slavery becomes even clearer in his response to this alleged justification: in cases in which purchasing enslaved people saves their lives, the purchaser is entitled to compensation for any related expenses. Hutcheson gives the example of a merchant who buys a hundred enslaved people, thereby saving their lives, and who has the right to be compensated for the purchase price, the "whole charges on the voyage," plus some profit and interest (*System* 2.14.3, 1755, 2: 84–85). This reference to a slave trade of such a scale, as well as to the "voyage," is obviously a reference to transatlantic slavery.

It is worth noting that Hutcheson does not here reject that kind of slave trade in general, but merely argues against inflicting perpetual bondage on the people whom one has "saved" by purchasing them. He appears to be fine—in cases in which the person's life was genuinely saved—with keeping them in slavery until all expenses have been repaid, which according to his calculation might, in the example of the merchant, take ten to twelve years, even if up to a third of the one hundred enslaved people die soon after the sale (*System* 2.14.3, 1755, 2: 85).[21] Nor does he dispute the claim that there are cases in which purchasing captives in "barbarous nations" is a way to save their lives. He does, however, end this discussion by reflecting on the reasons why people in a Christian nation with a strong sense of liberty—presumably England—do not react to specious excuses for perpetual slavery with the "abhorrence and indignation" that they clearly deserve. Hutcheson speculates that "custom and high prospects of gain" must have corrupted the conscience and natural sense of justice of these Christians (*System* 2.14.3, 1755, 2: 85). In other words, they have become accustomed to this type of slavery, and they are blinded by greed, due to the profitability of this trade. We need to be careful not to read too much into this passage, but it does suggest that Hutcheson is opposed to the transatlantic slave trade as it was practiced, that is, as imposing perpetual slavery on Africans and their descendants. At the same time, he appears to find temporary enslavement permissible in cases in which that is a way of saving someone's life.

---

[20] Examples of this type of defense include Turnbull 1786: 10–11; Long 1774: 389; Snelgrave 1734: 160–61; Beckford 1788: 60.

[21] Anstey speculates that Hutcheson might have qualified his critique of slavery in these ways in order to make it more likely that others would take his doctrines seriously (1975: 102).

2.2.3. Hutcheson's Arguments against Natural Slavery

We can now turn to Hutcheson's arguments against natural slavery. His most extensive discussion of natural slavery occurs in *A System of Moral Philosophy*, in a chapter about natural rights (*System* 2.5). As we saw earlier, he holds that natural rights—such as the rights to life and liberty—belong equally to all human beings. This natural equality, he points out, makes it impermissible for "the greatest or wisest of mankind to inflict any misery on the meanest, or to deprive them of any of their natural rights, or innocent acquisitions, when no publick interest requires it" (*System* 2.5.2, 1755, 1: 299). This, he contends, means that Aristotle's doctrine of natural slavery is wrong (*System* 2.5.3, 1755, 1: 301). No human being is naturally a slave; "no endowments, natural or acquired, can give a perfect right to assume power over others, without their consent" (*System* 2.5.2, 1755, 1: 300–301).[22] In other words, inferior capacities can never justify forcible enslavement, regardless of whether those capacities are innate or acquired. At most, he continues, those with superior capacities have an imperfect right to manage public affairs, if the members of the community are satisfied that these individuals will pursue the common good (*System* 2.5.2, 1755, 1: 300; see also *Short Introduction* 2.4.4, 2007: 131). It is true that the wisest humans are most suited for ruling, but that does not give them a right to subject others against their will.

Based on what I have said so far, it may sound as if Hutcheson's argument is almost identical to the arguments of other natural lawyers: the idea may simply appear to be that the natural equality of human beings entails that there are no natural slaves. Yet Hutcheson's version of this argument is actually quite different. In line with his moral philosophy, his argument bottoms out not in equal natural rights but in considerations about the general good and in considerations about the happiness and desires of individuals. We have already seen a hint of this: he claims that it is impermissible for the wisest people to deprive less wise people of their natural rights "when no publick interest requires it" (*System* 2.5.2, 1755, 1: 299).

Accordingly, Hutcheson ultimately argues that enslaving those with inferior capacities is wrong because "permanent power assumed by force over the fortunes of others must generally tend to the misery of the whole" (*System* 2.5.2, 1755, 1: 300). In other words, natural slavery is wrong because it is

---

[22] Note that the marginal heading for the paragraph under discussion is "None naturally slaves." See also *Short Introduction* 2.4.4, 2007: 130–31.

destructive of the general good. It is hence relevant that when paraphrasing Aristotle's doctrine, Hutcheson—correctly, I take it—ascribes to Aristotle the view that "by this subordination of the more stupid and imprudent to the wise and ingenious, the universal interest of the system is best promoted" (*System* 2.5.3, 1755, 1: 301). Thus, he thinks that Aristotle is, like him, advocating whatever is for the general good, but that Aristotle is mistaken in thinking that natural slavery promotes the general good. Instead, it is destructive of the general good.

To explain why exactly natural slavery is destructive of the general good, Hutcheson notes that even the weakest and least wise people differ from brute animals in being capable of forethought and reflection, which in turn gives them the capacity for far greater happiness and misery (*System* 2.5.2, 1755, 1: 300).[23] As a result, their interests must always weigh heavily in moral calculations.[24] And, he continues, certain aspects of human nature inevitably make life in slavery extremely miserable. One reason is that "Scarce any man can be happy who sees that all his enjoyments are precarious, and depending on the will of others of whose kind intentions he can have no assurance" (*System* 2.5.2, 1755, 1: 300).[25] In other words, one thing that makes enslavement hard to endure is the mere fact of being subject to the will of another person who has no obligation to act in one's best interest. This is the core idea of what we today call republican liberty: even if your master seems benign, the mere knowledge that you are completely at their mercy and subject to their arbitrary will is enough to make your situation dismal. This is presumably related to Hutcheson's point about the human capacity for forethought and reflection in the previous sentence. Unlike domestic animals—who may be content living in captivity as long as they are treated well—human beings are able to reflect on their situation and their future, thus becoming aware of its precariousness, which is extremely distressing.

Hutcheson then lists additional characteristics that set humans apart from animals and make it impossible for humans to be anything but miserable

---

[23] In this context, it is perhaps helpful to note that Aristotle describes natural slaves as lacking foresight (*Politics* i.2, 1984: 1986–87).

[24] For more on the differences between animals and humans with respect to happiness and misery, see *System* 2.6.3, 1755, 1: 311–12. It is important to note, however, that Hutcheson holds that animals are capable of some happiness and misery and that this carries moral weight; it is for instance morally wrong to inflict unnecessary suffering on animals. Yet since humans have a much greater capacity for happiness and misery, their interests weigh more heavily (*System* 2.6.3, 1755, 1: 311–12).

[25] As he puts it in another text, any human being will "count it next to death to have themselves and all that's dear to them, subjected to another's pleasure or caprice, and thus exposed to the greatest contumelies" (*Short Introduction* 2.4.4, 2007: 131).

while enslaved: "All men have strong desires of liberty and property, have notions of right, and strong natural impulses to marriage, families, and offspring, and earnest desires of their safety" (*System* 2.5.2, 1755, 1: 300). Enslavement prevents people from satisfying these strong desires, needs, and impulses: enslaved people are unfree, cannot own property, are deprived of their natural rights, cannot have a regular family life, and are forced to live in precarious circumstances. Slavery deprives them of all the main things that humans naturally desire.[26] That is a problem for two reasons. First, and most obviously, this means that enslavement causes immense suffering—not just physical pain, but the absolute misery of being permanently deprived of everything that humans naturally desire the most. Hutcheson suggests, after all, that it is impossible for human beings to be happy or live a good life while deprived of these things. Second, and relatedly, strong natural desires are morally relevant for Hutcheson because they tell us how God wants us to live and behave, which is also the natural and morally right way to live and behave. Thus, from the fact that all humans have the desires described in this passage we can infer that God does not intend any of us to live in slavery: there are no natural slaves. Hutcheson develops this idea more explicitly in the subsequent section, in a teleological argument that we will examine later.

A few pages earlier, Hutcheson describes the natural desire for liberty in more detail and explains why being deprived of liberty is so detrimental to human beings. There too, he has natural slavery in mind: he is responding to people who think it is morally permissible for more prudent people to enslave less prudent people forcibly (*System* 2.5.1, 1755, 1: 294–95). In this passage, Hutcheson explains that human beings have a natural right to liberty within the bounds of the law of nature; you have a right to do as you choose as long as you do not act in ways that hurt others or are incompatible with public interests (*System* 2.5.1, 1755, 1: 294). Governments may of course restrict the liberty of citizens in certain ways through laws and institutions, when that is necessary for the public good. Yet it is morally wrong to deprive law-abiding people of their liberty merely because they are not very prudent. After all, even for the weakest person, being deprived of natural liberty, and subjected to someone of whose benevolence and wisdom they are not assured, would cause "exquisite distress, and sink their souls into an abject sorrow, or

---

[26] This analysis of the inherent horrors of slavery stands in stark contrast to the insistence of other early modern authors that enslaved people can live quite comfortably because they do not have to worry about meeting their basic needs. See, for example, Grotius, *Rights of War* 2.5.27.2, 2005: 557.

kindle all the passions of resentment" (*System* 2.5.1, 1755, 1: 294–95). Thus, Hutcheson recommends either instructing those who are imprudent or convincing them "to submit voluntarily to some wise plans of civil power where their interests shall be secured" (*System* 2.5.1, 1755, 1: 295). In other words, forcible enslavement is not a permissible way to respond to the imprudence of others—at least as long as they are not a danger to others or to the public good (*System* 2.5.1, 1755, 1: 295). It is impermissible in part because of the strong natural sense of liberty that all human beings possess. Interestingly, Hutcheson adds that we desire liberty not only for self-interested reasons but also because our moral sense "represents our own voluntary actions as the grand dignity and perfection of our nature" (*System* 2.5.1, 1755, 1: 295). This means that there is something particularly valuable in acting on the basis of one's own choice because this capacity makes human beings special. The idea might be that it would be morally wrong to prevent a human being from exercising this special, God-given capacity.[27]

Even though Hutcheson describes the inherent horrors of slavery in the context of arguing against natural slavery, the same considerations can clearly be used to argue against slavery more generally. For Hutcheson, the enormous suffering that enslavement necessarily entails, as well as its incompatibility with the satisfaction of many strong natural desires, must always be taken into consideration. Forcible enslavement is permissible only when the public good requires it, that is, when the benefits outweigh the costs. As we saw earlier, he believes that this is sometimes the case, for instance, when someone commits a serious crime. With respect to natural slavery, Hutcheson's point is this: putting someone wiser in charge of someone less wise may have certain benefits, but these benefits are unable to justify forcible enslavement, at least in cases in which the less wise person is not a danger to others. The benefits can never outweigh the horrendous effects that slavery has on the enslaved. This means that the doctrine of natural slavery is wrong: differences in human abilities cannot justify enslaving someone against their will.

Hutcheson criticizes natural slavery in a few other ways. One criticism concerns Aristotle's claim that Greeks are generally natural masters and barbarians are generally natural slaves. In this respect, Hutcheson argues, Aristotle was simply misled by his own experience: in Aristotle's day, "Greece

---

[27] We find versions of this argument in several antislavery texts, including Hepburn 1715, which we examined in chapter 1.

indeed produced more great and ingenious men than perhaps the world ever beheld at once" (*System* 2.5.3, 1755, 1: 301). Yet subsequent history has shown that this superiority was contingent. In recent centuries, Greece has not achieved much at all. In contrast, the nations that Aristotle classified as barbarians and as natural slaves have recently produced many brilliant individuals.[28] Thus, Aristotle mistook contingent, temporary differences for natural and permanent ones, falsely judging Greeks to be naturally superior and others naturally inferior.

Hutcheson also raises a notable teleological objection against Aristotelian natural slavery. If nature or providence had indeed intended some nations to be slaves, it would have given the inhabitants of these nations not just the characteristics that Aristotle invokes, but several additional characteristics. The difference between natural masters and natural slaves would then be as clear and as big as that between humans and brute animals. The passage in which Hutcheson lists these characteristics is worth quoting in full:

> [These] nations would be found void of care, of fore-thought, of love of liberty, of notions of right of property, of storing up for futurity, without any wisdom or opinion of their own wisdom, or desires of knowledge; and perfectly easy in drudging for others, and holding all things precariously while they had present supplies; never disputing about the wisdom of their rulers, or having any suspicions or fore-boding fears about their intentions. (*System* 2.5.3, 1755, 1: 302)

However, he continues, there are no nations that fit this description. All humans love liberty and possess the other traits that Hutcheson earlier used to explain why life in slavery is inevitably miserable. Indeed, experience shows that individuals with lower intellectual capacities often have "the most delicate sense of liberty" and "the loveliest turn of temper for all the sweet social virtues in private life" (*System* 2.5.3, 1755, 1: 302). Thus, they are clearly not intended to be slaves. We can reconstruct this argument as follows:

1. If the doctrine of natural slavery is correct, some human beings possess natural traits that make life in slavery easy for them.

---

[28] We already saw a similar argument in chapter 1. Earlier authors who use this type of argument include the British missionary Morgan Godwyn (*The Negro's and Indians Advocate* 1.2.32–33, 1680: 34–36) and the German jurist Joachim Potgiesser (*Commentaries on German Law*, "Prolegomena" §7, 1736: 9). We will encounter some other instances later in the present chapter.

2. No human beings possess natural traits that make life in slavery easy for them.
3. Therefore, the doctrine of natural slavery is incorrect.

Proponents of natural slavery might, of course, reject either of the two premises. Yet each premise is quite plausible, particularly within Hutcheson's system. As we have seen, he holds that human desires and affects are a guide to how humans should live and how they should behave toward each other. If a certain way of life inevitably makes you miserable, then you are not naturally suited to this way of life. This strongly supports the first premise. Many of Hutcheson's contemporaries who disagree with his ethics also have good reasons to accept the first premise. One such reason is theological: if natural slavery is part of God's providential order, then it is plausible that God would give natural slaves all the traits that make someone suited to slavery. Another reason is philosophical and internal to the doctrine of natural slavery. Aristotle and many of his followers defend natural slavery by claiming not only that natural slaves are naturally suited for slavery due to their weak minds and strong bodies, but also that natural slaves benefit from slavery: the best life for them is the life of a slave. Thus, proponents of natural slavery have strong reasons to accept premise 1. This means that they may need to deny the second premise, which is difficult because this premise is supported by many early modern reports about the suffering of enslaved people in American colonies.[29] Later in the eighteenth century, the premise will also be supported by autobiographies of formerly enslaved people like that of Olaudah Equiano, which we will discuss in chapter 3.

Hutcheson includes one final argument against Aristotelian natural slavery in this chapter. This argument concerns the characteristics that give someone a right to rule others. Clearly, he contends, wisdom and intelligence are not sufficient, since these traits can occur in someone who is selfish and has a "corrupt temper," and who consequently would be a terrible ruler (*System* 2.5.3, 1755, 1: 302–3). Only someone who is known to be morally good can have a natural right to rule.[30] However, it is impossible to determine with certainty who has truly good intentions, as well as who has the

---

[29] In this context it is interesting to note that according to Pufendorf, some people are suited to slavery and able to "bear slavery with equanimity" (*Elements of Universal Jurisprudence* 1.3.7, 2009: 36). Thus, Pufendorf seems to reject the second premise of this argument.

[30] Presumably, this moral goodness must be known to the ruled because otherwise they would be miserable, uncertain that their ruler has their best interests in mind.

wisdom that is needed for governing (*System* 2.5.3, 1755, 1: 303; 2.3.7, 1755, 1: 267; see also *Short Introduction* 2.1.2, 2007: 105). Thus, no human being—unlike God, who is known to be perfectly good and wise—has a natural right to rule. A human being's right to rule can only derive from the consent of the governed, never from nature.[31]

Natural slavery comes up in a few other places as well. One such place is a chapter about the different tempers and characters that we find among human beings and their effects on happiness and misery (*System* 1.8). Hutcheson argues that even though no human affection is intrinsically bad, many of them are vicious when they are either misdirected or disproportionate to the other affections. For instance, a certain amount of selfishness is good for human beings, but excessive selfishness is detrimental for the individual as well as their community (*System* 1.8.1, 1755, 1: 150). Later in the same chapter, he explicitly mentions natural slavery in a section about "monstrous passions," that is, the most extreme excesses of selfish passions (*System* 1.8.9). He describes one of these monstrous passions as follows: "Civilized nations of great humanity, from false conceptions of the spirit and tempers of the rest of mankind, and from some absurd notions of dignity and preeminence in themselves, have thought them fit only to be slaves" (*System* 1.8.9, 1755, 1: 167). This can eventually make people in these "civilized" nations insensitive to the suffering of outsiders, and even lead them to "behold with joy the most horrid tortures of men truly innocent" (*System* 1.8.9, 1755, 1: 167). Among the examples he mentions are the joys of watching gladiator fights and the cruelty toward heretics. Yet the reference to the opinion that foreign nations are "fit only to be slaves" makes it clear that he is also thinking of cruelty toward those who are viewed as natural slaves.

Hutcheson makes a similar point in *Inquiry into the Original of our Ideas of Beauty and Virtue*. There, in the context of discussing various factors that can pervert or corrupt the moral sense, he explains that men sometimes limit their benevolence to small groups of people based on "foolish Opinions" (*Inquiry* 2.4.4, 2008: 142). Such men mistakenly form a low opinion of specific groups of people. For instance, they might mistakenly view members of those groups as dangerous or as "useless Burdens of the Earth." This false opinion—combined with the natural disposition for being less benevolent toward parts of mankind that one considers "useless or pernicious"—explains why "among Nations who have high Notions of Virtue, every Action toward

---

[31] For a discussion of this point, see Haakonssen 1996: 76.

an Enemy may pass for just," and it also explains "why Romans, and Greeks, could approve of making those they call'd Barbarians, Slaves" (*Inquiry* 2.4.4, 2008: 142). Here, it is clear that Hutcheson is diagnosing the origins of bias against other nations, and indeed extreme forms of bias, which lead the biased party to justify the enslavement of outsiders. It is particularly interesting that the mistaken opinions which, according to Hutcheson, lead to such a bias include not just the opinion that outsiders are dangerous, but also the opinion that they are "useless Burdens of the Earth." Perhaps he has in mind the attitudes of Europeans toward Africans and indigenous peoples in the Americas. After all, Europeans used the allegedly inferior ways of life of these groups to justify their exploitation and enslavement.

The textual evidence considered thus far suggests that Hutcheson is vehemently opposed to all versions of natural slavery. There is, however, one passage in which he comes close to endorsing a version of this doctrine. This passage occurs in the context of discussing various legitimate forms of slavery in *System of Moral Philosophy*. As already seen, he argues that it is permissible to subject someone to lifelong slavery if that is either an appropriate punishment for a crime or the only way for this person to repay a debt (*System* 3.3.1, 1755, 2: 201). Immediately after making this point, he criticizes nations that "favour liberty immoderately by never admitting perpetual servitude of any citizen" (*System* 3.3.1, 1755, 2: 202). Banning perpetual slavery altogether is a mistake, he continues, because

> perhaps no law could be more effectual to promote a general industry, and restrain sloth and idleness in the lower conditions, than making perpetual slavery of this sort the ordinary punishment of such idle vagrants as, after proper admonitions and tryals of temporary servitude, cannot be engaged to support themselves and their families by any useful labours. (*System* 3.3.1, 1755, 2: 202)

What he is saying here comes close to an endorsement of natural slavery, even though he presents it as a type of penal slavery. After all, he argues that it is permissible, and beneficial to the general good, to enslave individuals who cannot live fruitful lives in a state of freedom because they are prone to sloth and idleness. He is referring not to people who have committed crimes and deserve punishment, nor to people who have incurred a significant debt through negligence. Rather, he is referring to people who have become a "publick burden" due to flaws in their character (*System* 3.3.1, 1755,

2: 202).[32] This is not exactly natural slavery as Aristotle describes it, but it is quite close to some of the ways in which White Europeans defend trans-atlantic slavery in this period. After all, one common defense is the claim that Black people are naturally lazy and only work if compelled. To be sure, Hutcheson is not making this claim about Black people, nor about any other racialized group—at least not explicitly. Rather, his concern is with "idle-ness in the lower conditions" and among "vagrants," which suggests that he is referring to segments of British society.[33] Moreover, as noted, this passage is meant to illustrate the benefits of civil laws that allow the perpetual en-slavement of citizens in specific circumstances; it is not about the benefits of enslaving the inhabitants of foreign countries. Nevertheless, it is surprising to see Hutcheson argue for something so close to natural slavery.

2.2.4. Concluding Thoughts on Hutcheson

Hutcheson's attitude toward natural slavery is, as we have seen, notably dif-ferent from that of other natural lawyers. His sentimentalist moral sense ethics leads him to analyze the effects of slavery on the enslaved in a new way, which in turn allows him to argue against natural slavery quite differ-ently. Moreover, his framework leads him to analyze bias, unearned feelings of superiority, and cruelty toward outsiders in an extremely helpful and per-ceptive way. Even though he does not address transatlantic slavery as di-rectly as one might hope, it is no surprise that his writings influenced later abolitionists. Hutcheson's system contains the seeds for extremely powerful arguments against transatlantic slavery, such as his insights into how miser-able slavery is for human beings.

Even though Hutcheson's ideas have great potential for the antislavery cause, there are also elements of his system that can be used—or perhaps abused—to defend slavery. One such element is the proto-utilitarian idea that the forcible enslavement of an innocent person is permissible when

---

[32] Hutcheson's point here is similar to one of Potgiesser's, which I discuss in chapter 5. Potgiesser worries that without slavery, there would be large numbers of lazy vagabonds who are a burden on society. Another possible source for Hutcheson's point is the seventeenth-century Scottish author Andrew Fletcher, who proposes the forcible enslavement of Scottish vagabonds—whom he describes as "a burden and a curse upon us"—in his 1698 work *Second Discourse Concerning the Affairs of Scotland* (1698 2: 24–30). Thomas Hobbes made a similar proposal in 1651 (*Leviathan* 30.18–19, 1994: 228).

[33] Of course, British society in this period includes people of color. Yet there is no indication that Hutcheson is singling out any racialized group here.

some greater good requires it. This idea can easily be exploited by defenders of transatlantic slavery (Levecq 2008: 69–70). They can argue, in short, that transatlantic slavery is justified because of its enormous benefits for slave-holding societies; the suffering of the enslaved is outweighed by the benefits to slaveholders.[34] Hutcheson disagrees with this calculation, as we have seen. Nevertheless, it is true that utilitarians or proto-utilitarians cannot easily argue that enslaving innocent people is categorically wrong, no matter how much it increases the overall happiness. This is one advantage of natural law theories that view natural rights as absolute.

Another element of Hutcheson's thought that could be used to de-fend transatlantic slavery is his reliance on the moral sense. As mentioned earlier, William Paley argues that because we cannot distinguish our moral sentiments from prejudices and habits, moral sense theories can be used to defend existing practices such as racial slavery. Yet Hutcheson's version of moral sense theory is in a better position to avoid this problem than more flat-footed versions. One advantage of Hutcheson's version might—somewhat ironically—be its commitment to proto-utilitarianism and to uni-versal moral rules. According to him, we are not supposed to rely directly on our sense of right and wrong in all our actions, but rather on general rules, such as the natural law, and on calculations about which actions produce the greatest happiness for the greatest number.

2.3. David Hume

Our next author is by far the most widely known figure in this chapter: the White philosopher and historian David Hume (1711–1776). He did not write extensively about slavery and race. Yet his scattered comments paint an intriguing picture of an author who appears to criticize transatlantic slavery while espousing extremely racist beliefs. We will examine several relevant texts. Hume's most detailed discussion of slavery occurs in his essay "Of the Populousness of Ancient Nations," which he published in his collection of essays *Political Discourses* in 1752. This text appears to condemn transatlantic slavery, at least in some respects. Hume makes some additional remarks

---

[34] One author who defends slavery on utilitarian (or proto-utilitarian) grounds is Eliphalet Pearson, whom we briefly discussed in chapter 1 (Parsons and Pearson 1773: 9–17; 22–31). Pearson argues that transatlantic slavery benefits both the enslaved and their enslavers, and therefore maximizes overall happiness.

about slavery in his 1751 *Enquiry Concerning the Principles of Morals*, examining the question of whether any individuals or racial groups are natural slaves. There are also a few scattered comments about race in some of the essays that are included in Hume's *Essays Moral and Political*—published in many editions with various changes and additions starting in 1741—and in his 1752 *Political Discourses*. By far the most explicitly racist passage is a footnote that Hume added to his 1748 essay "Of National Characters" in the 1753 edition of the *Essays Moral and Political*.

Because Hume's remarks about race are neither detailed nor systematic, one might be tempted to think that his role in the history of this concept must have been negligible. Yet his racist footnote had a surprisingly large impact.[35] Several authors who use racist ideas to defend slavery cite Hume approvingly as an authority who supports their views. For instance, the influential White proslavery author, English politician, and Barbadian plantation owner Samuel Estwick writes in the second edition of his *Considerations on the Negroe Cause Commonly So Called* that upon reading Hume's essay "Of National Characters," he was "happy to observe the ideas of so ingenious a writer corresponding with my own," and proceeds to quote parts of Hume's footnote (1773: 77).[36] As we will see later, some antislavery writers—including James Beattie and James Ramsay—explicitly argue against Hume's racist claims. This seemingly obscure footnote was in fact widely known and played an important role in the early modern debate about race.

Before examining Hume's infamous footnote, let us take a look at his discussions of slavery.[37] In his 1752 essay "Of the Populousness of Ancient Nations," Hume brings up slavery in the context of comparing the numbers of inhabitants of ancient and modern nations. His background assumption is that the size of a population correlates with societal well-being: as a general rule, "wherever there are most happiness and virtue, and the wisest institutions, there will also be most people" (1752: 160).[38] This assumption

---

[35] See Willis 2018 and Gates 1987: 17–25 for helpful overviews of Hume's legacy regarding race.

[36] Other proslavery authors who approvingly quote Hume's footnote include Edward Long (*History of Jamaica* bk. 3, ch. 4, 1774: 476–77) and Richard Nisbet (1773: 21–22). Immanuel Kant also cites it approvingly, as we will see in chapter 5, though he does not use this racist claim to defend slavery.

[37] For a particularly helpful analysis of Hume's views on slavery, see Watkins 2013.

[38] In this context, it is interesting to note the important role that birth rates and death rates among transatlantic slaves play in early modern debates about slavery. Antislavery authors often point out that colonies require a constant influx of enslaved people in order to maintain their slave populations. This shows that colonial slavery is not a well-functioning or beneficial institution, since if it were, colonial slave populations would naturally increase without the need for importing large numbers of people every year. See for instance Benezet [1771] 2013: 161; Equiano [1789] 2003: 106. Proslavery

makes it important to determine whether ancient societies were more populous than their modern equivalents, since that would be evidence that their social and political institutions were superior. Immediately after explaining why this issue is important, Hume notes that the most crucial difference between the economies of ancient Greece and Rome on the one hand and early modern European nations on the other hand is the institution of slavery, which he claims has long been abolished in Europe, but which was widespread in classical antiquity. This leads him to consider the question of whether the practice of slavery increases the population, and more generally, whether slavery is beneficial for society.

Hume explicitly identifies the targets of his discussion of slavery's impact on society: early modern authors who idolize antiquity and who regret the loss of the institution of slavery (1752: 161).[39] These authors' main concern is political liberty. They claim that all submission to a monarch is a form of slavery, and they hence believe that there was more freedom in the ancient world than in their own day. At the same time, these authors "wou'd gladly reduce the greater part of mankind to real slavery and subjection" (1752: 161). Hume is clearly referring to European authors who criticize absolute monarchies while advocating for, or at least tolerating, certain forms of slavery. He finds that attitude ridiculous: it is clear that modern Europeans have far more liberty than the ancients and that personal slavery is "more cruel and oppressive than any civil subjection whatsoever" (1752: 161). This is a remarkable passage: Hume dismisses the claims of many other early modern authors that the subjection to a monarch is tantamount to slavery. For him, a monarchy that does not practice personal slavery is clearly preferable to a republic in which personal slavery is widespread.

Intriguingly, Hume then explicitly mentions modern colonial slavery: "The remains which are found of domestic slavery, in the *American* colonies, and among some *European* nations, wou'd never surely create a desire of rendering it more universal" (1752: 162). In short, he claims that the slavery in American colonies is so bad that nobody—or at least no reasonable

authors often feel the need to respond to such arguments (e.g., Adair 1790: 124–27). Hume mentions the negative population growth of West Indian slaves in a footnote to this essay (1752: 170).

[39] In the last sentence of this long essay, Hume again condemns those who idolize the past and criticize the present (1752: 262). As Margaret Watkins convincingly argues, it is important to keep this target in mind when reading Hume's discussion of slavery (2013). It means that Hume is not targeting "a political pro-slavery movement," but rather "a tendency to romanticize an earlier way of life," as a result of which we cannot classify Hume's discussion as genuinely abolitionist (2013: 113).

person—could want to expand it further.[40] His first reason for claiming that colonial slavery is detrimental for society is the inhumanity that is "commonly observ'd in persons accustomed, from their infancy, to exercise so great authority over their fellow creatures, and to trample upon human nature,"[41] which suffices "to disgust us with that authority" (1752: 162).[42] Here, Hume worries exclusively about slavery's effects on enslavers, rather than on the enslaved: the institution makes enslavers cruel and immoral. He speculates that this mechanism probably also explains how "barbarous" the ancient Greeks and Romans often were: slavery turned "every man of rank" into "a petty tyrant, . . . educated amidst the flattery, submission, and low debasement of his slaves" (1752: 162).[43]

Next, Hume enumerates some of the most horrific aspects of ancient slavery. He contrasts the absolute power of ancient slave masters with the much more limited power that early modern Europeans have over their hired servants, stressing that these hired servants cannot be treated nearly as inhumanely as ancient slaves (1752: 162). Over the next three pages, he lists evidence of the harsh treatment of ancient slaves before turning to the question of whether the institution of slavery might lead to an increase in the population. His answer is that the evidence is ambiguous. On the one hand, when enslaved people and their offspring are the property of masters, masters have an incentive to encourage them to procreate (1752: 166). The relevant incentives are exactly the same as the incentives of cattle farmers who profit from an increase in their herd, he notes. This comparison to cattle is "shocking" but "extremely just," he adds, since enslaved people indeed have a status very similar to that of cattle (1752: 167). On the other hand, there are also reasons for masters in populous and wealthy countries to discourage procreation among enslaved people. Raising children—just like

---

[40] Hume must have been aware that there were many people in Britain who did want to expand this trade further. Thus, this claim must either be read as downplaying the ongoing expansion of transatlantic slavery or as dismissing the reasons for such an expansion as ludicrous.

[41] This is reminiscent of John Woolman's description of the effects of slavery on free White children who grow up in slave-owning households, which I examined in chapter 1. Yet it seems unlikely that there was an influence in either direction, since Woolman apparently composed this text in 1746 but only published it in 1754, two years after Hume published his essay.

[42] In later editions of this essay, Hume changes "disgust us with that authority" to "disgust us with that unbounded dominion" (1772: 396). His reason for this change was presumably to stress the absoluteness of genuine slavery, which makes it very different from the practice of hiring servants over whom one has only limited authority.

[43] In a footnote, Hume mentions gladiator fights as an example of the inhumane customs of ancient people, adding that it is unsurprising that ancient "emperors shou'd treat the people in the same way the people treated their inferiors" (1752: 165).

raising cattle—is prohibitively expensive in densely populated areas, after all (1752: 167). He then mentions a host of other evidence against the claim that ancient slavery increased the population, concluding that "slavery is in general disadvantageous both to the happiness and populousness of mankind, and that its place is much better supply'd by the practice of hir'd servants" (1752: 177).

Interestingly, Hume also notes at the outset of his discussion of slavery's effects on population sizes that "if domestic slavery really encreas'd populousness, it wou'd be an exception to the general rule, that the happiness of any society and its populousness are necessary attendants" (1752: 166n). In other words, he is apparently far more confident that slavery is detrimental to the general good than that population size correlates with general well-being. He even gives a reason for why slavery might be an exception to the general rule: "A master, from humour or interest, may make his slaves very unhappy, and yet be careful, from interest, to encrease their number. Their marriage is not a matter of choice with them, no more than any other action of their life" (1752: 167n). The idea here is that in the case of enslaved people, fertility rates may not correlate with well-being or happiness because they are forced to procreate. Free people who live in miserable conditions would choose not to have children, but enslaved people do not have the freedom to make even this choice. This claim is noteworthy because it is evidence that Hume is deeply committed to the idea that slavery is a horrific institution—and indeed to the idea that it is horrific because of its negative effects not only on enslavers but also on the enslaved, whose unhappiness he here cites as evidence for the badness of slavery.

It is somewhat unclear what we should make of Hume's long discussion of slavery in "Of the Populousness of Ancient Nations." On the one hand, his main goal in this discussion is to criticize people who idolize classical antiquity—and thus ancient slavery—and who oppose modern monarchies. The early modern institution of slavery is only of marginal importance for this argument. Thus, this text does not provide evidence that Hume is overly concerned about transatlantic slavery or had a strong desire to effect its abolition.[44] Indeed, the fact that Hume does not appear to advocate abolition explicitly in any of his writings suggests that this issue was not very important to him. On the other hand, this essay does contain clear criticisms of chattel slavery: it argues that this institution can never be beneficial to society

---

[44] See Watkins 2013 for a slightly different argument that Hume should not be viewed as a genuine abolitionist.

because it makes enslavers inhumane and the enslaved miserable. Hume clearly thinks that it is far better for everyone concerned to replace enslaved people with hired servants. Moreover, he holds that transatlantic slavery supports his claims about the negative effects of slavery, which is a way of criticizing it. While Hume may not deserve to be called an abolitionist, he evidently views transatlantic slavery as, at the very least, regrettable.

Hume also refers to natural slavery, though in a completely different context and without using the term 'natural slavery'. The context is his discussion of justice in his 1751 *Enquiry Concerning the Principles of Morals*. In the relevant section, Hume examines the circumstances that are required in order for there to be laws of justice. He imagines a series of hypothetical scenarios in which such laws would be pointless or nonexistent—for instance, a situation in which all resources are so abundant that there is no need to worry about their allocation (3.1, 1975: 183–84). Later in the same section, Hume considers the Hobbesian state of nature, that is, a state without human institutions in which each person is at war with each other person. In such conditions, Hume states, the laws of justice would not be of any use and would therefore be suspended (3.1, 1975: 190).

Hume's next example of a scenario in which the laws of justice would be suspended is most relevant for present purposes: he imagines a situation in which humans coexist with "a species of creatures . . . which, though rational, were possessed of such inferior strength, both of body and mind, that they were incapable of all resistance, and could never, upon the highest provocation, make us feel the effects of their resentment" (3.1, 1975: 190). Our relation to these inferior creatures, Hume contends, could only be one of "absolute command . . . and servile obedience" (3.1, 1975: 190).[45] To put this slightly differently, we would be natural masters and they natural slaves. The natural inequality between us and them would be so enormous that the laws of justice would be useless and hence suspended (1975: 191). After all, these inferior creatures would not be able to have "any right or property," except by permission of their "arbitrary lords" (1975: 190), which means that we would not need laws of justice in order to solve conflicts of interest between us and them. He even adds that "no inconvenience ever results from the exercise of a power, so firmly established in nature" (1975: 191). Here, Hume sides with

---

[45] Thomas Hobbes makes a similar point: if anybody in the state of nature has "sure and irresistible power," they would thereby have "the right of ruling and commanding those who cannot resist" (*On the Citizen* 1.14, 1998: 31; italics removed; see also *Leviathan* 31.5, 1994: 235).

Hobbes's doctrine that irresistible might makes right; this goes against another influential school of moral philosophy according to which all rational creatures have moral rights, even if they are physically and mentally inferior to others. Indeed, Hume appears to embrace a version of the doctrine of natural slavery: if there are rational animals who are vastly inferior to us in mental capacities, it is permissible to enslave them. The resulting master-slave relationship would be absolute and unconstrained by the laws of justice, though Hume claims that "we should be bound by the laws of humanity to give gentle usage to these creatures" (1975: 190).

Does Hume believe that there are any natural slaves, or are his claims about inferior creatures merely a counterfactual thought experiment?[46] He considers three candidates for this status in the actual world: brute animals, "barbarous Indians," and women. Brute animals, he notes, are clearly inferior to human beings in precisely the way that the hypothetical creatures are.[47] With respect to women, his claims are much less straightforward. He notes that in some nations they are "reduced to like slavery," while elsewhere they "share with the other sex in all the rights and privileges of society" (1975: 191). Interestingly, Hume also states that the physical superiority of men enables them to keep women enslaved, and when women have equal rights, it is not because of their strength but because of their "insinuation, address, and charms" (1975: 191).[48] This is not the place to unpack this intriguing passage. Yet it is noteworthy that Hume does not describe women as mentally equal to men; he seems to suggest that when they gain an equal status it is not through rational discourse but through their charms. What he says is hence perfectly compatible with viewing them as naturally subordinate based on a physical and mental inferiority.

For our purposes, what is most relevant is what Hume says about American Indians in this context: he claims that "The great superiority of civilized Europeans above barbarous Indians, tempted us to imagine ourselves on the same footing with regard to them [as with regard to the hypothetical inferior

---

[46] For helpful discussions of this question, see Sebastiani 2013: 37; Valls 2005: 139–43; Willis 2018: 506–7; Roberts 2020.

[47] He does not take a stand on whether brute animals are rational, merely claiming that he will "leave it to others to determine" (1975: 191); if they are not rational, that would be one relevant difference between them and the creatures from the thought experiment.

[48] In this context, 'insinuation' means "The action of stealing into the favour or affections of any one by winning, persuasive, or subtle means" (OED, http://www.oed.com/view/Entry/96869). Similarly, 'address' refers to a personal approach or overture to another person, either of an amorous nature or as an appeal for help (OED, http://www.oed.com/view/Entry/2208).

creatures], and made us throw off all restraints of justice, and even of hu-manity, in our treatment of them" (1975: 191). In this passage, he endorses the claim that American Indians are inferior to Europeans to a significant extent. At the same time, it is unclear whether he believes that this inferiority is large enough to suspend the laws of justice and render the relation between Europeans and American Indians analogous to the relation between human beings and brute animals. After all, Hume merely states that Europeans were "tempted" on this basis to imagine themselves entitled to rule American Indians and as a result treated them without observing the rules of justice or even humanity. He does not say whether the Europeans' attitude and behavior was justified. If Hume thought that American Indians were clear examples of natural subordinates, he could have said so much more directly; the indirectness of his statement suggests that he either believes that this atti-tude was wrong, or that he at least does not want to commit himself publicly to its correctness.[49] His claim that Europeans, based on their imagined nat-ural right to rule, threw off even the restraints of humanity is clearly a criti-cism, since he explicitly stated earlier that if there are vastly inferior rational creatures, they ought to be treated humanely.

In this context, it is helpful to note what Hume says about human equality in his 1748 essay "Of the Original Contract": "When we consider how nearly equal all Men are in their bodily Force, and even in their mental Powers and Faculties, 'ere cultivated by Education; we must necessarily allow, that nothing but their own Consent cou'd, at first, associate them together, and subject them to any Authority" (1748: 291).[50] This is, of course, a central idea of the social contract tradition. What is interesting for our purposes is that Hume here describes all human beings as naturally "nearly equal" in their physical and mental powers, on which basis he rejects the idea that there could be natural rulers and natural subordinates among human beings. Given the lack of significant natural differences in physical or mental capacities, subordina-tion or rule must originally have resulted from consent. This passage is evi-dence that Hume does not believe that there are natural slaves among human beings, though he appears to believe that there could in principle be rational creatures who are naturally subordinated to us. The evidence is defeasible, however, because when Hume talks about the equality of "all Men," he could

[49] According to Valls, this passage suggests that this attitude was wrong (2005: 142).
[50] A little later in the same discussion, he refers to "the Equality, which we find in all the Individuals of [the human] Species" (1748: 292).

be implicitly restricting the scope to specific racial groups, in addition to excluding women.

In addition to the question of whether Hume believes in the natural right of one racial group to rule another based on natural differences in mental or physical capacities, there is another relevant question here: Does Hume believe in the right of "civilized" nations to rule "uncivilized" or "barbarous" ones? The two questions are clearly related, but not identical, since a commitment to differences in the degree of "civilization" is compatible with a commitment to an equality of natural capacities. As already seen, Hume claims in the *Enquiry Concerning the Principles of Morals* that there is a "great superiority of civilized Europeans above barbarous Indians," which prompted Europeans to treat American Indians unjustly and inhumanely (3.1, 1975: 191). On one interpretation, Hume believes that Europeans—due to their supposedly superior degree of civilization—possess a right to rule American Indians, though perhaps not the right to treat them unjustly and inhumanely. In particular, Hume might hold that Europeans have the right to conquer and "civilize" American Indians and other groups that he views as "barbarous." Evidence for this interpretation is found in the fifth volume of Hume's *History of England* (1754/1778) where Hume praises James I for "civilizing" Ireland forcibly (vol. 5, ch. 46, 1983b: 46–47), introducing "humanity and justice among the people, who had ever been buried in the most profound barbarism" (1983b: 49), and making them free citizens only after replacing their barbarous customs with English law (1983b: 48). Likewise, Hume describes some aspects of the Roman conquest of Britain in favorable terms in the first volume of his *History* (1762/1778): the Romans brought "laws and civility" as well as "letters and science" to the previously barbarous Britons (vol. 1, ch. 1, 1983a: 10). Hume is, however, critical of some aspects of the Roman conquest and by extension early modern European colonialism: he states that under Claudius, the Romans attempted to subdue Britain "Without seeking any more justifiable reasons of hostility than were employed by the late Europeans in subjecting the Africans and Americans" (1983a: 7–8).[51] Hence, Hume might hold that it is permissible for "civilized" nations to conquer "barbarous" ones in order to civilize them, but that this virtuous motive motivated neither the Roman conquest nor modern European colonialism.

---

[51] For a more detailed discussion of Hume's apparent approval of attempts to "civilize" barbarous nations, see Mori 2021.

It is finally time to turn to Hume's infamous racist footnote, which suggests that he views the differences between White Europeans and Black Africans to be far deeper than mere differences in customs and "civilization." Hume added this footnote to his essay "Of National Characters" in 1753—an essay he had first published five years earlier in the third edition of his *Essays, Moral and Political*.[52] After the note's first publication in 1753, in the fourth edition,[53] he slightly edited it for the 1772 and 1777 editions.[54] The original 1753 version of the footnote reads as follows, in its entirety:

> I am apt to suspect the negroes, and in general all the other species of men (for there are four or five different kinds) to be naturally inferior to the whites. There never was a civiliz'd nation of any other complexion than white, nor even any individual eminent either in action or speculation. No ingenious manufactures amongst them, no arts, no sciences. On the other hand, the most rude and barbarous of the whites, such as the antient *Germans*, the present *Tartars*, have still something eminent about them, in their valour, form of government, or some other particular. Such a uniform and constant difference could not happen, in so many countries and ages, if nature had not made an original distinction betwixt these breeds of men. Not to mention our colonies, there are *Negroe* slaves dispersed all over *Europe*, of which none ever discover'd any symptoms of ingenuity; tho' low people, without education, will start up amongst us, and distinguish themselves in every profession. In *Jamaica* indeed they talk of one negroe as a man of parts and learning; but 'tis likely he is admired for very slender accomplishments, like a parrot, who speaks a few words plainly. (1753: 291n)

A few aspects of this passage jump out right away. First, Hume describes nonwhite people as "naturally inferior" to White people and argues that

---

[52] The essay already contained some racist statements before the insertion of the footnote; for instance, Hume writes in the context of discussing the propensity for alcoholism among various groups, "You may obtain any Thing of the *Negroes* by offering them strong Liquors; and may easily prevail with them to sell, not only their Parents, but their Wives and Mistresses, for a Cask of Brandy" (1748: 286–87 / 1994: 91).

[53] The fourth edition of *Essays, Moral and Political* was published as the first volume of the four-volume work *Essays and Treatises on Several Subjects*.

[54] Hume died in 1776, before the 1777 edition appeared. He apparently worked on revisions to the 1772 edition in the last year of his life, but it is unclear which changes are his and which were introduced by others after his death (Haakonssen 1994: xxxviii). I will here follow other interpreters in assuming that Hume is responsible for the differences between the 1772 and 1777 versions of this footnote.

there is a natural "original distinction" between them. His evidence is the alleged dearth of civilization and individual achievement among nonwhite people, which he contends cannot be explained fully through differences in circumstances. The racism in this passage is patent. It is not the kind of racism that explicitly includes the claim that Black people are natural slaves or lack natural rights; what Hume says here is compatible with his claims elsewhere that transatlantic slavery is unjust. Yet the footnote is an instance of a more general type of racism that portrays White people as naturally superior in "ingenuity" as well as the capacity for speculation and the arts and sciences—superior in what we would today call intelligence.[55] Indeed, this footnote strongly suggests that Hume endorses polygenism, that is, believes that different racial groups have separate origins. After all, he concludes from what he takes to be empirical evidence that "nature . . . made an original distinction betwixt these breeds of men." In other words, he claims that these racial groups were different and separate from the very beginning.[56]

The two later versions of Hume's footnote differ only in small respects from the original version.[57] In the 1772 version, the claim that there has never been a "civilized" nation that was not White is slightly weaker than in the original version: "never was" in the note's second sentence is replaced with "scarcely ever was" (1772: 652). Yet this version retains the other seemingly universal claims, such as the claim that no Black people in Europe ever showed signs of ingenuity and that there are no arts, sciences, or ingenious manufactures among Blacks. The 1777 version contains a change that seems more significant: it limits its claims to the differences between Black and White people, omitting the reference to other races. The note's first sentence now reads, "I am apt to suspect the negroes to be naturally inferior to the whites"

[55] Some authors deny that this is sufficient for racism and prefer to call it 'racialism.' See, for example, Andrew Valls, who argues that Hume's footnote is not racist because it merely expresses a belief in racial superiority, unaccompanied by any claims about differences in moral status or any expressions of ill will (2005: 130).

[56] Several interpreters read this as an endorsement of polygenism (Popkin 1992: 65–66; Immerwahr 1992: 482; Sebastiani 2013: 34; Zack 2002: 14–17), but at least one interpreter disagrees (Valls 2005: 132). To me, the polygenist reading of this footnote is by far the most plausible. The only countervailing evidence of which I am aware is Hume's claim in "Of the Populousness of Ancient Nations" that "As far . . . as observation reaches, there is no universal difference discernible in the human species" (1752: 156). Valls rejects the polygenist reading because he claims the evidence in its favor is "slim"; strangely enough, he thinks that the main evidence is "Hume's use of the word *species* to refer to the different races" (2005: 132), which indeed would constitute slim evidence because the term 'species' was often used loosely in this period. Valls does not discuss the fact that Hume postulates an original natural distinction between racial groups, which surely is by far the strongest evidence for a polygenist reading.

[57] For more detailed discussions of these differences, see Immerwahr 1992; Garrett 2000; Sebastiani 2013: 120; Valls 2005: 132–35.

([1777] 1987: 208 n. 10). This change is important, but not directly relevant to our purposes here since the differences between Black and White people were already the main focus of the earlier versions of the footnote.

To better understand the footnote, let us examine its context. The essay "Of National Characters," to which this footnote was added, examines the extent to which differences in national characteristics are due to moral and physical causes. As Hume explains, moral causes are political, legal, economic, and cultural circumstances that "work on the mind as motives or reasons" and that hence are potential explanations for the characteristics of a particular nation ([1772] 1994: 78). For instance, oppressive forms of government—just like "poverty and hard labor"—make people "unfit for any science and ingenious profession" (1994: 79). Such moral causes might hence explain why some nations excel at the liberal arts while others do not. Physical causes, in contrast, are "qualities of the air and climate" that, according to some authors, have an insensible influence on "the temper, by altering the tone and habit of the body, and giving a particular complexion, which, though reflexion and reason may sometimes overcome it, will yet prevail among the generality of mankind, and have an influence on their manners" (1994: 78–79). Hume's aim in this essay is to argue against the widespread idea that physical causes are important for explaining national character. He tells us that he is "inclined to doubt altogether . . . that men owe any thing of their temper or genius to the air, food, or climate" (1994: 80–81) and asserts that "physical causes have no discernable operation on the human mind" (1994: 83). Instead, he argues, we can explain all observable differences far better through moral causes. These views are diametrically opposed to the views of many of Hume's contemporaries—perhaps most prominently Montesquieu[58]—who insist on the importance of physical causes.

It is worth stressing that according to Hume moral causes and their effects can change over time—as one would expect, since the political, legal, economic, and cultural circumstances of a particular nation can undergo significant changes. He mentions, for instance, that the national character

[58] Montesquieu's work *Spirit of the Laws*, which argues for the importance of physical causes and which we will discuss in chapter 4, appeared in the same year as Hume's "Of National Characters" (namely, 1748). It is unlikely that Hume read Montesquieu's work before composing his own essay (see Sebastiani 2013: 28; Harris 2015: 243–44). In fact, Hume already expressed very similar ideas in his 1739 work *A Treatise of Human Nature*. For instance, he argues that it is far more likely that the "great uniformity we may observe in the humours and turn of thinking of those of the same nation . . . arises from sympathy, than from any influence of the soil and climate" (*Treatise* 2.1.11.2, 1978: 316–17). After all, he explains, sympathy tends to communicate to us the passions of the people who are around us.

of modern Greeks has almost nothing in common with that of ancient
Greeks: while ancient Greeks were ingenious, industrious, and courageous,
and loved liberty, their modern descendants are stupid, lazy, cowardly, and
slavish (1994: 84). Similarly, the national character of Britons underwent significant changes after the Roman conquest; among other things, they have
become far less superstitious than they used to be (1994: 85).

At first, one might think that Hume's emphasis on moral causes and his
rejection of the impact of physical causes would tend to make his views less
racist. After all, it would make sense for someone who endorses this type of
theory to explain all apparent differences between racialized groups as the
effects of moral causes, that is, of contingent circumstances, rather than natural differences. Before the insertion of the footnote, that would have been
the most straightforward way to interpret Hume's views. Yet the footnote
clarifies that explanations in terms of moral causes only work within the
European context; Hume insists on explaining the differences between Black
and White people in a completely different way, namely, through a natural
and "original distinction." His purported evidence, as seen earlier, is the alleged observation that the characteristics of Black people stay the same regardless of the circumstances, whereas even "the most rude and barbarous of
whites . . . have still something eminent about them" (1753: 291n / 1994: 86n).
Hence, he claims that there are "uniform and constant" differences between
Black and White people that cannot be explained by moral causes and must
hence result from natural racial traits.[59] At the same time, as we have also
seen, he appears to reject explanations of racial difference in terms of physical causes such as climate, instead endorsing what sounds like a polygenist
account.

The immediate context of the footnote is noteworthy as well: Hume added
it to the last sentence of a paragraph in which he wonders whether the climate
might explain the apparent fact that "all the nations, which live beyond the
polar circles or between the tropics, are inferior to the rest of the species, and
are incapable of all the higher attainments of the human mind" (1994: 86).[60]
He then speculates that this apparent fact could be due to something other

[59] There is also a way in which Hume generally views national differences—not just those between
Black and White people—as more constant than Montesquieu: Hume claims that people retain their
national character no matter where they live (1994: 84).

[60] Hume makes a very similar claim in his essay "Of Commerce": "no people, living between the
tropics, could ever yet attain to any art or civility, or reach even any police in their government, and
any military discipline; while few nations in the temperate climates have been altogether deprived of
these advantages" ([1752] 1994: 104).

than physical causes, such as the "poverty and misery" of people in the north and the "indolence" of people in the south.[61] The paragraph ends with the claim that there is a large variety of national characters in temperate climates, and that it is difficult to make general statements about the character of peoples who live at the northern or southern end of these temperate climates (1994: 86). Presumably, the reason why Hume chose to insert the footnote into this paragraph is that the paragraph mentions the alleged inferiority of nations in polar regions and in the tropics; this perhaps prompted him to add a more detailed discussion of this purported inferiority and of his explanation for it.

Hume's racist statements may not be as systematic as those of some other authors, but they are clearly important and had an enormous influence. Because he opposes slavery, as we saw earlier, he is an excellent example of how even extreme forms of racism do not necessarily go hand in hand with a defense of transatlantic slavery in the eighteenth century.

2.4. George Wallace

George Wallace (1727–1805), a White Scottish jurist and cofounder of the Royal Society of Edinburgh, takes a particularly strong antislavery stance in his 1760 work *A System of the Principles of the Law of Scotland*.[62] The work includes a ten-page chapter on slavery (part 1, book 3, title 2), in which he argues not just against natural slavery but also against three widely accepted types of circumstantial slavery: war slavery, voluntary slavery, and hereditary slavery. On the basis of these arguments, he concludes that slavery is "a cruel, an inhuman, an unlawful institution" and that it "ought to be abolished" (*System* 1.3.2, §131, 1760: 91).[63] This is noteworthy because it may well make him the first British author to reject circumstantial slavery categorically and to advocate the abolition of all forms of slavery.[64] His discussion of natural

[61] Intriguingly, the explanation that Hume provides in "Of Commerce" for the lack of art, civility, police, and military discipline in nations between the tropics appears to invoke a physical cause: "It is probable that one cause of this phaenomenon is the warmth and equality of weather in the torrid zone, which render clothes and houses less requisite for the inhabitants, and thereby remove, in part, that necessity, which is the great spur to industry and invention" (1994: 104). He adds that when people have fewer possessions, there will be fewer conflicts and less need for police and or an army.

[62] For more on Wallace and the radical nature of his antislavery stance, see Davis 1971.

[63] Wallace appears to have had an impact on abolitionism and is sometimes cited by American abolitionists (e.g., Benezet 2013: 99–100).

[64] In this respect, he appears to be strongly influenced by Montesquieu, whom he cites and quotes repeatedly. Wallace does not mention penal slavery explicitly, but he appears to view the three types

slavery is interesting because it combines ideas from the natural law tradition with several other ideas. These other ideas include the Golden Rule, ideas about human affections and the general good that are reminiscent of Hutcheson, and ideas about the incompatibility of property and equality that are reminiscent of Rousseau. His discussion of slavery is largely theoretical, but in the chapter's final section, which is about three pages long, he applies his theoretical claims to slavery in British colonies in America. Each of his antislavery arguments, he states, "applies with peculiar force" to transatlantic slaves (*System* 1.3.2, §137, 1760: 95). He ends his discussion of transatlantic slavery with a long quotation from Montesquieu's *Spirit of the Laws*, which includes the passage in which Montesquieu ridicules racist justifications of slavery.[65]

Because Wallace's arguments against circumstantial slavery are very similar to Montesquieu's, I will concentrate on his arguments against natural slavery. This is the first philosophical justification for slavery that he discusses and refutes, immediately after explaining the legal status of slavery in Scotland. His starting point is the doctrine that all human beings are born equal and are hence naturally free. This means, he notes, that "No man has naturally dominion over another" and that "no man is by nature subject to any other, . . . and all that inequality, which is to be found among the individuals of human race, is derived from political and arbitrary institutions alone" (*System* 1.3.2, §131, 1760: 89–90).[66] In other words, he agrees with many authors in the natural law tradition that the natural equality and liberty of human beings directly contradicts natural slavery; subordination among human beings results not from nature but from human institutions.

Notably, though, Wallace does not stop there. He adds two additional principles that, he claims, prove that slavery is unnatural: the Golden Rule and the natural fondness for liberty, or natural hatred of bondage, that all

of circumstantial slavery as exhaustive (*System* 1.3.2, §132, 1760: 91), or to believe that undermining these three types automatically undermines all other justifications (*System* 1.3.2, §136, 1760: 95). As just seen, he states explicitly that the institution of slavery must be abolished completely.

[65] We will discuss Montesquieu and this passage in particular in chapter 4. For a helpful discussion of Montesquieu's influence on the Scottish debate about slavery, see Anstey 1975: 109–112.

[66] By 'arbitrary,' he probably means something like "based on consent or choice." He rejects natural slavery again a little later in this chapter by asking rhetorically, "Was any man born for no other end than to be used like a beast of burden, and to be made subservient to the grandeur of another?" (*System* 1.3.2, §131, 1760: 91). In the same context, he asks rhetorically whether enslaved people are not human beings with "human souls, human faculties, and human passions" (*System* 1.3.2, §131, 1760: 91). Later, he asks the same rhetorical question specifically about enslaved Black people in British colonies (*System* 1.3.2, §137, 1760: 96).

human beings share (*System* 1.3.2, §131, 1760: 90). He does not say very much about these two principles. Yet the idea behind the latter seems similar to the Hutchesonian argument that if all human beings are naturally miserable in a certain type of condition, this condition cannot be natural for any of them.[67] And the idea behind the former appears to be that, since each of us would hate being enslaved and would claim a right to liberty, the Golden Rule requires that we grant the same rights to others.

Wallace also explains that the only permissible instances of inequality in a society are the ones that are absolutely necessary to the welfare of this society; all unnecessary instances of inequality are unnatural and "ought to be destroyed" (*System* 1.3.2, §131, 1760: 90). This means that slavery must be abolished, since it is clearly not necessary—or even conducive—to the welfare of society (*System* 1.3.2, §131, 1760: 91). The enormous misery that slavery causes for huge numbers of people cannot be outweighed by the benefits it may have for the small number of people who are "wallowing in luxury and in opulence, purchased by the labor of others" (*System* 1.3.2, §131, 1760: 91). He makes a similar point later, when applying these principles to slavery in American colonies. Abolition may well bankrupt British colonies, but that is no justification for continuing the morally atrocious institution of slavery: "Let, therefore, our colonies be ruined, but let us not render so many men miserable" (*System* 1.3.2, §137, 1760: 96). In this context, Wallace mentions that one of the main obstacles to complete equality is private property. Property is "absolutely incompatible" with equality, but it is unfortunately rooted so deeply in society that it would be extremely difficult to abolish it (*System* 1.3.2, §131, 1760: 90). Nevertheless, even if we cannot eliminate inequality altogether, we must try to reduce it as much as we can. And one essential step of this reduction is the complete abolition of slavery, which is the largest source of inequality (*System* 1.3.2, §131, 1760: 91).

2.5. Adam Ferguson

The White Scottish philosopher and historian Adam Ferguson (1723–1816) is another important figure of the Scottish Enlightenment. After working as

---

[67] We will see another version of this teleological argument later, in the section about Ramsay. Another British author who uses a version of this argument is William Dickson, who argues that "the *passions* of the negroes prove that they were not created to be slaves" (*Letters on Slavery*, letter 9, 1789: 79).

a chaplain for the Royal Regiment of Scotland, and then as a librarian and a tutor, he became a professor at the University of Edinburgh, where he first held the chair of natural philosophy and later the chair of philosophy of mind (or "pneumatics") and moral philosophy. He published several works on history and ethics; the two works that are most relevant for our purposes are his 1769 textbook *Institutes of Moral Philosophy* and a two-volume work based on his lectures that he published in 1792 under the title *Principles of Moral and Political Science*. He discusses slavery in both works, and, while he treats this topic in a predominantly theoretical way, his statements warrant a brief examination because they differ in intriguing ways from the claims of his contemporaries.[68]

One noteworthy aspect of Ferguson's *Institutes* is that he briefly discusses racial differences in a section titled "Varieties of the Human Race" (1.1.4, 1769: 17–18). He distinguishes six races (1769: 18) and claims that the differences between these groups were originally caused by "climate, situation, and soil" (1769: 17). This is notable in part because it is in direct opposition to Hume, who—as seen earlier—rejects this type of environmental theory.[69] More importantly for our purposes, Ferguson notes that in addition to physiological differences there are differences in "animal and rational temperament," which he claims "has always possessed a distinguished superiority" in temperate climates (1769: 17). He does not elaborate on this, however, and does not mention slavery in the context of racial difference.

Slavery comes up in this textbook in a section about the right to command—a right that, as Ferguson explains in the beginning of the section, can only be acquired "by contract or forfeiture" (*Institutes* 5.10.3, 1769: 219). Thus, he clearly rejects natural slavery, or a right to command that is grounded in a natural superiority.[70] At the same time, he believes that there are licit instances of voluntary servitude—based on a "reciprocal contract" (1769: 219)—and of penal servitude (1769: 221). He does not use the word 'slavery' when describing these two licit types of bondage, however, referring to the former as a contractual agreement between a "master

---

[68] For background on Ferguson and his discussion of slavery, see Anstey 1975: 109–10 and Doris 2011b: 67–70.

[69] For an in-depth discussion, see Sebastiani 2013: 23–43.

[70] He makes this point more explicitly in *Principles of Moral and Political Science*: "It is . . . a manifest principle in the law of nature, that a right to command, or an obligation to obey, beyond what is required to the mere prevention of harm, can be founded in consent alone" (2.3.12, 1792: 244). With respect to forfeiture, he stresses that it cannot result in an unlimited obligation to obey, or in chattel slavery (2.3.13, 1792: 253).

and hired servant" (1769: 219) and to the latter as someone who is "bound" to make reparations "by his services" for some wrong he has committed (1769: 221). The reason for this terminological choice becomes clear at the end of this section in a passage that deserves to be quoted in full:

> No contract or forfeiture can deprive a man of all his rights, or render him the property of another. No one is born a slave; because every one is born with all his original rights. No one can become a slave; because no one, from being a person, can, in the language of the Roman law, become a thing, or subject of property. The supposed property of the master in the slave, therefore, is matter of usurpation, not of right. (1769: 221–22)

In short, Ferguson argues that there are no licit instances of slavery because being enslaved means being chattel or an item of property, and human beings can never be property. While human beings can alienate or forfeit some of their rights, they always retain some, and this means that they are always persons and never things or chattel.[71] There are no licit instances of chattel slavery because human beings cannot become the property of someone else in any way—neither through birth nor through rights forfeiture or voluntary agreements. This is quite similar to Carmichael's argument against chattel slavery that we examined at the beginning of this chapter, though Ferguson makes this point more forcefully and—because he understands slavery as chattel slavery—frames it as a general argument against slavery. Thus, like Wallace, Ferguson argues that there simply are no legitimate instances of slavery.

In the second volume of *Principles of Moral and Political Science*, Ferguson discusses slavery in much more detail, in a section on contractual agreements (*Principles* 2.3.12, 1792: 236–47) and a section about rights forfeiture (2.3.13, 1792: 248–56). After reflecting on social contracts, he turns to the question of whether any instances of slavery—again understood as involving the ownership of another human being—are compatible with the natural law (1792: 241). His answer is, of course, no. What is most interesting about this discussion and sets it apart from other antislavery arguments that we have encountered so far is how Ferguson frames the issue. Master-slave relationships, he notes, seem to originate in "violence or force, and not in consent" (1792: 241). To illustrate this, he mentions the practice of

---

[71] Unfortunately, Ferguson does not explain which rights a person can and cannot lose.

"barbarous nations" who sell their captives into slavery (1792: 241). This may be a reference to the practice of some African governments of selling captives to Europeans. What is unique about this framing is that Ferguson proceeds to ask whether an originally violent or forcible institution like slavery can become licit if everyone in the relevant society becomes "reconciled" to it and accepts it as morally justified (1792: 241). This question may be motivated by the proslavery argument that the African nations impacted by the transatlantic slave trade have long practiced slavery among themselves and view it as completely legitimate. According to this argument, transatlantic slavery is morally permissible because Africans view this type of slavery as justifiable. Alternatively, Ferguson's question could be motivated by another proslavery argument: transatlantic slavery is morally permissible because Africans do not mind being enslaved; they are better off in slavery than they would otherwise be and can be viewed as having consented tacitly to their own enslavement.

In response to this question, Ferguson provides a series of reasons to show that even though some enslaved people appear to be reconciled to their status, this does not allow us to infer that they have tacitly consented to their enslavement or that this enslavement is licit (1792: 241–42). One reason is that one can only be reconciled, and tacitly consent, to forms of treatment that one has already experienced. However, slavery gives masters unlimited power over enslaved people, which means that there will always be permissible forms of treatment that the enslaved person has not yet experienced and to which this person cannot have consented. As a result, an enslaved person who appears reconciled to their state should not be interpreted as having consented to their enslavement (1792: 242).

Ferguson then raises a much deeper objection to this alleged justification for slavery: those who seem reconciled to their enslavement will start feeling "injury and resentment" if their masters start treating them more severely. These sentiments are natural for human beings—indeed, they "characterise a *person*": all human beings view themselves as persons, not things, and consequently nobody can "abide the effects of capricious cruelty, without a pungent sense of his wrongs, and a just effort of nature to defend himself" (1792: 242). This means that no human being can be viewed as having tacitly consented to be treated like a thing, that is, to be subject to the unlimited and arbitrary power of another human being. Indeed, as Ferguson explains, it is impossible to consent to slavery, whether tacitly or explicitly, because such a consent would mean giving up one's status as a person and becoming a thing.

While someone "may consent to do what another commands, within the limits of possibility," a human being "must continue to be a person, having original if not acquired rights, and inspired by nature with a disposition to revolt, whenever he is galled with the sense of insufferable injury or wrong" (1792: 243). In other words, human beings cannot lose all their rights and cannot promise to allow themselves to be treated in whatever way another person chooses.

According to Ferguson, voluntary slavery is illicit for another reason. He notes that such a voluntary agreement would be "the resignation of every thing, in exchange for nothing" (1792: 243).[72] It would be completely irrational to enter into such an agreement. As a result, anyone who agrees to become a slave—giving up their right of self-defense and agreeing to endure even the most unjust treatment—is either devoid of reason or does not fully understand what they are agreeing to. Hence, such a contract is always invalid. In the former case, it is invalid due to the "insanity" of one of the parties; in the latter, it is invalid due to "*fraud* on the part of the supposed master," who entered into an agreement with someone who does not understand the contract's terms (1792: 243).

In the subsequent section of *Principles*, Ferguson turns to the question of whether someone can become a slave by forfeiting their rights, for instance by committing a heinous crime or incurring debts that one is unable to repay in any other way. As one would expect, his answer is once again no: "although a person may have forfeited his possession, his property, or his labour, to any amount, yet no one can forfeit all his personal rights, or from a *person* become a *thing* or subject of property" (2.3.13, 1792: 253). It is impermissible to subject anyone to "Capricious cruelties," no matter what they may have done (1792: 253–54). In this context, Ferguson explicitly discusses war slavery, arguing that it is rarely fair to hold individual soldiers responsible for the wrongs committed by their country. He adds that even in cases in which it is fair, and in which lifelong service is a just punishment, this can never amount to slavery (1792: 254–55). These war captives retain many of their rights, including the right to defend themselves against injustice and cruel treatment (1792: 255). Ferguson also rejects hereditary slavery (1792: 255). He concludes that there is simply no permissible instance of chattel slavery: "as no man is by nature the property of another, no more can he become so in any of the ways in which the right of property is acquired" (1792: 256). In short,

---

[72] This point is similar to one of Montesquieu's arguments, which we will examine in chapter 4.

chattel slavery is always wrong, no matter what natural capacities enslaved people possess, and no matter what circumstances obtain.

2.6. James Beattie

Another important antislavery author is James Beattie (1735–1803), a White Scottish professor of moral philosophy and logic in Aberdeen, who is known mainly for his attack on Hume's philosophy in his 1770 work *An Essay on the Nature and Immutability of Truth*. This text is noteworthy for our purposes because it contains a short discussion and rejection of Aristotelian natural slavery and of Hume's racism, which Beattie portrays as akin to natural slavery. Yet he discusses slavery and racism much more extensively in the second volume of his *Elements of Moral Science*, where he also reiterates his responses to Aristotle and Hume. This work was published in 1793, but Beattie claims that the sections on slavery stem from an unpublished treatise that he composed in 1778 (*Elements*, §656n, 1793: 217–18).[73] We will take a brief look at what he says about slavery and racism in his *Essay* and then turn to his more in-depth discussion in *Elements*.

In his *Essay*, Beattie brings up Aristotelian natural slavery to prove that he is not "a blind admirer of antiquity" (1770: 478).[74] He paraphrases Aristotle's doctrine as stating

> That men of little genius, and great bodily strength, are by nature destined to serve, and those of better capacity, to command; that the natives of Greece, and of some other countries, being naturally superior in genius, have a natural right to empire; and that the rest of mankind, being naturally stupid, are destined to labour and slavery. (1770: 478)[75]

This paraphrase reflects a plausible interpretation of Aristotle, expressed in eighteenth-century vocabulary. Beattie's response to Aristotle is quite short. First, he makes a point that we have already encountered in Hutcheson, namely that history has proven Aristotle wrong. Modern Greece has practically become enslaved by the Ottoman Empire, and the inhabitants of

---

[73] For a discussion of Beattie's reasons not to publish this antislavery text earlier, see Doris 2011a.

[74] As we saw earlier, Hume criticizes those who idolize antiquity in his essay "Of the Populousness of Ancient Nations."

[75] Beattie's paraphrase in *Elements* is quite similar (§605, 1793: 159).

countries that Aristotle classified as barbarian have since risen to promi-
nence. This shows that the alleged stupidity of these "barbarians" was neither natural nor permanent (1770: 479; see also *Elements* §605, 1793: 159).
Beattie speculates that Aristotle was simply trying to find an excuse for
slavery, which was widely accepted among ancient Greeks "to their eternal
reproach" (1770: 479). Interestingly, he also claims that it would have been
much worthier of Aristotle to argue that all human beings have a natural
right to liberty because all humans naturally desire liberty (1770: 479).

Immediately after dismissing Aristotelian natural slavery, Beattie quotes
Hume's claim that White people are superior to all other races, noting that
"Mr. Hume argues nearly in the same manner" as Aristotle (1770: 479). This
is already noteworthy because Hume does not use his racist claim to defend
slavery; the similarity to Aristotle merely consists in the claim about natural
superiority—or, as Beattie puts it elsewhere, "national prejudice" (*Elements*
§605, 1793: 159). Beattie's response to Hume is threefold. The first objection is similar to his main response to Aristotle: even if Hume were correct
that there are currently no signs of ingenuity in anybody who is not White,
this would not prove a natural inferiority. A brief look at history reveals that
nations who were once "barbarous" can become "civilised," and vice versa,
which means that these traits are not essential or natural (1770: 480). Beattie
then makes an epistemological point: to justify Hume's general claim about
the lack of ingenuity among Black people, one would need to be personally
acquainted with every single Black person, past and present (1770: 480). Since
that is impossible, nobody has sufficient evidence for this claim. Beattie's
third objection is that Hume's claim is not only unjustified, but clearly false,
since there are many counterexamples (1770: 481). Moreover, he adds, it is
unreasonable to expect there to be as many people famous for their ingenuity
among enslaved Blacks as among Whites, given that the former are typically
denied access to education and forced to live in circumstances that make it
nearly impossible to become famous for intellectual achievements. Among
other things, an enslaved Black person "has not a single friend on earth,
but is universally considered and treated as if he were of a species inferior
to the human" (1770: 482). This is an intriguing argument because instead
of focusing on opportunities for intellectual achievement, Beattie focuses on
opportunities for becoming famous for one's achievements. He presumably
views slavery as restricting both kinds of opportunities.[76] Yet, by focusing on

---

[76] He explicitly discusses the lack of opportunities for rational improvement in *Elements* (§628,
1793: 184).

the latter, he suggests that there may be many ingenious Black people whose achievements are simply ignored by White people due to racial bias and, as he also notes, language barriers. This, he proposes, is another reason why Hume may not have heard of significant achievements by Black people.

Let us now turn to Beattie's other work, the *Elements of Moral Science*, in which he discusses slavery at great length in part 2 of the second volume. This part is titled "Of Economicks" and discusses family life   or more specifically, the relation between husband and wife, parent and child, and master and slave. It is worth noting that Beattie spends only twenty-seven pages discussing marriage and parenthood (§§574–97, 1793: 124–50) and seventy-four pages discussing slavery (§§598–660, 1793: 150–223). Toward the beginning of his discussion of slavery, he distinguishes between servants and slaves, or servitude and slavery. Servitude, he claims, is contractual and is intended to benefit both the master and the servant (§598, 1793: 150–51). Slavery, in contrast, is not based on a mutual agreement and is intended to benefit only the master; masters also have much more extensive power over slaves than over servants (§601, 1793: 153–54).[77] He contends that slavery—unlike servitude—violates some of the most important natural rights (§602, 1793: 155). When arguing against Aristotelian natural slavery, he specifies one of the natural rights that slavery violates: "whether ingenious or dull, learned or ignorant, clownish or polite, every innocent man, without exception, has as good a right to liberty as to life" (§605, 1793: 160). In other words, all human beings regardless of their natural abilities have a right to liberty and hence a right not to be enslaved, at least if they are "innocent," that is, have not forfeited this right by committing a crime.[78] This means that Beattie rejects not just the empirical component of the doctrine of racial natural slavery—that some racial groups are naturally inferior in their abilities—but also the normative component, namely, that it is permissible to enslave individuals whose natural abilities are inferior. Indeed, Beattie rejects all traditional justifications for slavery (§611, 1793: 164); he argues not just against natural slavery, but also against war slavery (§607, 1793: 161), penal slavery (§608, 1793: 162),[79] voluntary slavery (§609, 1793: 162–63), and selling one's

---

[77] Beattie lists seven differences between slavery and servitude (§601, 1793: 153–55).

[78] Beattie denies that even criminals can licitly be enslaved, since he defines slavery as hereditary, and it would be unjust to enslave the descendants of criminals (§608, 1793: 162). Thus, he rejects penal slavery. Yet he holds that it is permissible to imprison criminals since they have forfeited their right to liberty (§640, 1793: 198).

[79] For Beattie's attitude toward penal slavery, see the previous footnote.

children into slavery (§610, 1793: 163–64). He appears to hold that slavery is never justified.[80]

Beattie returns to the topic of natural slavery later, when responding to what he takes to be the five most prominent proslavery arguments. The fifth of these proslavery arguments is a version of racial natural slavery, which Beattie describes as based on "this principle, that negroes are animals of a nature inferior to man; between whom and the brutes they hold, as it were, the middle place" (§640, 1793: 198).[81] In response, he first argues that even if this principle were true, it would not necessarily mean that White people have a right to enslave and abuse Black people (§640, 1793: 198). And, he is quick to add, this principle is clearly not true, and planters know too much about Black people to genuinely believe it (§640, 1793: 198–99). Moreover, there is no reason to doubt the biblical claim that all human beings have the same origin (§641, 1793: 199–200). After all, there are no differences with respect to the soul (§§642–43, 1793: 200–201) or the body (§§645–49, 1793: 203–10) that give us any reason to think that Black and White people belong to different species (§650, 1793: 211). Differences in climate, environment, and culture are perfectly good explanations for racial differences, including differences in skin color (§645–48, 1793: 203–8) and alleged differences in skull shape (§649, 1793: 209–10). It is also clear that Black people possess all the mental capacities that are characteristic of human beings, such as "reason, risibility, and a capacity of improvement" as well as "the faculty of speech, and consequently of forming, what philosophers call, general ideas" (§642, 1793: 200).[82] Beattie concludes that the apparent superiority of White Europeans "may be accounted for, without supposing the rest of mankind of an inferior species" (§655, 1793: 216). This appears to be an inference to the best explanation: the best explanation for apparent differences is climate, environment, and culture, rather than essential differences. The fact that Beattie discusses this argument at such length is further evidence that racial natural slavery was a prominent proslavery stance when Beattie composed these sections in 1778 and when he chose to publish them in 1793.

---

[80] Nevertheless, it becomes clear later that he advocates gradual abolition (§615, §637, §656, 1793: 169, 194, 217). That is disappointing and somewhat surprising, given how persuasively he describes the horrors and injustice of transatlantic slavery.

[81] A few sections later, Beattie also responds to an unnamed "very eminent naturalist, who maintained that negroes are of a species inferior to the human" (§644, 1793: 202).

[82] "Risibility" is the ability to laugh, which was traditionally thought to be a distinguishing feature of human beings.

2.7. James Dunbar

Our next author is the White Scottish philosopher James Dunbar (1742–1798). Dunbar was regent of King's College in Aberdeen, where he taught moral philosophy; he was also a founding member of the Royal Society in Edinburgh. We will focus on his 1780 work *Essays on the History of Mankind in Rude and Cultivated Ages*, in which he discusses differences among racial groups, slavery, and racism. As we will see, he is one of the first authors to describe internalized racism.

One of Dunbar's stated aims in *History of Mankind* is, "by an appeal to the annals of mankind, to vindicate the character of the [human] species from vulgar prejudices, and those of philosophic theory" (preface, 1780: n.p.). Judging by the essays that comprise this book, it is clear that he is referring to prejudices about the alleged natural inferiority of specific groups, particularly racial groups. To counter these misguided views, he explores the causes of the variety we observe among human beings and argues that this variety does not point to any essential differences.[83] For instance, his first essay discusses a conjectural primeval condition of human beings in which they are solitary and almost indistinguishable from brute animals. It then examines the factors that might prompt humans to evolve from this primeval condition by acquiring language, becoming social, and eventually establishing civil governments and improving their intellectual powers (1780: 1–3, 16).[84] In a later essay, he notes that this process can only occur in very specific favorable circumstances, and even after the process has commenced, it can easily be interrupted by various contingent factors. As a result, there is no basis for inferring that groups for whom this process happens much later or more slowly are naturally inferior (essay 5, 1780: 174; see also essay 8, 1780: 301).[85]

While the conjectural primaeval humans live almost exactly like brute animals, Dunbar stresses that they differ from lower creatures in essential ways, namely through "some inward consciousness, some decisive

---

[83] Like some of the other authors we have already discussed, Dunbar stresses the fact that nations who seem superior to other nations in one era seem inferior in another era, which shows that there is no essential or natural superiority (essay 5, 1780: 171–72).

[84] This essay is reminiscent of Rousseau's *Second Discourse*, which we will briefly discuss in chapter 4.

[85] As Dunbar eloquently puts it soon after, "Fortune governs events: and the magnitude of genius or capacity, in individuals or in tribes, cannot be fully estimated by the success of its exertions" (1780: 175). One important factor that has an impact on the process of improvement is climate, as Dunbar explains in depth in essay 6 (1780: 207–35). As he explains in essays 7–8, however, there are many other important factors (1780: 243–301).

mark of superiority" (1780: 14). He adds that this superiority is stronger in some stages of human development than in others: "savages, in some of the wilder forms, [are] inferior to civilized man in intellectual abilities" (1780: 15). Nevertheless, this inferiority is contingent and nonessential. After all, Dunbar holds that human evolution or improvement does not involve a genuine change in the powers or nature of the soul. Rather, it merely involves the exertion of powers that all human souls possess naturally but that lie dormant until there is occasion to exercise them (1780: 3–4). In other words, there are no essential differences between the least and the most developed human souls.

Even more relevant for our purposes than the first essay are essays 4, 5, and 12, which are respectively titled "Of the Criterion of Civilized Manners," "Of the Rank of Nations, and the Revolutions of Fortune," and "Of the Tendency of Moral Character to Diversify the Human Form." In essay 4, Dunbar rejects the division of nations into "barbarian" and "civilized" by claiming that this dichotomy is based on a misguided opinion about the degree to which Europeans differ from people in other parts of the world (1780: 145–46). The differences, Dunbar stresses, are actually much less significant than Europeans like to imagine (1780: 146–49). Along similar lines, he argues in essay 5 that many people in Europe falsely imagine that there are essential differences between them and other groups: Europe "affects to move in another orbit from the rest of the species. She is even offended with the idea of a common descent . . . and, by imagining specific differences among men, precludes or abrogates their common claims" (1780: 155).[86] Here, Dunbar describes his fellow Europeans as falsely believing that they are so superior to other groups that they belong to a distinct species and have a separate origin. He then explains how this polygenetic belief leads Europeans to deprive other groups of moral rights or a moral status:

> According to this theory [of separate origins], the oppression or extermination of a meaner race, will no longer be so shocking to humanity. Their distresses will not call upon us so loudly for relief. And public morality, and the laws of nations, will be confined to a few regions peopled with this more exalted species of mankind. (1780: 156)

---

[86] By "specific differences," Dunbar here seems to mean differences in species, that is, essential differences.

In this intriguing passage, Dunbar draws a direct connection between the belief that different racial groups have separate origins and the willingness of Europeans to oppress and exterminate allegedly inferior racial groups. Moreover, he describes the way in which this belief makes White people callous toward members of other racial groups and causes them to confine moral rights to members of their own group. This is a remarkably insightful description of racism.

Interestingly, Dunbar also discusses the history of racism, tracing it back to the beginning of European colonization of the Americas and the debates among Europeans about whether American Indians are humans or "Ourang Outangs," that is, subhuman (1780: 156–57). He also notes that while these specific beliefs are modern inventions, they build on "national vanity," which already existed in antiquity. National vanity, he explains, is the almost universal human tendency to view one's own nation as superior to others and one's own customs as the standard of morality and truth (1780: 158–59). Patriotism or national pride need not always be a bad thing, he adds, but it can easily turn into xenophobia if combined with ignorance (1780: 160).

In essay 12, which aims to argue against physiognomy, Dunbar discusses racism again, this time explicitly in connection to transatlantic slavery. When comparing ancient to modern slavery, he identifies modern racism and the lack of sympathy that it engenders as the main reasons why modern colonial slavery is so much worse. In this context, he also mentions natural slavery when noting that modern racist attitudes typically include the belief that Black people are naturally destined to be slaves:

> the negroes do not so easily excite [the sympathy of their masters]. Their features and complexion, regarded as natural badges of inferiority, seem to mark them out for servitude; and, furnishing an occasion for unreasonable contempt, or antipathy approaching to hatred, extinguish that fellow-feeling with their sufferings, by which their grievances would often be lightened, and the hand of the oppressor disarmed. (1780: 389)

Here, Dunbar describes the way in which racist attitudes enable colonial slaveowners to be far crueler and more callous. White Europeans view the physiological features of Black people as a mark both of natural inferiority and of natural slave status. Later in this essay, Dunbar describes racist defenses of transatlantic slavery as "repugnant to reason, [and] to humanity," and he laments the fact that the numerous recent refutations of these racist arguments have had little influence on the politicians who have the power to abolish the slave trade (1780: 391–92).[87]

In the same essay, Dunbar discusses the effects of slavery on enslaved people. He first points out, like other authors, that slavery naturally causes feelings of "Hatred, envy, and revenge" in enslaved people, and that it eventually erodes their natural appreciation for liberty (1780: 389; see also 1780: 397). Much more intriguingly, he then describes the effects of enslavement on the self-conception of enslaved people: "Self-reverence is gone; and emancipation itself cannot restore them to the honours of human nature. In time, they view themselves almost in the light in which they are viewed by their rulers" (1780: 389). This is the earliest explicit reference to internalized racism of which I am aware, and indeed to something resembling W. E. B. Du Bois's notion of double consciousness.[88]

2.8. James Ramsay

Let us examine one final White Scottish abolitionist: James Ramsay (1733–1789), who had direct knowledge of transatlantic slavery. One of his formative experiences occurred while he worked as a surgeon for the Royal Navy and inspected a British slave ship that was en route to the West Indies. Later, when a physical disability forced him to retire from the navy, he became an Anglican priest and worked as a clergyman and surgeon in the West Indies, on the island of Saint Kitts, from 1762 to 1777. There, he advocated both the conversion and the humane treatment of enslaved Black people. After his return to Britain, he published several influential antislavery works, including the nearly three-hundred-page *Essay on the Treatment and Conversion of Slaves in the British Sugar Colonies* (1784) and the sixty-page *Objections to the Abolition of the Slave Trade, With Answers* (1788). I will focus mainly on the former text here. Like his compatriots Wallace and Beattie, Ramsay rejects all traditional justifications of slavery, except certain instances of penal slavery.[89] What is

---

[87] Later in the same essay, Dunbar makes a fascinating point about the relation between enslaved American Indian and Black people in Spanish colonies. The Spaniards, he claims, purposely sow animosity between these two groups by ranking American Indians below Blacks. Yet Dunbar speculates that these two races might one day join forces to retaliate against their Spanish oppressors (1780: 394–95).

[88] We have already encountered another reference to internalized racism in chapter 1, when discussing Lemuel Haynes.

[89] As he explains in *Objections*, "I deny that a man can ever be an object of property, except in the case of an atrocious crime" (1788: 3).

noteworthy about him is both the radicality of his antislavery stance[90] and the unique way in which he argues against natural slavery based on his understanding of the purpose of society, the natural law, and the rights of all human beings. Moreover, he advances a detailed philosophical theory of the kinds of social arrangements that are justifiable and emphasizes the importance of protecting the rights of the most vulnerable members of society. He also discusses racism and racial natural slavery in a particularly interesting way. For instance, he distinguishes much more explicitly than most other authors between essential differences and contingent differences, and he examines alleged correlations between physical and mental differences.

One surprising feature of Ramsay's discussion of slavery is that he is sympathetic to one aspect of the doctrine of natural slavery: he agrees with Aristotle that human beings are naturally intended for different stations in life and are endowed with the natural abilities that befit their intended stations (*Essay* 1.0, 1784: 1). Thus, he holds that there are natural differences in human abilities, and that these differences indicate which social roles people are intended to fill. Yet he disagrees with Aristotle's claim that one naturally intended social role is that of a slave. After all, Ramsay argues, the enslavement of an innocent person is incompatible with the natural law. The natural law requires that "the feelings and interests of the weaker, or inferior members, are consulted equally with those of the stronger and superior" and that everyone is allowed to pursue life, liberty, and property, insofar as this is consistent with "the general improvement and happiness" of the human race (*Essay* 1.0, 1784: 2).[91] While some forms of subordination are beneficial for society and hence justifiable, slavery is not.

Ramsay adds another reason why the institution of slavery is contrary to the natural law: it is based on the wrongheaded principle that "power constitutes right" and that "according to the degree of his capacity of coercion, every man becomes his own legislator" (*Essay* 1.0, 1784: 3; see also 2.0, 1784: 102–3). Legitimate human institutions must be justified in terms of the general good or mutual benefit rather than power, and they must

[90] Notice, however, that while he provides radical arguments against all forms of slavery (except some instances of penal slavery), Ramsay only advocates gradual abolition, like Beattie. As we will see later, he holds that many enslaved people cannot be freed immediately because slavery has rendered them unfit for liberty (*Objections* 1788: 2; 1788: 35–36).

[91] The enormous value of liberty is one reason why Ramsey rejects all traditional justifications of slavery except penal slavery. As he puts it in *Objections*, "The act that reduces a man to slavery, is illegal and unjust; for it is impossible for a slave to receive a compensation for his liberty" (1788: 3). This point is reminiscent of Montesquieu, who also describes liberty as priceless. See my discussion in chapter 4.

always be regulated by laws that protect the rights of vulnerable members of society (*Essay* 1.1, 1784: 18). Thus, slavery is illicit, while contractual servitude, which gives servants extensive rights and protects them from oppression, is permissible (*Essay* 1.1, 1784: 15–17). Turning specifically to slavery in British colonies, Ramsay argues that this institution is "repugnant to humanity" because "the larger part of the community is literally sacrificed to the less; their time, their feelings, their persons, are subject to the interest, the caprice, the spite of masters and their substitutes, without remedy, without recompence, without prospects" (*Essay* 1.1, 1784: 17). This type of slavery directly contradicts the purpose of society and hence can never be licit (*Essay* 1.1, 1784: 18).

In addition to providing general arguments against slavery, Ramsay discusses racial natural slavery and racism. In his *Essay*, he devotes an entire chapter of over sixty pages to vindicating the natural capacity of enslaved Black people, and he even explains at the beginning of this chapter why such a vindication is necessary. It is necessary, he explains, because the hypothesis that Black people have a separate origin and are subhuman "has found powerful advocates," in part because this hypothesis "indulges pride [of White people], and saves the trouble of inquiry" (*Essay* 4.0, 1784: 197). Among these powerful advocates are David Hume and Edward Long, whom Ramsey discusses repeatedly (*Essay* 4.1, 1784: 198–203; 4.2, 1784: 214; 4.4, 1784: 231–32).

In order to vindicate the natural capacities of enslaved Black people, Ramsay makes some points that are already familiar from other authors, and some points that appear to be original. I will concentrate on the ones that I take to be original. One such point concerns the connection between viewing Black people as a separate race and viewing them as natural slaves who do not have the same rights as White people. Ramsay argues that there is no good reason to view Black and White people as belonging to different races—and by 'different races,' he apparently means different biological species, or groups with separate origins. Yet Ramsay also notes that even if there were evidence for a separate origin, it is unclear why that would entail anything about superiority and inferiority, let alone why that would justify enslavement. He uses animals as an analogy: horses and bulls belong to different species, but that by itself does not mean that one is superior to the other, nor that one can enslave the other (*Essay* 4.4, 1784: 231–32). It is fallacious to infer natural slave status and inferiority from an alleged natural difference. Yet many White people make this inference with respect to Black people: "if allowed to be a *distinct* race, European pride immediately concludes them an *inferior* race, and then it follows, of course, that nature formed them to be slaves to their superiors" (*Essay* 4.4, 1784: 231). These White slaveholders furthermore infer that they are "loosed [i.e., freed] from all obligations, but those of interest, in [their] conduct towards [Black people]" (*Essay* 4.4, 1784: 231). In other words, racist beliefs start with the idea of separate origins or separate races, from which White people are likely to infer fallaciously that Black people belong to an inferior race, are natural slaves, and lack moral rights. What leads people to make this inference is in part pride: White Europeans enjoy thinking of themselves as superior.

Earlier, Ramsay makes a sarcastic remark that adds another dimension to his account of racism: "Mr. Hume, because a tall and bulky man, and also a subtle philosopher, might have denied the capacity for metaphysical subtility to all who wanted [i.e., lacked] these his great bodily attributes, as well as suppose capacity and vigour of mind incompatible with a flat nose, curling hair, and a black skin" (*Essay* 4.2, 1784: 214). In addition to poking fun at Hume, Ramsay appears to be making a serious point: human beings have a tendency to think of people who are most like themselves as superior to people who are different. As a result, they base their judgments about mental abilities on criteria that are completely arbitrary and irrelevant, such as physiological traits.

Ramsay's discussion of physical differences between Black and White people also diverges from what we have seen so far. Among other things, he argues that these differences are simply instances of a more general phenomenon: each person looks slightly different from all others so that we can tell each other apart easily. At the same time, people from the same family typically resemble each other to some degree, which plays an important unifying role. The same is true at the level of provinces, nations, and continents: people from the same geographic region typically resemble each other, which unites them and makes it possible to distinguish them from people in other regions (*Essay* 4.1, 1784: 208–9). Physical differences between Black and White people are simply part of this broader and perfectly familiar phenomenon, and hence do not require special explanations. There is no reason to postulate distinct races or species to explain these differences. Nor is there a reason to assume that these physical differences correlate with differences in "animal or rational powers," since physical differences are merely arbitrary signs intended to unite us into societies (*Essay* 4.4, 1784: 235). To further help his White readers view Blackness as an instance of something familiar, Ramsay also suggests that black skin could perhaps be viewed as "an universal freckle" (*Essay* 4.2, 1784: 216).

Another noteworthy aspect of Ramsay's discussion is that he spends a lot of time examining one alleged reason to associate physical differences with intellectual differences—namely, the claim by some contemporaneous scientists that Black people have less capacious skulls and hence smaller brains. Ramsay expresses doubt that there are genuine racial differences in skull size. Yet his main strategy is not to dispute this empirical claim but to argue that even if it were true, it would not be a reason to infer essential differences in mental powers. His argument is threefold. First, he ridicules the assumption that the rational powers of individuals are directly proportional to the size of their brains. If that were true, he jokes, it would be easy to adjudicate any disagreement in the Parliament of Great Britain by simply measuring the skulls of the disputants (*Essay* 4.3, 1784: 222).[92] Next, he points out that even if the skulls of Europeans are larger on average than those of Africans, this does not hold for each individual in these two groups (*Essay* 4.3, 1784: 222–23). And finally, if there are differences in brain size, the most likely explanations are environmental factors, which means that they do not give us any reason to postulate essential differences in mental powers.[93] He speculates that having smaller brains and reduced mental powers might be an advantage for "savages," who have fewer opportunities and less need for abstract thinking (*Essay* 4.3, 1784: 224–25). Nature might simply adapt people's skulls to their way of life. Yet, Ramsay's speculation continues, there is every reason to think that such differences would disappear once the way of life changes, at least after a few generations (*Essay* 4.3, 1784: 224). He concludes that there is no "essential difference between the European and African mental powers," even though there may well be "an accidental or circumstantial difference" (*Essay* 4.3, 1784: 229). This is a major

[92] Ramsay also mentions that an investigation of animals confirms that there is no direct correspondence between brain size and mental powers. His example is somewhat strange: he says that despite similar brain sizes, monkeys are clearly inferior to dogs "in reasoning and sagacity" (*Essay* 4.3, 1784: 223).

[93] When introducing his discussion of alleged anatomical evidence for racial differences, he argues that if there is a natural inferiority, it must have "some benevolent and general purpose"; the purpose cannot be "to feed our pride, or indulge cruelty" (*Essay* 4.3, 1784: 220–21). Hence, even if it were the case that "negroes are an inferior race; it is a conclusion, that hitherto has lain hid and unobserved, and while it leads only to an abuse of power in the superior race, it is better concealed, than drawn out into notice. Perhaps Providence may keep it doubtful, till men be so far improved, as not to make an ill use of the discovery" (*Essay* 4.3, 1784: 221). He adds that since we know that arguments for the inferiority of Black people will likely be abused, such arguments must always be subjected to the "severest scrutiny" (*Essay* 4.3, 1784: 222).

concession, and it shows that Ramsay is most concerned to refute the existence of essential differences; he is quite comfortable conceding nonessential differences.

Ramsay also provides a particularly explicit version of the teleological argument against natural slavery that we have already encountered in Hutcheson:

> Had nature intended negroes for slavery, she would have endowed them with many qualities which they now want [i.e., lack]. Their food would have needed no preparation, their bodies no covering; they would have been born without any sentiment for liberty; and, possessing a patience not to be provoked, would have been incapable of resentment or opposition; that high treason against the divine right of European dominion.[94] (*Essay* 4.4, 1784: 234)

In other words, even when setting intellectual traits aside, it is clear that Black people are not natural slaves. To be a natural slave, a person would need to possess a whole range of characteristics that make life in slavery fitting and tolerable. These are the characteristics we notice in domestic animals, Ramsay explains, which is a clear sign that these animals are intended to serve human beings. Yet it is obvious that human beings lack these characteristics and are hence not intended for slavery. Among other things, human beings naturally love liberty and resent bondage. A genuine natural slave would not be attached to liberty and would hence not mind being enslaved.

One last aspect of Ramsay's discussion of physical and mental differences is worth noting: he uses the immateriality and simplicity of the human soul to argue against essential racial differences in mental powers.[95] Because the soul is simple, it is "not to be distinguished by squat or tall, black, brown or fair" (*Essay* 4.4, 1784: 235), which is to say that the physiological variety that we observe among human beings is not reflected in the soul itself. All human souls are fundamentally of the same type or species. Nevertheless, Ramsay also claims that the soul's simplicity makes it versatile: it "takes its manner and tincture from the objects around it; it universally appears to be fitted only for that character in which it is to act: but that this is not an

---

[94] The reference to "high treason" is clearly sarcastic, as is the reference to the "divine right of European dominion." Thus, this passage appears to be an indirect criticism of colonialism.

[95] This fits well with Justin Smith's argument that in the early modern period, substance dualism served as a "bulwark against the rise of modern racism" (2015: 18).

indelible character appears plainly in every page of the history of mankind" (*Essay* 4.4, 1784: 237). In other words, while there are differences in how well individuals can exercise their rational powers, these differences are due to the circumstances in which this person lives. They are not essential and un-changeable attributes and do not give us any reason to postulate different species of souls (*Essay* 4.4, 1784: 236–37).

Ramsay also provides a reductio ad absurdum argument against the claim that Black and White people have different types of souls: if observations of differences among human beings were to justify this claim, these observations would also justify the claim that "the peasant, . . . the mechanic, . . . [and] the man of learning" each have a different species of soul (*Essay* 4.4, 1784: 236). The idea here seems to be that the alleged mental differences between Black and White people are just like the mental differences that we observe among the different social groups in European societies. In both cases, the correct explanation is that human souls adapt to specific ways of life, rather than that there are multiple species of souls that differ essentially. Here it again becomes clear that Ramsay is comfortable with conceding a contingent mental inferiority; his aim is merely to refute an essential inferiority.

As we have seen, Ramsay rejects slavery categorically, except as a punish-ment for certain crimes. Nevertheless, he does not advocate the immediate abolition of slavery in British colonies. Like Benjamin Rush and some other North American antislavery writers whom we encountered in chapter 1, he merely argues for gradual abolition because he believes that many enslaved people are not ready for liberty. This becomes clear in the introduction of his 1788 work *Objections*, where he clarifies that he is merely proposing to end the slave trade but not to emancipate the enslaved people who are already in the colonies (1788: 1–2).[96] He explains his stance as follows:

All our slaves are not yet generally in a state, wherein full liberty would be a blessing. Like children, they must be restrained by authority, and led on to their own good. But it would be insidious not to declare, that humanity looks forward to full emancipation, whenever they shall be found capable of making a proper use of it. But this may be left to the master's discretion, and the effect of future arrangements, which even the planter acknowledges to be necessary. (1788: 2)

---

[96] He makes a similar point in the body of the tract: "it is not proposed to free them, till they shall have been civilized, and prepared for the government of law" (1788: 35).

This passage is yet another indication of how problematic it is to argue that enslaved Black people are unfit for liberty, even if this unfitness is viewed not as an essential difference but merely as a result of unfavorable circumstances: this idea can be used to argue against immediate abolition.[97] Of course, what Ramsay says here fits quite well with his claim that souls tend to adapt to the person's way of life. And he is far from the only antislavery author who believes that slavery can render enslaved people unfit for liberty. Yet the proposal to keep enslaved people in their present situation and to let masters decide when they are fit for liberty is difficult to square with Ramsay's doctrines about natural rights and the injustice of slavery. Moreover, it is entirely unclear why he would think that someone might become fit for freedom while in slavery—a condition that he describes as so horrible that it can hardly be conducive to human flourishing. He tries to justify his stance later in the introduction to the *Objections*: because enslaved people have a natural right to freedom, each slaveholder ought to restore his or her slaves to the condition in which they were before becoming enslaved, if that is possible. Unfortunately, Ramsay continues, this is not possible: "we cannot restore his cottage, his family, his relations, his country. If born a slave, we cannot often make him worthy of being a freeman. The only recompence we can make, is to treat him with consideration, and receive in return such service from him, as leaves him the reasonable enjoyment of himself" (1788: 4–5). If Ramsay truly means this and does not state it merely for pragmatic reasons as a way to get planters to support the abolition of the slave trade, it significantly weakens the radical claims he makes in his *Essay* about natural rights and the importance of protecting vulnerable members of society from exploitation.

---

[97] See chapters 1 and 4 for a more detailed discussion of this point.

3

English Debates about Slavery and Race

The next stop on our tour is England. Many people in eighteenth-century England knew about transatlantic slavery only from reading or hearing about it. However, there were also quite a few people who were intimately familiar with it because they were currently or formerly enslaved, current or former slaveowners, or had firsthand experience of the slave trade in some other capacity. English ships transported far more enslaved Black people to the Americas in the eighteenth century than the ships of any other nation.[1] England's economic dependence on slavery was enormous.

There are substantial similarities between the arguments of English and North American antislavery writers. This is unsurprising: these authors often read each other's works and, in some cases, corresponded or knew each other personally. Moreover, the English prided themselves on their love of liberty, almost as much as their American brethren. It was quite common for English authors to claim that while Britons are free, the citizens of other European nations are slaves. The well-known White novelist Daniel Defoe makes this point in a political pamphlet, as its title reveals: *A Word against a New Election, that the People of England May See the Happy Difference Between English Liberty and French Slavery; and Consider Well, Before they Make the Exchange* (1710).[2] Some antislavery authors used the idea that England is a beacon of liberty to argue for the abolition of slavery. Like North American authors, they sometimes emphasized the hypocrisy of valuing one's own liberty so highly while enslaving others. For instance, the 1777 poem "Mount Pleasant" by the White social reformer William Roscoe includes the lines

> Shame to mankind! But shame to Britons most,
> Who all the sweets of Liberty can boast;

---

[1] A searchable database is available at https://www.slavevoyages.org.
[2] Along similar lines, the anonymous author of *The Duty and Character of a National Soldier* refers to the "wretched, the crouching Slavery of France, of Spain, of Prussia, Germany, Turkey and Morocco, of which an Englishman cannot speak but with indignation and horror" (Anonymous 1779: 30).

Slavery and Race. Julia Jorati, Oxford University Press. © Oxford University Press 2024.
DOI: 10.1093/oso/9780197659236.003.0004

> Yet, deaf to every human claim, deny
> That bliss to others, which themselves enjoy. (Basker 2002: 196)

Nevertheless, there are also important differences between English and North American debates about transatlantic slavery. One difference is the specific sociopolitical context in which these texts were composed and to which they often explicitly responded. In England, one important step toward ending slavery came in 1772 with Lord Mansfield's judgment in the *Somerset v. Stewart* case. This judgment made it illegal for masters who had brought enslaved people to England to remove them forcibly from English soil. The ruling was an important victory for the antislavery cause, but it had no direct implications for slavery in British colonies.[3] American independence a few years later drastically reduced the number of Britain's slaveholding colonies. Around the same time, the debate over slavery intensified. By the late 1780s, there was a strong and well-organized antislavery movement in England. The Society for Effecting the Abolition of the Slave Trade was founded in 1787, and the Black antislavery society Sons of Africa was founded in the same year. Despite extensive lobbying efforts from both groups, a bill for the abolition of the slave trade in 1791 failed. Nevertheless, many people in England appear to have believed that abolition was inevitable and imminent. For instance, the White English novelist and poet Helen Maria Williams writes in her 1791 *Letters on the French Revolution* that it is only a matter of time until European nations abolish slavery because "Europe seems hastening towards a period too enlightened for the perpetuation of such monstrous abuses" (1791: 50).[4] The British Parliament would eventually ban the slave trade in 1807 and abolish slavery itself in 1833.

There are several major themes in English debates about slavery that are closely connected to race and to natural slavery. One important theme is dehumanization: several antislavery writers accuse their opponents of believing, or at least acting as if they believe, that Black people are sub-human and can therefore licitly be treated like brute animals. In response,

[3] Some abolitionists argued that it is inconsistent not to extend this ruling to Britain's colonies. For example, Granville Sharp, a leading English abolitionist, argues that "it is not enough, that the Laws of England exclude *Slavery* merely *from this island*, whilst the grand Enemy of mankind triumphs in a toleration, *throughout our Colonies*, of the most monstrous *oppression* to which human nature can be subjected!" (1776: 2).

[4] Roger Anstey contends that "little serious intellectual defence of slavery was any longer being attempted" in the late eighteenth century (1975: 95). However, that strikes me as an exaggeration; many proslavery texts were published in this period that at least aimed to be serious intellectual defenses of slavery, though of course one can dispute their success in achieving this aim.

many English antislavery authors argue explicitly that Black people are fully human and therefore entitled to the same rights and privileges as White people. Some, as we will see, argue this on theological grounds,[5] while others provide empirical and philosophical reasons. The long poem *Slavery, A Poem* (1788) by the White English social reformer Hannah More (1745–1833) is an excellent example of this strategy. It argues, among other things, that because Black people are human and created in God's image, there cannot be a right to enslave them, no matter what other characteristics they may possess:

> Respect *his* sacred image with they bear:
> Tho' dark and savage, ignorant and blind,
> They claim the common privilege of kind;
> Let Malice strip them of each other plea,
> They still are men, and men shou'd still be free. (1788: 10)

In other words, all human beings—even if they are "ignorant"—have a special moral status that includes the right to freedom. At the end of the stanza, More's poem explicates one implication of this special status: "The outrag'd Goddess with abhorrent eyes / Sees MAN the traffic, SOULS the merchandize!" (1788: 11). These lines echo a doctrine that we already encountered in Carmichael and other Scots in chapter 2: human beings, or beings with rational souls, simply cannot become merchandise. Being treated like a thing or like someone else's property—and hence chattel slavery—is incompatible with human dignity.[6]

A second and closely related theme in English antislavery writings is the origin of racial bias, and particularly, the origin of the racist belief that Black people are subhuman. Some authors in this chapter provide accounts of this origin that are different from the theories we encountered in chapter 1.

Another important theme concerns alleged differences in mental capacities between Black and White people, such as differences in intellectual capacities, moral character, and the capacity to feel sympathy or pain. Defenders of slavery sometimes invoke these alleged differences to justify

---

[5] One central aspect of the English debate that we will here neglect almost in its entirety concerns the question of whether Christian theology and the Bible can be used to defend transatlantic slavery, or whether they are incompatible with it. Two of the most important authors who discuss this question are Granville Sharp on the antislavery side (e.g., Sharp 1776) and Raymund Harris on the proslavery side (e.g., Harris 1788).

[6] The poem "The Negro's Complaint" by the White English poet William Cowper (1788) includes a similar claim: "Minds are never to be sold" (Basker 2002: 299).

slavery, for instance by arguing that these differences make Black people natural slaves, or by arguing that these differences make transatlantic slavery
less horrific than some people claim. In response, many antislavery authors
argue against these alleged mental differences. Hannah More's poem, from
which I already quoted, exemplifies one of the most popular argumentative
strategies in the following lines:

> Perish th' illiberal thought which wou'd debase
> The native genius of the sable race!
> Perish the proud philosophy, which sought
> To rob them of the pow'rs of equal thought!
> Does then th' immortal principle within
> Change with the casual colour of a skin?
> Does matter govern spirit? or is mind
> Degraded by the form to which 'tis join'd?
> No: they have heads to think, and hearts to feel,
> And souls to act, with firm, tho' erring zeal;
> For they have keen affections, kind desires,
> Love strong as death, and active patriot fires. (1788: 4–5)

More's main point here, which other antislavery authors echo, is that the only
natural differences between Black and White people are physiological,[7] and
physiological differences are clearly irrelevant for both mental capacities and
moral rights.[8] What matters is the soul, and the soul is clearly unaffected by
complexion or other physiological features. There simply are no differences
in the ability to think or feel; philosophers who think otherwise are guilty of
illiberality and pride.

---

[7] Later in the poem, the speaker seems more willing to concede some differences in the ability to
reason and concentrates on arguing that there is no difference with respect to feelings (1788: 10–12).

[8] Cowper's poem "The Negro's Complaint" (1788) is another excellent example of this strategy.
Among other things, it criticizes the claim that there are racial differences in the ability to feel. The
poem's speaker—who is an enslaved Black person—explains, "Skins may differ, but affection / Dwells
in white and black the same" (Basker 2002: 299). The poem ends with a demand addressed to the
speaker's white enslavers: "Prove that you have human feelings, / Ere you proudly question ours!"
(Basker 2002: 300). A further example is a fascinating anonymous poem, apparently composed in
1768 (or soon thereafter) as an epilogue to Isaac Bickerstaffe's comic opera *The Padlock* and published
in the *Gentleman's Magazine* in 1787. In this poem, the enslaved Black character Mungo—who in
Bickerstaffe's play serves mainly as a laughingstock—reminds his audience that he is a human being
who can think, feel, and desire in exactly the same way as his White masters (1787: 913–14 / Basker
2002: 185).

Some authors concede that there may be contingent mental differences between Black and White people, while rejecting any natural or essential ones. This, they sometimes point out, is sufficient to show that Black people cannot be natural slaves. The contingent differences, according to several authors, are due in part to cultural and educational factors: people in Africa and enslaved Black people in European colonies were thought to have fewer occasions to exercise and develop their intellectual capacities, and consequently to appear inferior. The basic idea is expressed nicely in the 1735 anti-slavery tract *The Speech of Moses Bon Sàam*: "only Education, and Accident, *not* Difference of *Genius*, have been the Cause of this provoking *Superiority*, that bids the Pride of a *white* Man despise and trample on a *black* one" (Krise 1999: 103). One instance of this general idea is what I have dubbed the effects-of-slavery strategy, that is, the argument that the alleged inferiority of Black people cannot justify the transatlantic slave trade because it is an effect of slavery. Life in slavery degrades the mind and makes significant intellectual achievements practically impossible. As direct empirical evidence that Black and White people possess the same natural capacities, several authors mention examples of famous Black intellectuals like the poet Phillis Wheatley, whom we encountered in chapter 1, and Ignatius Sancho, who was a prominent English prose writer.

In the remainder of this chapter, we will explore these themes in more detail by examining the writings of eight English authors in chronological order: Edward Trelawny, Thomas Rutherforth, the anonymous author of *Two Dialogues on the Man-Trade*, Thomas Clarkson, Dorothy Kilner, Quobna Ottobah Cugoano, Olaudah Equiano, and Mary Wollstonecraft. Many other authors could have been included; I will mention some of them in footnotes. My reason for selecting these eight is that they write in particularly detailed and innovative ways about the themes on which I would like to focus.

3.1. Edward Trelawny

The earliest text that we will discuss in depth is the 1746 pamphlet *An Essay Concerning Slavery, and the Danger Jamaica is Expos'd to from the Too Great Number of Slaves, and the Too Little Care that is Taken to Manage Them*. This pamphlet was published anonymously in London, but its author is most likely the White politician Edward Trelawny (1699–1754), who was the British governor of Jamaica at the time. As Jamaica's governor, Trelawny was obviously quite familiar with West Indian slavery. The pamphlet, which is written in the form of a dialogue, uses ideas from the natural law tradition to argue that colonial slavery is unjust, drawing explicitly on Samuel Pufendorf, John Locke, and William Wollaston. The dialogue's spokesperson advocates reforms to West Indian slavery and a gradual abolition, claiming that immediate abolition would be "a great Evil" and would lead to the financial ruin of many people (2018: 1134). What is most interesting for our purposes is that this text describes the racist attitudes of planters in the West Indies as the belief that Black people are subhuman and ties this belief explicitly to natural slavery.

The most relevant passage for our purposes occurs in section 2, in which the author's spokesperson speculates about planters' attitudes toward enslaved Black people:

> One would imagine that Planters really think that *Negroes* are not of the same Species with us [i.e., White people], but that being of a different Mold and Nature, as well as Colour, they were made intirely for our Use, with Instincts proper for that Purpose, having as great a Propensity to Subjection, as we have to command, and loving Slavery as naturally as we do Liberty. (2018: 1144)

He does not elaborate on this, but it is clear that he is ascribing to West Indian planters not just the belief that Black people belong to a subhuman species and have completely different natures but also that Black people are natural slaves. The way in which he describes natural slavery is interesting. He mentions the teleological idea that Black people were created exclusively to serve White people, as well as the idea that natural slaves have instincts and affects that make them desire slavery. The latter goes farther than the claim— often made by proponents of natural slavery—that natural slaves do not love freedom as much and can thus bear slavery more easily. This text claims that being a natural slave means positively loving slavery and having a propensity for it.

It is unclear to what extent the author genuinely believes that this is the attitude of West Indian slaveholders. The passage's main goal, it seems, is to claim that planters in Jamaica are overestimating the docility of enslaved people, acting as if large numbers of enslaved people will "most pleasantly submit to hard Labour, hard Usages of all kind, Cruelties and Injustice at the Caprice of one white Man" (2018: 1144). In other words, planters are acting as if the people they are enslaving love slavery and as if there were no reason to fear uprisings. The pamphlet—as its title already suggests—aims to warn about the danger of slave rebellions in Jamaica and to advocate measures that will reduce this danger. Nevertheless, in doing so, the text makes a fascinating point about natural slavery: in order to be a genuine natural slave, one would need to have a natural propensity for subjection and even a natural love for slavery. This also entails that rebellions among enslaved people and other forms of resistance—such as attempts to flee—are clear proof that they are not natural slaves.

3.2. Thomas Rutherforth

Our next author is Thomas Rutherforth (1712–1771), a White professor of theology at Cambridge and archdeacon of Essex.[9] Among historians of philosophy today, he is mostly known as one of Catharine Trotter Cockburn's primary targets and as a critic of Samuel Clarke's and David Hume's philosophy. For our purposes, Rutherforth is of interest because of his discussion of natural slavery in the first volume of his *Institutes of Natural Law* (1754), which is based on his lectures on Hugo Grotius's *Rights of War and Peace*. Rutherforth provides a whole battery of arguments against natural slavery; these arguments are completely theoretical, and he does not mention any implications for transatlantic slavery. We will focus on what I take to be his two most original and noteworthy arguments, which are based on the idea of self-ownership.

The first of these arguments ostensibly targets those who attempt to ground the natural right to enslave people in superior physical strength, but it contains the seeds of a more general argument. In the relevant passage, Rutherforth notes that there is an important difference between having the physical power to compel someone to obey and having the right to compel someone to obey. The former does not entail the latter because the mere fact that someone is physically weak does not mean that they lack self-ownership: "The weak mans mind and his body . . . are as much his own, as if nature had given him greater strength, and enabled him to make more effectual struggle in his own defence" (*Institutes* 1.20.3, 1754: 476). As a result, Rutherforth continues, if we are stronger, we have no right to force

---

[9] His last name is sometimes spelled 'Rutherford.'

this person, "against his inclination, to pursue our interest in such manner as we shall direct, without doing him an injury, without doing violence to that judgment and will of his mind, and to those active powers of his body, which nature has made his own" (*Institutes* 1.20.3, 1754: 476).[10] We can understand this as a general argument against natural slavery. The basic idea is quite simple:

1. No human being has the natural right to enslave those who naturally own their mind and body.
2. All adult human beings naturally own their mind and body.
3. Therefore, no human being has the natural right to enslave adult human beings.

This argument is nicely straightforward. Proponents of natural slavery could, of course, reject premise 2, that is, the claim that all human beings naturally own their mind and body. Nevertheless, given the popularity of the self-ownership doctrine in Rutherforth's intellectual milieu, the premise would be difficult to reject in this context. Premise 1 seems quite plausible as well, at least insofar as enslaved people are viewed as the property of their masters: it is hard to see how anyone for whom it is natural to be owned by someone else could still naturally own their body and mind. Interestingly, Rutherforth himself does not view enslaved people as the property of their masters. Rather, he insists that slavery only gives masters the right to direct the actions of the enslaved (*Institutes* 1.20.1, 1754: 474). The second argument, which we are about to discuss, works better for those who understand slavery in this way.

Rutherforth's second argument extends the idea of the previous argument:

If nature has made any thing a mans own, his mind and his body are so. . . . But no mans mind and body can be his own, unless the faculties of both, that is, his judgment, his will, and his power of acting are so. Now he, who has a right in his faculties of judging of chusing and of acting, is no slave. And since nature, which gave every man a right in his own mind and body, gave him a right likewise to these faculties, the consequence is, that nature has not placed any man in a state of slavery. (*Institutes* 1.20.3, 1754: 477)

---

[10] Rutherforth seems to be talking specifically about adult human beings here, namely, those who have judgment and will. This is not a problem, since he has separate arguments for the claim that children are not natural slaves (*Institutes* 1.11.5, 1754: 162–63; 1.20.3, 1754: 477).

We can reconstruct this passage as an argument against natural slavery generally:

1. By nature, each human being owns their mind and body.
2. Anyone who owns their mind and body also owns the faculties of their mind and body.
3. Thus, by nature, each human being owns the faculties of their mind and body (from 1, 2).
4. No human being who owns the faculties of their mind and body is a slave.
5. Therefore, by nature, no human being is a slave (from 3, 4).

This argument is a helpful expansion of the previous argument: instead of deriving the illegitimacy of natural slavery directly from the claim that all humans naturally own their minds and bodies, this argument inserts an additional step. This additional step is premise 2, that is, the claim that owning one's mind and body entails owning the faculties of one's mind and body. This claim is plausible. It also explains why natural self-ownership is incompatible with natural slavery, even if slavery is understood, in Rutherforthian fashion, not as the ownership of a person but rather as the right to direct their actions. The idea appears to be quite simply that if you naturally own the faculties of your mind and body, you ipso facto have the natural right to use them as you see fit. That is, you have the natural right to direct your actions, constrained only by the laws of nature. And, given Rutherforth's definition of slavery, this means that you are not a natural slave, since slaves lack the right to direct their actions. Premise 4 is difficult to deny for anyone who thinks that the master's right to direct the actions of the enslaved person is a necessary condition for slavery, which is fairly uncontroversial. Hence, this is a promising way to argue against natural slavery.

3.3. *Two Dialogues on the Man-Trade*

Our next text is the anonymous sixty-eight-page antislavery tract *Two Dialogues on the Man-Trade* (1760).[11] The two dialogues that comprise this

---

[11] This text had an enormous influence on abolitionism both in Britain and in America. For instance, Anthony Benezet quotes frequently and extensively from this text, even adding long extracts to his 1762 *Short Account* (2013: 49–66).

tract are conversations between two presumably fictitious characters: Mr. Allcraft, who has invested in the transatlantic slave trade but is starting to have scruples, and Mr. J. Philmore, the anonymous author's spokesperson, who slowly convinces Allcraft that this trade is, as he puts it, "a wicked trade" (1760: 4).[12] One remarkable aspect of the *Dialogues* is the strength of Philmore's antislavery stance. He argues, among other things, that slave traders are guilty of murder (1760: 36), as is the English government and anyone who is involved in the slave trade (1760: 44). Likewise, he argues that enslaved people have the right to kill their oppressors in order to escape and that everyone has the duty to help enslaved people attain freedom (1760: 54). He also rejects all justifications for chattel slavery, insisting that no human being can "on any supposition whatever, become the property, or part of the goods or estate of another man, as his horse, or his dog is" (1760: 8; see also 1760: 55). These claims presumably explain why the author chose to publish this text anonymously.

For present purposes, the most important aspects of the *Dialogues* are Philmore's argument for the humanity of Black people, his rejection of natural slavery and defense of natural equality, and his brief discussion of racial bias. These aspects are clearly central to this dialogue, since the first two are contained in the four "preliminary propositions" or principles that constitute the starting point for Philmore's antislavery argument: (a) Black people are human beings and do not differ in any significant ways from White people; (b) Black and White people are naturally equal, that is, there is no natural subordination; (c) Black and White people are subject to the same moral laws; and (d) Christians do not have authority over non-Christians in virtue of being Christians (1760: 6–10). Immediately after arguing for these principles, Philmore discusses racial bias in order to explain why it is necessary to state and defend these self-evident truths.

To defend the first proposition—namely, that Black and White people belong to the same species, have the same origin, and are equally human— Philmore considers two common ways to define 'human being' and points out that both definitions clearly encompass Black people. The first definition

---

[12] Some interpreters believe that J. Philmore is the real name of the tract's author (e.g., Hudson 2001: 562), perhaps because the tract ends with a letter addressed to "the Guinea-Merchants in England," which is signed "J. Philmore." Yet it is likely that this letter is simply part of the tract's pretense; Allcraft encourages Philmore to publish the conversation toward the end of the second dialogue, and readers are presumably meant to pretend that Philmore followed this advice and that they are reading the result. See Crosby 2013: 25–26 and 80 n. 79 for a brief discussion of the tract's anonymity.

is "a two leg'd animal, without feathers, and with broad nails" (1760: 6); the second is "rational animal" (1760: 7). Neither definition references skin color, Philmore points out, and Black people clearly meet these criteria just as well as White people.[13] Interestingly, he also notes that it is unimportant, and not possible to know, whether "our first parents were blacks, or whites" (1760: 6). Thus, he disagrees with contemporaneous racial theories that portray Blackness as a degeneration from the original skin color of humankind.[14]

Based on the doctrine that Black and White people belong to the same species, Philmore then argues for their natural equality and against any natural subordination or natural slavery. He stresses that the state of nature is not merely an imaginary or real primeval state, but exists in the present between different nations, such as between the inhabitants of Britain and of Guinea (1760: 7). This means that Britons do not have any authority over the inhabitants of Guinea, since nobody in the state of nature is "superior to another man, nor has any authority or dominion over him, any right to lay his commands upon him" (1760: 7). In short, nobody is naturally a master or a slave, and this directly undermines transatlantic slavery. Even if one person or group is stronger and wiser than another, the former does not have any natural right to command the latter (1760: 8).

In the second dialogue, Philmore invokes the effects-of-slavery strategy to explain apparent differences between Black slaves and free White people: it may be true that the former are "perverse, sullen, and mischievous," but that is simply a natural effect of being unjustly enslaved, removed from their native country, "treated worse than dogs, and made to work harder than horses" (1760: 50).[15] White people would exhibit precisely the same characteristics in these circumstances, which means that these differences are not natural and cannot be used to justify the transatlantic slave trade or the inhumane treatment of enslaved Black people.

Philmore's brief discussion of racism is perhaps the most interesting aspect of this tract. He acknowledges that hardly any defenders of slavery

[13] Philmore returns to the irrelevance of skin color in the second dialogue; he ridicules racists by stating, "I do not think this a good syllogism, the devil is black. The Africans are black. Therefore the Africans are devils" (1760: 51). Incidentally, we find refutations of the claim that Black people are devils in other British antislavery texts as well; for example, William Dickson, *Letters on Slavery*, letter 9 (1789: 62). Similarly, Scottish writer Alexander Geddes satirizes the idea that Black people are "*little more* than incarnate devils" because of physical features (1792: 23).

[14] James Beattie, whom we examined in chapter 2, is among those who hold that humankind was originally White (*Elements* §646, 1793: 205).

[15] Other English authors who use the effects-of-slavery strategy and spell it out in more detail include John Wesley (1774: 40–41), Joseph Woods (1785: 11–16), and Thomas Burgess (1789: 127–31).

state explicitly that Black people are subhuman or do not have the same natural rights as White people (1760: 12). The humanity of Black people and the equality of all humans is, after all, obvious. Yet Philmore continues,

> it is reasonable to suppose, that those, who are concerned in the man-trade, do not allow themselves to think on these truths impartially, seriously to consider them, and lay them to heart; but that, on the contrary, they have, some how or other, a kind of confused imagination, or half-formed thought, in their minds, that the blacks are hardly of the same species with the white men; but are creatures of a kind somewhat inferior. (1760: 12)

In short, Philmore argues that people who engage in the slave trade must implicitly accept racist beliefs and prevent themselves from seeing something that is evidently true. On some level, these people refuse to accept the humanity of Black people, or pretend that Black people are subhuman, in the face of clear evidence to the contrary. Philmore then explains why this is a reasonable assumption about people who own or trade in enslaved people:

> I do not know how to think, that any white men could find in their hearts, . . . to treat the black men, in that cruel barbarous manner, in which they do treat them, did [these White men] think and consider, that [Black men] have rational immortal souls, that . . . they have the same passions, senses, and feelings, as [White men] have, and are as susceptible of pain, and grief, and upon the same occasions, as they are. (1760: 12–13)

In other words, it is hard to see how any White person who is fully aware that Black and White people are completely equal could treat Black people the way that slaveowners and traders treat them. The most reasonable explanation for the enormous cruelty of transatlantic slavery is that the White people involved in this trade consider Black people to be subhuman and less susceptible to pain and suffering. This is, of course, no innocent mistake: as the earlier passage explains, these White people "do not allow themselves" to consider the clear evidence for racial equality. This suggests that their ignorance is culpable and even intentional.

3.4. Thomas Clarkson

Let us now turn to the prominent White abolitionist Thomas Clarkson (1760–1846), a founding member of the Society for Effecting the Abolition of the Slave Trade who devoted his entire adult life to the antislavery cause.[16] In 1785—two years after graduating from St. John's College, Cambridge—he composed a Latin essay on slavery for a competition, which he won. The essay was strongly influenced by James Ramsay's and Anthony Benezet's work, which we encountered in the previous two chapters. Clarkson subsequently published his essay in English, as *An Essay on the Slavery and Commerce of the Human Species, Particularly the African*. The first edition was published in 1786, followed by a revised and expanded edition in 1788 that addresses some criticisms. Clarkson's knowledge of transatlantic slavery was entirely secondhand, which led some West Indian planters to accuse him of misrepresenting the situation in slave-holding colonies.[17] Perhaps in part in response to such criticisms—but also in the service of the newly founded abolitionist society—he spent several months collecting accounts from English sailors and other people with direct knowledge of the transatlantic trade. This led to the publication of *The Substance of the Evidence of Sundry Persons on the Slave-Trade* (1789) and several other tracts, in quick succession. He does not appear to have interviewed enslaved or formerly enslaved people, or at least he did not include such firsthand testimony in his 1789 tract.

Many of Clarkson's publications concentrate on empirical information about the slave trade and on practical questions regarding abolition. I will here focus almost exclusively on his first work, the *Essay*, which differs from his other writings in its deep engagement with philosophical questions and the philosophical tradition. Clarkson examines natural law ethics and social contract theory in great detail. Having studied classics at St. John's College, he also discusses ancient conceptions of slavery in depth. When discussing Clarkson's *Essay*, I will rely on the revised edition from 1788, which is in most relevant respects identical to the first edition.[18] This work is divided into

[16] For more biographical information about Clarkson and his role in British abolitionism, see Smith 2010.

[17] For instance, Francklyn describes Clarkson's *Essay* as "merely an academical exercise, no more deserving an answer, and as equally a fable, as the Tragedy of Oroonoko" (1789: 2). *Oroonoko* is a fictional story originally composed by the English author Aphra Behn in 1688 and later adapted by several others, including Thomas Southerne. I discuss this tragedy in Jorati, forthcoming.

[18] Both versions of the *Essay* are available in recent editions: the Liberty Fund has published a transcription of the first edition (http://oll.libertyfund.org/title/1070), and Mary-Antoinette Smith has edited the revised edition (Clarkson 2010). Note that there are some differences in section numbering

three parts, the first of which is about the history of slavery, the second about the transatlantic slave trade and the question whether any type of slavery is justified, and the third about enslaved Black people in European colonies. Natural slavery comes up in all three parts, which is an indication of how central this doctrine is to Clarkson's antislavery argument. I will briefly highlight his most important points from each part.

In part 1, which discusses the history of slavery, Clarkson carefully distinguishes between circumstantial and natural slavery, stating that the former originates from specific circumstances such as war and piracy, whereas the latter originates from national pride and vanity (*Essay* 1.5, 2010: 86–87). Yet he argues that even circumstantial slavery led ancient people to adopt the belief that enslaved people are naturally inferior to masters. The basic idea of this argument is that once a society starts treating some human beings as commercial goods that can be bought and sold like cattle, members of this society inevitably start viewing enslaved people as having the same status as cattle in other ways as well. More specifically, enslaved people will start to be viewed and treated as brute animals and as "greatly inferior to the human species" (1.5, 2010: 85–86). Once that has happened, there is a vicious cycle: being treated like animals depresses the minds of enslaved people. This will prevent them from exhibiting "sparks of genius" and give them "the appearance of being endued with inferior capacities to the rest of mankind" (1.5, 2010: 86). This appearance, in turn, will strengthen the belief of free members of this society that enslaved people are "an *inferiour* order of men, and perfectly void of *understanding*" (1.5, 2010: 86). Last, masters will use the belief that enslaved people are inferior and irrational as an excuse to treat them with even more cruelty.

This description of ancient slavery is intriguing. It departs from the claim by other early modern authors that ancient slaves were treated far more humanely than modern chattel slaves.[19] Clarkson presumably wants his claims about ancient slavery to support his more general point that treating human beings as property inevitably leads to dehumanization, bias, and abuse;

between the two editions. Whenever that happens, I will reproduce both section numbers, starting with the first edition.

[19] See, for example, Dunbar 1780: 386–89; Cugoano [1787] 1999: 35; Carmichael, *Supplements* [1718], ch. 16, 2002: 144. Interestingly, Thomas Jefferson seems to agree with Clarkson: he claims that "among the Romans, about the Augustan age especially, the condition of their slaves was much more deplorable than that of the blacks on the continent of America" (*Notes on the State of Virginia* [1785], Query 14, 1984: 267).

there is no such thing as humane slavery. He spells this out most clearly in the very last chapter of part 3: "no man whatever can be brought or reduced to the situation of a slave, but he must instantly become a brute; he must instantly be reduced to the value of those things, which were made for his own use and convenience" (3.11/3.12, 2010: 214, italics removed; see also 2.4, 2010: 124–25). This is an extremely insightful point that I have not seen expressed elsewhere in this period.[20] Another relevant aspect of Clarkson's discussion of ancient slavery is that it draws a tight connection between circumstantial and natural slavery: the former, though not originally based on a belief in the natural inferiority of the people who are enslaved, inevitably spawns this belief. Clarkson's description of the vicious cycle is also remarkable, and I have not seen it explicitly in other authors. When applied to the transatlantic slave trade, it is a plausible account of how racial slavery and racism are related.

After describing the vicious cycle, Clarkson turns explicitly to natural slavery, which he characterizes as an additional excuse for slavery among the Greeks and Romans. Their vanity and national pride led them to view all foreigners as barbarians who were "*defined* by nature to *obey*," and who ought to be treated like brute animals or even plants (1.5, 2010: 87). There are many ways to refute this doctrine, Clarkson notes, for instance by emphasizing that all human beings are born equal (1.5, 2010: 88). Yet his preferred strategy is simply to list several examples of enslaved people in antiquity who produced excellent works of literature and are thus clear counterexamples to the alleged inferiority of enslaved people (1.5, 2010: 88–90).

Clarkson's discussion of natural slavery in part 2 of the *Essay* is similarly interesting. This part is ostensibly about the transatlantic slave trade, but the first eight chapters provide a general moral framework for evaluating the legitimacy of all forms of slavery. Clarkson defends a natural law ethics that stresses the natural equality and natural liberty of all human beings as well as a social contract theory of legitimate rule (2.1–3, 2010: 119–24). On this basis, he not only rejects natural slavery but also argues that nobody can become enslaved without their consent and that no human being can have absolute property rights over the liberty of another human being (2.4, 2010: 124–26). He even discusses and rebuts specific types of circumstantial slavery. The most relevant portion of this discussion concerns hereditary slavery. Clarkson argues

---

[20] It is, however, related to a point made by John Woolman and others whom we already encountered in the previous two chapters: slavery itself causes racist attitudes.

that the only possible justification for believing that the children of enslaved people are automatically enslaved is the belief that the parents are brute animals, which is clearly absurd (2.8, 2010: 136). The idea here seems to be that such a hereditary ownership is possible only with respect to subhuman animals; human beings are always born free. This is noteworthy because it is yet another place in which Clarkson stresses that the belief in the subhuman status of the enslaved is crucial for the institution of slavery.

Clarkson's most extensive discussion of natural slavery occurs in part 3 of the *Essay*. There he characterizes racial natural slavery as the doctrine that "Africans are an inferiour link of the chain of nature, and are made for slavery" (3.7/3.8, 2010: 176). This doctrine, he states, is the last resort of defenders of transatlantic slavery: they unfailingly turn to this doctrine when their other attempts to justify slavery have been refuted (3.7/3.8, 2010: 176). Clarkson then helpfully divides natural slavery into two subcategories and refutes each separately: (a) the doctrine that Black people are natural slaves because they are inferior in their capacities, which he points out was also what ancient proponents of natural slavery believed about barbarians (3.7/3.8, 2010: 176–185), and (b) the doctrine that Black people are natural slaves because of their skin color and other physiological characteristics (3.8/3.9, 2010: 185–201). He separately discusses and rebuts the doctrine that Black people are "made for slavery" (*Essay* 3.8/3.9, 2010: 201–2), but he does not present it as a third subcategory—presumably because this claim is typically based on allegedly inferior capacities or on physical marks and is hence a version of (a) or (b).

In order to refute the first subcategory of racial natural slavery, the version that ties natural slave status to inferior capacities, Clarkson uses two strategies that we have already seen elsewhere. First, he uses the effects-of-slavery strategy: he argues that the apparent inferiority of enslaved Black people is merely an effect of slavery, rather than a natural or racial difference (3.7/3.8, 2010: 177). Second, he invokes empirical evidence for the equality of capacities. According to Clarkson, there is no evidence whatsoever that Black and White people differ in intellectual or artistic achievements if they are in the same circumstances and have the same opportunities (3.7/3.8, 2010: 178–79). Quite to the contrary, there is clear empirical evidence that when Black people receive the same education as White people, they are capable of the same things. One such example is Phillis Wheatley, whose poetry we examined in chapter 1, and about whom Clarkson states, "if [she] was designed for slavery, . . . the great part of the inhabitants of Britain must lose their claim to freedom" (3.7/3.8, 2010: 181).[21] In other words, if Wheatley's intellectual capacities make her unfit for freedom, then hardly anybody in Britain is fit for freedom.[22] Clarkson concludes that the first subcategory of the doctrine of natural slavery is "wholly malevolent and false" (3.7/3.8, 2010: 185). And when he later turns to the question of whether Black people were in some sense made for slavery, he uses a third strategy that we have also seen already: he argues that if Black people were made for slavery, they would exhibit very clear signs of their status, such as an indifference toward liberty and an inability for contemplation. Yet there are no such signs, which means that Black people cannot be made for slavery (3.8/3.9, 2010: 201–2).

Clarkson's refutation of the second subcategory of racial natural slavery, according to which natural slave status is based on physiological differences, also employs arguments we have already seen in other authors. He first argues against two biblical versions of this doctrine, namely, that Black people descend from Cain or from Ham, and that their Blackness is a physical mark that signals their status as natural slaves (3.8/3.9, 2010: 185–89). Then he provides nontheological arguments for monogenesis and defends a climate theory of skin color (3.8/3.9, 2010: 194–95); he also endorses Ramsay's hypothesis that Black skin is practically a huge freckle (3.8/3.9, 2010: 200). On this basis, he concludes that physiological differences do not make Black people natural slaves.

3.5. Dorothy Kilner

Another fascinating antislavery writer is the White English novelist and children's book author Dorothy Kilner (1755–1836). In her didactic two-volume novel *The Rotchfords; or, the Friendly Counsellor: Designed for the Instruction and Amusement of the Youth of Both Sexes* (1786), she educates her young readers about racial equality and the injustice of slavery, among

---

[21] Clarkson also mentions evidence that free Black people in Africa are often extremely accomplished in the mechanical arts, mathematics, and writing (3.7/3.8, 2010: 183–84). In another work— the 1791 *Letters on the Slave-Trade*—Clarkson adds another piece of empirical evidence, which he might have borrowed from Cugoano: Black people in Africa are clearly capable of establishing and maintaining complex political systems as well as systems of jurisprudence (letter 9, 1791: 77–78).

[22] Many other antislavery writers mention Wheatley's poetic talents as clear evidence against racist claims about intellectual inferiority. For instance, Robert Boucher Nickolls quips that "nothing has been written by the late defenders of slavery, that discovers half the literary merit or ability of . . . Phillis Wheatley. . . . I never heard of poems by a monkey" (1788: 46). See also Thomas Burgess (1789: 131), Thomas Cooper (1787: 30) and Joseph Woods (1785: 14).

other things.[23] This novel is about a fictional White English couple—Mr. and Mrs. Rotchford—and their six children. The plot repeatedly gives the parents occasion to instruct their children on various important issues. The portion of the book that is most relevant for our purposes is a long episode that takes up half of the second volume: the Rotchfords take in a twelve-year-old Black boy whose name is Pompey and who had been enslaved in Barbados before being brought to England.[24] His former master, Lyncus Chromis, had abused him and eventually kicked him out after the half-starved boy took some food. The Rotchford children's initial attitude is marked by pity and a desire to help Pompey, but also by racial bias. Mr. and Mrs. Rotchford teach them, in a series of conversations, that racism is irrational and that racial slavery is unjust.[25] They also explain that Pompey's initial prejudices against White people and against Christians are completely reasonable, given his experiences (1786: 93, 130). What is most interesting for our purposes are their arguments against racial natural slavery and their description and refutation of racial bias.

Mrs. Rotchford argues against natural slavery toward the beginning of the episode about Pompey: she explains to one of her sons that the "vile practice . . . of buying and selling slaves" is based on the notion that "being possessed of money, enjoying many superior blessings, and having the understanding more enlightened . . . give[s] one nation a right over the *lives*, *liberties*, and *possessions* of another" (1786: 84–85). This notion is clearly false, she adds: "God and nature have given no such authority to any one" (1786: 85). Here she appears to endorse the claim that Europeans are more enlightened, but she denies that this or other contingent advantages can justify transatlantic slavery. These differences do not make Africans natural slaves. Later she stresses that in all morally relevant ways, Black and White

---

[23] Kilner is not the only early modern children's book author who educates her readers about the injustice of slavery. Another example is the enormously popular six-volume work *Evenings at Home* (1792–96) by John Aikin and Anna Laetitia Barbauld. Volume 6 includes a fascinating fictional dialogue between a master and an enslaved person (1796: 81–88). Frederick Douglass reports having read this dialogue over and over in his childhood, when he was enslaved, and having found it extremely encouraging (*Life and Times of Frederick Douglass,* part 1, ch. 11, 1882: 57–58).

[24] 'Pompey' was, at this time, a stereotypical name for Black male servants and slaves.

[25] One commentator describes these arguments as "one of the fiercest fictional [antislavery] statements by a female writer before abolition" (Ferguson 1992b: 123). Unfortunately, Pompey himself does not argue against slavery directly; the Rotchfords mostly speak for him. Yet Pompey repeatedly illustrates the enormous brutality of transatlantic slavery by reporting his many horrific experiences, including how he and his mother were physically abused and separated and how his brother Tankey was tortured and killed in Barbados (1786: 88–90). One aspect of *The Rotchfords* that is highly problematic by present-day standards is Kilner's attempt to capture Pompey's creole English. For a brief discussion, see Aravamudan 1999: 30.

people are equal. She justifies this equality by explaining that all people are "created by the same God, susceptible of the same pleasures, the same pains, and equally endowed with souls immortal" (1786: 94). Thus, slaveowners are clearly committing a horrible sin by treating Black people like domestic animals, or as completely lacking understanding and as less capable of physical sensations than White people (1786: 87). Mr. Rotchford makes a similar point: he argues that because Black people have immortal souls, it is wrong for White people to treat them differently, and specifically to oppress and enslave them "as if they were only beasts of burden: nay, even sometimes worse than that, as if they had no feeling at all" (1786: 110; see also 1786: 121–22).

The novel's main argument against racial natural slavery, then, is the familiar point that because of the fundamental or essential sameness of all humans, no racial group is naturally destined for slavery, and everyone is morally equal. One aspect of the Rotchfords' argument that is particularly interesting is that they stress not only the equality with respect to the soul, the mind, or the understanding, but also the equality of feelings or susceptibility to pain.[26] This is not an entirely original point—we have already seen it, for instance, in the anonymous *Two Dialogues* (1760: 12–13)—but it is noteworthy since it suggests that alleged differences in sensitivity had become a prominent component of proslavery arguments.[27]

The topic of racial bias comes up repeatedly throughout this episode. When the Rotchford children first meet Pompey, they express various prejudices, for instance, by describing his complexion as ugly and dirty (1786: 82–83) and assuming that his blood and bones must be completely different from their own (1786: 105–10). In each case, the parents patiently correct their children's misapprehensions. Mrs. Rotchford also describes and refutes widely held racist beliefs in a way that is closely connected to her claims about natural slavery. She notes that Pompey's skin color

> exposes him to contempt and barbarity, from many unkind and unthinking people; many of whom seem to imagine, that because a person's complexion

---

[26] In this context, it might be relevant that the Rotchfords also argue that it is wrong to be cruel to domestic animals (1786: 150–52), which suggests that they—and by extension Kilner, whose spokespersons the Rotchfords clearly are—believe that the ability to feel pain is important for morality. At the same time, it is clear that they view human beings as having a special status because of their immortal souls and their special mental abilities, and they repeatedly stress—as already seen—that there are no racial differences in that respect either.

[27] Even some antislavery authors claim that Black people are almost entirely incapable of feeling pain, for instance Benjamin Rush (1799: 292; see the discussion in Kendi 2016: 128).

differs from their own, and is *black*, therefore, they cannot *feel*: without reflecting, that the tint of the skin affects not the sensibility either of the body
or mind; but that the sensations of pain, are equally exquisite in people of all
complexions, and of all countries. (1786: 84)

Mrs. Rotchford here portrays racist beliefs as ridiculous and describes their
content primarily as the proposition that Black people do not feel pain. Later,
Pompey's former master, Mr. Chromis, expresses a racist belief that is even
more directly related to natural slavery. He claims that Pompey is not only
lazy and stupid but also "like the rest of his colour, fit only to be kept to toil
and hard labour" (1786: 112). Over the next several pages, Mr. Rotchford
and one of his sons painstakingly argue that Chromis's claims are based on
"a narrow-minded prejudice" against all Africans or all Black people and that
his negative portrayal of Pompey is therefore not credible (1786: 113–16).
Kilner's goal is, clearly, to help her readers overcome prejudices of precisely
this type and to realize that the judgments of slaveowners are not trustworthy.

3.6. Quobna Ottobah Cugoano

Let us now turn to Quobna Ottobah Cugoano (c. 1757–after 1791), another abolitionist and the author of the influential 1787 book *Thoughts and
Sentiments on the Evil and Wicked Traffic of the Slavery and Commerce of
the Human Species, Humbly Submitted to the Inhabitants of Great-Britain,
by Ottobah Cugoano, a Native of Africa.*[28] Unlike the authors discussed in
this chapter so far, Cugoano was Black and had firsthand experience of enslavement. Moreover, unlike many other Black antislavery writers in Europe
and North America, he had extensive firsthand knowledge of Africa: until
the age of about thirteen he lived in what is today Ghana, immersed in Fanti

---

[28] Cugoano published a shorter version of the book in 1791 (1999: 115–43), but I will focus exclusively on the longer 1787 version. One thing that is intriguing about the shorter version is its title,
which reads *Thoughts and Sentiments on the Evil of Slavery, or, the Nature of Servitude as Admitted by
the Law of God, Compared to the Modern Slavery of the Africans in the West-Indies; In an Answer to the
Advocates for Slavery and Oppression. Addressed to the Sons of Africa, by a Native.* This is significant in
part because it signals that the book is addressed to members of the Sons of Africa, whereas the original version of the book is addressed to the inhabitants of Great Britain in general. Smith speculates
that the shorter version was intended as a handbook for Afro-British antislavery activists (Smith
2010: 24). Something that is noteworthy about both title pages is that Cugoano—unlike Equiano,
whom we will discuss next—chose to include only his African name. As Cugoano mentions in a short
biographic note printed immediately after the table of contents of the longer version, his slave name
was 'John Stewart' (1999: 7).

culture.[29] Thus, he can confidently rebut racist descriptions of life in West Africa without having to rely on travel reports by White outsiders. At around thirteen, he was kidnapped and sold to European slave traders, as he recounts in the short autobiographical portion of his book. He spent some time in slavery in the West Indies and eventually England before becoming free. He stayed in England and became part of the antislavery movement there by joining the Sons of Africa, a Black political organization with close ties to the Society for Effecting the Abolition of the Slave Trade.[30]

The antislavery arguments that Cugoano provides in *Thoughts and Sentiments* draw on Christian theology and the natural law tradition as well as on his intimate knowledge about Africa, the slave trade, and the capacities of Black people. As we will see, there are indications that he uses a creolized version of natural law doctrines, which makes his contributions to abolitionism particularly intriguing. Something else that distinguishes Cugoano from most of the other authors discussed in this chapter so far is that he argues for immediate, not just gradual, abolition (1999: 98), which was extremely rare among British authors at the time. This makes him one of the most radical abolitionists in this period.[31]

Cugoano is important for our purposes in part because some of his arguments against slavery are clearly responses to the doctrine of racial natural slavery. The most direct reference to natural slavery occurs toward the beginning of the book, where Cugoano anticipates the disparaging racist reactions of his White contemporaries. Some people, he predicts, will surely say that an African like him is capable neither of high degrees of knowledge nor of theorizing about morality because "nature designed him for some inferior link in the chain, fitted only to be a slave" (1999: 11–12). In other words, his opponents believe that Black people occupy a lower place in the Great Chain of Being and are either destined by nature to be slaves, or at least unfit to be anything but slaves. He also notes in the next sentence that some people treat Black people as if they were not human but "beasts"—that is, subhuman. Later in the book, he notes, along similar lines, that slaveowners rank enslaved Black people "with brutes" and use them "as a kind of engines

---

[29] For the importance of Cugoano's familiarity with Fanti culture, see Jeffers 2017: 137.

[30] For more on Cugoano's life and his milieu, see Hanley 2018: 171–202; Gates 1988: 146–52.

[31] On this issue, see Bernasconi 2019: 34; Gunn 2010: 629–30; Wheeler 2001: 17. For other reasons to interpret Cugoano's stance as radical, see Bogues 2003: 25–46; Peters 2017.

and beasts of burden" (1999: 23).[32] Thus, Cugoano's book is at least in part a refutation of the doctrine of racial natural slavery.

There is further evidence that racial natural slavery is one of Cugoano's main targets in his book: he explicitly rebuts several proslavery arguments, including (a) the argument that Africans are by nature "poor, ignorant, dispersed, unsociable people" and are therefore better off in slavery (1999: 22), (b) the argument that Africans do not love liberty nearly as much as Europeans, which makes it permissible to enslave them (1999: 22–23), and (c) the argument that "Africans are peculiarly marked out by some signal prediction in nature and complexion for [the] purpose [of slavery]" (1999: 28). Argument (a) is common among authors who invoke natural slavery to justify transatlantic slavery. According to these authors, Africans live without stable political and social institutions, which is allegedly evidence that they are incapable of self-government and hence that they are natural slaves, unable to live good lives outside of slavery.[33] This is closely related to argument (b), that is, the claim that Africans do not value liberty. As Cugoano himself notes, authors who make this argument typically allege that Africans sell each other and even their own family members without the slightest scruples (1999: 23).[34] Argument (c) is also connected to natural slavery, since it states that Africans are intended for slavery and that either their complexion or something else in their nature signals this intention. Thus, the first and second arguments refer to psychological or behavioral characteristics that allegedly make Africans natural slaves, whereas the third refers additionally to physiological characteristics.

Cugoano attacks each of these arguments in several different ways, using empirical evidence as well as moral and theological considerations. He summarizes his own position as follows: "there is nothing in nature, reason, and scripture . . . in any manner or way, to warrant the enslaving of black people more than others" (1999: 45). In short, transatlantic slavery is

---

[32] Elsewhere, Cugoano states that European seamen "have such a prejudice against Black People, that they use them more like asses than men, so that a Black Man is scarcely ever safe among them" (1999: 106).

[33] See, for instance, Thomas Maxwell Adams 1788: 30–35.

[34] Examples include David Hume, who claims that one "may easily prevail with [Negroes] to sell, not only their parents, but their wives and mistresses, for a cask of brandy" ("Of National Characters," 1748: 286–87 / 1994: 91). Another example is Thomas Maxwell Adams, who writes that Africans "sell even their nearest relations, *wives and children* not excepted" (1788: 32). Some authors make the more general claim that Africans do not understand the value of liberty; see, for example, Rowland Cotton, who argues that "Negroes could never form the least idea" of liberty (1778: 17). The trope that Africans routinely sell their family members will play an important role in chapter 4.

inconsistent with empirical facts (or "nature"), moral principles (or "reason"), and theological doctrines (or "scripture").

Let us first look at the ways in which Cugoano uses empirical facts and moral principles to argue against racial natural slavery. In response to the claim that Africans are better off enslaved because they are "poor, ignorant, dispersed, unsociable people" (1999: 22), he states that this argument is

> without any shadow of justice and truth, and, if the argument was even true, it could afford no just and warrantable matter for any society of men to hold slaves. But the argument is false; there can be no ignorance, dispersion, or unsociableness so found among them, which can be made better by bringing them away to a state of a degree equal to that of a cow or a horse. (1999: 23)

This passage makes several important points. In the last sentence, Cugoano notes that the condition of Africans is clearly not such that it would be improved through enslavement. It is false that Africans are so ignorant and unsociable that becoming enslaved would benefit them. The passage also hints at a more general point, namely, that it is ridiculous to claim that being a chattel slave is beneficial for anyone. How could it possibly be good for any human being to have the same status as a domestic animal? The idea here seems to be that even if it were morally justifiable to coerce someone into a different way of life for their own good, chattel slavery clearly cannot be justified in that way since being enslaved cannot benefit any human being. Along similar lines, Cugoano points out in the first sentence of this passage that even if it were true that Africans are "poor, ignorant, dispersed, unsociable people" (1999: 22)—which they are not—it would nevertheless be morally wrong to enslave them. He repeats this point later on: "as to the Africans being dispersed and unsociable, if it was so, that could be no warrant for the Europeans to enslave them" (1999: 25). Here, he objects to the normative principle behind natural slavery, rather than to an empirical claim: it is simply not true that a person's ignorance or incapacity for political self-government can justify enslaving them. This objection might be based on an antipaternalist principle that prohibits coercing people into doing what is beneficial for them.

Cugoano also cites empirical evidence against proslavery arguments, including the three that I listed earlier. For instance, he explains that it is clearly false that Africans are unsociable and incapable of political self-government:

even though they may have many different feuds and bad practices among
them, . . . the numerous inhabitants [of Africa] are divided into several
kingdoms and principalities, which are governed by their respective kings
and princes, and those are absolutely maintained by their free subjects.
(1999: 25)

In short, the proslavery claim that Africans live in a state of nature without
political institutions is completely false. Cugoano also adduces empirical
evidence against the claim that Black people do not love liberty as much as
Europeans do. As mentioned earlier, some proponents of slavery use this
claim as evidence that Black people are natural slaves. Cugoano responds
that this is a lie: "Those people annually brought away from Guinea, are
born as free, and are brought up with as great a predilection for their own
country, freedom and liberty, as the sons and daughters of fair Britain"
(1999: 27). Black people love their liberty "with as much zeal and fervour" as
anyone else (1999: 28). With respect to the claim that Africans sell their own
family members into slavery because they do not value liberty, he notes that
"nothing can be more opposite to every thing they hold dear and valuable"
(1999: 27). In short, it is clearly false that Africans do not appreciate liberty as
much as Britons. Cugoano also objects to the empirical claim that Africans
are less intelligent than Europeans: "the Africans, though not so learned, are
just as wise as the Europeans" (1999: 28). The point here is clear: Africans
might be on average less educated than Europeans, but these two groups are
equal in their mental capacities.

   The book also contains a general condemnation of slavery: "what the light
of nature, and the dictates of reason, when rightly considered, teach, is, that
no man ought to enslave another" (1999: 28). In other words, it is simply always wrong to enslave other human beings, no matter what those human
beings are like. Cugoano refers approvingly to the tradition that argues for the
"universal natural rights and privileges of all men" (1999: 28). Presumably, he
is referring to the commonly accepted natural law doctrine that all human
beings naturally have the same rights, which include the right to liberty.[35]
Thus, in addition to denying that Black people possess the characteristics
ascribed to them by proponents of natural slavery, Cugoano argues against
the legitimacy of enslaving any human being, even those (if there are any)

---

[35] He invokes these ideas elsewhere as well, for instance when entreating Britons "to restore that
justice and liberty which is our natural right" (1999: 96).

who possess such characteristics. He rejects the doctrine of natural slavery categorically, not just its applicability to Black people.

Even though Cugoano invokes ideas from the natural law tradition, there are hints that his own conception of liberty is ultimately somewhat different from standard natural law conceptions. As one interpreter argues persuasively, Cugoano blends the prevalent European conception of natural liberty as an individual right with a romanticized West African conception according to which liberty is linked "to the collective care of the community" and is hence a collective right (Dahl 2020: 913; see also 2020: 915–16 and 909).[36] One particularly strong piece of evidence for this interpretation is a passage near the end of Cugoano's book. While discussing what wages might be fair for free laborers in the West Indies after the abolition of slavery, Cugoano criticizes European countries that oppress the poor and exploit their labor and in which many industrious citizens are unable to find work (1999: 103). People who live in such circumstances, he argues, are not genuinely free. Indeed, Africans "may boast of some more essential liberties than any of the civilized nations in Europe enjoy; for the poorest amongst us are never in distress for want, unless some general and universal calamity happen to us" (1999: 103). In other words, true liberty requires taking care of the most vulnerable members of society and ensuring that nobody is "oppressed and screwed down to work for nothing" (1999: 103).[37] This is not only a notable expression of solidarity with poor people in Europe (Dahl 2020: 913; Levecq 2008: 118) but also a reference to a social or collective conception of liberty. The idea, it seems, goes beyond the claim that poor people are personally unfree because the rich oppress and exploit them: Cugoano appears to say that societies that oppress and exploit the poor are collectively unfree. In this respect, African nations are far superior to European nations. This

---

[36] More specifically, Dahl argues that Cugoano creolizes the natural law conception of liberty (2020: 909). Creolization is a process of blending two traditions that are weighted unequally and that stand in asymmetrical power relations; this process transforms the ideas of both traditions (Dahl 2020: 910). Chike Jeffers makes a similar point: "for Cugoano, . . . the idea of natural rights is not really embedded within a modern European intellectual tradition. Certain formulations of it may be paradigmatically European, but it is ultimately a concept that transcends cultural boundaries. . . . Cugoano, I believe, represents modern Africana philosophy as a convergence of African and European intellectual trajectories" (2017: 138).

[37] Cugoano also defends the duty to take care of vulnerable members of society earlier in the book, but without explicitly connecting it to liberty: he states that governors have a duty "to order and establish such policy, . . . that every thing should be so managed, as to be conducive to the moral, temporal and eternal welfare of every individual from the lowest degree to the highest; and the consequence of this would be, the harmony, happiness and prosperity of the whole community" (1999: 20).

social conception of liberty makes Cugoano's arguments unique; he does much more than merely apply natural law doctrines to transatlantic slavery.

Let us now turn to Cugoano's theological arguments against natural slavery.[38] One of his main points is summarized nicely in the following passage: "the scriptures . . . afford us this information: 'That all mankind did spring from one original, and that there are no different species among men. For God who made the world, hath made of one blood all the nations of men that dwell on all the face of the earth'" (1999: 29). In other words, we know from the Bible that all human beings were created equal and descend from the same ancestors. This is the doctrine of monogenesis: all humans have the same origin or are consanguineous. Interestingly, Cugoano then concludes from this theologically motivated endorsement of monogenesis that

> there are no inferior species, but all of one blood and of one nature, . . . there does not an inferiority subsist, or depend, on their colour, features or form, whereby some men make a pretence to enslave others; and consequently, as they have all one creator, one original, made of one blood, and all brethren descended from one father, it never could be lawful and just for any nation, or people, to oppress and enslave another. (1999: 29)

In short, he is saying that theology teaches us that racial natural slavery is wrong. Because all human beings have the same origin and are all equally children of God, there are no naturally inferior groups, marked out by physical differences, whom it is permissible to enslave.

Cugoano also provides an interesting analysis of the moral irrelevance of complexion and the irrationality of racism. Differences in skin color, he argues, were established by God after the descendants of Noah had settled in different parts of the globe, in order to allow them to endure the climate in their places of residence (1999: 29–30). Addressing the objection that people in the same latitude sometimes have very different complexions, he argues that customs and differences in ways of life can also have an impact on skin color (1999: 30). Cugoano then examines and refutes the scripture-based argument that Blackness is either the mark of Cain or a sign of Ham's curse (1999: 30–33). He concludes that only ignorance and a corrupted imagination could possibly make someone "think that the stealing, kid-napping,

---

[38] Theology plays a large role in Cugoano's book; I can only mention one small aspect of the theological argumentation. For a more in-depth analysis, see Wheelock 2016.

enslaving, persecuting or killing a black man, is in any way and manner less criminal, than the same evil treatment of any other man of another complexion" (1999: 34). It is clear that differences in human skin color are morally irrelevant. Black lives matter just as much as White lives, and Black liberty and well-being carry as much moral weight as the liberty and well-being of Whites.

Along similar lines, Cugoano stresses in a wonderfully vivid passage a few pages later how ridiculous it is to think that skin color is an essential difference, especially in light of the immortality of the soul. He says, "when a man comes to die, it makes no difference whether he was black or white, whether he was male or female, whether he was great or small, or whether he was old or young; none of these differences alter the essentiality of the man, any more than he had wore a black or a white coat and thrown it off for ever" (1999: 41). His point is clearly that physiological features are ultimately irrelevant for human beings, since all that truly matters is the soul. Our bodies are like coats that we shed and leave behind when we die. What makes us human and what makes us morally and theologically equal is the soul. Contingent features of the body—and hence race, sex, age, and so on—are utterly irrelevant.

Cugoano's book is, without question, an extremely important contribution to eighteenth-century debates about slavery. His antislavery arguments often go beyond those of his White contemporaries. Moreover, Cugoano's first-hand knowledge of West Africa and transatlantic slavery allows him to add a perspective to English antislavery literature that was previously missing and to provide reliable empirical information about Africa from an insider's point of view. His philosophical arguments for abolition are shaped by this perspective and are therefore particularly valuable.

3.7. Olaudah Equiano

One of the most prominent Black abolitionists in eighteenth-century Britain was Olaudah Equiano (c. 1745–1797), whose autobiographical work *The Interesting Narrative of the Life of Olaudah Equiano, or Gustavus Vassa, the African* (1789) was an almost instant bestseller.[39] In this work, Equiano depicts his early childhood in Igboland, in what is today Nigeria, and states that he was

---

[39] 'Gustavus Vassa' is Equiano's slave name, which he continued using after he became free. For more on these two names and the ways in which Equiano used them, see Lovejoy 2016.

kidnapped and sold into slavery at the age of eleven. According to the *Narrative*, he was first taken to the West Indies, then to Virginia, then to England, and later back to the West Indies, where he was able to gain his freedom in 1766. He moved back to England about a year later.[40] Intriguingly, there is some evidence that his claims about his early life might be partly fictional: Equiano may have become enslaved at an even younger age than he claims and may even have been born into slavery in South Carolina (Carretta 1999 and 2016). This thesis is very controversial.[41] If correct, it would mean that Equiano found it important to invent an African identity for himself in the *Narrative* (Carretta 2003: xi; Levecq 2008: 122–29). If incorrect, his book is a source of valuable information about Igbo culture in the eighteenth century by an insider.

When Equiano joined the English abolitionist cause in the late 1770s as a member of the Sons of Africa, he closely collaborated with several of the other authors whom we have already encountered, including Ramsay, Clarkson, and Cugoano. In addition to his *Narrative*, Equiano published several open letters in the journal *Public Advertiser*, in which he castigates proslavery authors like James Tobin, Gordon Turnbull, and Raymund Harris and appeals to British politicians to abolish slavery.[42] I will return to these letters at the end of this section, after discussing Equiano's most famous and longest work, the *Narrative*. This book contributed to abolitionism in part by describing the middle passage and slavery from the perspective of an enslaved man, rather than the far more commonly published perspective of a White observer.[43] While Equiano also engages in reflections about slavery in the book, it contains far fewer antislavery arguments than Cugoano's book. Equiano instead concentrates on narrating his own experiences, which to this day are gripping to read. As with other Black authors, the very act of writing and publishing a book contributed to the antislavery cause by providing a clear counterexample to claims about intellectual inferiority.[44] First-personal narratives like Equiano's furthermore help White readers to

---

[40] For more on Equiano's life, see his *Interesting Narrative* as well as Hanley 2018: 51–75; Carretta 2005; Gates 1988: 152–58.

[41] For criticisms of Carretta's interpretation, see Acholonu 2009; Ukaegbu 2009; Lovejoy 2016.

[42] These letters are included in Appendix E of Carretta's edition of Equiano's *Narrative* (Equiano 2003: 327–71).

[43] Equiano's *Narrative* was not the first autobiography composed in English by a formerly enslaved Black person in the eighteenth century; earlier examples include James Albert Ukawsaw Gronniosaw's *A Narrative of the Most Remarkable Particulars in the Life of an African Prince, as Related by Himself* (1772) and John Marrant's *A Narrative of the Lord's Wonderful Dealings with John Marrant, a Black* (1785).

[44] As we will see later, Mary Wollstonecraft's review of Equiano's book discusses the question of whether the book is such a counterexample.

imagine the realities of slavery from the point of view of an enslaved person. What is most relevant for our purposes, however, are Equiano's reflections about racial slavery, which are directly connected to natural slavery.

One relevant passage occurs in the first chapter of the *Narrative*. In the last few paragraphs, Equiano theorizes about the origins of modern Africans and sides with authors who argue that Africans descend from the biblical Abraham and his second wife or concubine Keturah (ch. 1, 2003: 44). He then sides with Clarkson's climatological theory of differences in complexion. More interestingly, Equiano also addresses racism, arguing against the belief that Africans are naturally inferior to White Europeans because of their dark skin. Specifically, he claims that there are "causes enough to which the apparent inferiority of an African may be ascribed, without limiting the goodness of God, and supposing he forbore to stamp understanding on certainly his own image, because 'carved in ebony'" (ch. 1, 2003: 45). In other words, it is unreasonable—and theologically dubious—to think that God created Africans without intellects, since there are many far more likely explanations for their ostensible inferiority to Europeans. These explanations, he goes on to explain, clearly include language barriers, cultural differences, a lack of access to education, dehumanization, slavery itself, and the "rude and uncultivated" condition of Africans. This is a version of the effects-of-slavery strategy: a partial explanation of the apparent inferiority of enslaved Africans is that they are not "treated as men" and that "slavery itself depress[es] the mind, and extinguish[es] all its fire, and every noble sentiment" (ch. 1, 2003: 45). The overall argument appears to be an argument to the best explanation. Dark skin is clearly the effect of differences in climate and has nothing to do with intelligence; the best explanation for apparent differences in intelligence is not a natural or divinely intended inferiority but rather a difference in opportunities and contingent circumstances.

Toward the end of the fifth chapter, Equiano again reflects about racial differences and slavery and makes some new points. One noteworthy aspect of this reflection is Equiano's claim that the slave trade has devastating effects on White slaveowners and traders: it makes them cruel and incapable of sympathy (ch. 5, 2003: 111). Even more relevantly for our purposes, he then invokes ideas from the natural law tradition to argue that the slave trade is unjust:

> this traffic . . . violates that first natural right of mankind, equality and independency, and gives one man a dominion over his fellows which God

could never intend! For it raises the owner to a state as far above man as it depresses the slave below it; and, with all the presumption of human pride, sets a distinction between them, immeasurable in extent, and endless in duration! (ch. 5, 2003: 111)

The general point of this passage is familiar: humans are naturally equal and free, which means that no human being has a natural right to completely dominate another. Yet Equiano makes this point differently from other authors we have encountered so far. Slavery violates natural rights by raising slaveowners to a level that is too high for a human being, giving them an almost godlike authority over enslaved people; at the same time, it lowers the enslaved to a level that is too low for a human being, giving them a status more like that of a brute animal.[45] And to make matters even worse, this immense and unnatural power imbalance is lifelong.

In the same paragraph, Equiano invokes the effects-of-slavery strategy again, in a slightly different way. It is absurd and unfair for slaveowners to claim that the people they enslave naturally lack virtue, understanding, and the ability to learn, since slavery itself is clearly the main cause of these alleged characteristics. With respect to the apparent lack of virtue, Equiano notes that slaveowners by their own behavior set "an example of fraud, rapine, and cruelty," while also compelling the people they enslave to live "in a state of war" with them (ch. 5, 2003: 111). The reference to the state of war is particularly interesting; the idea seems to be that it is unreasonable to expect civility from those with whom one is at war—and particularly, one might add, from those whom one has attacked without justification. With respect to alleged intellectual differences, he notes that slaveowners "stupify [their slaves] with stripes, and think it necessary to keep them in a state of ignorance" (ch. 5, 2003: 111). The latter claim is intriguing, since it suggests that slaveowners purposely keep enslaved people ignorant because this is necessary for maintaining their status. We saw a similar claim in Jones and Allen's 1794 pamphlet that we discussed in chapter 1, but it is rare.[46]

Of Equiano's open letters, two are particularly relevant to our purposes: the one addressed to James Tobin, author of the proslavery tract *Cursory Remarks upon the Reverend Mr. Ramsay's Essay* (1785), and the one

---

[45] This interpretation is confirmed later, when Equiano describes slaves as "humbled to the condition of brutes" and not permitted to "enjoy the privileges of men" (ch. 5, 2003: 111).

[46] It is noteworthy that Jones and Allen used to be enslaved; like Equiano, they have presumably experienced this phenomenon firsthand.

addressed to Gordon Turnbull, author of the proslavery tract *An Apology for Negro Slavery* (1786). Both letters were published in early 1788. Equiano attacks these two defenders of slavery in delightfully direct and astute ways. For instance, he calls Turnbull a "fool" and warns him that according to the Bible, "Fools perish for lack of knowledge" (2003: 334).[47] Along similar lines, he calls Tobin a "malicious slanderer" who shamelessly misrepresents the situation in the West Indies to further his own wicked interests (2003: 331). Equiano also notes that Tobin's fondness for flogging others proves that he is "deserving of flagellation" himself (2003: 330). Moreover, he warns Tobin of God's vengeance; the tortures experienced by enslaved Black people at the hands of oppressors like Tobin will pale in comparison to the punishment that God has in store for these oppressors (2003: 331).

One particularly intriguing aspect of the letter to Tobin is its discussion of interracial marriage and interracial sex. As seen in earlier chapters, many White authors in this period—even authors who argue for the abolition of slavery—oppose miscegenation. Equiano is one of very few authors who explicitly defend it. First, he argues that it is iniquitous and cruel to shackle not only the bodies but the inclinations of Black men by banning interracial relationships. This ban forces Black men who have fallen in love with White women to languish, unable to follow the strongest inclinations of their hearts (2003: 331). Such bans, he explains, are premised on the worry that "the offspring should be tawney," which is clearly a ludicrous thing to worry about: "A more foolish prejudice than this never warped a cultivated mind." After all, skin color is completely irrelevant for moral virtue; God does not care about the color of our skin, and neither should we (2003: 331). Next, he turns to the question of what repealing this ban would mean for Black women. His answer is that it would be extremely beneficial because there would no longer be "such a strong propensity toward the black females" (2003: 331). His explanation deserves to be quoted in full:

> Nature abhors restraint, and for ease either evades or breaks it. Hence arise secret amours, adultery, fornication and all other evils of lasciviousness! hence that most abandoned boasting of the French planter, who, under the

---

[47] Interestingly, Equiano also argues in his letter to Turnbull that racial natural slavery is incompatible with Christian ethics, which after all commands "meekness, justice, . . . charity, and above all, . . . brotherly love" (2003: 333). He asks rhetorically, "can any man be a Christian who asserts that one part of the human race were ordained to be in perpetual bondage to another?" (2003: 333).

dominion of lust, had the shameless impudence to exult at the violations he had committed against Virtue, Religion, and the Almighty—hence also spring actual murders on infants, the procuring of abortions, enfeebled constitution, disgrace, shame, and a thousand other horrid enormities. (2003: 331–32)

He makes several important points in this passage. The basic idea is that bans on interracial marriage have horrendous implications for Black women because when laws prevent White men from satisfying their desires in virtuous ways, they will satisfy their desires in immoral ways. One of the immoral acts that Equiano mentions here is consensual extramarital sex, but it is almost impossible not to read this passage as also containing veiled references to the rape of enslaved Black women by White men, such as in the remark about the French planter. Bans on interracial sex have other horrendous consequences as well, he adds, including infanticide and the abortion of mixed-race fetuses. There is an easy way to stop these immoral actions, Equiano points out: "why not establish intermarriages at home, and in our Colonies? and encourage open, free, and generous love upon Nature's own wide and extensive plan, subservient only to moral rectitude, without distinction of the colour of a skin?" (2003: 332). In 1788, this proposal would have shocked many White readers, even among those who favored the abolition of slavery; this makes Equiano one of the most radical and audacious proponents of racial equality in this period.

3.8. Mary Wollstonecraft

Our last author in this chapter is the White English philosopher Mary Wollstonecraft (1759–1797), mainly known today as an advocate of women's rights and a critic of Edmund Burke and Jean-Jacques Rousseau. In her writings on political philosophy, she often uses the term 'slavery' to describe the subjection of women—like many other early modern feminists—as well as the unfreedom of citizens in unjust political systems. She sometimes discusses transatlantic slavery, albeit never in very much detail. These discussions occur in her two best-known philosophical works, *Vindication of the Rights of Men* (1790) and *Vindication of the Rights of Woman* (1792), as well as in her 1795 *Historical and Moral View of the Origin and Progress of the French Revolution* and in her anonymously published book review of Olaudah Equiano's

Interesting Narrative from 1789.[48] Moreover, she discusses race and ethnicity in her 1796 work *Letters Written during a Short Residence in Sweden, Norway, and Denmark* and in two additional anonymous book reviews: a 1788 review of Samuel Stanhope Smith's *Essay on the Causes of the Variety of Complexion and Figure in the Human Species* and a 1797 review of François Le Vaillant's *New Travels into the Interior Parts of Africa*. The most relevant aspects of her discussions of transatlantic slavery are that she mentions natural slavery in several places, that she explicitly advocates abolition, and that she opposes slavery based on an original theory about the importance of freedom for human flourishing. With respect to race, we will see that she argues for the moral equality of all human beings while also holding that "civilization" is necessary for the full development of human rationality and that there are significant natural differences in mental and physical capacities.[49]

Some background information about Wollstonecraft's political philosophy will help us understand her attitude toward slavery. The first thing to note is that she views liberty as a "natural and imprescriptible[50] right of man" (*French Revolution* 2.4, 1989: 115), or as a birthright that society can licitly take away only from someone who has forfeited this right through a crime (*Rights of Men*, 1995: 53). In the state of nature, human beings are completely free, but they have strong reasons to surrender some of this liberty by entering into a social contract (*French Revolution* 2.4, 1989: 115). After all, as we will see later, living in a well-organized society is necessary for human flourishing. Wollstonecraft builds this idea into her definition of the right to freedom: man's birthright is "such a degree of liberty . . . as is compatible with the liberty of every other individual with whom he is united in a social compact, and the continued existence of that compact" (*Rights of Men*, 1995: 7). Unfortunately, she continues, no existing government grants its citizens this amount of freedom; all existing nations encroach on the human birthright to some extent because they prioritize property rights over freedom (1995: 7)

---

[48] I will refer to Wollstonecraft's main works with shortened versions of their titles: *Rights of Men*, *Rights of Woman*, and *French Revolution*.

[49] For more on Wollstonecraft's views on race, see Juengel 2001; Rickman 2005. For her views on slavery, see Howard 2004; Ferguson 1992a; Tomaselli 2021: 69–72.

[50] Saying that a right is imprescriptible typically means that it "cannot in any circumstances be legally taken away or abandoned" (OED, http://www.oed.com/view/Entry/92708). According to this definition, "imprescriptible" is stronger than "inalienable," because it means that the right in question cannot even be forfeited. Yet Wollstonecraft appears to hold that the right to liberty can be forfeited through certain crimes (*Rights of Men* 1995: 53). Wollstonecraft may be borrowing this expression from the French Declaration of the Rights of Man and the Citizen (1789), which talks of "natural and imprescriptible rights" (*droits naturels et imprescriptibles*) (art. 2, in Rials 1988: 22).

and cement injustice by making property and arbitrarily assigned honors hereditary (1995: 8–9). The English, she remarks sarcastically, have practically redefined liberty as the security of property; they sacrifice genuine liberty in order to secure the selfish interests of the rich (1995: 13).

Liberty is extremely important for Wollstonecraft because it is a necessary condition for becoming "either a reasonable or dignified being" (*French Revolution* 2.4, 1989: 115). Thus, people who are unfree cannot acquire rational capacities and are prevented from living in a way that befits human beings. For instance, those who live under despotic governments are unable to develop their mental capacities and are forced to live like brute animals, or like mere instruments for the despot's purposes, which is incompatible with dignity (2.4, 1989: 115). Political systems that deprive citizens of "natural, equal, civil and political rights" also degrade the moral character of these citizens, turning the rich into tyrants and the poor into slaves, which in turn leads the poor to resort to fraud, theft, and other crimes (5.4, 1989: 234; see also *Rights of Men*, 1995: 62). Wollstonecraft applies this doctrine to the French ancien régime, claiming that most of its citizens were nearly as ignorant as "barbarians" due to their unfreedom (5.3, 1989: 221). She uses the same idea elsewhere to explain why women seem intellectually inferior to men in many societies: due to their unfreedom, they lack opportunities for intellectual development (*Rights of Woman*, ch. 2, 1995: 105). This is analogous to the effects-of-slavery strategy, which we have already encountered in many other authors.

As we have just seen, Wollstonecraft views freedom as a necessary condition for acquiring rationality. It is not sufficient, however. A second necessary condition for developing rational capacities is society: in the state of nature, in which humans are fully free, they nevertheless cannot "unfold [their] intellectual powers" because humans are naturally social beings (*French Revolution* 2.4, 1989: 115). This means that there are two ways of life in which human beings are unable to develop their rational capacities: life without a government and life under an oppressive or despotic government. Only good forms of government allow humans to flourish, that is, to actualize their potential for rationality and hence live in accordance with the dignity of their nature. Accordingly, Wollstonecraft describes "savages," or people who are completely "uncivilized"—by which she presumably means that they do not live in well-organized, just societies—as not yet having "extended the dominion of the mind, or even learned to think with the energy necessary to concatenate that abstract train of thought which produces principles" (*Rights of Woman*, ch. 13.3, 1995: 286). In short, she holds that without a good government, human beings can hardly exercise their rational capacities at all.

Wollstonecraft also endorses the doctrine that all human beings are naturally equal, though with significant caveats.[51] All humans naturally possess the basic capacity for reasoning, which she defines as "the simple power of improvement; or, more properly speaking, of discerning truth" (*Rights of Woman*, ch. 4, 1995: 127).[52] This power must belong to all humans because it is an emblem of the divine image and thus connected to our special status as immortal creatures (ch. 4, 1995: 126–27). The nature of this power is the same in all humans, she adds, even if it is "less . . . conspicuous in one being than another" (ch. 4, 1995: 127). This suggests that while all human beings can learn to exercise their rational capacities to some extent, there are important natural differences in this respect. Indeed, Wollstonecraft claims elsewhere that nature has "made men unequal, by giving stronger bodily and mental powers to one than to another" (*French Revolution* 1.1, 1989: 17) and that "there is a superiority of natural genius among men" (5.3, 1989: 220).

Yet—and this is important—these natural differences do not give governments the right to oppress those who are naturally inferior. Quite to the contrary, Wollstonecraft argues that "the end of government ought to be, to destroy this [natural] inequality by protecting the weak" (*French Revolution* 1.1, 1989: 17). As she explains, it is a mistake to think that due to these natural differences, "men of every class are not equally susceptible of common improvement" (5.3, 1989: 220). The idea seems to be that even those whose natural capacities are inferior can improve their reasoning abilities significantly, if given the opportunity. As a result, it is "a monstrous tyranny, a barbarous oppression," and detrimental to the general good when governments deny a large proportion of their citizens such opportunities for improvement (5.3, 1989: 220). In short, natural differences do not justify oppression; all human beings are capable of rationality and governments have an obligation to enable all citizens to develop their mental capacities.

Another text that helps us understand Wollstonecraft's views about natural differences is her 1796 work *Letters Written during a Short Residence in Sweden, Norway, and Denmark*. When discussing the differences between Swedes and Norwegians, she criticizes the widespread tendency to

---

[51] For an excellent discussion of Wollstonecraft's views on human inequality, see Tomaselli 2021: 65–111 and 162–64.

[52] This is similar to Jean-Jacques Rousseau's notion of perfectibility (*Second Discourse* 1.16, 2019a: 144).

ascribe such differences to "national character," because such ascriptions fail to separate differences that are truly natural from differences that are acquired (letter 5, 1989: 266). A more thorough investigation, she predicts, would show natural differences to be limited to "the degree of vivacity or thoughtfulness, pleasure, or pain, inspired by the climate," and that all other differences stem from political and religious disparities (letter 5, 1989: 266).[53] Here she endorses a climate theory of human difference while also arguing that very few observable differences stem from climate and are hence natural. As the context makes clear, this means that no ethnic or racial group is "stupid by nature," and it also means that there are no natural differences in moral character (letter 5, 1989: 266). As we will see later, she appears to use the same idea to reject racial natural slavery. Yet this passage also reveals that Wollstonecraft acknowledges some natural differences between ethnic groups, including intellectual ones—differences in what she calls "thoughtfulness"—and differences in sensitivity to pain.[54]

Wollstonecraft elsewhere argues that many people exaggerate the natural differences between Africans and Europeans. The reason for such exaggerations is not only that people tend to mistake acquired differences for natural ones but also that the vast majority of European reports about Africa are utterly unreliable due to hasty generalizations and cultural prejudices (review of Smith 1788: 433n; see also letter 5, 1989: 266). She warns that some authors who write about Africa, whom she labels "metaphysical romancers,"[55] have malignant motives for portraying Africans as naturally inferior and even as subhuman: these writers have an interest in proving "that morality ha[s] no foundation in the natural dispositions and affections" (review of Le Vaillant 1797: 465). Proving this would enable these writers to conclude that if they can "degrade a part of the human species below the brutes, the moral obligation to act up to the character of man would be less binding on the whole race" (1797: 465). In other words, Wollstonecraft accuses some Europeans of dehumanizing Black people in an attempt to morally justify colonialism and slavery. In her review of Le Vaillant, she makes this point specifically with respect to reports about the "hottentots"—that is, the Khoekhoen of southwestern Africa. Prior to Le Vaillant's work, she notes,

---

[53] In an appendix to this work, she provides some examples of social and political factors that result in significant differences: "The poverty of the poor, in Sweden, renders the civilization very partial; and slavery has retarded the improvement of every class in Denmark" (1989: 346).

[54] It is not entirely clear to me what she means by "thoughtfulness."

[55] In other words, these writers make metaphysical claims that are invented or wildly exaggerated.

Europeans have typically described this group as the most "disgusting and brutal" ethnicity and as having "dirty customs" (1797: 465). She praises Le Vaillant for correcting this unfair and inaccurate representation (1797: 465). Interestingly, she also identifies another reason why most reports about this ethnic group are so unreliable: the reports are mainly based on encounters with Khoekhoen who have been corrupted through close contact with immoral Europeans (1797: 465).[56] Indeed, she writes that European traders and planters in Africa cruelly oppress and dehumanize the local population, which makes the former much more deserving of the label 'savage' than the latter (1797: 466).[57] Khoekhoen who have not had extensive contact with Europeans are "just and affectionate, with the distinctive characteristics of man" and possess "domestic virtues, and moral sensibility" (1797: 465).

Wollstonecraft also denounces transatlantic slavery in a few places—as one would expect, given her emphasis on the importance of freedom for human flourishing and on the natural right to liberty. When criticizing Burke in *Rights of Men*, she warns that his "servile reverence for antiquity, and prudent attention to self-interest," if taken to their logical conclusion, entail that American slavery never ought to be abolished (1995: 13). She uses this as a reductio ad absurdum of Burke's principles: the transatlantic slave trade is an "inhuman custom" that violates human dignity and "outrages every suggestion of reason and religion" (1995: 13). The fact that our ignorant ancestors sanctioned this trade and that abolition would violate the property rights of those who profit from it cannot be a good reason to continue such an "atrocious insult to humanity" (1995: 13). Along similar lines, she later refutes the argument that abolition would infringe on the rights of planters by stating that it is clearly "consonant with justice, with the common principles of humanity, not to mention Christianity, to abolish this abominable mischief" (1995: 53). After all, all humans who have not committed a crime must be "allowed to enjoy their birth-right—liberty" (1995: 53). Even though she

[56] She invokes a similar mechanism to explain why under the French ancien régime, "the great bulk of the people were worse than savages; retaining much of the ignorance of barbarians, after having poisoned the noble qualities of nature by imbibing some of the habits of degenerate refinement" (*French Revolution* 5.3, 1989: 221). This passage, like the review of Le Vaillant, suggests that human beings naturally possess some noble traits that they tend to lose when they are exposed to perverted or degenerate forms of civilization. Thus, perverted forms of civilization are worse for human beings than no civilization at all.

[57] Wollstonecraft explains this inhumane behavior of Europeans in part as a corrupting influence of power: this behavior illustrates that "half civilized men are [unfit] to be entrusted with unlimited power" (review of Le Vaillant, 1797: 466).

does not spell out these antislavery arguments in much detail, it is apparent that she staunchly supports abolition.

In *Rights of Woman*, she invokes transatlantic slavery when comparing the unfreedom of all women to the unfreedom of transatlantic slaves. If women are immortal, she argues, they are capable of living freely, rather than in subjection to men (ch. 9, 1995: 234–35). Thus, it is unjust for women, "like the poor African slaves, to be subject to prejudices that brutalize them" (ch. 9, 1995: 235). Indeed, she adds, this is "indirectly to deny woman reason . . . for a gift is a mockery, if it be unfit for use" (ch. 9, 1995: 235). While this passage is primarily about women's rights, it is clear that she thinks the same argument applies to enslaved Black people. They too are immortal and therefore capable of rationality and liberty; it is hence unjust to treat them like brute animals and pretend that they are not rational, or that they cannot use the divine gift of rationality. This is not a direct reference to racial natural slavery, but it comes close: Wollstonecraft is clearly arguing against the idea that the subjection of Black people is licit because they are incapable of using their reason. Moreover, she describes sexism and racism as comprising a belief in the subhuman status of women and Black people, respectively, by claiming that these prejudices "brutalize" their targets.

Wollstonecraft refers to natural slavery more directly in other texts. One is her somewhat unfavorable review of Equiano's *Interesting Narrative*, which she published anonymously in the *Analytic Review* in 1789. She starts this review as follows:

> [Equiano's book] is certainly a curiosity, as it has been a favourite philosophic whim to degrade the numerous nations, on whom the sun-beams more directly dart, below the common level of humanity, and hastily to conclude that nature, by making them inferior to the rest of the human race, designed to stamp them with a mark of slavery. (1789: 27)

In other words, she states that many of her contemporaries view Black people not only as inferior to White people but as natural slaves. Her description of this inference as hasty and her usage of the term "philosophic whim" strongly suggest that she views the doctrine of racial natural slavery as misguided.[58] In the continuation of this passage, she then states that this review is not the

---

[58] This suggestion is, of course, also supported by her claims about equality, liberty, and slavery in her other works, which we have already examined.

place to discuss the causes of Blackness, nor the place "to draw a parallel between the abilities of a negro and European mechanic" (1789: 27). This appears to be an oblique reference to specific arguments against the claim that Africans are naturally destined for slavery, namely arguments that dark skin is not a mark of slavery or of essential differences, and arguments that Black people have abilities that resemble at least those of European artisans.[59] Instead of discussing these types of arguments, Wollstonecraft turns to the question of whether Equiano's autobiography refutes the doctrine that Africans are natural slaves—not through the arguments it contains but by providing evidence of the intelligence of its author. Her answer appears to be affirmative, though not unequivocally so:

> if these volumes do not exhibit extraordinary intellectual powers, sufficient to wipe off the stigma, yet the activity and ingenuity, which conspicuously appear in the character of Gustavus,[60] place him on a par with the general mass of men, who fill the subordinate stations in a more civilized society than that which he was thrown into at his birth. (1789: 27)

Her assessment, in short, is that Equiano's autobiography suggests that his intellectual powers are equal to those of common people in "civilized" countries, but not extraordinary.[61] She appears to think that this does not suffice to "wipe off the stigma" of Blackness entirely. Nevertheless, since she does not hold that common people in Europe are natural slaves, she presumably thinks that this is evidence against the claim that all Africans are natural slaves.[62] In the remainder of this short review, she provides only a very rough overview of the book's contents, though she notes that Equiano's descriptions of the middle passage and of slavery in the West Indies "make the blood turn its course" (1789: 28).

---

[59] The latter might be a reference to James Ramsay, who argues—as we saw in chapter 2—that the mental differences between Black and White people are no greater than the differences between a European "man of learning" and a European mechanic (*Essay* 4.4, 1784: 236). With respect to the causes of Black complexion, it is worth noting that in her review of Samuel Stanhope Smith's *Essay on the Causes of the Variety of Complexion and Figure in the Human Species*, she praises Smith's arguments for monogenesis as well as his climate theory of human diversity (1788: 431–32).

[60] Equiano's slave name, as mentioned earlier, was 'Gustavus Vassa.'

[61] She complains about Equiano's writing style later in the review, claiming that there is a contradiction between "many childish stories and puerile remarks" and "rather tiresome" expressions of religious sentiments on the one hand, and "some more solid reflections" and "a few well written periods" on the other (1789: 28).

[62] This statement may, then, be a version of the argument that the mental capacities of Africans resemble those of European artisans, which she mentioned earlier.

Another relevant text is *Letters Written during a Short Residence in Sweden, Norway, and Denmark*. After noting that it is very important to distinguish between natural and acquired differences among different nations or ethnic groups, Wollstonecraft criticizes those who characterize a specific group as "stupid by nature." These people fail to realize that "slaves, having no object to stimulate industry, have not their faculties sharpened by the only thing that can exercise them, self-interest" (letter 5, 1989: 266).[63] In other words, the apparent stupidity of subordinated groups is not natural but acquired; life in slavery affords no opportunities for developing one's rational capacities. What she says in this text fits well with her theory that liberty is a necessary condition for becoming fully rational, which we discussed earlier. Interestingly, the text continues as follows: "Others have been brought forward as brutes, having no aptitude for the arts and sciences, only because the progress of improvement had not reached the stage which produces [arts and sciences]" (letter 5, 1989: 266). This might be a reference to racist prejudices against Africans or other racialized groups who are sometimes portrayed as subhuman, such as the Sami. Wollstonecraft repudiates this portrayal by pointing out that the relevant differences are entirely due to contingent historical factors and are hence not essential or natural differences.

Wollstonecraft also mentions natural slavery in *View of the French Revolution*, but in the context of political rather than personal slavery. When discussing the revolution in France, she notes that everybody should feel joy "at seeing the inhabitants of a vast empire exalted from the lowest state of beastly degradation to a summit, where, contemplating the dawn of freedom, they may breathe the invigorating air of independence; which will give them a new constitution of mind" (2.1, 1989: 52). This also fits with Wollstonecraft's doctrine that political unfreedom degrades human beings to an animal-like condition and depresses the human mind. Intriguingly, she then goes on to ask, "Who is so much under the influence of prejudice, as to insist, that frenchmen are a distinct race, formed by nature, or by habit, to be slaves; and incapable of ever attaining those noble sentiments, which characterize a free people?" (2.1, 1989: 52). The presupposition here is clearly that the ancien régime would only be an acceptable political system if the citizens of France were natural slaves, unable to live freely. And that, she implies, is

---

[63] This statement is reminiscent of Adam Smith's economic argument against slavery in his 1776 *Wealth of Nations*: slavery violates economic laws by eliminating the main incentives for productive labor (3.2.9, 1986: 488–89). Smith makes a similar argument in his *Lectures of Jurisprudence* in 1762/63 (1978: 185).

clearly not the case. She even suggests that if this were the case, it would make the French "a distinct race"—presumably because it would make them fundamentally different from all other human beings, who are naturally capable of living freely.

As we have seen in this section, Wollstonecraft's theory of the importance of liberty is different from the theories we have encountered thus far. While she does not discuss transatlantic slavery in great detail, she uses her theory in a few places to advocate abolition. She is committed to equal rights and argues that governments have an obligation to protect the most vulnerable members of society and to counteract natural inequalities. Moreover, she acknowledges the ways in which the prejudices and self-interest of Europeans distort their assessment of the natural capacities of Black people. The doctrine that Black people are natural slaves is one result of such distorted assessments, and she refutes this doctrine quite effectively.

4

Francophone Debates about
Slavery and Race

Jean-Baptiste Belley (1747–1805), a formerly enslaved Black man who served as the deputy for northern Saint-Domingue—present-day Haiti—argued as follows in a 1794 pamphlet:

> Fellow citizens, do you believe that Nature is unjust, that it has created some men to be the slaves of others, as the colonists claim? Do you not see in this shameful assertion the true principles of these detestable ravagers of the human species? . . . The executioners of the blacks impudently lie when they dare to claim that these oppressed men are brutes. If they lack the vices of Europeans, they have the virtues of Nature; they are sensitive and grateful beings. . . . [They] were invigorated on hearing the unexpected sound of happiness and freedom. You . . . have returned to human life and happiness unfortunate men whom the colonists . . . have for a long time classed among the animals and treated with great inhumanity. (Belley 1794: 5–6 / 2014: 113; translation altered)[1]

Belley composed this text shortly after France announced the abolition of slavery in its colonies, which included Saint-Domingue; this announcement is the "unexpected sound of happiness and freedom" that Belley references. The passage touches on three themes that are central to francophone debates about slavery: the doctrine of racial natural slavery, the importance of liberty, and the equality of all human beings.

France and its colonies were host to some of the most intriguing debates about slavery and race in the eighteenth century. One of the factors shaping these debates was the French Revolution. French revolutionaries, like their American counterparts, argued against the legitimacy of tyrannical forms of rule and for the importance of liberty and equality. At the same

---

[1] For more information about Belley, see Levecq 2019: 75–159.

Slavery and Race. Julia Jorati, Oxford University Press. © Oxford University Press 2024.
DOI: 10.1093/oso/9780197659236.003.0005

time, France participated directly in the transatlantic slave trade and—like England—had several colonies in the Americas that depended on the labor of enslaved Black people. Thus, francophone debates were sparked in part by a tension similar to the one we have already encountered in English and North American contexts: France prided itself on its firm commitment to enlightenment ideals and struggled to reconcile this self-conception with its involvement in, and economic dependence on, transatlantic slavery.[2] The content of French debates about slavery and race also overlaps with its British and North American counterparts. This is no coincidence since intellectuals and activists in these three regions often exchanged ideas and influenced one another. Nevertheless, certain aspects of the French debates are distinctive, due in part to the fact that France was home to some of the most radical political philosophers and freethinkers of this period. We will examine some of them in this chapter.

A very brief sketch of the historical background will be helpful for contextualizing the debates that are at the core of this chapter.[3] One important component of the legal background is the infamous *Code noir* or Black code, which governed slavery in French colonies during most of this period. It defined the legal status and rights of enslaved Black people as well as of free people of color,[4] outlawed certain types of punishments while mandating others, and regulated many other aspects of colonial slavery. This code was originally passed in 1685 and was amended twice in the 1720s. Some eighteenth-century authors viewed this code favorably, as a way to prevent masters from treating enslaved people with excessive cruelty. Others viewed the code's provisions as horrendously unjust and cruel.

The second half of the eighteenth century, in which nearly all these debates occurred, was a time of enormous political and social upheaval in France. From 1754 to 1763, France and Great Britain clashed over the control of North American colonies in the French and Indian War, which in

---

[2] This tension already existed before the French Revolution; for book-length discussions of this tension and its manifestations during the ancient régime, see Peabody 1996; Boulle 2007. For book-length discussions of race and slavery in eighteenth-century France, see Pluchon 1984; Sala-Molins 2006; Ehrard 2008; Curran 2011.

[3] I will only provide background information about France and its colonies even though one of the authors I will discuss—Jean-Jacques Rousseau—was from Geneva. Rousseau spent significant portions of his career in France and was a member of French intellectual circles. Hence, even though it is crucial to keep his Genevan roots in mind, the French context is important for understanding his ideas as well.

[4] In the French context, the term 'people of color' (*gens de couleur*) is used for the mixed-race descendants of Black colonial slaves. For an eighteenth-century explanation of this term by a free person of color, see Raymond 1791, who also discusses the prejudices against free people of color.

1756 became part of the Seven Years' War. This conflict did not end well for France—in the 1763 Treaty of Paris, it agreed to give up most of its colonies in North America. It was, however, allowed to retain some of its Caribbean colonies, including Martinique and Saint-Domingue. In addition, France regained control over parts of Senegal, which was one of the hubs of the transatlantic slave trade. Nevertheless, France's defeat had far-reaching economic and political consequences and shaped francophone debates about slavery.[5]

Another tremendously important political event was the French Revolution (1789–99) and concomitant debates about natural rights and legitimate rule, as already mentioned. Many of the political ideas that were at the heart of the Revolution are expressed in the Declaration of the Rights of Man and of the Citizen (Rials 1988), adopted by the National Constituent Assembly in 1789. Antislavery activists in French colonies and in France— many of whom were active in the abolitionist organization Society of the Friends of the Blacks (Société des amis des Noirs)—argued that racial slavery is incompatible with these political principles.[6] For instance, the White civil commissioner of Saint-Domingue, Léger-Félicité Sonthonax, writes in 1793, "Men are born and remain free and equal in rights. There you have it, citizens: the Gospel of France. . . . The French Republic wants all men without distinction of color to be free and equal" (1793: 1–2 / 2014: 107). Free people of color in French colonies also used these ideas to argue that they deserve the same political rights as free White colonists. For instance, Vincent Ogé— a man of color from Saint-Domingue—states in 1789: "this word Liberty that can only be uttered with enthusiasm, this word which embodies the idea of happiness, . . . this Liberty, the greatest and first of all goods, is it made for all men? I believe so. Should it be given to all men? Again, I believe so" (1789: 5 / 2014: 49; translation altered).[7]

As we will see later in this chapter, the Revolution also sparked discussions about the extent to which violent uprisings are a licit response to violations of natural rights. Additional fodder for these debates was supplied by

---

[5] For a discussion of the ways in which the Seven Years' War impacted French politics and its debates about slavery, see Thomson 2017: 252–53.

[6] For more on this society and its various campaigns, see Drescher 2009: 151–63. French women's rights activists also used these ideas for their cause, perhaps most famously Olympe de Gouges, whom we will discuss at the end of this chapter.

[7] Ogé also led a revolt of free people of color in 1790, which White administrators brutally repressed. For English translations of additional primary sources from this context, see Geggus 2014; Hunt 1996; Dubois and Garrigus 2006. Scans of many of the original French texts are available through https://gallica.bnf.fr.

the revolts of enslaved people in Martinique (1789) and, more important, Saint-Domingue (1791), which were at least partially inspired by the French Revolution. Saint-Domingue's revolt was the beginning of the Haitian Revolution, which would lead to Haiti's independence in 1804. News about these revolts had a significant impact on French debates about slavery in the last decade of the eighteenth century. Intriguingly, both sides portrayed these events as supporting their cause. On the one hand, as we will see when discussing Olympe de Gouges, some slavery apologists blamed antislavery writers like Gouges for these revolts and used this accusation to try to silence abolitionists. On the other hand, these revolts made the tension between France's revolutionary ideals and its participation in transatlantic slavery much harder to ignore, as antislavery authors liked to point out. Why would the French people be entitled to oust their tyrannical rulers, while enslaved Black people in the West Indies are not? Moreover, and more importantly, the revolts changed the political and economic situation significantly: France's West Indian colonies had become unstable and far less profitable. To make matters worse, Spain and Britain were threatening to take control of these colonies. While the National Assembly had reaffirmed its support for slavery in French colonies in a 1790 decree, it completely changed course only four years later by abolishing slavery in French colonies in 1794.[8] Unfortunately, this abolition was short-lived: Napoleon Bonaparte reintroduced slavery to French colonies in 1802.

This chapter will focus on a small number of authors: Montesquieu, Rousseau, Voltaire, a few contributors to Diderot and D'Alembert's *Encyclopedia*, Raynal, Diderot, Pechméja, Condorcet, and Gouges. One thing that will become clear is that some French authors were far less radical in their opposition to transatlantic slavery than one might expect, given their reputation as freethinkers or as champions of liberalism. While many of them criticize slavery in a general or theoretical respect, some are either silent about transatlantic slavery or appear unconcerned by it. Of the authors whom we will examine, only Diderot, Pechméja, and perhaps Condorcet express the type of staunch antislavery stance that one would expect. We will also see that natural slavery—the doctrine that some human beings are naturally destined for slavery—is an important theme in francophone debates.

---

[8] For more details on the 1790 decree and the ways in which the changing geopolitical situation convinced the National Assembly to abolish slavery, see Drescher 2009: 157 and 162–63. For more on the political and legal background and the ways it impacted the French antislavery movement, see Cole 2011: 163–72.

So, indeed, is the racialized version of this doctrine, which I have been calling racial natural slavery.[9] Several of the authors we will encounter in this chapter accept versions of this doctrine, though some argue against it.

4.1. Charles-Louis de Secondat, Baron de Montesquieu

Our first author is the White Frenchman Charles-Louis de Secondat, Baron de Montesquieu (1689–1755). We will focus on his 1748 work *Spirit of the Laws* (*De l'esprit des lois*), which had an enormous influence on the eighteenth-century debate about slavery in France and elsewhere.[10] The most relevant portion of this work is book 15, which is titled "How the laws of civil slavery are related with the nature of the climate," and which in the English translation is eighteen pages long (1989: 246–63). This book, which is divided into nineteen very short chapters, starts by defining slavery (15.1) and then argues that enslavement cannot licitly originate in war, self-sale, or birth (15.2), nor in customs (15.3), religion (15.4), or race (15.5). Intriguingly, as the book's title suggests, Montesquieu ultimately argues that slavery can, in some sense, originate in climate (15.7) and in despotic forms of government (15.6), which he views as natural in hot climates. The remainder of the book examines the ways in which slavery is inappropriate in European nations (15.8–9) and then makes suggestions for how to regulate slavery (15.11–19).

Montesquieu portrays slavery as wrong at the theoretical level, but he does not advocate the abolition of transatlantic slavery. He notes at the very beginning of his discussion that slavery is "not good by its nature" and not useful to anyone, since it prevents both enslaved people and masters from living virtuously (15.1). He also describes it as contrary to the natural and civil law (15.2) and argues that while slavery is "useful to the small, rich, and voluptuous part of each nation," its wrongness becomes clear when we consider the public good and the desires of everyone, including those who would end up enslaved (15.9). Incidentally, this passage is somewhat reminiscent of the Rawlsian veil of ignorance: Montesquieu argues that nobody "would want to draw lots to know who was to form the part of the nation that would be

---

[9] One French proponent of racial natural slavery is Jacques-Philibert Rousselot de Surgy (1766: 164–67).

[10] I will cite this text by book and chapter numbers, which are identical in the French edition (Montesquieu 1968) and in the English translation (Montesquieu 1989), from which I will be quoting unless I indicate otherwise.

free and the one that would be enslaved" (15.9). Even though he argues that slavery is wrong, he does not support its immediate abolition. Quite to the contrary, he insists that "Slaves must not be freed suddenly in considerable numbers by a general law" (15.18). He does not even advocate a gradual abolition but merely describes the danger of too many enslaved people, particularly in nondespotic states (15.13), and he recommends regulating slavery to avoid some of its worst abuses and to make it less perilous for free people (15.11, 15.16–17).[11] It appears to be his overall goal to argue that there should be no slavery in Europe, but he seems willing to accept the continuation of transatlantic slavery.[12]

Because Montesquieu's discussion of slavery is highly complex and raises a host of interpretive issues, I will concentrate almost exclusively on his comments about racial and natural slavery, though I will briefly mention his arguments against circumstantial slavery. These arguments are worth noting because he rejects the legitimacy not just of voluntary and hereditary slavery—which John Locke and others had already criticized—but also of war slavery. He is among the first European authors to argue categorically against the permissibility of enslaving prisoners of war.[13] When it comes to racial and natural slavery, what is most intriguing is that he ridicules racial justifications for slavery but nevertheless appears to embrace a version of natural slavery—and arguably, a version of racial natural slavery. After all, he claims that the enslavement of people from excessively hot regions is far more natural than the enslavement of people from moderate climates. This explains the somewhat paradoxical reception of this text: both proslavery and antislavery authors sometimes cite *Spirit of the Laws* as supporting their cause.[14]

---

[11] For an in-depth analysis of Montesquieu's views on slavery—albeit, in my estimation, too charitable—see Schaub 2005. For another extremely helpful analysis, see Ehrard 2008: 141–61.

[12] It is worth noting that Montesquieu's 1721 epistolary novel *Persian Letters* contains an explicit critique of transatlantic slavery. The Persian character Usbek—who owns slaves himself—at one point describes transatlantic slavery and then states that "Nothing can be more outrageous than to cause the death of an incalculable number of men in order to remove gold and silver from the depth of the earth" (letter 114, 2008: 159). The novel also contains a few general criticisms of colonialism (e.g., letter 117, 2008: 162–64).

[13] There are earlier authors who argue against war slavery on the basis of an endorsement of natural slavery: the only people who can licitly become enslaved are natural slaves, which means that war slavery is not generally permissible (e.g., Felden 1664: 3).

[14] An example of a proslavery author who approvingly cites Montesquieu is Turnbull (1786: 7–8). This influence continued into the nineteenth century: the proslavery author Albert Taylor Bledsoe, for instance, argues that Montesquieu's philosophy justifies American slavery (1856: 264–65). See Davis 1966: 395 for a discussion of the ways in which Montesquieu's claims were used to support the alleged inferiority of Black people.

Montesquieu starts book 15 by defining "civil slavery"—which we can understand as referring to chattel slavery, or slavery in its core sense—as a right that gives masters absolute power over the life and goods of the enslaved (15.1).[15] Interestingly, he adds almost immediately that slavery is far more tolerable in despotic countries, where people are already politically unfree and ought to be glad simply to have their basic needs met (15.1). In contrast, slavery is inappropriate under nondespotic regimes, that is, in monarchies, aristocracies, and democracies (15.1). This comment foreshadows Montesquieu's later claims about natural slavery, which we will examine in due course. Let us first take a quick look at his rejection of voluntary, hereditary, and war slavery.

Montesquieu's argument against war slavery targets the doctrine that enslaving prisoners of war is permissible because it is a merciful alternative to killing them. His counterargument is based on the normative principle that it is only permissible to kill enemy soldiers when it is necessary, that is, when there is no other way to prevent them from doing harm. Yet "when a man has made another man his slave, it cannot be said that he had of necessity to kill him, since he did not do so" (15.2). In other words, if you can capture enemy soldiers, you do not have the right to kill them, and this means that there is no basis for a right to enslave them.[16] Montesquieu undermines the legitimacy of voluntary slavery in several ways, at least some of which appear to be original to him. One intriguing argument is that the idea of selling oneself into slavery is incoherent because "A sale assumes a price; if the slave sold himself, all his goods would become the property of the master; therefore, the master would give nothing and the slave would receive nothing" (15.2). The idea appears to be that sellers must receive something in exchange for what they sell, but enslaved people—according to Montesquieu's definition—cannot receive anything because whatever they have belongs to the master. He adds other reasons to reject voluntary slavery, including the claim that liberty is priceless as well as the claim that civil laws are meant to divide goods among citizens and hence cannot treat citizens as goods (15.2). Montesquieu's argument against hereditary slavery builds on his rejection of the other types: in order for someone to be born a slave, this person's ancestors must have been legitimately enslaved through war or voluntary agreements. Hence, if there are no licit war slaves or voluntary slaves, then nobody is born a slave either.

[15] This definition is reminiscent of John Locke's (*Two Treatises* 2.24, 1988: 285). Many other early modern authors, in contrast, do not think that masters have absolute power.

[16] Many later antislavery writers adopt this argument—for instance, Rousseau, as we will see in the next section, and Scottish author George Wallace, *System* 1.3.2, §133, 1760: 92.

As just seen, Montesquieu rejects voluntary, hereditary, and war slavery categorically. Yet he appears quite ambivalent toward natural and racial slavery. He addresses racial justifications for slavery in chapter 5 of book 15, which is titled "On the slavery of Negroes." This chapter, which is only one page long, consists of a list of claims the author would make if he "had to defend the right we had of making Negroes slaves" (15.5). Given the absurdity of some of the items on this list, it is clearly meant to be satirical. Montesquieu aims to uncover the ridiculousness of racial justifications for slavery.[17] First on the list are two economic reasons for enslaving Black people that are perhaps less obviously satirical than the remaining items. The satire becomes increasingly evident as we progress through the list. After mentioning economic reasons, Montesquieu quips that it is nearly impossible to feel sympathy for someone with Black skin and a flat nose, and that it is hard to see why a wise God would "put a soul, above all a good soul, in a body that was entirely black" (15.5). While the claim about sympathy could be interpreted as a mere description of common racist attitudes among White Europeans,[18] the claim about souls is clearly meant to illustrate the absurdity of holding that people with Black skin are subhuman. After all, Montesquieu simply states—very bluntly and without providing a reason—that it is unclear why God would attach a soul to a Black body.

The next item on the list cites the alleged Asian practice of castrating Black men as evidence that it is "natural to think that color constitutes the essence of humanity" (15.5). The idea appears to be that turning a man into a eunuch is a way of making him different from other men in a permanent and "distinctive way" (15.5). In this context, it is relevant that Montesquieu argues in a later chapter—sincerely, it seems—that eunuchs cannot be fully free citizens because they cannot have families of their own, as a result of which they "are bound to a family by their nature" (15.19).[19] Still, the claim about

---

[17] Not everyone reads the text like this; some interpreters appear to think that Montesquieu was quite serious. For instance, Justin Smith discusses this chapter briefly without marking it as satirical (2015: 238). See also Pius Adiele, who appears to interpret at least portions of this chapter as serious (2017: 198). Likewise, the editor of an English edition of *Spirit of the Laws* in 1878 states in a footnote to this chapter, "The above arguments form a striking instance of the prejudice under which even a liberal mind can labor" (Montesquieu 1878: 257n). Yet most interpreters appear to agree that it is satire (Seeber 1937: 33; Davis 1966: 403; Peabody 1996: 66–67; Garrett 2006: 194; Schaub 2005: 73; Miller 2008: 65; Ehrard 2008: 151; Curran 2011: 130–33; Harvey 2012: 160; Watkins 2017: 3–4). Readers in the eighteenth century also interpreted this chapter as satire, for instance George Wallace (*System* 1.3.2, §137, 1760: 97–98); Voltaire, *Works* 41: 212.

[18] This is how Smith interprets this claim (2015: 238).

[19] See Schaub 2005: 73. The naturally unfree (and perhaps subhuman) status of eunuchs in Asia—including Black eunuchs—is also a major theme in *Persian Letters* (e.g., letter 65, 2008: 90–91).

the alleged Asian practice seems to be intended satirically: readers are presumably supposed to be shocked by the idea of castrating people because of their skin color and to realize that it is ridiculous to view differences in complexion as essential differences.

If any doubts remain about the satirical nature of this chapter, Montesquieu removes them with the subsequent three items on his list. The next one is about hair color, which he notes correlates with skin color: the Egyptians, whom he describes as the world's best philosophers, took hair color so seriously that they killed anyone with red hair (15.5). This is clearly meant to illustrate the arbitrariness of viewing one specific complexion as inferior: readers are presumably supposed to realize that such judgments are culturally relative and can just as easily be used to justify violence against White as against Black people. The next point is unmistakably satirical as well: Montesquieu claims that Black people value glass necklaces more than golden ones, which is "proof that Negroes do not have common sense," since gold is valued much more highly in "civilized nations" (*nations policées*) (15.5; translation altered). Here again, he points to something that is culturally relative—namely, the value of gold—in order to show that racial justifications for slavery are based on arbitrary and morally insignificant characteristics.[20] This point is reminiscent of an earlier chapter, in which Montesquieu ridicules the Spanish for attempting to justify the enslavement of American Indians through differences in customs, for instance through the fact that Indigenous Americans eat insects, smoke tobacco, and fail to "cut their beards in the Spanish fashion" (15.3).

The penultimate item on Montesquieu's list is the most relevant for our purposes.[21] It reads, in its entirety: "It is impossible for us to assume that [Black] people are men because if we assumed they were men one would begin to believe that we ourselves were not Christians" (15.5). The sarcasm is quite clear. Montesquieu is describing the perverse reasons that lead White Europeans to deny the humanity of Africans: if they were to accept that Black people are human, they would have to acknowledge that transatlantic slavery is immoral, or at least unchristian. Thus, White people must believe, or pretend, that Black people are subhuman in order to justify this profitable trade to themselves. This cannot be meant as a legitimate reason for this racist

---

[20] One of the characters in *Persian Letters* points out that gold and silver "are in themselves completely useless, and are only seen as wealth because they have been chosen as its symbols" (letter 114, 2008: 159).

[21] The final item on the list is less relevant: it accuses European governments of hypocrisy (or indifference) by stating that the injustice against Africans cannot be as bad as some people claim, since European governments would have reached an agreement to end this practice otherwise (15.5).

claim; Montesquieu is clearly describing a twisted psychological motivation for racist beliefs that cannot function as an epistemic or moral justification. Thus, his point appears to be that racist beliefs are not based on empirical evidence; rather, they are adopted by White people who profit from the slave trade as an excuse for their horrendously immoral practices.

Let us briefly take stock. Chapters 1–5 of book 15, as already seen, appear to reject all common defenses of slavery. Montesquieu argues that slavery cannot be based on war, voluntary agreements, birth, customs, religion, or race. If this were the entirety of his discussion of slavery, we could classify him as a categorical opponent of all traditional justifications for slavery. Yet the discussion does not stop there, and the subsequent chapters complicate the situation significantly. The chapter that satirizes racial justifications for transatlantic slavery appears to conclude the portion of the book in which Montesquieu rejects various defenses of slavery. In the two subsequent chapters, he turns to justifications of which he approves. This is clear from their titles: chapter 6 is titled "The true origin of the right of slavery," and chapter 7 "Another origin of the right of slavery." These are the chapters in which Montesquieu discusses natural slavery, which means that he is at least to some extent sympathetic to it. Because the type of natural slavery that he discusses is arguably racialized, this raises questions about its relation to the racial justifications for slavery that he rejects in chapter 5. Let us first take a look at the arguments of chapters 6 and 7 and then investigate whether they are compatible with the previous chapter.

Montesquieu opens chapter 6 by announcing that "the true origin of the right of slavery" must be sought in the nature of things. He does not say why. Perhaps he takes himself to have arrived at this insight through a process of elimination: the previous chapters were supposed to show that slavery cannot licitly originate in conventions, circumstances, or nonessential and arbitrary physical differences such as complexion. If slavery cannot originate in those things, then perhaps the only other option is that it originates in the nature of things. He appears to understand 'nature' rather broadly in this context because the first possibility that he examines—and embraces—is that despotic forms of government can render slavery natural and reasonable. More specifically, he argues that "gentle" forms of slavery can licitly originate under despotic governments, where citizens are already politically unfree and where it is hence possible to sell oneself into slavery (15.6).[22] On the face

---

[22] As briefly mentioned earlier, Montesquieu already makes this point in chapter 1, where he claims that people in despotic countries can endure slavery far more easily because in such countries

of it, this contradicts Montesquieu's argument against voluntary slavery from chapter 2. Yet we can reconcile them by interpreting the argument in chapter 2 as implicitly restricted to people in nondespotic states. One piece of evidence in favor of this interpretation is the stated conclusion of Montesquieu's argument against voluntary slavery: "a freeman can[not] sell himself" (15.2). If the subjects of a despotic government are not strictly speaking "freemen" because they are politically unfree, they are not covered by this argument. Montesquieu supports this idea in chapter 6 by stating that "political slavery more or less annihilates civil liberty" (15.6), which suggests that people living under despotic regimes are automatically unfree in both the political and the civil sense. Another piece of evidence is that Montesquieu uses the pricelessness of liberty as a premise in one of his arguments against voluntary slavery (15.2). Because he claims in chapter 6 that under a despotic government one's liberty is "worth nothing" (15.6), this also suggests that the argument in chapter 2 is implicitly restricted to people who are politically free.[23]

In chapter 7, Montesquieu describes another licit origin of slavery. It covers not just the "gentle" type of slavery discussed in the previous chapter, but also "that cruel slavery seen among men" (15.7), which is presumably a reference to transatlantic slavery. While the previous chapter grounds a right of slavery in the nature of government, this chapter grounds it in climate and the effects of climate on human beings. It is here that Montesquieu explicitly discusses natural slavery.

To contextualize Montesquieu's discussion of natural slavery, it is useful to take a quick look at what he says elsewhere about the natural differences between people in various parts of the world. In book 14—the book directly preceding the one about slavery—he argues that the climate has a tremendous impact on "the characteristics of the mind and the passions of the heart" (14.1; translation altered). This in turn means that different political regimes and different laws are appropriate in different climates (1.3; see Garrett 2006: 195). For instance, he claims, people in excessively hot climates possess less virtue, "no curiosity, no enterprise, no generous sentiment" (14.2). He adds that "inclinations will all be passive there; laziness there will

---

"the condition of the slave is scarcely more burdensome than the condition of the subject" (15.1; see also 15.13).

[23] This hypothesis does not directly address Montesquieu's argument that self-sale is incoherent (15.2). Yet this argument only works against forms of slavery in which masters have absolute power over enslaved people and their possessions; perhaps the "gentle" form of slavery in chapter 6 does not give masters absolute power.

be happiness; most chastisements there will be less difficult to bear than the action of the soul" (14.2).[24] Based on these character traits and others, Montesquieu argues in book 16 that the domestic servitude of women is natural in hot climates, and in book 17 that political servitude, or despotism, is likewise natural there.[25] He repeatedly contrasts Europe, which has "a genius for liberty," with Asia, Africa, and America, where "a spirit of servitude" reigns, due to climate and other geographic features (17.6).[26] Political power in Asia and regions with a similar climate, he asserts, "should always be despotic" (17.6).[27] Book 15 must be understood in this context; its goal is to argue that chattel slavery is also natural in hot climates, or at least more natural than in cold climates.[28] This means that the short chapter about natural slavery in book 15 is of enormous importance because it establishes the connection between climate and slavery that constitutes the book's main goal.

In the chapter about natural slavery, Montesquieu builds on his earlier claims about the effect of climate on human character, arguing that slavery "runs less counter to reason" in excessively hot climates, where heat "enervates the body and weakens the courage so much that men come to perform an arduous duty only from fear of chastisement" (15.7).[29] This passage already reveals one reason why slavery is more natural in such climates, for Montesquieu: people there will only work hard if they are threatened with severe punishment; they are too lazy to work voluntarily. Another reason is connected to Montesquieu's claims in the previous chapter about despotism: since governments in hot climates are naturally despotic, "civil slavery there is again accompanied by political slavery" (15.7). As already seen, he holds that this makes civil slavery easier to endure and hence less horrific.

---

[24] In *Persian Letters*, one of the characters makes similar claims about "savages," describing them as having a strong aversion to work (letter 116, 2008: 161).

[25] Montesquieu may have been influenced by John Arbuthnot's 1733 *Essay Concerning the Effects of Air on Human Bodies*. Arbuthnot argues, for instance, that excessive heat makes people "lazy and indolent," which in turn naturally leads to a "slavish Disposition" (6.19, 1733: 152). He also claims that despotic governments are "most improper in cold Climates" (6.19, 1733: 153).

[26] Interestingly, a very similar claim occurs in *Persian Letters*: "Asia and Africa have always been oppressed by despotism. . . . It seems as if liberty is made for the spirit of the peoples of Europe, and servitude for that of the peoples of Asia" (letter 125, 2008: 175).

[27] It is worth noting that Montesquieu appears far more interested in Asia than in Africa or America; he mentions the two latter continents a few times but spends far more time discussing Asia.

[28] There are several reasons, in addition to this context, for thinking that this is the main goal. The title of book 15 is "How the laws of civil slavery are related with the nature of the climate," for instance, and the book on political servitude starts with the sentence "Political servitude depends no less on the nature of the climate than do civil and domestic servitude" (17.1).

[29] A similar claim occurs in *Persian Letters*, where one character describes the Persian army as "composed of slaves who are cowardly by nature, and can only overcome their fear of death with the fear of punishment" (letter 87, 2008: 121).

Elsewhere, he appears to add a third reason: peoples in southern climates naturally have fewer needs because nature makes subsistence much easier for them; this leads to laziness, and it also makes servitude natural. After all, "as they can easily do without wealth, they can do even better without liberty" (21.3). Montesquieu contrasts southern peoples with northern peoples who "need liberty" because they have more extensive needs and because liberty is the means for satisfying these needs (21.3). This means that life in slavery is not a great burden for people from the south because, unlike people in colder climates, they do not need liberty.

Montesquieu even states that if Aristotle is correct that there are natural slaves, then they are the inhabitants of these excessively hot regions (15.7). He does not commit himself to the existence of natural slaves and stresses that Aristotle has not demonstrated it (15.7). Nevertheless, the idea seems to be that slavery in these regions is at least somewhat appropriate and less obviously wrong. The proximity to Aristotle's doctrine is disturbing.[30] Montesquieu also speculates that slavery might be necessary in countries where, due to the climate, free people are unwilling to do grueling work such as mining, though he wonders whether the right incentives might make this work sufficiently attractive even in the hottest climates (15.8).

Interestingly, Montesquieu stops short of stating categorically that slavery is natural in hot climates. He insists that it is, in one crucial sense, unnatural everywhere: "as all men are born equal, one must say that slavery is against nature" (15.7). Yet he immediately adds that "in certain countries it may be founded on a natural reason, and these countries must be distinguished from those in which even natural reason rejects it, as in the countries of Europe" (15.7). Thus, in hot climates, slavery is natural in one sense and unnatural in another. It is natural in the sense that there are good reasons to practice slavery in such climates, and fewer reasons not to practice it, since it is more tolerable there. These reasons are "natural" since they are grounded in the climate and other features of the natural environment as well as in the national character. At the same time, slavery is unnatural everywhere in the sense that the natural state of all human beings is one of equality. Unfortunately, Montesquieu does not tell us what role this second sense should play in our assessment of the moral permissibility of slavery in hot climates. His main goal appears to be to argue that, as he puts it in the subsequent chapter, "natural slavery must be limited to certain particular countries of the world"

---

[30] This is also Laurent Estève's assessment (2002: 61, 68).

(15.8), or in other words, that natural slavery only exists outside of Europe. Because he has already rejected the main forms of circumstantial slavery, this presumably means that there are no justifiable forms of chattel slavery in Europe. Unfortunately, this leaves transatlantic slavery untouched—or worse, it suggests that transatlantic slavery is justifiable.[31] While Montesquieu may not directly defend the transatlantic trade in this text, he certainly does not seem overly troubled by it, and he does not reject it explicitly.[32]

One important question is to what extent Montesquieu's distinction between people in different climates—particularly between Europeans, Asians, Africans, and American Indians—should be interpreted as a racial distinction. As we saw in the introduction, one relevant factor is the stability of these differences: paradigmatic racial traits do not change when one moves to a different climate. There are some indications that Montesquieu views these differences as quite unstable. For instance, he claims in one passage that Europeans who grew up in India often exhibit some of the characteristics of people who have lived there for generations: "Indians are by nature without courage; even the children of Europeans born in the Indies lose the courage of the European climate" (14.3).[33] This suggests that the traits that Montesquieu ascribes to Asians, Africans, Europeans, and Americans are not hereditary (see Bok 2018: §4.3), which in turn makes them seem less paradigmatically racial.

It is also worth noting that Montesquieu stresses in some places that the climate is not the only factor that shapes the characters of human beings. The general spirit or character of each nation, he holds, is influenced not just by natural causes such as climate and geology, but also by what early modern authors often

---

[31] Diana Schaub puts a positive spin on this argument. According to her, Montesquieu makes the concession that there is natural slavery (in some sense) outside of Europe in order to advance the antislavery cause since this concession serves to "quarantine [slavery], to place it beyond the pale of civilization" (2005: 74). She claims that this serves the antislavery cause because Montesquieu does not explicitly say which non-European countries are the unfortunate ones where slavery is somewhat natural; rather, she contends that "he capitalizes on the inclination of each nation to count itself among the fortunate" and that he thus takes advantage of his readers' "snobbishness and ethnocentrism" (2005: 75). This is an intriguing proposal, but I am not fully convinced. After all, in the context of the rest of this work, it is quite clear to which countries Montesquieu is referring. Moreover, Montesquieu's theory does not state that European slavers are "beyond the pale of civilization," but rather that the people whom they are enslaving are. Thus, it is unclear to me how this theory could aid the antislavery cause.

[32] As mentioned earlier, one of the characters in *Persian Letters* does criticize transatlantic slavery, though mainly for causing the deaths of large numbers of Africans for a worthless cause (letter 114, 2008: 159).

[33] In one place, it sounds as if the impact of hot or cold air on human character can be almost instantaneous: "Put a man in a hot, enclosed spot, and . . . he will fear everything, because he will feel he can do nothing" (14.2).

call moral causes,[34] that is, social, cultural, and political factors. As Montesquieu puts it in book 19, these latter factors include "religion, laws, the maxims of the government, examples of past things, mores, and manners" (19.4). As a result, some interpreters deny that Montesquieu embraces a "simple climatological determinism" (Garrett 2006: 195; see also Bok 2018: §4.3). As already seen, he holds that some of these moral causes are themselves influenced by climate, but others may not be. If that is the case, the natural environment does not fully determine the characteristics of each nation.

In chapter 8 of book 15, Montesquieu even toys with the idea that the characteristics of people in hot climates that make slavery somewhat natural are effects of flawed political systems rather than the climate. In a fascinating passage starting with the disclaimer that he is unsure whether this idea originates in his mind or his heart, he wonders whether it could be the case that "Because the laws were badly made, lazy men appeared; because these men were lazy, they were enslaved" (15.8). This makes the relevant characteristics sound less paradigmatically racial. Unfortunately, this suggestion is extremely tentative. Moreover, it may not ultimately matter whether the climate causes the relevant character traits directly or merely in an indirect way, by necessitating political regimes that in turn cause the relevant characteristics. After all, as we saw earlier, Montesquieu holds that political despotism is inevitable in hot climates.

Importantly, Montesquieu also holds that the various causes of national characters operate differently in different geographic regions: "To the extent that, in each nation, one of these causes acts more forcefully, the others yield to it" (19.4). He does not explain why one of these causes might be stronger in some nations than in others but merely describes the effects of these differences: "Nature and climate almost alone dominate savages; manners govern the Chinese; laws tyrannize Japan" (19.4). In other words, moral causes have practically no effect on "savages," whose characteristics are determined almost entirely by natural causes.[35] "Savages," as Montesquieu clarifies elsewhere, are "small scattered nations which, for certain particular reasons, cannot unite" and who are usually hunters (18.11);[36] these nations

---

[34] We already encountered this term in chapter 2, when discussing Hume. Montesquieu sometimes uses the term 'moral cause,' for instance, in 14.5.

[35] Curran (2011: 134) and Estève (2002: 62) make a similar point. Montesquieu also says about the East Indies that its climate and geography fix its manners and mores forever: "The Indies have been, the Indies will be, what they are at present" (21.1).

[36] Montesquieu distinguishes between savages and barbarians; the latter are "small nations that can unite together," and they are usually pastoral (18.11).

include the majority of "the peoples on the coasts of Africa" (21.2) as well as many or all American Indians (5.13, 17.9). Hence, while Montesquieu holds that moral causes can have a significant impact on national characters, he appears to think that such causes are insignificant in the coastal regions of Africa and among American Indians. Natural causes determine nearly every aspect of life for people in these regions. This moves Montesquieu's theory of human diversity closer to paradigmatically racial theories and makes it possible to interpret his claims about the naturalness of slavery in hot climates as a form of racial natural slavery.

One potential objection to interpreting Montesquieu as embracing a form of racial natural slavery is that, as already seen, he ridicules racial justifications for slavery in chapter 5 of book 15. Are his claims in chapter 5 compatible with accepting racial natural slavery? I think they are. It is perfectly consistent to claim that skin color cannot directly justify enslavement and that Blackness itself cannot make people inferior or subhuman, while also claiming that differences in climate can to some extent justify slavery. After all, complexion on its own would be an arbitrary criterion for natural slavery. In contrast, Montesquieu clearly thinks that climate is a nonarbitrary criterion because it causes character traits and gives rise to political systems that in turn constitute a "natural reason" for slavery (15.7). If these differences in climate are also among the causes of differences in skin color, specific skin colors might in the end correlate with natural slave status. Yet skin color is not a natural reason for slavery, unlike some of the other effects of climate.

There is another potential objection to my claim that Montesquieu embraces racial natural slavery, or that he views slavery as natural in some parts of the world. This objection is based on what can be interpreted as a general rejection of natural slavery in chapter 2 of book 15. There, Montesquieu considers the doctrine that people who are "incapable of earning their living must be reduced to servitude" (15.2). He immediately rejects this doctrine by claiming that "one does not want such slaves as these" (15.2). The idea seems to be that people who are physically or mentally unable to support themselves through work would not be useful when enslaved. One could read this as a general argument against natural slavery,[37] but I do not think that is plausible. First of all, Montesquieu does not seem to be discussing natural slavery in this passage. The context is an examination of circumstantial slavery, or slavery in Roman law. More specifically, the context is the question

---

[37] Schaub reads it that way (2005: 74).

of whether civil laws that permit slavery can be useful to enslaved people, in the same way in which criminal laws are useful even to citizens who at some point become convicted by these laws. In this context, Montesquieu examines and rejects the possibility that the laws of slavery are useful to enslaved people in cases in which they would not be able to provide for themselves outside of slavery. This question about usefulness is not directly related to the doctrine of natural slavery. Moreover, and more importantly, the people in hot climates whom Montesquieu views as potential natural slaves are clearly able to support themselves through work. According to him, they do not lack the natural ability to perform hard work, but merely have a strong aversion to work that can only be overcome through force. Hence, the argument from chapter 2 does not apply to them and therefore does not undermine natural slavery in general.

We have now seen some of the reasons that Montesquieu's *Spirit of the Laws* was a mixed blessing for the antislavery cause. On the one hand, it provides powerful arguments against circumstantial slavery and exposes the absurdity of some racial justifications for slavery. These ideas had an enduring influence on antislavery discourse. On the other hand, Montesquieu portrays the enslavement of Africans as in some sense natural; he also claims that people in hot climates do not need liberty and can bear slavery quite easily. This strongly suggests that Montesquieu embraces a version of racial natural slavery. And even if he does not, these ideas can easily be used—and indeed have been used—to defend transatlantic slavery.

4.2. Jean-Jacques Rousseau

Let us now turn to Jean-Jacques Rousseau (1712–1778), the prominent Genevan philosopher who spent significant portions of his career in France and whose political philosophy had a large impact on the French Revolution. His two most relevant works for our purposes are the 1755 *Discourse on the Origin and the Foundations of Inequality Among Men* (*Un discours sur l'origine et les fondemens de l'inégalité parmi les hommes*), which scholars typically call the *Second Discourse*, and the 1762 work *The Social Contract* (*Du contrat social*).[38] Rousseau puts forward a social contract theory strongly

---

[38] I will cite Rousseau's political works by paragraph numbers—and if applicable, book and section numbers—as in Gourevitch's editions (Rousseau 2019a and 2019b). All translations are from

influenced by Thomas Hobbes, Algernon Sidney, and John Locke,[39] which is relevant to our purposes because contractarians typically hold that all licit domination is based on a contractual agreement. One fascinating aspect of Rousseau's version of contractarianism is that he describes not just an ideal social contract resulting in a just society but also a nonideal one that explains why existing political systems benefit the rich and exploit the poor (*Second Discourse* 2.31–37). This nonideal social contract is a version of what Charles Mills calls a domination contract (Mills 2007b: 82–83).

While Rousseau does not discuss slavery in much detail, he makes a few scattered remarks that are worth examining. One of these remarks is a rejection of natural slavery, based on the natural freedom of all human beings and the contractarian doctrine that licit domination requires consent. What is particularly interesting about this brief discussion is Rousseau's argument that the doctrine of natural slavery gets things backward: being enslaved causes people to have the characteristics of natural slaves, rather than the other way around. Another noteworthy aspect of Rousseau's discussion is that he rejects all forms of circumstantial slavery, including hereditary slavery, war slavery, and voluntary slavery.

4.2.1. Rousseau, Transatlantic Slavery, and Race

Before examining Rousseau's theoretical discussions of slavery, let us take a brief look at his views on race and at the extent to which he discusses transatlantic slavery. As we will see later, there appears to be only one place in his oeuvre—and not in a philosophical work—where he explicitly mentions the enslavement of Africans. This is presumably in part because Rousseau is far more interested in political slavery, or political unfreedom, than in personal slavery. Yet even when discussing personal slavery, he typically does so in an abstract, theoretical, or historical way, without acknowledging the existence of this institution in the early modern world. He appears to discuss personal slavery mainly in order to support his claims about political liberty. Even worse, in one passage, he appears to erase transatlantic slavery more directly.

Gourevitch unless I note otherwise. The French versions of these texts are in volume 3 of Rousseau's *Oeuvres Complètes* (Rousseau 1964).

[39] I discuss these three authors, their versions of social contract theory, and their stance on slavery in Jorati, forthcoming.

In this passage, he first states that there can be circumstances in which the freedom of citizens depends on the complete enslavement of others, and then mentions that this was the case in Sparta, where citizens were able to enjoy complete political liberty because enslaved people did all the work. One might expect him to draw a parallel to European countries in his own day, whose prosperity depended on slave labor and the exploitation of colonies. Yet instead he contrasts the circumstances in ancient Greece with the circumstances of his readers, whom he considers to be politically unfree: "As for you, modern peoples, you have no slaves, but are yourselves slaves; you pay for their freedom with your own. Well may you boast of this preference; I find in it more cowardice than humanity" (*Social Contract* 3.15.10).

The claim that his contemporaries do not own slaves is astonishing.[40] It appears to dismiss the relevance or importance of transatlantic slavery and suggests that nothing similar to ancient Greek slavery exists in the eighteenth century. An even more troubling aspect of this passage is Rousseau's apparent suggestion that it would be better to live like the ancient Greeks, that is, to adopt a system where citizens have complete political liberty, while others live in slavery and thereby allow citizens to be completely free. Rousseau appears to say that it is cowardice to pay for the liberty of those who would otherwise be enslaved with one's own political liberty, that is, to prefer the situation in eighteenth-century Europe to the situation in ancient Greece. This sounds as if he advocates personal slavery, which is peculiar since he elsewhere argues against its legitimacy, as we are about to see. We could read this passage more charitably as simply stating that his audience's motive for not having slaves is cowardice rather than humanity. He might hold that doing so out of humanity would be a good thing but that Europeans are doing it for the wrong reasons. If that is correct, he may not be advocating slavery after all. Yet that still leaves his erasure of colonial slavery.

What should we make of Rousseau's silence about transatlantic slavery? As Mills notes in this context, "Textual silence can speak volumes" (2007a: 253). Several other commentators also condemn Rousseau for failing to denounce the transatlantic slave trade.[41] As one scholar puts it, Rousseau appears alarmingly unconcerned about the slavery in French

---

[40] Mills discusses this claim as well and argues that it is "a bizarre claim, if his reference class is transracial, as most readers have assumed" (2007a: 253).

[41] Interestingly, as Ehrard points out (2008: 165), this criticism is not new. Even in the eighteenth century, some people criticized Montesquieu and other philosophers of writing about slavery "as if this crime were not something that occurs today, and in which half of Europe takes part" (Bernadin de Saint-Pierre 1773, 1: 204).

and British colonies, since he invokes chattel slaves merely as symbols of political subjugation (Peabody 1996: 96). Another interpreter makes this point more bluntly: "Rousseau did not care two hoots about enslaved blacks" (Sala-Molins 2006: 81; see also 2006: 73). Of course, Rousseau is not the only European political philosopher to be silent on this topic. Yet it becomes increasingly difficult around the middle of the eighteenth century to excuse this omission, given how much the transatlantic trade—as well as European awareness of it—had grown. Rousseau is writing in a time and place where transatlantic slavery has become a hotly debated issue; he is, after all, writing after the publication of Montesquieu's *Spirit of the Laws* (1748). Thus, it is worth asking why Rousseau does not so much as mention transatlantic slavery in his major philosophical writings, especially since he discusses topics that are closely related. This silence supports Mills's thesis that Rousseau, like other European political theorists in this period, uses a racially restricted notion of personhood, that is, that he does not count nonwhites as full persons (Mills 2007a: 253).

The only place in which Rousseau mentions the enslavement of Africans appears to be his 1761 epistolary novel *Julie, or the New Heloise*. One letter in this novel, written to Julie by St. Preux, contains the following passage: "I have seen those vast and unfortunate countries that seem destined only to cover the earth with herds of slaves. At their lowly appearance I turned aside my eyes in contempt [*dédain*], horror, and pity, and seeing the fourth part of my equals [*mes semblables*] turned into beasts for the service of others, I rued being a man" (*Julie*, part 4, letter 3, 1997: 340). This does appear to be a reference to transatlantic slavery, but it is unclear what we should make of it, in part because these are the words of a character in a novel and in part because the passage does not unequivocally condemn transatlantic slavery. The description of the inhabitants of these—presumably African—countries as seemingly destined for slavery need not be an endorsement of natural slavery. Yet the reference to "equals" or perhaps better "fellows" (*semblables*) need not entail a commitment to full equality, either. It is true that the emotions that this character claims to feel when contemplating transatlantic slavery suggest disapproval, which may be taken as indicative of Rousseau's own feelings.[42]

---

[42] Klausen argues that St. Preux's emotions, and hence possibly Rousseau's, appear ambivalent in this passage: he "demonstrates an inability to redignify [African slaves] as human beings. St. Preux's struggle to pity—in the rich Rousseauian sense of that term . . . —could stand in for the author Rousseau's own ambivalence toward those held as chattel" (Klausen 2014: 84).

If this is indeed Rousseau's attitude, however, it is surprising that he does not discuss and condemn transatlantic slavery in his political writings.

In order to determine Rousseau's views on race, it is helpful to examine his claims about various groups that he describes as 'savage.'[43] First, Rousseau uses the label 'savage' for human beings in his hypothetical state of nature. They live extremely primitive and solitary lives, and they have only an extremely rudimentary language, no foresight, and no ability for abstract thinking (*Second Discourse* 1.23–31, 2.9–14). Interestingly, though, Rousseau denies that this condition would be terrible; he disagrees with Thomas Hobbes's infamous claim that the state of nature is a state of war. In fact, he describes man's natural state as idyllic and, in many ways, superior to the condition of modern Europeans: humans in this state are stronger, healthier, less miserable, and less fearful than "civilized" people (*Second Discourse* 1.4–10, 1.32).

While Rousseau's state of nature is hypothetical, he holds that there are some groups of modern humans who live in a very similar state and whom he invokes multiple times to illustrate features of the hypothetical state of nature. He sometimes calls these groups 'savage' as well. For instance, he illustrates the fearlessness of natural man by claiming that "Negroes and savages," and particularly "the Caribs of Venezuela," are similarly fearless and for the same reasons (*Second Discourse* 1.6, added in 1782 edition).[44] Later in the same text, he states that "the Caribs . . . of all existing Peoples [have] up to now moved least far from the state of Nature" (*Second Discourse* 1.43). He also claims that members of this group, just like natural man, completely lack foresight, which leads them to sell their bed in the morning and buy it back in the evening (*Second Discourse* 1.20).[45] Moreover, Rousseau contends that the languages spoken by "various Savage Nations" in the modern world resemble the crude languages of natural man (*Second Discourse* 2.10). He even states that children in "Savage Nations, such as the Hottentots[46] . . . [and] Caribs of the Antilles" walk on all fours for much longer than European children because they are neglected by their parents (*Second Discourse*, Note 3.1). In the same context, he mentions "savage" children in Germany and Lithuania who were raised by animals and also prefer walking on all fours (*Second*

---

[43] Mills contends that this term is racial or proto-racial in this period (2007a: 249–50).

[44] By 'Carib,' Rousseau is referring to the indigenous peoples of the Caribbean.

[45] Rousseau's claim that American Indians lack foresight is interesting in part because lack of foresight is one of the characteristics of Aristotelian natural slaves (Aristotle, *Politics* i.2, 1984: 1986–87).

[46] 'Hottentot' is the historical name for the Khoekhoen of southwestern Africa.

Discourse, Note 3.1). Finally, he invokes modern "savages" to support his claim that the middle stage of human development—halfway between the primitive state and the state of present-day Europeans—is "the best for man" (*Second Discourse* 2.18): American Indians, "Hottentots," and the inhabitants of Greenland and Iceland prefer their "savage" lifestyle to the European or Christian lifestyle, no matter what efforts are made to "Civilize" or convert them (*Second Discourse*, Note 16.1–4).

How should we interpret Rousseau's various claims about "savages"? One possibility is that they are evidence of racism. After all, he describes some groups as significantly inferior in their mental abilities and as very similar to animals, even while also describing them as in some sense ideal human beings.[47] Charles Mills argues for this interpretation (1997: 68–69). Other interpreters argue that there is insufficient evidence for racism in Rousseau. For instance, Bernard Boxill argues that Rousseau's description of modern "savages" is not racist because he views all differences between ethnic groups as the results of environmental differences, rather than innate differences (2005: 160–61). Rousseau, after all, holds that the reason that some ethnic groups have not developed as far as Europeans is simply their way of life, which in turn is explained by climate and other environmental factors (2005: 160–61). Nevertheless, I agree with Mills that this is not enough to get Rousseau off the hook, since many paradigmatically racist theories explain racial differences through environmental factors.

Independently of the question of whether Rousseau's views are racist, it is worth noting that some of the traits he ascribes to modern-day "savages" are incompatible with natural slavery. While he describes them as lacking foresight and a fully developed language, he also claims that they have a much keener sense of liberty than Europeans and prefer death to slavery. He contrasts this with the servile character of "civilized" man, who is "proud of his slavery" (*Second Discourse* 2.57). This fits with a claim that Rousseau makes about the effects of slavery, which we will examine later: unfreedom—whether political or personal—corrupts the human mind and gives rise to the characteristics of natural slaves. "Savages" are uncorrupted and hence are much farther from natural slavery than Europeans.

---

[47] For a detailed discussion of the idea of 'noble savages' in Rousseau and some other Enlightenment thinkers, see Muthu 2003: 11–71.

4.2.2. Rousseau's Rejection of Circumstantial Slavery

Let us now take a look at Rousseau's arguments against circumstantial slavery. Like other prominent contractarians, Rousseau holds that human beings can only attain legitimate authority over others through the latter's consent. Human beings are naturally free, or "born free," which means that "no one may, on any pretext whatsoever, subjugate [a man] without his consent" (*Social Contract* 4.2.5). As a result, Rousseau argues, it is impermissible for parents to sell their children into slavery: these children have a natural right to freedom and cannot licitly lose their freedom without their consent. Likewise, slavery cannot be hereditary since each human being is born free (*Social Contract* 1.4.5; *Second Discourse* 2.42). Rousseau quips that "To decide that the son of a slave is born a slave is to decide that he is not born a man" (*Social Contract* 4.2.5; similarly in *Second Discourse* 2.42). Like Montesquieu, Rousseau furthermore argues against war slavery based on the observation that there is no right to kill an enemy soldier after this soldier has surrendered (*Social Contract* 1.4.11). This undercuts the most common defense of war slavery, namely, the argument that since it is permissible to kill enemies in a just war, it is a fortiori permissible to enslave them.

Rousseau furthermore argues against voluntary slavery: liberty, like life, is a priceless gift of nature, which means that "it would be an offense against both Nature and reason to renounce them at any price whatsoever" (*Second Discourse* 2.42). Likewise, he claims that alienating one's liberty would mean renouncing "one's quality as a man, the rights of humanity, even its duties" (*Social Contract* 1.4.6). He also contends—like Montesquieu—that it does not make sense to sell one's own liberty, since a sale is by definition an exchange, but enslaved people cannot get anything in return for agreeing to become enslaved. By becoming enslaved, their rights become the master's, just like their property, which means that they can gain neither rights nor property in exchange for agreeing to become enslaved (*Social Contract* 1.4.6, 1.4.14). Because Rousseau argues that subjugation requires consent and that it is impossible to consent to slavery, he holds that there is no licit form of enslavement: "from whatever angle one looks at things, the right to slavery is null, not only because it is illegitimate, but because it is absurd and meaningless. The words *slavery* and *right* are contradictory; they are mutually exclusive" (*Social Contract* 1.4.14).[48] Thus, Rousseau rejects slavery in general.

---

[48] Rousseau says something similar in his 1755 *Discourse on Political Economy*: "slavery . . . is contrary to nature, and no right can authorize it" (§4).

4.2.3. Rousseau on Natural Slavery

Based on Rousseau's claims about natural liberty and the general impermissibility of slavery, it makes sense that he rejects the doctrine of natural
slavery. And that is precisely what he does in *Social Contract*. What is surprising, however, is that he seems to accept one aspect of the doctrine. After
describing Aristotle's claim that some people are natural slaves and others
natural masters, Rousseau states:

> Aristotle was right, but he mistook the effect for the cause. Any man born
> in slavery is born for slavery, nothing is more certain. Slaves lose every-
> thing in their chains, even the desire to be rid of them; they love their ser-
> vitude, as the companions of Ulysses loved their brutishness.[49] Hence, if
> there are slaves by nature, it is because there were slaves contrary to na-
> ture. Force made the first slaves, their cowardice perpetuated them. (*Social
> Contract* 1.2.8)

In other words, once someone is reduced to the unnatural condition of
a slave, they lose their natural love for liberty and acquire the characteristics of a natural slave. Rousseau makes a similar point in the *Second
Discourse*: slavery degrades human beings; enslaved people become used to
the absence of liberty and even "boast of the peace and quiet they enjoy in
their chains" (*Second Discourse* 2.39).[50] This means, of course, that Aristotle's
doctrine cannot justify anyone's original enslavement; only those who are already enslaved have the characteristics of natural slaves. Nobody has these
characteristics naturally, and the fact that people acquire these characteristics as a result of being enslaved is itself a sign that slavery is deeply unnatural
and has devastating effects.

As seen in earlier chapters, this type of strategy—which I call the effects-
of-slavery strategy—is quite problematic.[51] First of all, it can be used to

---

[49] This is a reference to Homer's *Odyssey*, in which the goddess Circe turns Ulysses's companions
into pigs. Perhaps Rousseau's point is that even if these men enjoy themselves while they are pigs, that
does not mean that this condition is natural or good for them.

[50] Here Rousseau appears to be influenced by Algernon Sidney, who also claims that some nations
mistake their political unfreedom for peace (Sidney, *Discourses* 2.15 [1698], 1996: 160).

[51] Another French text that uses the effects-of-slavery strategy is a reply to a proslavery letter from
an American in the journal *Les Ephémérides du citoyen*. This reply is probably composed by Nicolas
Badeau (1730–1792), the journal's founder (no. 11, 1766, vol. 6: 176). As we will see later, Diderot and
Condorcet also use this strategy.

justify the continued enslavement of people who are currently enslaved. If they are no longer fit for freedom or can no longer appreciate the benefits of freedom, then one can argue that they ought to remain in slavery for their own benefit and the public good.[52] Second, while this strategy denies that there are natural differences among humans that mark out some people as natural slaves, it concedes that currently enslaved people are not just different but also inferior to free people. When applied to transatlantic slavery, this concession is racist on some definitions of racism, and it also shares some of the central features of our paradigm.[53] Rousseau's discussion is an excellent illustration of this second problem: in the passage under discussion, he describes enslaved people as cowardly, that is, as morally deficient, and even blames the perpetuation of slavery on their alleged cowardice. Moreover, his claim that anyone who is "born in slavery is born for slavery," when taken literally, suggests that children born to enslaved parents are natural slaves from the very beginning, not just after having grown up with the indignities and deprivations of slavery. This would mean that the effects of enslavement are hereditary. And finally, this passage is further evidence that Rousseau's discussion is bewilderingly detached from contemporaneous literature about transatlantic slavery, since this literature is filled with reports about enslaved people who revolt, escape, or choose death over slavery. Rousseau's claim that enslaved people automatically lose their desire for freedom, become cowards, and love their chains clearly ignores swaths of data about transatlantic slavery to which Rousseau had access. Perhaps we can find a charitable explanation for this. For instance, perhaps Rousseau is only interested in political slavery and exaggerates the corrupting effects of unfreedom for rhetorical purposes. Yet, even if that is the case, it seems problematic for someone in the mid-eighteenth century to discuss slavery in this way, in the midst of the horrors of transatlantic slavery and an increasingly heated discussion among intellectuals about its moral permissibility.

---

[52] Rousseau's reference to Homer's *Odyssey* might be an indication that he rejects this justification for continued enslavement. After all, in the *Odyssey*, Ulysses's companions are rescued and turned back into men. The background assumption in the story appears to be that it would be horrible for them to remain pigs. Yet this may be reading too much into Rousseau's reference to this story.

[53] For instance, Kendi argues that "the abolitionist theory that slavery made Black people inferior [is racist]. Whether benevolent or not, any idea that suggests that Black people as a group are inferior, that something is wrong with Black people, is a racist idea" (2016: 98).

4.2.4. Concluding Thoughts on Rousseau

There is clearly much more to say about Rousseau; his discussions of slavery and his attitude toward race are enormously complex. This section has shown, however, that Rousseau is important for the history of racial slavery for two main reasons. First, he is among the first major political philosophers to reject all forms of slavery categorically. But, second, his silence about transatlantic slavery and his comments about natural slavery suggest that he is, at best, indifferent toward the enslavement of Black people. Rousseau thus constitutes evidence for Mills's thesis that canonical Enlightenment thinkers viewed their moral principles as applying primarily or exclusively to White Europeans.

4.3. Voltaire

Let us next take a look at the White French freethinker, satirist, and philosopher François-Marie Arouet (1694–1778), better known under his pen name, 'Voltaire.' He was enormously prolific and composed works in a vast number of different genres.[54] For our purposes, he is important in part because he is one of the few early modern proponents of polygenesis, the doctrine that racial groups have separate origins. He combines this doctrine with paradigmatically racist claims about physiological and intellectual differences among racial groups. With respect to transatlantic slavery, he may at first look like a staunch opponent, but a closer examination reveals that this is not the case. Indeed, he either embraces or at least flirts with a version of racial natural slavery, claiming that there is something natural and perhaps inevitable about the enslavement of Black Africans by other racial groups. I first examine and evaluate the passages that one could view as evidence that Voltaire was opposed to transatlantic slavery, and then I present contrary evidence, including his statements about race.[55]

Voltaire is a satirist who appears to enjoy poking fun at practically everyone and shocking or provoking his readers. One of his favorite targets is

[54] I will cite Voltaire's writings by providing the volume and page numbers from the *Complete Works* (Voltaire 1968–2022), preceded by '*Works*'. When an English translation is available, I will cite that as well.
[55] For an extremely helpful discussion of Voltaire's views on slavery and race, see Curran 2011: 137–149; Ehrard 2008: 112–17.

religion—both organized religion, particularly Christianity, and religious practices and beliefs more generally. This satirical attitude sometimes makes it difficult to discern Voltaire's actual views. The problem is heightened by the fact that he often writes in the form of a dialogue or from the perspective of a fictional character, rather than in his own voice. As a result, it is natural to wonder to what extent Voltaire genuinely embraces the radical polygenetic racism he sometimes expresses. Might this be an instance in which he mainly intends to provoke his readers and challenge the traditional Christian doctrine of the kinship of all humans? And might some of his seemingly racist and proslavery statements be intended satirically, to ridicule people who genuinely accept these types of doctrines, similarly to Montesquieu's satirical list of possible defenses of racial slavery? Some scholars think so.[56] Nevertheless, I do not ultimately find this reading sustainable, and most scholars appear to agree with my doubt.[57]

4.3.1. Voltaire's Ambiguous Antislavery Statements

Voltaire's most famous discussion of transatlantic slavery—and the one that interpreters usually cite when they claim that he was a staunch opponent— is from the 1759 novel *Candide, Or Optimism* (*Candide, ou l'optimisme*), which is among Voltaire's most widely read works. The novel as a whole satirizes Leibnizian optimism, the doctrine that we live in the best of all possible worlds. Its plot centers around the titular character Candide, a young believer in this doctrine, who travels the world and experiences the most horrific things imaginable, gradually losing his confidence in optimism. One of the many horrors he witnesses is transatlantic slavery: in Surinam, a Dutch colony in South America, Candide and his travel companions meet an enslaved Black man whose left leg and right hand have been amputated (ch. 19, *Compete Works* 48: 194–95 / 2003: 76). When they ask him what happened, he explains: "When we work in the sugar factory, and the mill happens to snatch off a finger, [our masters] instantly chop off our hand;

---

[56] For instance, Claudine Hunting argues that Voltaire used satire as a very effective tool to combat slavery, like Montesquieu (1978: 418); she does not read Voltaire as racist either (1978: 413 n. 11), which makes her an outlier. Aaron Garrett has a more nuanced assessment. He refers to Voltaire's views on race as "sarcastic polygenism" (2006: 198) and comments that "disturbing and bigoted as it was, [Voltaire's polygenism] mocked the vanity of the unity of mankind more than it attempted to provide a real explanation" (2006: 187).

[57] See Smith 2015: 237; Abanime 1979: 251; Boulle 2007: 27–28.

and when we attempt to run away they cut off a leg. Both these things have happened to me; and it is at this cost that you eat sugar in Europe" (*Compete Works* 48: 195–96 / 2003: 77).[58] Later, he notes that "Dogs, monkeys, and parrots are a thousand times less wretched than I" (*Compete Works* 48: 196 / 2003: 77). After hearing the man's testimony, Candide announces that he has come to reject optimism, "and so saying, he turned his eyes towards the poor negro, and shed a flood of tears; and in this weeping mood he entered the town of Surinam" (*Compete Works* 48: 196 / 2003: 77).

This episode from *Candide* clearly contains a criticism of transatlantic slavery: Voltaire presumably wants his European readers to be shocked by the cruelty of colonial slaveholders—or at least join Candide in feeling sympathy or pity for the enslaved man—and to realize that their consumption of sugar and other colonial products makes them at least partially responsible for this cruel institution. The passage does not contain explicit philosophical arguments for abolition, but it arguably constitutes a sentimentalist denunciation or criticism of transatlantic slavery. Incidentally, Voltaire makes a very similar point about the consumption of colonial goods in his *Essay on the Customs and the Spirit of the Nations* (*Essai sur les moeurs et l'esprit des nations*), a text he apparently started composing in the late 1730s for Émilie Du Châtelet and then revised and expanded until at least the 1770s. It is Voltaire's longest work, comprising eight volumes of the *Complete Works* and consisting of almost two hundred chapters. In chapter 152, Voltaire mentions a statistic about Saint-Domingue: in 1757, its inhabitants included 30,000 "persons" and "100,000 negro and mulatto slaves who . . . shorten their lives to flatter our new appetites, by fulfilling our new needs, which were unfamiliar to our fathers" (*Works* 26A: 284–85).[59] Like *Candide*, this texts appears to criticize Europeans for consuming colonial goods whose production causes many enslaved Black people to suffer and die.[60]

The unnamed enslaved man in *Candide* says a few other things, however, which complicate our assessment of Voltaire's attitude toward slavery. Immediately after describing the human cost of sugar, he tells us how he

[58] Voltaire references the same form of punishment in his *Essay on Customs*: "if they [i.e., colonial slaves] want to run away, one cuts off a leg" (ch. 152, *Works* 46A: 285).

[59] Incidentally, this passage suggests that Voltaire did not consider enslaved Black people to be persons—at least in some sense—since he does not include them in the number of persons. Alternatively, this may be sarcasm.

[60] Voltaire is not the only French author around this time to raise this point. Another example is Claude Adrien Helvétius, who calls for a boycott of sugar in his *De l'esprit*, after describing the enormous human cost of its cultivation (1758: 25n). Jean Ehrard observes that this theme became an "obsession" in these debates (2008: 125).

came to be enslaved: his own mother, he claims, sold him into slavery and said to him, "My dear child, bless our fetishes; adore them for ever; they will make you happy; you have the honour to be a slave to our lords the whites, by which you will make the fortune of your parents" (*Compete Works* 48: 196 / 2003: 77). Here Voltaire invokes not just a stereotype about the alleged fetishism of Africans but also a racist proslavery trope—namely, the trope that Africans happily sell their own children and other relatives into slavery.[61] Indeed, he even represents the man's mother as believing that it is an honor for Black people to serve White people, whom she describes as "our lords," which can be understood as a reference to racial natural slavery.[62]

This passage is difficult to interpret. On the one hand, readers are presumably supposed to disapprove of the woman's choice to sell her son into slavery. Perhaps they are also supposed to disagree with her claim that being enslaved by White people is an honor and that White people are generally the lords of Black people, though this is less clear. On the other hand, this passage paints a racist picture of Black Africans and even portrays them as actively enabling the transatlantic slave trade. Voltaire could easily have described the enslaved man as tragically kidnapped in Africa and thereby highlight the injustice of transatlantic slavery, but instead, he chose to describe him as sold into slavery by unloving, superstitious, ignorant, and greedy parents. He may be criticizing White slaveowners in this episode of *Candide* for their cruelty, but he also ridicules Africans and embraces racist stereotypes. This suggests that Voltaire's primary aim here is not to make an antislavery point, but rather to supply yet another example of how gruesome our world is and thereby to weaken Candide's naive faith in humanity. In other words, perhaps the treatment that this Black man has received from his parents is supposed to have exactly the same effect on readers as the treatment he has received from his Dutch master. Perhaps neither aspect of the story is meant to make

---

[61] Many antislavery writers refute this racist trope explicitly. Two French examples are Jean-Baptiste-Christophe Fusée-Aublet (1775: 114) and Benjamin Frossard (1789, vol. 1: 193–96). Apparently, many Frenchmen in the eighteenth century believed that it was common for Africans to sell their loved ones; see, for example, Jacques Christophe Valmont de Bomare (1764, vol. 3: 576); Jacques-Philibert Rousselot de Surgy (1766, vol. 10: 162); Jacques Savary des Bruslons and Philemon Louis Savary (1723, vol. 2: 859). As we saw earlier, Montesquieu also claimed in 1748 that people in Asia and Africa—and more generally, people who are accustomed to living under despotic governments—sell themselves and each other easily because "their liberty is worth nothing" (*Spirit of the Laws* 15.6).

[62] Voltaire makes a similar claim in the *Essay on Customs*: "negroes . . . believe themselves to be born in Guinea to be sold to whites and to serve them" (ch. 141, *Works* 46A: 247–48).

a larger political point, but they are simply supposed to illustrate the cruelty with which human beings treat one another.

The enslaved man says something else that complicates our interpretive task further:

> The Dutch fetishists who converted me tell me every Sunday that the blacks and whites are all children of one father, whom they call Adam. I'm no genealogist, but if what these preachers say is true, we are all second cousins; and you must admit that no one could treat his own relations in a more horrible manner. (*Compete Works* 48: 196 / 2003: 77)

At first blush, this portion of the speech appears to criticize the hypocrisy of Christians who preach human equality while enslaving their fellow humans. As we saw in earlier chapters, it is quite common for antislavery authors to invoke the theological doctrine that all human beings are brethren in order to argue against slavery. Yet given Voltaire's own attitude toward Christianity and human kinship, this interpretation becomes questionable. After all, Voltaire is a harsh critic of Christianity and religion more generally, and— as we will see later—a proponent of polygenesis. He does not believe that all racial groups descend from one man. Instead, he insists that Black and White people have completely separate origins and different natures. This means that he would reject antislavery arguments that are based on the doctrine that all races have the same natural traits and capacities. While Voltaire clearly wants to ridicule Christian slaveholders in this passage, he does not seem to be providing antislavery arguments that he endorses. Indeed, we could interpret him as ridiculing Christians at least in part for their belief in monogenesis, or in a common origin of all human beings.

There are other texts by Voltaire that one could interpret as criticisms of transatlantic slavery. One such text is the article "Slavery" ("Esclavage"), published in 1774 as part of Voltaire's *Questions about the Encyclopedia* (*Questions sur l'Encyclopédie*), which is his response to Diderot and D'Alembert's *Encyclopedia*. This article comprises two dialogues between an Englishman who defends transatlantic slavery and a Frenchman who opposes it. The latter brings up the slave trade in the first dialogue as one of the few things that anger him about the world; he mentions that he enjoyed Montesquieu's chapter "On the slavery of Negroes," which he describes as "very comical" (*Works* 41: 212). In response, the Englishman admits that Europeans do not have a *natural* right to force citizens of Angola to work on

232 SLAVERY AND RACE

sugar plantations in Barbados, but he insists that they have a *conventional* right. This means, presumably, that he does not view transatlantic slavery as an instance of natural slavery but rather as a licit instance of circumstantial slavery. He reveals that he believes some transatlantic slaves to be voluntary slaves when asking rhetorically, "Why does the negro sell himself? Why does he allow himself to be sold? I bought him, he belongs to me; how am I wronging him?" (*Works* 41: 212–13). When the Frenchman asks—presumably inspired by Montesquieu—whether human persons can sell their own liberty, which is priceless, the Englishman responds, "Everything has its price. Too bad for him if he sells me something so precious at a cheap price. Call him a fool, but do not call me a villain" (*Works* 41: 213). He elaborates on this point in the second dialogue: "the negro who sells himself is a fool, and the Black father who sells his child is a barbarian; but I am a sensible man when I buy this negro and make him work on my sugar plantation" (*Works* 41: 217). Thus, the Englishman defends both voluntary slavery and the sale of children by their parents as licit justifications for transatlantic slavery.

As for the treatment of enslaved people in colonial plantations, the Englishman argues that European soldiers are not treated any better (*Works* 41: 213) and draws a comparison to the treatment of horses (*Works* 41: 217). The Englishman also defends war slavery, arguing that if an enemy soldier whom you are about to kill begs you to enslave him instead, there is nothing wrong with doing him this favor (*Works* 41: 214). At this point in the dialogue, however, the discussion is no longer about transatlantic slavery, but about various forms of bondage practiced in Eastern Europe and Mediterranean countries. The vast majority of the second dialogue is not about transatlantic slavery either, but about "slavery of the spirit," or the kind of unfreedom existing in a society that restricts free expression and free thought (*Works* 41: 218).

These two dialogues are intriguing, but it is hard to know what to make of them. One might expect the Frenchman to be Voltaire's spokesperson, but this is not entirely clear. The Frenchman's replies to the Englishman's proslavery arguments are very feeble; he pushes back only in very few places and never provides fleshed-out counterarguments. One gets the impression that the Englishman is presented as having the upper hand in the relevant portion of the dialogue. His defenses of slavery—unlike the arguments in Montesquieu's chapter about racial slavery—do not sound satirical.[63] As a

---

[63] Abanime makes this point as well, adding that the Englishman's arguments are too eloquent to count as a caricature or satire (1979: 246).

result, this text is not straightforward evidence for Voltaire's opposition to colonial slavery.

Another text that one could interpret as evidence for Voltaire's opposition to transatlantic slavery is the thirteen-page article "Slaves" ("Esclaves"), published in 1771 as part of his *Questions about the Encyclopedia*. The vast majority of this article is about the etymology of the term 'slave,' slavery in the Bible, the ancient history of slavery, and forced labor in early modern France. Parts of the article are seemingly intended to show that slavery was accepted nearly everywhere for nearly all of history. The most significant statement about transatlantic slavery occurs at the very end of section 1: after describing Barbary Coast piracy, Voltaire mentions that "Those who call themselves whites proceed to purchase negroes at a good price, in order to resell them for a high price in America. The Pennsylvanians alone have solemnly renounced this traffic recently, which seemed dishonest to them" (*Works* 41: 227).[64]

This is not a condemnation of the transatlantic slave trade, or at least not a direct one. Voltaire merely reports that people in Pennsylvania view the trade as dishonest, but he does not say whether he agrees. At most, one could interpret the first sentence of this passage as making a point about hypocrisy similar to the one we already saw in *Candide*: Europeans trade in human beings while calling themselves "whites," which arguably suggests that Voltaire sees a tension between participation in the transatlantic slave trade on the one hand, and Whiteness on the other. His idea might be that trading in human beings is unworthy of White, supposedly "enlightened" Europeans.[65] Thus, this passage might contain a criticism of transatlantic slavery, though at most a very indirect one that is based on a racist presupposition.

The article "Slaves" makes some other noteworthy claims about slavery, albeit not specifically about transatlantic slavery. The most noteworthy comment occurs in section 2, where Voltaire responds to the claim that enslaved people are far better off than free poor people because the former are "fed and cared for by their masters like their horses." His reply is that while this is true,

---

[64] Voltaire mentions transatlantic slavery in two other places in this article, but only in passing. For an article of this length about slavery composed in the 1770s, it is astonishing that transatlantic slavery plays such a miniscule role.

[65] He makes a similar point in the *Essay on Customs*: "We tell [Black colonial slaves] that they are humans like us, that they are redeemed by the blood of a God who died for them, and then they are made to work like beasts of burden. . . . After that we dare to speak of the law of nations" (ch. 152, *Works* 46A: 285).

it does not justify slavery because humans dislike having to depend on others and value freedom over food security (*Works* 41: 228). He elaborates,

> it is for the people about whose condition we are disputing to decide which condition they prefer. Question the vilest laborer covered with rags, fed on black bread, and sleeping on straw in a half-open hut; ask this man whether he would like to be a slave, better fed, clothed, and bedded—not only will he respond by recoiling in horror, but there are some to whom you would not dare propose it. Then ask a slave if he would like to be freed, and you will see what he will answer. By this alone the question is decided. (*Works* 41: 230)

This is a persuasive response to paternalist defenses of slavery. Alas, it is unclear whether Voltaire had transatlantic slavery in mind when writing these lines, that is, whether he extends the right to decide one's own way of life to enslaved Black people in European colonies.[66] In this article and elsewhere, one gets the impression that Voltaire was far more concerned about various types of unfreedom experienced by White people in France than about transatlantic slavery.[67]

4.3.2. Voltaire on Race, Racial Slavery, and Natural Slavery

To gain a deeper understanding of Voltaire's attitude toward transatlantic slavery, we need to examine his discussions of race and some of his comments on racial slavery. This examination will show that despite the passages discussed so far, Voltaire does not deserve to be called a staunch opponent of transatlantic slavery. I will start with a quick look at Voltaire's comments about race before turning to more explicit comments about racial slavery.[68]

---

[66] Relevant context for this passage is that this section is Voltaire's criticism of Simon Nicolas Linguet's book *Théorie des lois civiles, ou principes fondamentaux de la société* (1767), which in turn is to a large extent a criticism of Montesquieu. The passage under discussion is a response to a passage from chapter 30 of Linguet's book (1767, vol. 2: 464–65); this passage is not an explicit discussion of transatlantic slavery.

[67] Abanime argues this more extensively, based on several texts (1979: 243–45); see also Miller 2008: 75–76. As Abanime points out, Voltaire even states explicitly in a letter to Nicolas Toussaint Le Moyne Des Essarts in 1776 that unfree people in the part of France that borders Switzerland "are far more unhappy than [enslaved] negroes" (letter 19954, *Works* 126: 428).

[68] For a more detailed discussion of Voltaire's anthropology, see Duchet 1971: 281–321.

One of Voltaire's earliest discussions of race occurs in his 1734 *Treatise on Metaphysics* (*Traité de Métaphysique*), which he composed for Émilie Du Châtelet. In this text, he writes from the perspective of an alien "from Mars or Jupiter" who visits Earth for the first time. Voltaire explains that he adopts this perspective in order to examine important philosophical questions without prejudice (Introduction, *Works* 14: 419). Racial differences are the topic of the first chapter, which is titled "The different species of humans," and which depicts the alien narrator's attempts to study human nature. The first stop on his travels around the earth is Cafrerie, in the south of Africa. In his search for human beings, he finds monkeys, elephants, and "negroes." He initially struggles to decide which of these three types of creatures are rational and hence human, since they all use a type of language, seem to pursue ends in their actions, and exhibit an imperfect type of reasoning. Only after learning the language of the "negroes" does he conclude that they are the human beings, since their language is somewhat superior to that of the monkeys and elephants (*Works* 14: 420–21). Based on this first encounter, he comes up with a preliminary definition of human beings: "a black animal with wool on its head, walking on two paws, almost as well-postured as a monkey, less strong than other animals of its size, having slightly more ideas than they, and a greater capacity to express them; otherwise subject to all of the same needs" (*Works* 14: 421; trans. Curran 2011: 140). When he later encounters human beings from other racial groups, he revises his definition and concludes that there must be multiple species of human beings (*Works* 14: 421).

When the alien traveler visits Goa, he meets a Christian priest who explains that all human beings descend from one man. The traveler is suspicious about this doctrine and asks whether a Black couple could produce White offspring with blond hair, blue eyes, and an aquiline nose. The priest responds that this is not the case and that Black people transplanted to Germany will nevertheless produce Black children. People cannot change their species, the priest admits, and "no educated person has ever argued that unmixed species degenerate" (*Works* 14: 422). Based on this information, the traveler concludes that the priest's belief in monogenesis must be mistaken. He decides that humans are like trees: just as different types of trees do not originate from one original type, the different species of humans do not descend from one man (*Works* 14: 423).

The chapter we just examined suggests that according to Voltaire, the distinction between human racial groups is undeniable and would be among the first things noticed by an unprejudiced observer. Indeed, he views it as obvious that the doctrine of monogenesis is false: the different racial groups could not have originated from common ancestors but must have had completely separate origins. It also becomes clear that for Voltaire, the difference between humans and animals is less obvious than traditionally thought. This latter idea is confirmed in chapter 5 of the same work, where Voltaire represents humans as continuous with animals and locates Black people at the bottom of the human species: the alien visitor explains that some of the humans he has observed are superior to Black people in the same way in which Black people are superior to monkeys and monkeys to oysters (*Works* 14: 452). When he is confronted with the philosophical doctrine that human beings have immaterial souls that make them completely different from other animals, he finds it ridiculous (*Works* 14: 452–53).

Voltaire elaborates in later works on the ideas about race that he already explores in *Treatise on Metaphysics*. One particularly explicit passage is from *Philosophy of History* (*La philosophie de l'histoire*), which Voltaire published as the introduction to his *Essay on the Customs and the Spirit of the Nations*, but which he originally intended to be a self-contained work. In the second chapter, which is titled "Of the different races of man," Voltaire states that "Only a blind person can doubt that the whites, the negroes, the Albinos, the Hottentots, the Laplanders, the Chinese, the Americans, are completely different races" (*Works* 59: 92).[69] As evidence for the distinctness of Black people, he briefly discusses the differences between Black and White skin, noting that Black people cannot lose their blackness. He also mentions other traits that he claims are characteristic of Black people and that support his thesis that they belong to a completely separate race: "their round eyes, their flat noses, their invariably fat lips, the wool on their head, even the extent of their intelligence reflects prodigious divergences between them and other species of men" (*Works* 59: 92, trans. Curran 2011: 14). This is important because he mentions not just physiological differences but also differences in mental capacities.[70] As in the *Treatise on Metaphysics*, he then adduces evidence that these differences are permanent and not merely the effect of

[69] It is interesting that Voltaire lists 'albinos' here as a separate race; for a helpful discussion, see Curran 2011: 142–45.
[70] Another text in which Voltaire discusses alleged differences in intelligence is his 1769 *Lettres d'Amabed*: Amabed writes, when traveling to the southern coast of Africa, that the inhabitants are brutish and ignorant of all the arts; he adds, "Our sages have said that man is the image of God. Behold a pleasant image of the eternal Being with a flat black nose and little or no intelligence!" (*Works* 70A: 389).

climate: Black people who are "transported" to colder parts of the world always produce "animals of their species" (*Works* 59: 92).[71]

In chapter 141 of the *Essay on Customs*, Voltaire elaborates on his claim that there are intellectual differences between Black and White people:

> The race of negroes is a species of men different from ours.... [O]ne can say that if their intelligence does not belong to a different species than our understanding, it is very inferior. They are not capable of great attention; they plan [*combinent*] very little, and seem made neither for the advantages nor for the abuses of our philosophy. (*Works* 26A: 147)[72]

Here he enumerates concrete ways in which he views the intellects of Black people as inferior to the intellects of Whites. In the subsequent paragraph, while discussing various "species of negroes," Voltaire distinguishes two degrees of "stupidity": the lowest degree consists in thinking only about the present and about bodily needs, whereas the second degree allows for semiforesight, but also includes superstition and the inability to form stable societies (*Works* 26A: 148). He appears to view Black Africans as being in the second category. The reference to an inferiority in foresight, planning, and self-government is relevant for our purposes, of course: these alleged deficiencies are not only widespread racist tropes but also among the traits typically associated with natural slaves.

The *Essay on Customs* also contains passages suggesting that Voltaire views transatlantic slavery at least as a necessary evil, if not as something that is entirely unproblematic. Some passages even suggest that he embraces a version of racial natural slavery. In one of these passages, he once more turns to the allegedly common African practice of selling one's children into slavery. The context is worth noting: after praising the medieval pope Alexander III for banning servitude as much as possible, he notes that while there is still serfdom in Poland, Christians only practice civil servitude, whereas Asians practice domestic servitude. Of course, Voltaire is well aware that

[71] He adds that mulattoes are a "bastard race" similar to mules, which are the offspring of parents belonging to two different species (*Works* 59: 93). This is presumably meant to address the objection that Black and White people, since they can procreate, must belong to the same biological species. He does not mention the fertility of the offspring here, which early modern authors typically use to show that the case of mules is completely different from that of mixed-race human beings.

[72] In the portion of this passage that I omitted, Voltaire makes a surprising comparison, claiming that the difference between Black and White people is like that between spaniels and greyhounds. It is unclear to me what the upshot of this comparison is, in part because I am unsure how Voltaire views the difference between spaniels and greyhounds.

this is untrue: enormous numbers of Black people are enslaved by European Christians as domestic slaves in the eighteenth century. He acknowledges this but immediately argues that it somehow does not count as a refutation of his more general point: "We do not buy domestic slaves, except from negroes. We are criticized for this trade, [but] a people who trade in their children are even more reprehensible than the buyer; this trade demonstrates our superiority; he who gives himself a master is born to have one" (ch. 197, *Works* 26C: 322). Here Voltaire is clearly defending, or at least excusing, transatlantic slavery. While it was somewhat unclear how to interpret his references to parental sale in *Candide* and in the dialogues between the Frenchman and the Englishman, it is obvious in this text that he thinks this alleged African practice makes it acceptable for Europeans to buy enslaved Black people.[73] The real villains of the transatlantic trade, he suggests, are the Africans themselves who sell each other into slavery. What Europeans are doing may be bad, but it is far better than what Africans are doing. At the end of this passage, he goes even further and appears to embrace a form of racial natural slavery: because Africans willingly sell each other into slavery, they must be naturally inferior to Europeans and born to be slaves, that is, meant to be subordinated to Europeans.[74]

There is at least one other place in *Essay on Customs* where Voltaire appears to endorse racial natural slavery: in chapter 145, after stating once more that Black people do not change color if they live in colder climates, he claims that

this is manifest proof that there is in each species of humans, as in plants, a principle that differentiates them. Nature has subordinated to this principle the different degrees of genius, as well as national characteristics that one sees so rarely change. It is on this basis that negroes are the slaves of other men. One purchases them on the coast of Africa like brute animals. (*Works* 26A: 200)[75]

---

[73] This would make Voltaire's position similar to that of the proslavery writer and plantation owner Pierre Victor Malouet, who invokes the alleged fact that Africans sell each other as one of the reasons why colonial slavery is an acceptable practice (1788: 26–27). He also argues that while transatlantic slavery violates the natural law, it is a natural evil and must be accepted because abolishing it would not make the world any better (1788: 25–27).

[74] Condorcet also understood this passage as an endorsement of natural slavery, as we will see later.

[75] Voltaire also mentions in a few other places that enslaved Black people are treated like animals, for instance, in chapter 148: "negroes [were] bought in Africa and transported to Peru like animals destined to serve humans. Neither the negroes nor the inhabitants of the New World were, in fact, ever treated like a human species" (*Works* 26A: 242). As in the passage from chapter 145, Voltaire takes a descriptive tone and does not explicitly tell us whether he approves of treating Black people "like animals destined to serve humans." One can read an implicit criticism into this passage, but it is not entirely clear how morally problematic Voltaire finds this.

In short, he contends that there are permanent physiological differences between racial groups which are naturally tied to differences in intelligence. These differences, in turn, naturally result in the enslavement of Black people by other racial groups. Thus, while Voltaire does not explicitly say that racial differences make racial slavery morally permissible, he does seem to portray it as natural and does not appear to view it as an urgent moral problem.

A final text that is helpful for understanding Voltaire's attitude toward natural slavery is the article "Equality" from his 1764 *Philosophical Dictionary* (*Dictionnaire Philosophique*). This article starts with the memorable claim that unlike brute animals—who do not depend on each other—human beings have received "the ray of divinity which one calls reason, and whose fruit consists in being slaves in nearly the entire earth" (*Works* 36: 42).[76] Voltaire adds that no human being would enslave another in a hypothetical paradisaical environment in which everyone can easily find enough food and the climate is suitable for humans. Indeed, he claims that the very idea of slavery would be absurd in such an environment because there would be no need for it; all human beings would necessarily be equal (*Works* 36: 43–44 / 1977: 113).

Of course human beings in the actual world do not live in paradisaical conditions; our resources are limited and often difficult to obtain, which according to Voltaire necessitates inequality and, even worse, dependence or servitude (*Works* 36: 43–44 / 1977: 113).[77] It is necessary for human societies in the actual world to comprise two classes: "the one the rich who command, the other the poor who serve" (*Works* 36: 44–45 / 1977: 114). He quips that equality is "at once the most natural thing and the most chimerical," since humankind would not be able to survive without a nearly endless supply of "useful men who possess nothing at all" (*Works* 36: 46–47 / 1977: 115; translation altered). Voltaire appears to find this situation regrettable but insists that the poor and powerless must accept it. The cook of a cardinal might view himself as equal to his master, but he must nevertheless "do his duty, or else all human society is disordered" (*Works* 36: 48 / 1977: 116). Even though Voltaire does not mention slavery explicitly in this article, these claims

---

[76] A later version of this article starts by saying that human beings are equal "in the enjoyment of their natural faculties," including the faculties of the understanding (*Works* 36: 42 n. 2 / 1977: 112).

[77] In the 1767 edition of the *Dictionary*, Voltaire also includes the article "Master" (*Maître*). This article addresses the question of how one man can become the master over others by paraphrasing a South Asian and an East Asian fable about the origins of subordination (*Works* 36: 331–32). Voltaire concludes that in the order of nature, "humans all being born equal, it was violence and ability that created the first masters, and laws that created the last" (*Works* 36: 333).

suggest—if taken at face value—that he viewed inequality and bondage as necessary evils, which it would be both dangerous and futile to try to remedy.[78]

4.3.3. Concluding Thoughts on Voltaire

As we have seen, Voltaire embraces many paradigmatically racist ideas. Indeed, he goes farther than most other intellectuals in this period by explicitly defending polygenesis and thereby positing an enormous and unbridgeable gulf between Black and White people. Voltaire furthermore views Black people as markedly inferior to White people, both intellectually and morally. Due to this alleged natural inferiority, he either embraces a version of racial natural slavery or at least does not find the enslavement of Black people particularly atrocious. Andrew Curran may well be correct that Voltaire ultimately views Black people as a subhuman racial group "for whom bondage seemed the logical but regrettable extension of the race's many shortcomings" (2011: 148). While Voltaire appears to dislike slavery in general and sometimes portrays transatlantic slavery as inhumane, he never provides extensive philosophical arguments for its abolition. In fact, he appears far more concerned about various types of unfreedom in Europe than about colonial slavery.

4.4. Diderot and D'Alembert's *Encyclopedia*

We now turn to an enormously influential text: the *Encyclopedia or Reasoned Dictionary of the Sciences, Arts, and Trades* (*Encyclopédie, ou Dictionnaire raisonné des sciences, des arts et des métiers*), edited by two White Frenchmen, Denis Diderot (1713–1784) and Jean Le Rond d'Alembert (1717–1783), and published in seventeen volumes between 1751 and 1765.[79] Many authors contributed to this monumental work, and, while some entries list their authors, the authorship of quite a few entries is unclear. Some entries were

---

[78] There are other reasons to believe that Voltaire views transatlantic slavery as a necessary evil; see Abanime 1979: 247 and 251.

[79] An electronic edition is available at https://encyclopedie.uchicago.edu. I will cite the *Encyclopedia* as EDR, followed by the volume and page numbers of the original edition (Diderot and d'Alembert 1751–65), which are also included in the electronic edition. If available, I also include a reference to an English translation of the relevant article.

original compositions, but many drew on previously published work, often reproducing long passages verbatim or in paraphrase. These borrowings are typically unacknowledged, which can make it difficult to determine whether a particular passage is borrowed. It makes sense that much of the content is recycled from other sources because the *Encyclopedia*'s aim was to serve as an up-to-date compendium of knowledge and as a general reference work (Clark 2016: xx). The articles that are most directly relevant to our purposes were mainly composed by Louis de Jaucourt (1704–1780), a White French Calvinist who spent most of his formative years in Geneva and who was the author of the bulk of the *Encyclopedia*—an astonishing 17,288 entries in total.[80]

Jaucourt's entry "Slavery" ("Esclavage"), which was published in volume 5 in 1755, borrows freely from Montesquieu, as well as to some extent from John Locke and other seventeenth-century natural law theorists.[81] The entry starts with a long discussion of the history of slavery before arguing that slavery is "contrary to natural and civil right, that it is offensive to the best forms of government, and finally, that it is useless in itself" (EDR 5: 936–37 / 2016: 176). Jaucourt also stresses the distinction between property rights over persons and property rights over things: like Samuel Pufendorf, he argues that alleged property rights over persons are much more restricted than property rights over things and do not include the right to use, consume, or destroy the person in one's possession.[82] Thus, he concludes, "one cannot, properly speaking, have property rights in persons" (EDR 5: 937 / 2016: 177–78). Drawing primarily on Locke and Montesquieu, he then argues against voluntary slavery (EDR 5: 937 / 2016: 178) and later against war slavery and hereditary slavery (EDR 5: 938 / 2016: 180). Like Montesquieu, he also claims that slavery is useless for master and slave because it prevents both parties from living virtuously (EDR 5: 937 / 2016: 179). More interesting is his argument that slavery violates human dignity and degrades "humanity itself," which, in combination with his arguments against various forms of circumstantial slavery, means that "nothing in the world can render *slavery*

---

[80] For helpful overviews of the *Encyclopedia* articles on slavery and race, see Curran 2011: 149–61 and 181–86; Ehrard 2008: 165–84.

[81] For a paragraph-by-paragraph concordance between Jaucourt's article and Montesquieu's *Spirit of the Laws*, see Ehrard 2008: 169–70. Another *Encyclopedia* entry that summarizes Montesquieu's discussions of slavery is d'Alembert's "Eulogy for President Montesquieu" ("Eloge de M. le Président de Montesquieu"), published in 1755 as a preface to volume 5 (EDR 5: iii–xviii / 2016: 122–138).

[82] Pufendorf states these views in *Duty of Man* 2.4.5, 1991: 130. See my discussion of the distinction between persons and things in chapters 2 and 5.

legitimate" (EDR 5: 937–38 / 2016: 179). This sounds like a firm and completely general rejection of slavery.[83]

The most noteworthy aspect of Jaucourt's entry "Slavery" is his discussion of natural slavery. He calls the Greek doctrine of natural slavery "an arrogant presumption" that is founded on "the prejudices of pride and ignorance," adding that the same applies to Christians who pretend that their religion gives them the right to enslave those who are not Christians (EDR 5: 938 / 2016: 181). Finally turning explicitly to transatlantic slavery, he ridicules those who draw analogies between the political unfreedom of Europeans and the unfreedom of colonial slaves (EDR 5: 938 / 2016: 182). At the end of the entry, however, Jaucourt repeats—approvingly—Montesquieu's claim that in hot climates slavery is natural in an important sense and is "scarcely more burdensome than the subject's condition." In these climates slavery is founded on a natural reason, even though it is still contrary to nature (EDR 5: 938–39 / 2016: 182). Thus, Jaucourt does not truly go beyond Montesquieu in this article, nor does he discuss transatlantic slavery in detail.

In some of his later entries, Jaucourt takes a stronger and more explicit stance against transatlantic slavery. For instance, he is most likely the author of the short entry "Natural Liberty" ("Liberté naturelle"), published in 1765 as part of volume 9. In this entry, he criticizes Christians for defending slavery. He asks, "how is it that the Christian powers have not judged that this same religion, independent of natural law, cries out against the enslavement of the Negroes? it's because they need them for their colonies, their plantations, and their mines. *Auri sacra fames* [*O accursed hunger for gold*]!" (EDR 9: 471–72 / 2016: 330). Thus, he explicitly accuses proponents of slavery of bad faith: the true reason why they support slavery is their economic self-interest, but they invent specious moral and religious justifications to defend it.

Jaucourt's most radical denunciation of transatlantic slavery occurs in the entry "Traffic in Negroes" ("Traite des Nègres"), which is included in volume 16, also published in 1765.[84] As David Brion Davis has shown, this entry

---

[83] He does, however, accept penal slavery (EDR 5: 937 / 2016: 177).

[84] There is also an entry "Negroes (Trade)" ("Nègre [Commerce]"), which overlaps to a significant extent with the entry "Negres" in Jacques Savary des Bruslons and Philemon Louis Savary's *Dictionnaire universel de commerce* (1723, vol. 2: 858–860). The anonymous author of the *Encyclopedia* entry does not take a clear stance on transatlantic slavery, but does mention—perhaps with an implicit criticism—that Europeans "try to justify what is abhorrent and contrary to natural law in this trade by saying that these slaves ordinarily find the salvation of their souls in the loss of their freedom; that the Christian instruction that we give them, joined to the indispensable need that we have of them for the cultivation of sugar, tobacco, indigo, and so on, soften what seems inhuman in a trade where men buy and sell others, like brute animals" (EDR 11: 79).

borrows extensively from the Scottish author George Wallace, whom we discussed in chapter 2 (Davis 1971). Following Wallace, Jaucourt argues that every single enslaved Black person in European colonies has the right to be freed because "Men and their liberty are not articles of trade; they cannot be sold, bought, or paid for at any price," which means that the sale of a human being is always "null and void" (EDR 16: 532 / 2016: 613). Also like Wallace, he argues that if the emancipation of all colonial slaves entails the ruin of these colonies, "let the European colonies be destroyed rather than create so many poor wretches!" (EDR 16: 533 / 2016: 614). Economic considerations cannot make it legitimate to deprive human beings of their sacred moral rights. Yet, he adds, it is not even true that the abolition of slavery would bankrupt Europe's colonies. Quite to the contrary, it would make America far more populous and prosperous (EDR 16: 533 / 2016: 614).

It is worth noting that Jaucourt also repeats many racist tropes. For instance, in the entry "The river Senegal" ("Sénégal, riviere de"), he describes the "Negroes" living on one side of this river as "tall, fat, and without genius," also claiming that they are "sedentary and have kings who enslave them" (EDR 15: 13). In his entry "The kingdom of Senegal" ("Sénégal, le royaume de"), he describes the Senegalese king as a plunderer and claims that the king's subjects are no better: "they steal from each other, and try to sell each other to the Europeans who trade in slaves on their coasts"(EDR 15: 13).

Slavery also comes up in entries by other authors. Diderot himself appears to express an antislavery stance in a very short remark in his entry "The human species" ("Humaine espece"): after discussing various African ethnic groups, he exclaims, "We have reduced [the Negroes], I do not say to the condition of slaves, but to the condition of beasts of burden. And we are reasonable! And we are Christians!" (EDR 8: 347). One particularly interesting discussion—though not of colonial slavery in particular—occurs in the extremely long entry "Five Percent Tax" ("Vingtième"), which is included in volume 17. The authorship of this text is unclear, but it may have been composed by Etienne Noël Damilaville (1723–1768), a White French government official, probably with input from Diderot (Clark 2016: 623). At one point, this entry rejects the idea that there are some people who are destined to be rulers. The author associates this idea with Hugo Grotius, rather than Aristotle, claiming that Grotius misrepresented Aristotle's doctrines.[85]

---

[85] A few paragraphs later, the entry provides its own interpretation of Aristotle: Aristotle merely meant that some people are born with a greater talent for ruling, and "others with the need to be

He then calls the idea "absurd" and explains that "No one has received from nature the right to command his fellow creature. No one has the right to buy him" (ERD 17: 861–62 / 2016: 647). He even adds, "The slave who sold himself yesterday has so little power to do so that according to natural right, he could today tell whoever bought him that he is his own master if he had the strength to back it up" (ERD 17: 862 / 2016: 647–48). Thus, this entry suggests that natural slavery and voluntary slavery are illicit.

Entries about transatlantic slavery by other authors have a completely different tone. Take, for instance, the entry "Negroes considered as slaves in American colonies" ("Negres, considérés comme esclaves dans les colonies de l'Amérique"), composed by Jean-Baptiste-Pierre Le Romain (d. 1780), a White French engineer who lived and worked in the West Indies and composed some of the *Encyclopedia*'s entries relating to the Caribbean. This entry claims, among other things, that Black people who are enslaved in American colonies are far better off than free Black people living in Africa (EDR 11: 80). It also describes the slave trade in great detail, portraying it as overall quite humane. While Le Romain acknowledges that some colonial masters are far too cruel to their slaves, he appears to hold that the *Code noir* is the correct solution to this problem, since it bans unreasonable forms of punishment (EDR 11: 82).

In the end, then, it is clear that the *Encyclopedia* is not consistently antislavery. Some contributors denounce slavery, others condone it; several entries furthermore embrace racist stereotypes about Black people. The antislavery arguments that the *Encyclopedia* does contain are primarily copied from other publications. Thus, this text—like Montesquieu's *Spirit of the Laws*—is a mixed blessing for the antislavery cause, simultaneously supplying ammunition for both sides.

4.5. Guillaume-Thomas Raynal, Denis Diderot, Jean-Joseph de Pechméja, and the *History of the Two Indies*

Another immensely influential eighteenth-century text is the *Philosophical and Political History of the Settlements and Commerce of Europeans in the Two Indies* (*Histoire philosophique et politique des établissemens & du commerce des*

---

governed and with the inclination to let themselves be ruled" (ERD 17: 862 / 2016: 648). Perhaps the claim here is that Aristotle did not think that these natural aptitudes justify forcible enslavement.

Européens dans les deux Indes), which is typically referred to as the *History of the Two Indies* (*Histoire des deux Indes*). As the title suggests, it is an encyclopedia of the commerce between Europe, Asia, and America, though it also discusses Africa extensively. This work was first published in 1770 in six volumes; significantly revised editions with varying numbers of volumes appeared in 1774, 1780, and 1820. It was also published in English translation in many editions and appears to have influenced English-speaking abolitionists enormously (Anstey 1975: 123). Guillaume-Thomas Raynal, or abbé Raynal (1713–1796), was the work's official author, but large portions were written by other people: Raynal asked many of his acquaintances to write various sections, and he also lifted many portions from existing sources.[86] In this way, this text is quite similar to Diderot and D'Alembert's *Encyclopedia*. One major difference is that the *History of the Two Indies* is structured more like a monograph than like an encyclopedia. Many of its chapters include material by multiple authors without giving the reader any direct indication of this fact.[87] In many cases, these authors have very different and sometimes even contradictory perspectives.

On the basis of the *History of the Two Indies*, some scholars describe Raynal as one of France's staunchest opponents of slavery and colonialism in the eighteenth century.[88] Many people in the early modern period viewed him in similar ways.[89] Yet as Ann Thomson convincingly argues, he does not deserve this reputation. The explicit antislavery portions of the *History of the Two Indies* were composed by other people—in the 1780 edition mainly by Diderot, who built on Jean-Joseph de Pechméja's contributions to the first and second editions. Raynal's own position on colonialism, slavery, and race appears to be far less radical. For instance, in a passage from the 1770 edition,

---

[86] For a more detailed overview of the authorship and publication history of the *History of the Two Indies*, see Thomson 2017. For other in-depth treatments of this text and its discussions of slavery and colonialism, see Terjanian 2013: 54–92; Biondi 2015; Curran 2011: 191–99; Ehrard 2008: 191–206.

[87] The new critical edition of this text helpfully indicates the authorship in footnotes. The portions of the work on which I will focus are included in volume 3 of the critical edition (Raynal 2020).

[88] See, for instance, Thomas 1997: 483–84; Anstey 1975: 121–23; Davis 1966: 418. For a helpful discussion of how radical the *History of the Two Indies* was in general, but how little credit Raynal deserves for these radical ideas, see Israel 2011: 413–42.

[89] The American antislavery author Anthony Benezet, for instance, quotes antislavery passages from the *History of the Two Indies* and attributes them to Raynal, whom he calls "that celebrated philosopher and friend to mankind" (2013: 231–33). The passages he quotes are from book 11, chapter 30 (or, according to the table of contents, chapter 31) of the 1774 edition, titled "Slavery is repugnant to humanity, reason, and justice." These passages, according to Thomson, were primarily written by Jean-Joseph de Pechméja, rather than Raynal himself (Thomson 2017: 260). Many early modern authors—perhaps particularly those outside of the French context—were unaware that the antislavery passages in the *History of the Two Indies* were not written by Raynal.

Black people are portrayed as "more effeminate, lazier, weaker, and unfortunately more suitable to become slaves" than other groups (1770: 120, see Curran 2011: 192). And this passage is not an outlier—the work as a whole presents the capacities and prospects of Black Africans in an extremely pessimistic light (Curran 2011: 194) and portions of it attempt to justify colonialism (Thomson 2017: 254–57).[90]

I will concentrate here on the most explicit antislavery passages contained in the 1780 edition of this work, which were composed by Diderot but incorporate portions of Pechméja's text.[91] This discussion is remarkable, not only because of how radical it is but also because it makes some points that I have not encountered in earlier texts. For instance, it describes the callousness of White slave traders in a particularly memorable way and raises the question of whether proslavery arguments even deserve or require refutations. The passages on which I will focus occur in book 11, chapter 24, which is titled "Origin and progress of slavery. Arguments devised to justify it. Responses to these arguments." We can view this chapter as implicitly divided into six parts: a short preamble (§§1–2), a discussion of the historical origins of slavery from a state of equality (§§3–18),[92] an antislavery argument based on the doctrine that liberty is a natural right (§§19–23), proslavery arguments and refutations of these arguments (§§24–46), a concrete proposal for a way to end transatlantic slavery gradually (§§47–55), and then an appeal to European self-interest with a warning of slave uprisings and other dire consequences for White Europeans if they do not abolish slavery (§§56–58). I will only comment on a few aspects of this chapter that are particularly relevant for our purposes.

One noteworthy aspect of the chapter is that it defines slavery as a state of a human being who has lost self-ownership and of whom a master can dispose as of a thing that belongs to the master (§2). Conversely, it defines liberty as self-ownership (§19) or "ownership of one's body and enjoyment of

---

[90] See Benot 2005: 107–123 for an in-depth discussion of the evidence for and against an anticolonial reading of this text.

[91] The 1780 edition is also the basis for the recent critical edition of this text (Raynal 2020), on which I will be relying. I will cite this work by book, chapter, and paragraph, as labeled in Raynal 2020. For differences between the 1780 edition's version of this chapter and the two earlier editions, see Raynal 2020: 561–63; see also the discussion in Wolpe 1957: 153–59.

[92] As the editors of Raynal 2020 helpfully document, this portion of the chapter is based mainly on two works: The 1771 work *Observations Concerning the Distinctions of Ranks in Society* by the Scottish author John Millar, and the 1769 work *The History of the Reign of the Emperor Charles V*, by the Scottish historian William Robertson.

one's mind" (§21), adding that natural liberty is the natural right of all human beings to dispose of themselves based on their own choices (§19). Diderot points out how crucial this natural right is: directing one's actions with one's own will is what distinguishes us from animals, and it is the foundation of all morality, human relationships, and human institutions (§§20–21). Taking away someone's liberty is tantamount to denying their human nature, reducing them to the level of brute animals, and even to "homicide" (§§21–22); liberty is so essential to human beings that "no power under heaven" can dispose of it (§21). This entails that slavery is never justified.

In a particularly striking passage, Diderot—repeating almost verbatim passages composed by Pechméja for the 1770 edition—describes the barbarity, callousness, and greed of White Europeans involved in the transatlantic slave trade, as well as their shockingly businesslike attitude as they trade in human beings:

> Look at the shipowner who, bent over his desk, calculates, pen in hand, the number of attacks he can make on the coasts of Guinea; who leisurely examines how many guns he will need to get a negro, chains to keep him bound on his ship, whips to make him work; who calculates, in cold blood, the price of each drop of blood with which this slave will sprinkle his dwelling; who debates whether the negress will give more or less to his land by the labors of her weak hands than by the dangers of childbirth. (§22)[93]

This passage may well be the most incisive early modern description of the moral absurdity that is involved in treating human beings like merchandise. Diderot then—again recycling material from the 1770 edition—criticizes Christianity for its complicity in the slave trade: not only has the church been shockingly silent about the injustice of transatlantic slavery, but it has also actively sustained it by imposing draconian punishments on fugitive slaves. He asks rhetorically whether this type of behavior does not necessitate "suffocat[ing] the ministers under the debris of their altars" (§22).

When refuting specific proslavery arguments, Diderot rejects several alleged justifications for transatlantic slavery, including natural slavery (§§29–30), hereditary slavery (§§31–32), voluntary slavery (§§35–36), war slavery and the

---

[93] For the corresponding passage in the 1770 edition, see Raynal 2020: 561 / 1770: 170.

claim that the captives in question would be executed if Europeans did not buy them (§§37–38), penal slavery (§§39–40), the argument that Africans are better off in American colonies than in Africa (§§41–42), and the argument that transatlantic slavery is justified because it saves the souls of enslaved people by Christianizing them (§§45–46).

We can focus here on what Diderot says about natural slavery; we have already seen versions of the other arguments in other authors. First, note that Diderot directly addresses what I call racial natural slavery, which of course makes sense since he is responding to alleged defenses of transatlantic slavery. The way he describes this doctrine—a description he takes verbatim from the 1770 edition—is already interesting: "negroes are a species of men born for slavery. They are limited [*bornés*], deceitful, wicked; they themselves recognize the superiority of our intelligence, and almost recognize the justice of our rule" (§29).[94] This description is notable because this version of the doctrine suggests not only that every single Black person is automatically a natural slave and inferior in intelligence and virtue, but also that Black people view themselves as inferior and come close to seeing themselves as natural slaves. Diderot's response to this doctrine—in which he again borrows heavily from the 1770 edition—is a version of what I have called the effects-of-slavery strategy. In other words, he concedes that enslaved Black people are inferior, but he insists that this inferiority is caused by transatlantic slavery and can hence not serve as a justification for it. Transatlantic slavery degrades the minds of enslaved Black people. As for their moral character, it is fitting and permissible to be mean and deceitful toward one's oppressors (§30). He also describes racial natural slavery as a ruse and claims that defenders of the transatlantic slave trade have "almost succeeded in persuading [enslaved people] that they were a singular species, born for abjection and dependence, for work and punishment" (§30).[95] It is utterly ridiculous, he adds, to accuse Black people of being vile when one has done everything in one's power to degrade them.

One final noteworthy aspect of Diderot's contribution to the *History of the Two Indies* is his reflection on whether proslavery arguments even deserve painstaking refutations. After providing brief arguments against some of the

---

[94] For the corresponding passage in the 1770 edition, see Raynal 2020: 562 / 1770: 170–71.

[95] This is an instance of internalized racism. We have already encountered eighteenth-century descriptions of internalized racism in chapters 1–2, when discussing Lemuel Haynes and James Dunbar.

most common defenses of transatlantic slavery, he notes that he could have provided much stronger and more extensive refutations. But, he asks,

> are they worth it? Do we owe great efforts, all the contention of our minds, to someone who speaks in bad faith? Is the contempt of silence not better suited than a disputation with someone who pleads for his interest against justice, against his own conviction? I have said too much for the honest and sensible man; I cannot say enough for the inhuman trader. (§47)

This is a fascinating point that I have not encountered in earlier texts, at least not as explicitly—though the 1770 edition might hint at something similar when it states that "Anyone who justifies such an odious system [that is, slavery] merits a contemptuous silence from the philosopher and a stab of a dagger from the negro" (1770: 167–68). Diderot, in the 1780 edition, claims that it is ultimately futile to try to effect the abolition of slavery through philosophical arguments. Proponents of slavery, according to him, are not arguing in good faith and are guided by pure self-interest. They support slavery not because they are unaware of its injustice but because it is extremely profitable for them. Later in the same chapter, Diderot expresses an even more general pessimism about the power of philosophical argumentation to shape people's behavior: "let us stop making the useless voice of humanity heard by the peoples and their masters: perhaps it has never been consulted in public dealings" (§56). In other words, he questions whether nations ever make political decisions on the basis of moral principles. In the remainder of this chapter, Diderot heeds his own advice: instead of supplying additional moral arguments, he provides reasons for abolishing slavery that are founded in European self-interest. If Europe does not abolish slavery, he warns, enslaved Black people will eventually find a way to take vengeance and gain the upper hand; "the *Code noir* will disappear and the *Code blanc* [that is, White code] will be terrible, if the victor consults only the right of retaliation!" (§§57–58).[96]

---

[96] As several commentators point out, these sections include a reference to the fascinating utopian novel *The Year 2440* (*L'an 2440*), published by Louis-Sébastien Mercier in 1771 (e.g., Harvey 2012: 162–63, 191–95), which I unfortunately cannot examine here.

4.6. Marie Jean Antoine Nicolas Caritat,
Marquis de Condorcet

We now turn to another fairly radical antislavery author: the White French mathematician and philosopher Marie Jean Antoine Nicolas Caritat, Marquis de Condorcet (1743–1794). In addition to composing several antislavery texts, Condorcet was an active member of the French abolitionist organization Society of the Friends of the Blacks. His longest antislavery tract is *Reflections on the Slavery of the Negroes* (*Réflexions sur l'esclavage des nègres*), which he published in 1781 under the pseudonym "M. Schwartz, Pastor of Saint Evangile in Bienne and member of the Economic Society of B***." This text will be my main focus, though I will also have occasion to mention a few other texts.[97]

Condorcet's *Reflections* contains several antislavery statements that would have been considered radical in 1781—though, as we will see, it also contains claims that, at least from our point of view, are disappointing. The work begins with a dedicatory letter to enslaved Black people, which opens with an endorsement of human equality: "My friends, although I am not of the same color as you, I have always viewed you as my brothers. Nature has formed you to have the same mind, the same reason, the same virtues as white people" (2003: 3). The first chapter starts with a similarly direct pronouncement, this time about the moral impermissibility of slavery: "To reduce a man to slavery, to buy him, sell him, or keep him in servitude, these are genuine crimes, and they are worse than theft" (2003: 7). Condorcet does not mince words in this text.

In chapters 2–4, he then refutes many common defenses of slavery, including the argument that transatlantic slaves are licit war or penal slaves (2003: 8–9) and the argument that voluntary slavery and hereditary slavery are licit (2003: 10–12).[98] He concludes in chapter 4 that there is no instance of slavery whatsoever that is compatible with natural law (2003: 12).[99] In this context, his most original contribution appears to be his argument against

[97] For a helpful overview of Condorcet's views on slavery, see Popkin 1992: 50–63.

[98] In chapter 12, Condorcet refutes some additional defenses of transatlantic slavery, for instance, that Black people do not mind losing their freedom as much as White Europeans do, that colonial slaves are no worse off than peasants in Europe, and that the self-interest of masters will ensure the humane treatment of slaves (2003: 43–47).

[99] Condorcet includes a similarly general denunciation of slavery in his 1789 text "On the Admission of Representatives of the Planters of Saint-Domingue in the National Assembly": he ascribes to a representative of a free nation belief that "A man cannot be the property of another man" and that it is unjust "to sell the liberty of other human beings for a sum of money" (2003: 67).

penal slavery in chapter 2. A necessary condition for just punishments, he argues, is that their form and duration are clearly defined by the law. This means that it is permissible to condemn a criminal to perform tasks for the government or for the public.[100] However, it is impermissible to condemn a criminal to be the slave of a private individual because then the form and the duration of the punishment would depend on the caprice of this master, rather than the law (2003: 10). I have not seen this intriguing argument against penal slavery elsewhere. Unfortunately, proponents of slavery seem to have ways to respond. For instance, they could reply that a just punishment for capital crimes is the lifelong and absolute subjection to another person, and that the law might specify this. Moreover, they could argue that the government can pass laws that describe the forms that slavery can take, and it could sentence criminals either to lifelong slavery or to a specific number of years. Luckily, Condorcet does not rest his entire case on this argument: he also points out that "it is as absurd as it is atrocious to dare to suggest that most of the unfortunate people bought in Africa are criminals" (2003: 10). Thus, even if penal slavery were in principle justifiable, it would not justify the transatlantic slave trade.

When Condorcet turns, in chapter 5, to what legislators ought to do about transatlantic slavery, he—quite disappointingly—becomes far less radical. The chapter starts with the promising claim that legislators have an obligation to repeal unjust laws and repair injustices, even going so far as to call it a crime to tolerate unjust laws when one has the power to change them (2003: 13). Unfortunately, Condorcet also argues that it is sometimes in the interest of the victims of an injustice, and necessary for public tranquility, to delay repealing unjust laws and to make changes only gradually. The abolition of slavery, he claims, is precisely such a case. Like some of the authors we have encountered before—mainly in chapter 1—he argues that immediate abolition would be dangerous because slavery has rendered enslaved people unfit for liberty:

> If the slaves in European colonies have become incapable of fulfilling the functions of free men—due to their upbringing, the stupidity [*abrutissement*] acquired in slavery, the corruption of manners, and as a necessary consequence

---

[100] Traditionally, this kind of punishment would probably be considered public slavery. Thus, Condorcet appears to accept the legitimacy of public slavery and rejects only private or personal slavery.

of the vices and example of their masters—one can (at least until the use of freedom will have given them back what slavery made them lose) treat them like men whom misfortune or illness has deprived of a portion of their faculties. One cannot grant the full exercise of rights to such people without the risk that they will do harm to others or to themselves. They need not only the protection of the laws, but the care of humanity. . . . By giving them their freedom abruptly, we would reduce them to misery. (2003: 14)

Later in the same chapter, he elaborates that "before placing slaves at the rank of free men, the law must ensure that in this new capacity they will not disturb the safety of citizens," and one must also keep the public safe from potentially violent outbursts of former slave masters (2003: 15). From a present-day perspective, this is extremely problematic: Condorcet suggests that Black people must be treated like people with mental illnesses or intellectual disabilities that make them dangerous to society.[101]

On the basis of his concern for public safety, Condorcet favors a gradual abolition: even though he recognizes how horrendously unjust transatlantic slavery is, he does not think it ought to be abolished immediately.[102] He argues that public tranquility is one permissible reason for delaying abolition, and another one is a consideration of the interests of enslaved people themselves, for whom he believes a sudden emancipation would not be beneficial. To his credit, he explicitly denies that economic or financial reasons can be taken into consideration: "the interest of power and wealth of a nation must disappear before the right of a single man; otherwise there would be no difference between a well-regulated society and a group of thieves" (2003: 15).[103] While he holds—as he argues in chapter 6—that the abolition of slavery would be economically beneficial for Europeans, he stresses that even if things were otherwise, that would not be a moral justification for delaying abolition.

---

[101] For a discussion of how problematic this is, see Sala-Molins 2006: 17–19.

[102] Chapter 9 contains the details of Condorcet's proposal for a gradual abolition (2003: 26–33). For more on Condorcet's gradual abolitionism and its context, see Harvey 2012: 172–79.

[103] Condorcet makes a similar point in his 1789 text "On the Admission of Representatives of the Planters of Saint-Domingue in the National Assembly": he ascribes to a representative of a free nation the conviction that "any infringement of one of the natural rights is a crime which the financial interests of those who committed it cannot excuse" (2003: 67). In contrast, he ascribes to planters the opposite conviction: financial interest can legitimize infringing on other people's rights, taking away their liberty, treating them barbarously, and even killing them (2003: 68). He uses this difference to argue that planters should not have representatives in the French National Assembly.

It is clear from what we have already seen that, according to Condorcet, slavery has extremely negative effects on the minds and characters of enslaved people. He elaborates on this in chapter 6 in the context of discussing the economic consequences of abolition. When a certain group of people is lazy, he explains, it is always due to bad laws and never due to the climate, geography, physiology, or national character (2003: 17). He describes enslaved Black people as clear examples of this: they are lazy, stupid, and morally depraved, but these traits are simply natural effects of life in slavery. These are not their natural characteristics. Quite to the contrary, Black people are "naturally gentle, industrious, and sensible," and if they were free, they would soon become a "thriving nation" (2003: 21). Here, Condorcet sharply distances himself from the kind of geographic or climatological determinism advocated by Montesquieu and others (see Garrett 2006: 194).

Condorcet uses a more explicit version of the effects-of-slavery strategy in his 1788 text "On Slavery: Rules for the Society of the Friends of the Blacks." In the preamble, he points out how absurd it is that White Europeans "deprive the Negro of all his moral faculties and then declare him inferior to us, and consequently destined to carry our chains" (2012:150). In other words, there is nothing natural about the characteristics that proponents of slavery invoke when claiming that Black people are natural slaves. The slave trade itself deprives enslaved people of "all their human characteristics" (2012: 150) and there is nothing at all in the "customs, colour or moral character" of Africans that can justify this trade (2012: 149). Condorcet adds that European slave traders ruin the moral character not only of the people they enslave, but also of free Africans who, through their interactions with corrupt Europeans, become so greedy that they are willing to sell their own family members (2012: 149). Thus, Condorcet appears to accept the widely held belief that Africans routinely sell their loved ones but argues that this behavior is a product of the transatlantic slave trade.

In a comment on Voltaire, Condorcet reiterates that Europeans bear the responsibility for the alleged vices of Africans and that Africans are not natural slaves. As seen earlier, Voltaire states in chapter 197 of his *Essay on Customs* that it is more reprehensible to sell one's children than to buy slaves, and that "he who gives himself a master is born to have one" (*Works* 26C: 322). Condorcet comments that "this expression must be understood in the same sense in which Aristotle said that there are natural slaves"—in other words, he understands Voltaire as endorsing a version of natural slavery. He then criticizes Voltaire's reasoning, arguing that European traders bear an enormous responsibility and compares the claim that "certain humans de-serve to be slaves" to the claim that "misers deserve to be robbed." He also argues that even though Africans who sell their countrymen into slavery are clearly doing something wrong, these crimes are ultimately the Europeans' fault, who inspired this type of crime and pay Africans for committing it (1804: 287–88).

One final aspect of Condorcet's discussion of slavery is worth noting: he sometimes comments on the perspective of enslaved Black people them-selves. In his 1790 "Address of the Society of the Friends of the Blacks to the National Assembly," he ridicules the idea that Black people see themselves as natural slaves: "when a slave . . . knows that there are vast regions where all men are free, when he hears freedom proclaimed around him as an impre-scriptible, inalienable right, belonging to all men, can he still believe himself condemned by nature to eternal servitude?" (2003: 76).[104] In short, the idea that colonial slaves accept their own enslavement as natural is preposterous, particularly during the Enlightenment era, when the natural right to liberty is widely discussed. Condorcet makes a similar point in his 1791 "Review of the Work of the First Legislature," when reflecting on the beginnings of the Haitian Revolution: enslaved people in the colonies who hear about the French declaration of rights can easily see that their own enslavement is a violation of their rights. He asks rhetorically, "is it not the height of imbe-cility to suppose that, in order to regard servitude as an unjust oppression, the African in the colonies needs a European philosopher to come and make him see it?" (2003: 82). In short, colonial slaveholders are mistaken if they think that enslaved people are unaware of the enormous injustice of their sit-uation and will simply accept it as justified or natural.

4.7. Olympe de Gouges

Our last author in this chapter is one of the most intriguing: Olympe de Gouges (1748–1793), a White French political activist and playwright, and the most vocal female antislavery writer in eighteenth-century France.[105] Her enormous

[104] This is reminiscent of the description of natural slavery in the *History of the Two Indies*, which includes the allegation that Black people view themselves as inferior to White people and come close to viewing themselves as natural slaves (book 11, chapter 24, §29).

[105] Her birth name was 'Marie Gouze,' and she briefly used the name 'Marie Aubry' after mar-rying Louis Yves Aubry in 1765. She changed her name to 'Olympe de Gouges' after her husband's death in 1766, sometimes also calling herself 'Marie-Olympe de Gouges'; 'Olympe' was her mother's

success as an intellectual is all the more impressive given her background. She was born in Montauban, in the Occitania region of southern France, and her first language was Occitan. Her family was part of the middle class—her father was a butcher, and her mother came from a somewhat influential bourgeois family.[106] Gouges received some formal education (Bergès 2022: 2), though far less than the other authors in this chapter. Against all odds, she became a member of the intelligentsia after moving to Paris as a young woman. Among her many publications are several fascinating texts about slavery, which will be our main focus here. Gouges also advocated other causes, including women's rights—most famously in her 1791 "Declaration of the Rights of Woman and Female Citizen" ("Déclaration des droits de la femme et de la citoyenne"). This text was Gouges's response to the 1789 Declaration of the Rights of Man and [Male] Citizen (Déclaration des droits de l'homme et du citoyen), which she criticized for failing to embrace gender equality. Her political activism also extended into several other domains. She argued, for instance, that the people should choose their form of government, and she campaigned against the execution of the French king and queen during the Revolution. This activism eventually led to her arrest and execution by guillotine.

Gouges's first major antislavery text was the prose drama *Zamor and Mirza, or the Happy Shipwreck* (*Zamor et Mirza, ou l'heureuse naufrage*), originally composed in 1783.[107] She revised it extensively until 1792, when she also changed its title to *Black Slavery, or the Happy Shipwreck* (*L'esclavage des noirs, ou l'heureux naufrage*).[108] The play contains strong political messages and caused quite a stir.[109] Some contemporaries even accuse Gouges of having instigated the slave revolts in Martinique and Saint-Domingue.[110]

---

middle name. For in-depth discussions of Gouges and her views on slavery and colonialism, see Miller 2008: 109–40; Orrù 2020; Le Hir 1994. For an overview of Gouges's philosophical views, see Bergès 2022.

[106] Gouges's paternity is controversial; she sometimes claimed to be the illegitimate daughter of the writer Jean-Jacques Lefranc, Marquis de Pompignan, rather than of her legal father, her mother's husband (Bergès 2022: 1).

[107] In some editions, including the 1788 edition, 'Zamor' is spelled 'Zamore.'

[108] When the play was first performed in 1789, it bore yet another title: *The Slavery of the Negroes, an Indian Drama* (*L'esclavage des nègres, drame indien*); see Orrù 2020: 102.

[109] For helpful background information about the play and the controversies it caused, see Orrù 2020; Le Hir 1994; Miller 2008: 113–28. I will cite *Black Slavery* using the act and scene numbers from the 1792 edition, which is also the basis for the edition of the French text with an English translation that I will, for the most part, use (Gouges 1994). The scenes are numbered differently in the 1788 edition; some of the content is also different.

[110] Gouges mentions this accusation in several places, including the 1792 preface to *Black Slavery*, 1994: 87/232.

Gouges's other writings on slavery include the 1792 preface to the play, a 1790 article titled "Response to the American Champion" (*Réponse au champion américain*), in which she defends herself against the accusation that she is partially responsible for slave revolts in America, and finally her 1788 essay "Reflections on Negroes" (*Réflexion sur les hommes nègres*). She also makes some short remarks about slavery in her 1790 "The Comedians Unmasked" (*Les comédiens démsasqués*).

Let us first examine the fascinating play *Black Slavery*.[111] In the 1792 edition, all three acts are set in "the Indies"—that is, presumably, the West Indies.[112] It tells the intertwined stories of four characters: Zamor, Mirza, Sophie, and Valère.[113] Zamor and Mirza are lovers; they are Black and used to be enslaved by M. de Saint-Frémont, the governor of an unnamed West Indian Island. At the beginning of the play, the couple lives in hiding on a nearby otherwise uninhabited island. They took refuge there after Zamor killed the master's overseer in self-defense and in defense of Mirza, who had angered the overseer by refusing his sexual advances.[114] Sophie and Valère are White. They are a young married couple from France who came to the West Indies in search of Sophie's father and become shipwrecked on the island where Zamor and Mirza are hiding. Zamor saves Sophie from drowning and later tells the French couple the reason for his and Mirza's precarious situation.[115] Soon after this, the governor's new overseer arrives on the island, captures Zamor and Mirza, and brings them back to the main island, where they are supposed to be executed. Sophie and Valère—along with many

---

[111] I will concentrate mainly on the aspects of the play that are directly related to slavery and race. The play has other dimensions. As some interpreters point out, it is also a play about gender (Le Hir 1994: 70–73; Cole 2011: 173–78). Moreover, it contains noteworthy criticisms of colonialism. In the first scene, for instance, Zamor says about White Europeans in the West Indies that "They came to these regions, seized the lands, the fortunes of the Native Islanders, and these proud ravishers of the properties of a gentle and peaceable people in its home, shed all the blood of its noble victims, sharing amongst themselves its bloody spoils and made us slaves as a reward for the riches that they ravished, and that we preserve for them" (1.1).

[112] Intriguingly, the 1788 edition is set in the East Indies instead, and Zamor and Mirza are not Black but (East) Indian. For more on the change of setting, see Miller 2008: 121–24; Brown 2001: 392; Vanpée 2014: 108–9. As Miller argues, Gouges at times seems to mix East Indian with West Indian elements in her play.

[113] Of these four characters, the two central heroes are Zamor and Sophie; Mirza and Valère are less central.

[114] What exactly the overseer did to Mirza is not entirely clear. There might be hints that he attempted to rape her.

[115] The general situation of the first act—former colonial slaves and members of the White ruling class on a desert island where the power structures of their former societies cannot be retained—is reminiscent of Pierre de Marivaux's 1725 play *The Island of Slaves* (*L'île des esclaves*), though the plot is otherwise completely different. We can view the island as symbolic of the state of nature, in which all human beings—Black and White, male and female—are equal.

enslaved people—plead with the governor to pardon the two prisoners. The governor initially refuses, but when he discovers that Sophie is his long-lost daughter, he frees Zamor and Mirza.

Even aside from the specifics of the plot, it is significant that Zamor and Mirza, a Black couple, are among the four central characters—and indeed heroes—of the play.[116] This is a political statement in itself. The audience is clearly meant to sympathize with Zamor and Mirza and hope that they will not be executed. These two characters are portrayed in extremely positive ways. Both are heroic and noble-minded, exhibiting generosity and courage when helping Sophie and Valère and when facing execution. Mirza is additionally described as beautiful—Valère exclaims that he has never seen a more beautiful Black woman (1.7)—and Zamor as highly educated, having been raised almost like a son by Governor Saint-Frémont (1.8). The play portrays Zamor's reasons for killing the overseer as noble, and Mirza bravely insists on being executed alongside Zamor because she cannot fathom living without him and blames herself for his deed. When the governor commands Zamor's execution, Zamor gives a speech in which he selflessly and courageously accepts his punishment "for the good of the Colony" (3.11). In short, Gouges gives the audience an abundance of reasons to admire and sympathize with Zamor and Mirza.

Some of the White characters—including not just Sophie and Valère but also Governor Saint-Frémont and his wife—are also portrayed as exceptionally benevolent. Mirza describes Saint-Frémont as "the best of all Masters," and Zamor agrees (1.1). Even while Saint-Frémont is fully committed to having Zamor executed, Zamor expresses his love and admiration for his master, exclaiming pathetically that as long as his master cherishes him, he can die happy (3.11). Indeed, the play depicts Saint-Frémont as genuinely wishing to pardon the two prisoners, though he initially sees himself forced by political considerations to have them executed (2.6). The planters and overseers on his island insist that Zamor's execution is necessary for restoring order and preventing a slave uprising. Here Gouges presumably

---

[116] This play is, however, not the first European play with a Black hero. Earlier examples include the English play *Oroonoko*, which is Thomas Southerne's 1699 dramatization of Aphra Behn's 1688 novel of the same title. There are a few interesting parallels between the plots of these works. For instance, *Oroonoko* is also the story of a pair of enslaved Black lovers in a European colony in the Americas who are described as exceptionally well educated and beautiful; the story also features a White European woman whose father went to the New World to be the lieutenant-general of a colony. In the end, however, the two Black heroes of *Oroonoko* are tortured and killed, while their counterparts in *Black Slavery* live happily ever after. It is worth noting that *Oroonoko* was well known in eighteenth-century France (Curran 2011: 187; Ehrard 2008: 83).

wants to illustrate the ways in which unjust political institutions like colonial slavery can force even well-intentioned people who are in power to do horrific things. She makes a similar point in the second act when Coraline, an enslaved woman, explains that "in order to be good, one must be neither master nor slave" (2.2).[117] Being a slave is dreadful and negatively affects one's character, but being a master is incompatible with virtue as well.[118] The institution of slavery corrupts everything that it touches and needs to be abolished in order to enable people to live virtuously.

The fact that Zamor has received the education of a member of the French ruling class—unlike the other enslaved characters in this play—is significant. One of the very first things Zamor says is, "The education that our governor had given me added to the sensibility of my rude manners and rendered the frightful despotism [of the overseer's behavior] . . . even more intolerable" (1.1). Later in the same scene, Zamor generalizes this point, stating that education makes enslaved people far less likely to accept their fate: "[Planters] take care not to instruct us. If by chance our eyes were to open, we would be horrified by the state to which they have reduced us, and we would shake off a yoke as cruel as it is shameful" (1.1). In other words, West Indian planters keep enslaved people ignorant on purpose because otherwise it would be impossible to keep them enslaved. Zamor even admits that he does not reveal his way of thinking to other enslaved people, presumably because he believes that spreading this knowledge would have horrendous consequences. He also states at one point that White people in the colonies are at a huge advantage because of their education: "instruction has made Gods of them, and we are only men" (1.1). The governor appears to agree with Zamor's assessment of the effects of education on enslaved people, speculating that Zamor would

---

[117] Interestingly, Coraline—like Zamor—is literate; she mentions that she read in a book that "to be happy one need only be free and a good Farmer" (2.2). As in several other scenes—as we are about to see—wisdom here is associated with Western education. Interestingly, Gouges sometimes describes herself as having acquired her knowledge not from a formal education but from nature: "I know nothing, Sir: nothing, I tell you, and I have learned nothing from anyone. Student of simple nature, abandoned to her care alone, she thus enlightened me, since you think me completely informed" ("Response to the American Champion," 1994: 122/268; see Bergès 2022: 2). If this is not a mere expression of modesty or a rhetorical tool, it suggests that she does not ultimately view a formal Western education as necessary for acquiring moral knowledge. Bergès argues that according to Gouges we need virtue, rather than education, in order to be fit for liberty. Virtue can be based on natural inclinations rather than education, and these natural inclinations can easily be overpowered by unjust social and political conditions or by the wrong kind of formal education (Bergès 2022: 33, 51).
[118] This also becomes clear when Zamor tells Sophie that it is pointless to try to convince the new overseer to be lenient: "his soul is hardened and does not know kindness. It is his daily task to make his rigor conspicuous" (1.9).

not have killed the overseer if he were uneducated, because he would never have dared to disobey (2.6).

The play also portrays education as the best way to end slavery: Coraline describes a hopeful future in which colonial slave masters free her and her fellow slaves, who will then "instruct themselves, recognize the laws of humanity and justice, and our superiors will find in our attachment, in our zeal, the reward for this kindness" (2.2). Once enlightened, emancipated slaves would not want to become masters themselves, she explains; rather, they would want to continue working for their former masters, and they could jointly become a happy, free society (2.2). This vision might be an expression of Gouges's faith in the power of enlightenment ideas; it is presumably also an attempt to reassure European colonizers that if they end slavery, emancipated slaves would not want to turn the tables or take revenge. Quite to the contrary, she is suggesting that abolishing slavery would be beneficial for planters as well.[119] Being educated makes slavery harder to tolerate, according to her, but it makes free people more likely to obey the law and is a necessary condition for a peaceful and free society.

Natural slavery plays a major role in this text. For instance, toward the beginning of the drama, Mirza asks Zamor, "why do Europeans and Planters have such advantage over us, poor slaves, even though they are made like us? We are men like them! Why, then, such a great difference between their kind and ours?" (1.1; translation altered). Zamor answers: "The difference is very small; it consists only in color. But the advantages that they have over us are huge. Art has placed them above Nature" (1.1; translation altered).[120] His point is clear: White people are not naturally superior to Black people; their advantage is simply that they are more educated and possess more advanced technology. Sophie makes a similar argument when the new overseer, an "Indian," refers to enslaved Black people as a "cursed race" who "would slit

---

[119] In "Reflections on Negroes," she also discusses the effects of emancipation. She starts out with a positive vision in which there would be no need to fear "Deadly conspiracies" and in which Black people "cultivate freely their own land like the farmers in Europe" (1994: 85/231). Yet she also mentions potentially negative effects. For instance, she worries that emancipation would likely "produce a large number of idle, unhappy, and bad persons of all types," and that there might not be enough people willing to work on farms. Nevertheless, she suggests that wise laws might be able to mitigate these negative consequences (1994: 86/231; translation altered).

[120] In "Reflections on Negroes," Gouges elaborates on her point that complexion is the only natural difference and that this difference cannot possibly make White people superior. She asks, "If [Black people] are animals, are we not also like them? How are the Whites different from this race? Is it in the color[?] . . . Why do blonds not claim superiority over brunettes who bear a resemblance to Mulattos? . . . Ottomans exploit Whites in the same way we exploit Blacks" (1994: 85/230; ellipsis in original text).

our throats without pity," adding that "even Slaves who have received some instruction . . . are born to be savages and tamed like animals" (1.9). Sophie replies, "What frightful prejudice! Nature did not make them Slaves; they are men like you" (1.9).[121] Thus, one of the play's main messages appears to be the natural equality of Black and White people and the absurdity of racial natural slavery.

There appears to be another message in the play, however, which makes Gouges far less radical than some of the other authors we have seen so far. This is the message that the common good and public tranquility trump individual rights, which means that violence and lawbreaking are never permissible means for remedying injustices like slavery.[122] Zamor expresses this idea himself. As already mentioned, he accepts his own execution as "necessary for the good of the Colony" even while describing himself as innocent (3.11). In the same speech, he begs the other enslaved people not to defend him and thereby render themselves guilty. His advice to them is "never deliver yourselves into excess to escape slavery; fear breaking your irons with too much violence; time and divine justice are on your side; stand by the Governor and his respectable spouse" (3.11). Thus, Zamor both condemns violent uprisings and expresses optimism that the abolition of slavery is inevitable and perhaps imminent.[123]

The governor, as mentioned earlier, is also willing to have Zamor executed for the good of the colony, even though it pains him greatly and he believes Zamor to be innocent. He stresses the importance of law and order in the final lines of the play. Addressing the enslaved people who are present when he frees Zamor and Mirza, he first expresses his regret that he cannot free all of them. He then gives them the following advice:

if ever your destiny were to change, do not lose sight of the love of the public good, which until now has been unknown to you. Know that man, in his liberty, needs still to submit to wise and humane laws, and without disposing

---

[121] Gouges makes a very similar point in "Reflections on Negroes." She claims that when she was a child, she was told that Black people were "brutes, cursed by Heaven," but later she realized that prejudices were the reason Black people were enslaved, that "Nature plays no role" in slavery, and that colonial slavery is practiced because of the power and interests of White people (1994: 84/229). She also stresses that "People are equal everywhere" (1994: 84/230).

[122] Le Hir discusses this theme in detail (1994: 76–77).

[123] Coraline expresses the same kind of optimism: "I have a presentiment that we shall not always be in irons, and perhaps before long . . ." (2.2; ellipsis in original text). Likewise, Valère explains to Mirza in the first act that "Frenchmen have a horror of slavery. One day, when they are more free, they will see about tempering your fate" (1.7; translation altered).

yourselves to reprehensible excesses, place all your hopes in a benevolent
and enlightened Government. (3.13)

It is quite bizarre to give this kind of advice to enslaved people who have no
immediate prospect of emancipation. Perhaps Gouges chose to end her play
in this way because many White Europeans feared that emancipated slaves
would be unable or unwilling to become law-abiding citizens. The governor's
speech might be intended as a model of what the abolition of slavery should
look like: "enlightened" Europeans teach formerly enslaved people about the
duties of citizenship and the importance of submitting to benevolent rulers.
Gouges may additionally have seen the governor's final speech as a chance to
stress the importance of law and order one last time.

Intriguingly, there are some crucial differences between the 1788 and the
1792 version of the play that are related to the idea of law and order. The
1788 edition has additional characters, including Félicio, who is Valère's and
Sophie's servant and who survives the shipwreck. In the last scene of the first
act—scene 12 in the 1788 edition—Félicio criticizes colonial laws and even
suggests that they are not worth obeying. The context of this criticism is as
follows. Sophie expresses her intention to get Zamor pardoned, and Félicio
responds that there is no hope because "We are in a land of savages and the
most civilized [*policés*] are the most hard-hearted" (1788: 24). Then, the
overseer explains that Zamor's and Mirza's execution is necessary to restore
peace; he expresses puzzlement that "all the citizens demand an example,
but moan at their destiny even though the law requires it" (1788: 25). Félicio
retorts, "What laws! Will men never be able to live in peace? Will we always
have to see them spend their lives tormenting and destroying each other?"
(1788: 25). What he appears to be saying is that when laws are not conducive
to peace but sanction violence, they are not worth obeying.

Félicio and his perspective are entirely absent in the 1792 edition; all skep-
ticism about the validity of colonial laws is removed. In its place, we find new
passages—such as the ones discussed earlier—in which violent uprisings are
explicitly condemned. The most likely reason for this change is that the revolt in Saint-Domingue, or the Haitian Revolution, had begun in 1791, between the two editions, and another slave revolt had occurred in Martinique
in 1789. As mentioned earlier, Gouges was accused of having incited these
revolts through her play. In these circumstances, it makes sense for Gouges
to remove passages that may seem to justify slave revolts and insert others
that explicitly tell enslaved people not to attempt to free themselves through

violent means. Indeed, when she defends herself against these accusations elsewhere, she stresses that she has "tempered [the play's] effect" since its original composition, while also denying that the original version advocated revolts ("Response to an American Champion," 1994: 124/270).

It is not entirely clear whether Gouges made these changes to her play for pragmatic reasons or whether she merely clarified a position that she actually embraced all along—or perhaps had come to embrace after living through parts of the French Revolution and learning about the revolts in the West Indies. In any case, she denounces violent uprisings even more fervently in her preface to the 1792 edition of the play. After expressing a desire for peace and describing herself as "an earwitness of the disastrous accounts of the troubles in America," she argues that her play could not have been a cause of these "troubles" and that her moral maxims are pure (1994: 87/232–33). Many colonists are inhumane wretches. Yet she insists that what she has written actually serves to safeguard the property and interests of these colonists (1994: 88/233). Here again, she portrays colonial slavery as wrong but simultaneously claims that property rights and other laws must be respected, even in an unjust system. She makes this point far more bluntly later in the same text, when addressing enslaved Black people directly:

> perhaps I have incontestable rights to blame your ferocity: cruel ones, you justify tyrants when you imitate them. Most of your Masters were humane and charitable, and in your blind rage you do not distinguish between innocent victims and your persecutors. Mankind was not born for irons, and you prove that they are necessary. . . . You make those moan who wanted to prepare a kinder fate for you by temperate means, a fate more enviable than all those illusory advantages whereby the authors of the calamities in France and America have misled you. (1994: 88/233–34; translation altered)

Here Gouges clearly condemns the recent slave revolts. She not only criticizes enslaved people who use violence to fight for their freedom; she also describes colonial slaveholders as largely benevolent and claims that enslaved people would be better off if they had waited for their compassionate masters to reform colonial laws. Indeed, she even goes so far as to state that the cruelty that enslaved people have exhibited during the revolts proves that they deserve to be kept enslaved. She elaborates on this idea later in the same text: "If the savage, a ferocious man, fails to recognize [the law that all men are brothers], then he is made for irons, to be tamed like a brute." She asks Black people to "recognize these gentle laws and show that an enlightened Nation was not mistaken to treat you like men" (1994: 88–89/234).[124] In short, she argues that if enslaved people do not respect the law—by which she appears to be referring to something like the natural law, or perhaps the principles codified in documents like the Declaration of the Rights of Man and Citizen—they deserve to remain in slavery. This is not quite an endorsement of racial natural slavery because Gouges does not claim that there are racial traits that prevent Black people from recognizing and obeying these laws. Indeed, she expresses the hope that arguments like hers have the power to convince enslaved people to accept these laws. Nevertheless, she blames Black people here for their own enslavement and suggests that it is their responsibility to prove—by acquiescing to their unjust enslavement, paradoxically—that they are worthy of liberty.[125] She requires enslaved people to temporarily accept an unjust institution that brutalizes them and obey cruel masters, patiently waiting for benevolent and enlightened White politicians to reform the system.

Gouges confirms in another text that she intended her play to be exactly the opposite of "a signal for insurrection": if it were performed in America, she expects that it would "bring black men round to their duties while expecting the abolition of the black slave trade and a happier fate from colonists and the French nation" ("Response to the American Champion," 1994 [1790]: 123–24/270). Along similar lines, she explains in her 1790 "The Comedians Unmasked" that if her drama were performed in front of Black audiences, "it would encourage submission; . . . it exudes propriety and obedience to the laws" (1790: 48). Unfortunately, we can only speculate to what extent such statements express Gouges's genuine beliefs and to what extent they are motivated pragmatically.

In the end, whatever the reasons may be, Gouges's antislavery writings are far less radical than they might initially seem. While these texts acknowledge the injustice of transatlantic slavery, they ultimately value public tranquility

---

[124] What she says next is perhaps even worse from a present-day perspective. She tells Black people to remember that their situation in Africa would be even worse: "your Fatherland condemns you to a frightful servitude and your own parents put you up for sale: men are hunted in your frightful climes like animals are hunted elsewhere. The true Philosophy of the enlightened man prompts him to snatch his fellow-man from the midst of a primitively horrible situation where men not only sold one another, but where they still ate each other" (1994: 89/234). Here, she repeats several proslavery talking points: that Africans routinely sell family members and other Africans, that transatlantic slaves would be enslaved in Africa if they had not been purchased by Europeans, and that Africa is a horrendous place filled with cannibals where life is worse than the life of colonial slaves.

[125] Orrù makes a similar point (2020: 114–15).

over individual rights and demand that enslaved people wait patiently and passively for their eventual emancipation.[126] At the same time, these texts are truly remarkable and contain some important radical ideas. For instance, Gouges appears to be more committed to racial equality than most or all of the other authors in this chapter. Her play includes Black characters who are extremely intelligent and virtuous and who are not inferior to any of the White characters in any way. While Gouges does appear to believe in the superiority of European enlightenment culture, she does not essentialize cultural differences in the way that many of her contemporaries do. She firmly denies that White people are naturally superior to Black people, and she does not seem to believe that there are any major obstacles to the establishment of peaceful and prosperous multiracial societies after the abolition of slavery. For these reasons, Gouges is an extremely important voice in French debates about slavery and race.

---

[126] The claim that public tranquility trumps individual rights is a significant parallel between Gouges and Condorcet.

5

Dutch and German Debates about
Slavery and Race

The two final stops on our tour are Germany and the Netherlands. Germany—unlike the other European nations discussed in this book—did not play a major part in the transatlantic slave trade.[1] It was, however, an enormously important player in eighteenth-century scholarly debates about race and in the inception of scientific racism; some German authors also theorized about slavery. In contrast, the Netherlands was an important slave-trading nation and possessed plantation colonies in the Americas, including Surinam, or Dutch Guiana. Surprisingly, there was no significant abolitionist movement in the Netherlands in the eighteenth century, even though there were some debates about slavery.[2] It did not abolish slavery in its colonies until the second half of the nineteenth century.

Each of these two nations deserves a chapter of its own. Sadly, I will only be able to discuss one author from each. First, we will examine the Black Dutch-African philosopher Jacobus Elisa Johannes Capitein, who composed a Latin treatise about slavery in 1742. One aspect of this treatise that is particularly relevant for our purposes is an argument against natural slavery that helpfully derives the moral equality of human beings from their natural similarity via two bridge principles. There are also strong but ultimately inconclusive reasons to think that Capitein embraces a version of biblically sanctioned slavery based on the curse of Ham.

The only other author whom we will discuss in depth is the White German philosopher Immanuel Kant. He is significant in part because he flirts with racial natural slavery in some texts and explicitly endorses paradigmatically racist claims. These claims are part of an influential and systematic theory

---

[1] Germany played a larger role in transatlantic slavery than typically thought; see Raphael-Hernandez and Wiegmink 2017 for an overview. Nevertheless, the other nations in this book were clearly involved far more extensively.

[2] For helpful analyses of the dearth of Dutch abolitionism in this period, see Sens 1995 and Kuitenbrouwer 1995.

Slavery and Race. Julia Jorati, Oxford University Press. © Oxford University Press 2024.
DOI: 10.1093/oso/9780197659236.003.0006

of race. Unlike most other authors in this book, Kant was an important par-ticipant in scientific debates about race. This raises the question of whether he condoned transatlantic slavery. As we will see, the question is difficult to answer because Kant says surprisingly little about transatlantic slavery, and much of what he says is ambiguous. While he theorizes about circumstantial slavery and argues that most forms are illicit, these theoretical discussions do not have direct implications for his views on transatlantic slavery. He appar-ently did not view it as an important issue.

There are many other important eighteenth-century authors who could have been included in this chapter. One particularly relevant White Dutch author is Willem Bosman (born 1672), a merchant who worked for the Dutch West India Company. He published the enormously influ-ential book *Accurate Description of Guinea's Gold, Ivory, and Slave Coast* (*Nauwkeurige beschryving van de Guinese Goud- Tand- en Slave-kust*) in 1704, which appeared in an English translation a year later. In this book, Bosman describes Guinea and its inhabitants in great detail. Even though his account is in part fictional, many later authors rely on it. With respect to the transatlantic slave trade, he mostly describes its workings in de-tached, matter-of-fact ways, acknowledging its brutality only in passing and claiming that it cannot be stopped. For instance, after describing the ways in which European traders purchase and brand enslaved Black people in Guinea, he notes, "I doubt not but this trade seems very barbarous to you, but since it is followed by mere necessity it must go on; but we yet take all possible care that they are not burned too hard [when branded], espe-cially the women" (letter 19, 1705: 364–65; spelling modernized). Bosman also summarizes what he claims to be a common African theory about the origins of racial differences. According to this theory, God created Black and White people separately and allowed them to choose among two gifts: gold or the knowledge of reading and writing. Black people chose gold, whereas Whites chose knowledge, and to punish Black people for their avarice, God "resolved that the Whites should for ever be their Masters, and they obliged to wait on them as their Slaves" (letter 10, 1705: 146–47). Thus, Bosman claims that some Africans view the transatlantic slave trade as sanctioned by God.

Another White Dutch author whom I would have liked to include is Elisabeth Maria Post (1755–1812), who published an epistolary novel titled *Reinhart, or Nature and Religion* (*Reinhart, of natuur en godsdienst*) in 1791–92. This novel is one of very few Dutch texts from this period that criticize transatlantic slavery explicitly and incisively. Unfortunately, this text appears to be available only in Dutch, which I cannot read.[3]

One noteworthy German author whom I will not be able to discuss in detail is Anton Wilhelm Amo (c. 1703–c. 1759), a Black Nzema man who was born in what is today Ghana. He was brought to Germany as a young boy in about 1707 to be raised at the court of Anton Ulrich, the duke of Brunswick-Wolfenbüttel. He later studied law in Halle and received a doctorate in philosophy from the University of Wittenberg, after which he taught philosophy in Halle and Jena. Today, he is known mainly for his important contributions to the philosophy of mind and philosophical methodology. What is most relevant for our purposes, however, is his disputation "On the Right of the Moors in Europe" (*De jure maurorum in Europa*), which he defended in 1729.[4] According to a short summary that was published in the newspaper *Hallische Nachrichten*, Amo's disputation "investigated how far the freedom or servitude of Moors purchased by Christians extends in Europe according to the commonly accepted laws" (Ludewig 1729: 273, trans. Jeffers 2017: 132). Unfortunately, the short summary contains only a few hints of what exactly Amo argued with respect to the rights of enslaved "Moors," and no copies of the disputation appear to have survived.[5] Amo does not discuss slavery in the texts that are available to us.

Another German author who is relevant to my project is Johann Gottlieb Heineccius (1681–1741). He was an influential natural law theorist who stresses the natural liberty and equality of all human beings but also adopts something akin to natural slavery (*Universal Law* 2.4.47, [1738] 2008: 384–85). In addition, several German authors are important for the history of race and racism, some of whom also comment on transatlantic slavery. These authors include Johann Gottfried Herder (1744–1803), Christoph Meiners (1747–1810), Johann Friedrich Blumenbach (1752–1840), Johann Georg Adam Forster (1754–1794), and Samuel Thomas Sömmerring (1755–1830).[6] Finally, it is worth noting that Gottfried Wilhelm Leibniz (1646–1716) is

---

[3] For a brief summary of the novel's plot, see Blakely 1993: 173. Blakely also discusses several other Dutch authors who are relevant to my project. For additional information on Dutch literature about slavery and colonialism, see Hermans 2009: 325–30.

[4] The term 'Moor' and its German equivalent *Mohr* can be difficult to interpret; it sometimes appears to refer to all Africans and sometimes only to North Africans. Some authors refer to North Africans as 'Tawny Moors' and to sub-Saharan Africans as 'Black Moors' or 'Blackamoors' (Lewis 2019: 27). Amo was often described as a "baptized Moor" (e.g., Ludewig 1729: 271).

[5] For helpful discussions, see Lewis 2019: 29–33; Jeffers 2017: 131–34; Abraham 1996: 430–31; Smith 2015: 210–11.

[6] For more on these figures and other important German authors, see Eigen and Larrimore 2006.

highly relevant for my project. He wrote about slavery and race in several texts, including some texts from the early eighteenth century. Yet, because many of the relevant texts are from the seventeenth century, I chose to include him only in my book about slavery and race in the sixteenth and seventeenth centuries (Jorati, forthcoming; see also Jorati 2019).

5.1. Jacobus Elisa Johannes Capitein

In 1742, Jacobus Elisa Johannes Capitein (1717–1747), whose birth name is unfortunately unknown,[7] published a Latin treatise on slavery, which he had originally delivered as a lecture at the University of Leiden. The title of this treatise is *Political-Theological Dissertation about Slavery, Not Contrary to Christian Freedom* (*Dissertatio politico-theologica de servitute, libertati Christianae non contraria*).[8] This work is informed by firsthand knowledge of slavery. Capitein was born near the Guinea coast, in what is today central Ghana, and he was sold into slavery at the age of seven or eight after becoming an orphan. Three years later, his owner took him to the Netherlands, which made him legally free, though he was still dependent on his former master. In the Netherlands he received a classical education, was baptized, studied theology at the University of Leiden, and was ordained by the Dutch Reformed Church in order to return to West Africa as a chaplain.[9] Thus, Capitein possessed much deeper and more intimate knowledge of what is at stake in debates about slavery than White, European-born authors.[10]

Capitein's *Dissertation* was enormously popular—it was almost immediately translated into Dutch and went through many editions. It engages with

---

[7] Some sources from the nineteenth century apparently claim that his birth name was 'Asar,' but it is unclear whether that is true (Parker 2001: 10).

[8] The chapters of this work are divided into short numbered sections in the original edition (Capitein 1742) and in Grant Parker's English translation (Capitein 2001), so I will cite this text as *Dissertation*, followed by chapter and section numbers. The only exception is the work's preface, which is not divided into sections and which I will cite by page numbers. All translations are from Capitein 2001, unless otherwise noted. Incidentally Parker, in his English translation, provides a slightly different title for this work: *Political-Theological Dissertation Examining the Question: Is Slavery Compatible with Christian Freedom or Not?* (*Dissertatio politico-theologica, qua disquiritur, Num libertati Christianae servitus adversetur, ut ne?*). In the original Latin edition, this title is printed immediately preceding the first chapter heading (Capitein 1742: 17), but the title page of the book features the other version of the title, that is, the one that does not have the form of a question.

[9] For more information about Capitein's life, see Capitein, *Dissertation*, preface; Levecq 2019: 19–74; Parker 2001: 7–11; Prah 1992: 37–54.

[10] As David Kpobi points out, however, Capitein had not experienced the treatment of enslaved people in colonial plantations (2002: 86).

a broad range of philosophers, including Grotius, Selden, Thomasius, More, Seneca, Augustine, and Bodin. Sadly, this text has scarcely received attention from historians of philosophy. Part of this neglect is likely due to the rather unpalatable main thesis of the work: as the title suggests, Capitein argues that slavery is perfectly compatible with Christianity.[11] More precisely, he aims to show (a) that it is permissible for Christians to own slaves and (b) that Christians are not required to free enslaved people who have converted to Christianity (see *Dissertation* 1.2). Another reason for the neglect might be the impression that Capitein is not a very original thinker and that his arguments are more theological than philosophical. Yet, as we will see, that impression is unwarranted.

What makes Capitein's *Dissertation* important for our purposes is that in addition to arguing for the compatibility of slavery and Christianity, it contains a brief but intriguing argument against natural slavery. This argument will be our main focus.[12] It is based on the doctrine that all human beings are equal and free, but it is interestingly different from other natural-law-based arguments.

Before turning to Capitein's argument against natural slavery, it will be helpful to take a quick look at his conception of slavery. This will reveal that, despite some indications to the contrary, he is very much concerned with the contemporaneous transatlantic slave trade in his work, and he is discussing chattel slavery rather than something broader. Next, we will examine his argument against natural slavery. One thing that makes this argument unique is that it employs two highly plausible bridge principles in order to derive the moral wrongness of natural slavery from the descriptive claim that human beings are naturally similar. This way of arguing against natural slavery has advantages over extant arguments, and it is, to the best of my knowledge, original to Capitein. In addition to reconstructing and evaluating this argument, I will briefly explore a series of questions about its relation to the rest of the *Dissertation*: How significant is it that Capitein includes this argument in the first place? Can we infer anything from its inclusion about Capitein's overall attitude toward slavery? Might this argument make Capitein's work

[11] Some scholars describe this work as a defense of slavery (e.g., Parker 2001: 3–4; Levecq 2013: 151, 154; Amponsah 2013: 432; Prah 1992: 62), but others argue that this is not entirely accurate since one can argue for the compatibility of two entities without defending either one (Menn and Smith 2020: 12).
[12] The few interpreters who discuss Capitein's *Dissertation* do not say much about this argument. Levecq, for instance, mentions it only in passing and then says that the relevant chapter "sounds more like social and political science than like theology or philosophy" (2013: 153; 2019: 47).

more subversive than it initially appears? These questions are difficult to answer, but nevertheless instructive to investigate. Finally, I will examine two passages from Capitein's *Dissertation* that suggest that he might endorse a version of the doctrine of natural slavery or a version of biblically sanctioned slavery.

5.1.1. Capitein's Conception of Slavery

When Capitein discusses slavery, what exactly does he have in mind? At least on the surface, his argument against natural slavery is framed as a theoretical and historical issue, not tied to specific modern instances. He argues against it to make the case that slavery originated from human laws and historical accident, rather than from nature. The argument seems to target ancient proponents of natural slavery rather than those who use this idea in the early modern period to defend the enslavement of Africans. One can get the same impression with respect to the main argument of the book, namely, the argument that Christian liberty is compatible with slavery. Capitein frames this argument almost exclusively as a theoretical or theological problem rather than as an issue that arises in the context of early modern slavery.

Yet there are strong reasons—both textual and contextual—for thinking that Capitein's main concern in the *Dissertation* is enslaved Black people who owned and traded by early modern Europeans. One relevant piece of contextual evidence is that Capitein composed the *Dissertation* as part of a university education whose express purpose it was to allow him to return to Guinea as a chaplain and missionary. More specifically, he would return to Elmina—a major hub of the slave trade that was under Dutch control at the time—as an employee of the Dutch West India Company. There was also an ongoing debate, to which Capitein refers repeatedly throughout his book, about whether transatlantic slaves who convert to Christianity must be freed. Putting these two pieces together, it is clear that for someone training to be a Christian missionary in Elmina in the mid-eighteenth century, the question of whether Christianity and slavery are compatible is tied intimately to questions about the status of converted transatlantic slaves. Indeed, it is exceedingly likely that this is the reason Capitein chose to, or was asked to, write about the question in the first place. The connection is even clear on the title page of Capitein's *Dissertation*, in both the Latin and the Dutch editions: it features a picture of Elmina Castle with a Dutch ship in the background as well as imagery symbolizing salvation: a sun and an angel holding a scroll with the Greek word meaning 'gospel.'[13]

There is also textual evidence to support this hypothesis. One potentially relevant passage occurs in chapter 2, during Capitein's examination of the historical origins of slavery: he sides with those who trace slavery back to Ham, one of Noah's sons in the Old Testament who is cursed to slavery (*Dissertation* 2.3). As Capitein is surely aware—though he does not mention it—this biblical story is often used in the early modern period to justify the enslavement of Africans, who are portrayed as the descendants of Ham and therefore intended by God to be slaves. Even more directly relevant is the fact that Capitein motivates the book's project toward the end of his Preface by pointing out that "some Christians fear that through evangelical freedom slavery will disappear entirely from those colonies which Christians own, to the great detriment of the overseers of those colonies" (1742: xvi / 2001: 93). He then announces his intention of allaying these fears in his *Dissertation*—a task that he claims his "own present situation demands" (1742: xvi / 2001: 93). Likewise, he starts chapter 3—which contains the main arguments for his thesis—by lamenting the fact that most of his contemporaries in the Netherlands "wish to persuade themselves and others . . . that Christian freedom can in no way walk in step with slavery in the proper sense" (*Dissertation* 3.1). He draws the connection between the thesis of his *Dissertation* and missionary work in European colonies even more explicitly in the final section of the book, which constitutes its conclusion: he states that his argument for the compatibility of Christianity and slavery shows "that slavery does not impede the spread of the Gospel in those Christian colonies where it prevails right up to the present day" (*Dissertation* 3.27). In the two last sentences of the work, Capitein mentions the contemporaneous Dutch theologian Henrik Velse,[14] an early advocate of Capitein's missionary education, who examines whether in European colonies "the teachings of the Gospel . . . can be handed down to slaves without ill effect" (*Dissertation* 3.27). Thus, despite Capitein's extensive references to ancient slavery, he is clearly conceiving of the arguments in the *Dissertation* in the context of his own future missionary work in Elmina and hence in the context of transatlantic slavery.

---

[13] This image is by B. F. Immink. For more on the meaning of this image, see Emmer and Gommans 2020: 124.

[14] For more information about Velse, see Parker 2001: 8, 63–64.

Let us now take a brief look at the definition of slavery that Capitein provides in the first chapter, which also indicates what type of slavery he is discussing. He defines slavery as "a status in which someone is unwillingly [*invitus*] subjected to the authority [*dominium*] of another" (*Dissertation* 1.1). He indicates in the subsequent paragraph that the kind of subjection he is referring to is chattel slavery, or the "possess[ion of] other human beings in the manner of personal goods" (*Dissertation* 1.2). As Capitein points out himself, his definition of slavery excludes those who enter servitude through a voluntary agreement. He contends that the latter should not be called 'slaves' but merely 'attendants' or 'servants' (*Dissertation* 1.1).[15] This is an unusual definition. Even though Capitein describes his definition as being that of the jurists, many prominent early modern jurists define 'slave' in a way that includes those who enter servitude voluntarily.[16] Capitein's definition is closest to that of Thomas Hobbes, who insists on reserving the term 'slave' for individuals who have not made any voluntary agreements with their masters or captors (*Leviathan* 20.10–12, 1994: 130–31).[17] It is not entirely clear why Capitein chooses to define slavery in this way.[18] Perhaps he holds that one cannot voluntarily subject oneself to the absolute rule of another—though it would be unusual to build that into the definition.[19] Alternatively, this might be further evidence that Capitein primarily has transatlantic slaves in mind, who are enslaved involuntarily.

5.1.2. Capitein's Argument against Natural Slavery

Armed with a better understanding of Capitein's conception of slavery, we can now turn to his argument against natural slavery. In the relevant

---

[15] Here, 'slave' translates the Latin terms *servus* and *mancipium*, whereas 'attendant' and 'servant' translate *famulus* and *minister*. This passage is evidence against Menn and Smith's claim that Capitein's arguments "were primarily oriented by a conception of slavery that did not distinguish it from the forms of servitude familiar from antiquity and surviving still in parts of Europe" (2020: 12).

[16] Two prominent Dutch jurists in the seventeenth century are a case in point: Hugo Grotius explicitly includes those who enter slavery voluntarily in his definition of slavery (*Rights of War* 2.5.27, 2005: 556–57) and so does Ulrik Huber (*De jure civitatis* 2.4.6–22, 1684: 372–74).

[17] Yet Capitein does not follow Hobbes in claiming that as soon as enslaved people are no longer imprisoned or chained, they should be viewed as having made a voluntary agreement with the master and have hence become servants.

[18] He quotes Seneca as support for his definition (*Dissertation* 1.1), but that does not answer the question of why he departs from the common early modern definition.

[19] Another early modern author who defines slavery in a way that excludes voluntary or contractual bondage is James Beattie, as we saw in chapter 2 (*Elements of Moral Science* §601, 1793: 153–54), but that is long after Capitein's *Dissertation*.

chapter, he paraphrases Aristotle's doctrine—which he calls "thorny"—as follows: "Aristotle . . . judges that in the natural state the difference among people must be recognized, that while one person is free by nature, another may be born a slave" (*Dissertation* 2.1). Thus, he interprets Aristotle as claiming that in the state of nature some individuals are free and others are slaves.[20] As we will see momentarily, Capitein argues against this doctrine by using ideas from the natural law tradition. Interestingly, he also portrays this doctrine as ridiculous and arrogant: Aristotle's argument "plainly exhibits either humor in a serious context or the arrogance of the Peripatetic school in matters such as this" (*Dissertation* 2.1). In the subsequent section of the chapter, he then points out that other pagan authors in antiquity rejected Aristotle's doctrine; they instead viewed slavery as established by the law of nations and as contrary to the law of nature (*Dissertation* 2.2). He concludes that clearly it was "not nature but human law and accident which have made humans into slaves" (*Dissertation* 2.2).

As already mentioned, Capitein then sides with the theological doctrine that slavery originated soon after Noah's flood, when Ham was condemned to slavery (*Dissertation* 2.3). It is somewhat paradoxical that Capitein uses the curse of Ham to counter Aristotelian natural slavery, since the curse of Ham is often used as a theological justification for something very much like natural slavery. David Amponsah proposes one way to resolve this paradox: perhaps Capitein presents the myth of Ham as showing not that Africans are naturally inferior and destined for slavery, but merely that they were inferior initially, and that this inferiority can be cured by conversion to Christianity (2013: 436). This interpretation is intriguing but speculative, since Capitein does not make this point explicitly. I will suggest another way to resolve this paradox toward the end of my discussion of Capitein.

Capitein's philosophical argument against Aristotelian natural slavery is extremely short. He starts out by agreeing with the "most learned people [who] propose that, without a shadow of doubt, every human being is under his own authority [*sui juris*][21] according to natural law, and that the common condition of early humankind permitted equal freedom to all humans" (*Dissertation* 2.1). Thus, he aligns himself with the natural law tradition that

---

[20] Aristotle does not describe his doctrine in terms of a state of nature in the early modern sense, but he does talk of some individuals as marked out for slavery from birth (*Politics* i.5, 1984: 1990). Thus, this paraphrase seems so capture Aristotle's views quite well.

[21] The term *sui juris* is a legal term that is in use to this day. It describes those who are not under someone else's power—as a child or a slave is—but instead have the full rights of a free person.

views all human beings as naturally equal and free, and thus as naturally their own masters. It is interesting that he does not rest content with an appeal to the authority of the "most learned people." Rather, he goes on to provide an argument for the equal rights of human beings. This argument is very brief. It consists simply of the claim that "we are all similar by origin" and the following legal maxims: "There is similar reasoning for similar things and the same reasoning for the same things, and where there is the same reasoning, there is the same law or right [*jus*]" (*Dissertation* 2.1; translation altered).[22] The basic idea, then, is that because human beings are originally similar, they have the same natural rights. After all, viewing individuals who are naturally similar as having different natural rights would violate the principle that it is wrong to apply different legal or moral standards to similar cases. It would be arbitrary or unreasonable, and hence contrary to natural law, to view individuals who are naturally so similar as nevertheless having vastly different natural rights.

One important question about this argument is what Capitein means by saying that "we are all similar by origin" (*omnes origine simus similes*). One possibility is that he is referring to monogenesis, that is, the theory that all human beings have common ancestors or the same origin. But there is another possibility: he could be referring to the doctrine that in the state of nature, human beings are very similar in their capacities. This reading strikes me as more plausible because of the way Capitein talks in the remainder of this short paragraph: as already seen, he mentions "the common condition of early [*primaevum*] humankind" just before the argument. And directly after the argument, as we have also seen, he notes that Aristotle views human beings as different "in the natural state" and claims that some are "free by nature" while others are born slaves. Thus, it seems most likely that "similar by origin" simply refers to a similarity in the state of nature, conceived as either a real or a hypothetical original condition of humankind, prior to human institutions.

If that is correct, we can reconstruct Capitein's argument as follows:

---

[22] These maxims appear in many texts by other authors, sometimes in slightly altered versions, but it seems likely that Capitein is taking them from a work by Johan van den Honert, who was the chair of Capitein's dissertation committee. Honert uses these maxims in one of his books, in a very different context, but in precisely the same wording and even with exactly the same (and somewhat unusual) punctuation: *Nam similium similis, & eorundem eadem est ratio: & ubi eadem est ratio, idem est jus* (Honert, *Dissertationes Apocalypticae*, 1736: 40). Identical wording and punctuation also occur in a disputation by one of Honert's earlier students, Johann Wilhelm Kals (*Disputatio theologica de natura theologiae typicae*, 1728: 23). I was unable to find this exact wording anywhere else. These maxims are italicized in Capitein's work, which suggests that they are meant to be quotations.

1. All human beings are similar in the state of nature.
2. It is wrong not to apply similar reasoning to similar things.
3. Thus, it is wrong not to apply similar reasoning to all human beings in the state of nature (from 1, 2).
4. If it is wrong not to apply similar reasoning to something, it is wrong not to apply similar laws and rights to it.
5. Thus, it is wrong not to apply similar laws and rights to all human beings in the state of nature (from 3, 4).
6. The doctrine of natural slavery does not apply similar laws and rights to all human beings in the state of nature.
7. Therefore, the doctrine of natural slavery is wrong (from 5, 6).

This argument is quite persuasive. Premises 2 and 4 are plausible principles about when it makes sense to apply different reasonings and different laws—in the broad sense of 'law' (*jus*), which includes moral rights and obligations. Indeed, they can be interpreted as correlates of the Principle of Sufficient Reason. Premise 6 is difficult to deny, since the doctrine of natural slavery ascribes to some human beings the natural right to enslave others and states that only some human beings are naturally entitled to freedom. Thus, proponents of natural slavery are most likely to reject the first premise.

There are at least two ways to interpret the first premise of this argument, that is, the claim that all human beings are naturally similar. One possibility is that this premise is meant as a metaphysically necessary truth, perhaps based on the idea that all individuals with a human nature are necessarily similar to a significant extent, or in the relevant ways. Another possibility is that the natural similarity of human beings is intended to be a contingent empirical fact.[23] Either interpretation could work, and I do not see strong reasons to prefer one over the other. On either interpretation, the argument uses highly plausible bridge principles—namely, premises 2 and 4—to derive the normative claim about equal natural rights from the descriptive claim about natural similarity. Thus, this argument helpfully spells out why exactly it is problematic to acknowledge the natural similarity of all humans while denying that all humans have the same natural rights: one would need to reject the bridge principles.

Of course, Aristotle and his followers insist that there are significant differences in the natural abilities of human beings. Hence, the argument

---

[23] This seems to have been Hobbes's view, as I argue in Jorati, forthcoming.

would need to be supplemented with evidence for the first premise. If this natural similarity is a metaphysical necessity, such evidence would presumably consist in a philosophical analysis of human nature combined with reasons that the similarity that all human beings possess qua human beings is sufficient to make this argument go through. If, in contrast, the natural similarity is supposed to be a contingent fact, then the relevant supplementary evidence would consist either in empirical data about the natural similarity of human beings, or in theological reasons to hold that all humans were created equal in the relevant sense. Unfortunately, Capitein does not tell us how he would argue for the first premise.

One important question about Capitein's argument against natural slavery is whether its content, or the fact that he includes it in the first place, makes the *Dissertation* more subversive than it might otherwise appear. In other words, one might wonder—as Parker does (2001: 76)—whether Capitein's rejection of natural slavery tempers his argument that slavery is compatible with Christianity. Given the context in which Capitein composed this text,[24] it is after all plausible that he felt pressure to argue for the compatibility of slavery and Christianity.[25] Thus, one might wonder whether his choice to include the argument against natural slavery in the beginning might be his way of signaling his disapproval of the way in which his White contemporaries were practicing and justifying slavery. One reason to be suspicious of this interpretation is that it was not unusual in this period to reject natural slavery while embracing other justifications for enslavement, as we have already seen. When viewed from that perspective, there is nothing surprising or subversive about the argument against natural slavery. Likewise, the fact that Capitein chose to include the discussion of natural slavery is not particularly surprising either, since it is common in early modern discussions of slavery to start with speculations about the historical origins of slavery and an examination of the relation between slavery and natural law. On the other hand, Capitein is writing at a time when many Europeans view Africans as natural slaves and hold that this is one of the main justifications for transatlantic slavery. Thus, Capitein could have intended to subtly challenge the ways in

---

[24] Part of the relevant context is that Capitein's patrons, some of whom were involved in the slave trade, supported his university education specifically so that he could later go to West Africa as a missionary. This is relevant because if conversion to Christianity is compatible with slave status, missionary endeavors—like the one in which Capitein was about to engage—are much more likely to find support among those who benefited from the slave trade.

[25] See, for example, Kpobi 2002: 84; Amponsah 2013: 441–42.

which slavery was currently practiced by undermining this particular justification. Unfortunately, we can only speculate about this.

5.1.3. Potential Complications regarding Capitein's Opposition to Natural Slavery

Before concluding our discussion of Capitein, it is worth examining two last passages from the *Dissertation* that might be relevant for determining his views about natural slavery. One passage is from chapter 3, in which Capitein argues for the compatibility of Christian freedom and slavery. His main strategy consists in distinguishing between spiritual and physical freedom. Since enslaved people lack only physical freedom, slavery is compatible with Christian liberty, which is spiritual. What is relevant for present purposes is that toward the end of this chapter (*Dissertation* 3.26), he quotes—approvingly, it seems—a text that endorses a version of natural slavery. This text is the popular sixteenth-century work *Turkish Letters* by White Flemish writer Ogier Ghiselin de Busbecq. In the quoted passage, which is from the third letter, Busbecq argues that slavery is beneficial for society because some individuals are not capable of living freely. The passage starts by extolling the benefits of a public slavery that is administered "justly, leniently and according to the precepts of Roman law" (Busbecq 1771: 147; trans. Capitein 2001: 130). This form of slavery, Busbecq claims, would prevent crimes of poverty and make the death penalty superfluous. He then shifts from talking about crime and poverty to talking about differences in natural human abilities:

> Not everybody's nature [*ingenium*] can endure resourceless freedom and not everyone is born so that they can govern [*regere*] themselves and know how to use their own judgment [*arbitrio*] properly. They need the leadership and rule of superiors, like a prop; in no other way will they put an end to their wrongdoing. They are like certain animals whose fierceness is always to be feared unless constrained by chains. Indeed the weaker mind is ruled by a master's authority and the master lives by the slave's work. (Busbecq 1771: 147–48)[26]

---

[26] My translation is based on Parker's translation of Capitein's *Dissertation* 3.26, that is, 2001: 130. For a helpful but somewhat loose nineteenth-century English translation of this passage and its context, see Busbecq 1881: 210.

Here Busbecq clearly embraces a version of the doctrine of natural slavery: he describes some people as naturally unable to govern themselves and as fit only for slavery. He even compares them to wild animals and ascribes specific cognitive deficits to them.

Capitein cites another text in support of the claim that slavery can be beneficial, immediately after quoting the passage from Busbecq: the "Prolegomena" of White German jurist Joachim Potgiesser's 1736 work *Commentaries on German Law Regarding the Status of Slaves* (*Commentariorum iuris germanici de statu servorum*).[27] Instead of quoting from Potgiesser verbatim, Capitein paraphrases his views as follows. Without the institution of slavery,

> there would be a massing of dishonest and lazy people who would wander around and consume the food of their fellow-citizens and others, thereby weakening them, an evil that would come about unless slavery continues to proliferate on a large scale among all Christians. (*Dissertation* 3.26)[28]

Potgiesser makes this point almost immediately after quoting from Busbecq—in fact, he quotes the same passage that Capitein includes in his own work, with three additional sentences at the beginning. What Potgiesser is saying in this passage is not quite an endorsement of Aristotelian natural slavery—indeed, he argues against that doctrine earlier in the same text.[29] Yet Potgiesser appears to agree with Busbecq that it is beneficial and permissible to enslave those who are unfit for freedom and hence a burden on society.[30] Thus, he appears to be endorsing a version of natural slavery, though not Aristotle's version.

What should we make of the fact that Capitein cites these texts without explicitly disavowing their apparent endorsement of natural slavery? Is this evidence that Capitein accepts a version of natural slavery himself? One thing to note is that he cites these texts not in the context of discussing natural slavery but rather to make the point that slavery is compatible with Christian freedom. The immediate context is Capitein's response to the question of why, if Christianity and slavery are compatible, so many Christian countries have

---

[27] This work is an expanded version of Potgiesser's 1707 book *De conditione et statu servorum apud Germanos.* The "Prolegomena" that Capitein cites are not included in the 1707 book.

[28] This is a rough summary of what Potgiesser says in "Prolegomena" §35, 1736: 41–42.

[29] See "Prolegomena" §7, 1736: 8–9; see also *De conditione et statu servorum apud Germanos* 1.1.2, 1707: 2.

[30] As we saw in chapter 2, Francis Hutcheson defended a similar justification for slavery (*System* 3.3.1, 1755: 202).

stopped practicing slavery. Capitein's initial replies are that many of those countries still practice some forms of slavery, and that the reasons for banning other forms of slavery are political rather than theological (*Dissertation* 3.24–25). In the section in which he cites Busbecq and Potgiesser, he adds a further reply, namely, that there are "learned and meritorious persons" who argue for reintroducing slavery in Christian nations because of its benefits (*Dissertation* 3.26). His two examples of such learned people are Busbecq and Potgiesser. Given this context, there are no compelling reasons to think that Capitein endorses these authors' claims about natural slavery. The purpose of mentioning them is merely to show that some learned people think that it would be beneficial to reintroduce slavery in Christian countries, and hence that Christianity and slavery are compatible. Indeed, Capitein states explicitly in the subsequent section that he "by no means" agrees with everything that these learned authors say, but that the discussion has shown that slavery does not contradict Christian liberty (*Dissertation* 3.27). Thus, he signals disagreement with some unspecified aspect of these authors' views and merely commits to agreeing with them about the compatibility of Christianity and slavery. Given his argument against natural slavery in the previous chapter, it makes sense to interpret this claim as a sign that he disagrees with the authors' endorsement of natural slavery.

Another passage that complicates Capitein's opposition to natural slavery occurs in the Preface, in which he briefly summarizes his earlier treatise *On the Calling of the Heathen* (*De vocatione ethnicorum*). This treatise, which he composed around 1738, is unfortunately lost. In the Preface of the *Dissertation*, Capitein notes that the first chapter of this lost treatise was devoted to the thesis that "The promises made concerning Japheth and Ham are found [*inveniri*] in the calling [*Vocatione*] of their descendants, according to God's true word" (Preface, 1742: vii / 2001: 81; translation altered). He does not explain what exactly he means by this, but it is plausible that the calling to which he is referring is slavery and mastery. After all, the relevant biblical promises include the promise that Ham's descendants— or some of them—will be the slaves of Japheth and Shem. As already seen, Capitein sides with those who believe that the curse of Ham is the origin of slavery. Moreover, as Capitein was surely aware, it was widely believed that modern Europeans are descendants of Japheth and modern Africans of Ham. On a straightforward reading, this suggests that Capitein accepts a theological justification for racial slavery: in God's providential order, some people—namely Africans, the descendants of Ham—are destined for slavery, while others—namely Europeans, the descendants of Japheth—are destined for mastery.[31] Accepting this justification is compatible with rejecting natural slavery, since the latter doctrine justifies slavery in terms of inferior capacities, while the former justifies it through divine intentions and divine punishments for sins. If that is indeed Capitein's view, it would be very interesting—he would be rejecting racist justifications for the enslavement of Africans that invoke alleged differences in natural capacities while embracing the theory that Africans are destined by God to be the slaves of Europeans. That, in turn, might suggest that he is not generally opposed to transatlantic slavery. Unfortunately, because *On the Calling of the Heathen* is lost, it is not entirely clear that this is the correct interpretation.

5.1.4. Concluding Thoughts on Capitein

Based on what we have seen in this section, it should be clear that Capitein's argument against natural slavery deserves the close attention of historians of philosophy. It is different from other early modern arguments since it uses bridge principles that do not occur in anyone else's argument, to the best of my knowledge. Instead of merely stating that there cannot be natural slaves because all human beings are naturally equal—as other authors do—Capitein uses his bridge principles to derive the equality of natural rights from the descriptive claim that all humans are naturally similar. This is a promising philosophical move, and it may even constitute a veiled criticism of transatlantic slavery. After all, as I have shown, it is clear that transatlantic slavery is very much on Capitein's mind in this work.

5.2. Immanuel Kant

Our last author is the White German philosopher Immanuel Kant (1727–1804). He is important for several reasons. First, he is among the most influential moral philosophers of this period, which gives his views on race and slavery enormous historical significance. Second, Kant's ethics appears to

---

[31] Parker interprets this passage differently. According to him, Capitein invokes this curse merely "as a way of underlining the need for the conversion of (African) non-Christians" and in order to stress that "the New Covenant of Christianity promises deliverance to all people, even to those under the curse" (2001: 38). Yet my reading strikes me as far more straightforward.

provide excellent resources for arguing against slavery and European colonialism. These resources include the duty to respect the dignity and freedom of all human beings and, as Kant puts it in the second formulation of his categorical imperative, the obligation never to use other human beings "merely as a means," but "always at the same time as an end" (*Groundwork* Ak 4: 429 / 1996: 80).[32] Chattel slavery seems to be among the clearest instances of using someone merely as a means—after all, many definitions of slavery categorize enslaved people as mere tools for advancing the master's ends.[33] As a result, Kantian ethics seems to have great potential for the abolitionist and anticolonial cause. It is hence worth examining whether Kant himself used his principles in this way, and if he does not, why not. Another reason for Kant's importance is that he wrote about race extensively and systematically, unlike most other early modern authors who currently count as canonical. Indeed, Kant has a central place in the history of race and racism; some scholars go so far as to call him "the inventor of race" (Bernasconi 2001; Larrimore 2008: 341). Regardless of whether he invented the modern concept of race, he is clearly of immense importance for our understanding of racism and its legacy. Kant also theorizes about slavery in several texts— though less extensively than about race—and argues against some forms of human bondage while embracing others.

There are, furthermore, important questions about whether—and if so, how—Kant's discussions of race, his arguments concerning the permissibility of slavery, and his normative ethics fit together. His moral principles are phrased in universalist ways: it seems that they are supposed to apply to all human beings. Yet Kant's discussion of race and slavery—like his discussion of gender—suggests that he does not view his moral principles as applying to all human beings equally. In some of his writings, he expresses deeply racist views. This raises the question, which Kant scholars have discussed at great length, of whether Kant is simply inconsistent, or whether his moral principles are not meant to be truly universalist—that is, are not meant to apply to all racial groups. As Pauline Kleingeld put it in an influential paper, the question is whether we should read Kant as an "inconsistent universalist" whose

---

[32] I will typically cite Kant's works using the volume and page numbers of the Akademie edition (Kant 1902–), preceded by the abbreviation "Ak." Whenever an English translation is available, I will cite that as well. For works that are not included in the Akademie edition, I will cite other editions in the original language and English translations, where available.

[33] As we will see later, Kant himself endorses a similar definition (Ak 6: 330 / 1996: 471). For a careful explication of Kant's prohibition of using others merely as a means and its applicability to slavery, see Kleingeld 2020, especially 2020: 406.

racist views contradict the universalist moral principles he endorses, or as a
"consistent inegalitarian" whose moral principles exclude nonwhite people
and are therefore consistent with racist views (2007: 576). Some—including
Kleingeld herself—argue that Kant started out as an inconsistent universalist
but later abandoned his racist views and became a consistent universalist
(Kleingeld 2007).[34] Others—most prominently Charles Mills—argue that
we should read Kant as a consistent inegalitarian whose moral principles are
not meant to apply to all racial groups (Mills 2005; 2014). Huaping Lu-Adler
argues for an intriguing third option: Kant might have been a consistent universalist throughout his career because his moral principles might apply universally to human beings *in abstracto*, but not *in concreto*. Being a universalist
in the abstract sense is compatible with holding racist views about concrete
groups of human beings (Lu-Adler 2022b: 272–73; 2023: 43–54).

Kant's views about race have received a great amount of attention from
many excellent scholars in recent years.[35] His attitude toward slavery has received far less attention. Scholars writing on Kant's theory of race often mention his claims about slavery in order to draw conclusions about his views
on race, but very few scholars have made Kant's views on slavery their main
focus.[36] Indeed, scholars often appear to misunderstand Kant's comments on
slavery, assuming for instance that Kant is discussing transatlantic slavery in
passages that only discuss bondage within Europe. Because there is already
such a wealth of literature about Kant's theory of race, I will concentrate
mainly on what Kant says about slavery. I will discuss his views on race rel-
atively quickly, focusing on the aspects that are particularly relevant for determining his attitude toward slavery. Because of the enormous complexity
of the relevant texts, I will not attempt to solve all the important interpretive
issues here. My goal is mainly to present these issues and discuss some of the
most relevant evidence for various interpretations. I do hope to show, however, that Kant's views on transatlantic slavery are far less clear than some
scholars claim.[37] He mentions transatlantic slavery only a few times and

[34] Other scholars argue that there is no evidence that Kant ever abandoned his racist views (e.g.,
Bernasconi 2011; Larrimore 2008: 358–59; Lu-Adler 2023).
[35] To name some examples, see Allais 2016; Bernasconi 2002 and 2011; Boxill 2017; Eberl 2019;
Eze 1997; Harfouch 2018; Hedrick 2008; Kaufmann 2019; Kirkland 2017; Kleingeld 2007; Larrimore
1999 and 2008; Lu-Adler 2022b and 2023; Mensch 2013: 92–109; Mills 2005 and 2014; Sandford
2018; Valdez 2017.
[36] One notable exception is Lu-Adler 2022a, which nicely complements what I will say here.
[37] Kleingeld claims, for instance, that in the 1790s, Kant was "unambiguously opposed to [colonial]
chattel slavery" (2007: 587; see also 2012: 111–13).

never provides a detailed moral argument against it. It seems that he did not view it to be a pressing moral issue. Most of his discussions of slavery are not about transatlantic slavery and do not answer the question whether he views this early modern institution as morally permissible.

5.2.1. Kant on Circumstantial Slavery

One of Kant's most extensive discussions of circumstantial slavery occurs in the *Metaphysics of Morals* (1797)—mainly in the first part of the *Doctrine of Right*, which is about private right or private ownership. After discussing property rights in general as well as various ways to acquire ownership of a thing, Kant devotes an entire section to "Rights to persons akin to rights to things" (Ak 6: 276 / 1996: 426), that is, to relations among persons within a household that resemble rights to things. He examines three such household relations—the husband-wife relation, the parent-child relation, and the master-servant relation (§23, Ak 6: 277 / 1996: 426)—and explains to what extent each of them resembles a right to things. In this context, as we will see, Kant mainly discusses master-servant relations that are voluntary— more specifically, a contractual, nonabsolute form of bondage. Yet he also mentions penal slavery, which is more relevant for our purposes because it is the strictest form of bondage that Kant endorses explicitly. I will devote a large portion of this section to penal slavery, which incidentally raises intriguing philosophical questions about Kant's seemingly universalist moral principles. We will also take a look at Kant's arguments against other traditional forms of slavery, namely, hereditary slavery, war slavery, and absolute forms of voluntary slavery.

First, however, it is helpful to examine the terminology that Kant uses to talk about bondage. In the *Doctrine of Right*, he mostly uses the German word *Gesinde*, a now obsolete term that refers to domestic servants, farmhands, and more generally menial staff.[38] I will translate it as 'servant,' rather than 'slave,' and use the term 'servitude' for this type of bondage. In some places, Kant uses the Latin term *servus* (slave) interchangeably with the German words *Leibeigener* (literally 'serf' and sometimes translated 'bondsman') and

---

[38] In some places, Kant uses the German term *Knecht* (servant), for instance in Ak 6: 254. In his lecture course on natural law, Kant uses the Latin term *famulus* for servants (Naturrecht Feyerabend, Ak 27: 1380).

Sklave or *Sclav(e)* (slave).[39] I will use the term 'slave' to translate these latter terms and 'slavery' to refer to this type of bondage. As we are about to see, the difference between slavery and servitude is important: Kant holds that a master's power over enslaved people is nearly absolute, whereas a master's power over servants is far more restricted. Either type of bondage can be licit, according to Kant, though he stresses that there are very few circumstances in which slavery is permissible. The only justification for slavery that he endorses in the *Doctrine of Right* is punishment for a crime; he explicitly rejects hereditary slavery, war slavery, and voluntary slavery. Yet he holds that voluntary servitude is perfectly legitimate. For reasons we will examine later, he contends that a person can voluntarily subject herself to a limited and contractually delineated type of bondage, but not to slavery or to a practically unlimited type of bondage.

One interesting aspect of the section "Rights to persons akin to rights to things" in *Metaphysics of Morals* is Kant's description of the legal status of servants. As we saw in chapter 2, there was a debate in early modern jurisprudence about whether enslaved people have the legal status of things or of persons. Gottfried Wilhelm Leibniz asserted in an early juridical text that they are, legally speaking, things rather than persons (*Nova Methodus* 2.15 [1667], 1923–: 6.1, 301 / 2017: 51). Other philosophers—including Samuel Pufendorf—insisted that no human being can ever have the same legal status as a thing.[40] Gershom Carmichael, as we saw in chapter 2, used this Pufendorfian doctrine to reject chattel slavery categorically: it is never permissible to treat another human being as a piece of property. Kant seems to take an intermediate position with respect to servants—though arguably not with respect to slaves, as we will see later. As the section's title already suggests, he argues that the right over servants is similar to a right to things, though it is still a right to a person.[41] To carve out this intermediate category, he distinguishes between the matter and the form of the right of a head of household (*Hausherr*) over his servants.[42] As far as the form is concerned—that is,

---

[39] At one point, he glosses *Leibeigener* with the Latin phrase *servus in sensu strictu*, "slave in the strict sense" (Ak 6: 330 / 1996: 471). For a helpful discussion of Kant's usage of these terms, see Schönecker 2021: 610–12.

[40] Pufendorf describes this doctrine as follows in his 1660 *Elements of Universal Jurisprudence*: enslaved people "are understood to have no citizenship in the state and are enrolled under the head of things, and not of persons" (1.3.7, 2009: 35). As we saw in chapter 2 when discussing Carmichael, Pufendorf argues against this doctrine.

[41] Pascoe argues that this is an extremely important innovation on Kant's part (2022: 14–20).

[42] I will use masculine pronouns to refer to heads of household because for Kant, they are always men and because the term *Hausherr* is clearly gendered. For more on Kant's views about women and gender roles, see Varden 2017.

the way of being in possession (*Besitzstand*)—this right is "like a right to a thing," because the head of household can retrieve runaway servants against their will, just like an owner of things can retrieve lost possessions (§30, Ak 6: 283–84 / 1996: 431–32). There is another sense in which servants are not persons: they "lack civil personality," that is, cannot vote or be active citizens, due to their subordination to the head of the household (§46, AK 6: 314 / 1996: 458).[43] Based on this subordination, Kant describes the existence of servants—as well as of wives and children—as "inherence" in the head of household (§46, AK 6: 314 / 1996: 458), and elsewhere compares servants to "parasitic plant[s]" (Ak 23: 137). With respect to the matter, however—that is, with respect to the use that the head of household can rightfully make of his servants—he can "never behave as if he owned them," and can hence never be a slave master (*dominus servi*) (§30, Ak 6: 283 / 1996: 431). Later in the *Metaphysics of Morals*, Kant explains that the right to a person akin to a right to a thing is a right "of not *treating* persons in a similar way to *things* in all respects, but still of *possessing* them as things and dealing with them as things in many relations" (Ak 6: 358 / 1996: 493–94). Thus, despite formal similarities between the possession of a thing and rights over a servant, heads of household cannot use their servants as they use things in all respects.

The reason it is impermissible for heads of household to use their servants like things in all respects, Kant elaborates, is that the relationship between heads of household and servants is based on a contract, and one cannot fully renounce one's freedom and personality through a contract (§30, Ak 6: 283 / 1996: 431–32). Here, Kant appears to borrow an argument from Jean-Jacques Rousseau:[44] "a contract by which one party would completely renounce its freedom for the other's advantage would be self-contradictory, that is, null and void, since by it one party would cease to be a person and so would have no duty to keep the contract but would recognize only force" (§30, Ak 6: 283 / 1996: 431; see also Ak 19: 547).[45] In other words, a person cannot become a thing through a contractual agreement, because things cannot have

---

[43] Kant stresses that they are, nevertheless, free and equal "*as human beings*" (§46, AK 6: 315 / 1996: 458). Moreover, they are passive citizens, according to him, which means that they are protected by civil laws (see Moran 2021).

[44] As we saw in chapter 4, Rousseau puts forward a version of this argument in *Social Contract* 1.4.6, 2019b: 47. Kant was deeply influenced by Rousseau in several respects, and this appears to be an instance of this influence.

[45] Kant restates this idea in the second part of the *Doctrine of Right*: "No one can bind himself to this kind of dependence, by which he ceases to be a person, by a contract, since it is only as a person that he can make a contract" (Ak 6: 330 / 1996: 472). See also "Naturrecht Feyerabend" (1784), Ak 27: 1335.

contractual duties. Hence, a head of household cannot use his servants ex-actly like things, which for Kant means that he cannot use them in a way that "would amount to using them up [*Verbrauch*]" as one might use up one's other possessions (§30, Ak 6: 283 / 1996: 432).[46] Kant adds that this means that servants are not slaves (*Leibeigene*), which suggests that enslaved people, unlike servants, can be used as things. In short, Kant rejects contractual or voluntary slavery; contracts cannot result in the complete loss of liberty and personality. He does, however, accept voluntary servitude.

What it would mean to have a right to human beings that is exactly like a right to a thing—and hence includes the right to use them up—becomes clear later: such a right would authorize the master "to use the powers of his subject as he pleases," which means that he "can also exhaust [these powers] until his subject dies or is driven to despair" (Ak 6: 330 / 1996: 472). This, tellingly, is one of the rare places in which Kant mentions transatlantic slavery. He notes that the masters of "the Negroes on the Sugar Islands" often drive their slaves to death or despair by using up their powers (Ak 6: 330 / 1996: 472). Unfortunately, Kant does not say anything else about this impor-tant real-world instance of slavery in this passage. He does not tell us whether what happens in the Sugar Islands—that is, presumably, the West Indies—is morally permissible. Instead, he merely brings it up as an example of a kind of bondage that cannot licitly originate in a contract.[47]

As we just saw, Kant argues that a voluntary agreement can never result in a master-slave relationship, that is, it cannot give masters the right to use their subordinates as things in all respects. Kant rejects voluntary slavery. He acknowledges only one licit justification for using human beings as things in the *Doctrine of Right*, and hence one licit justification for slavery: it is pos-sible for a human being to "forfeit . . . his personality by a crime" (§30, Ak 6: 283 / 1996: 431), that is, cease to be a person by committing a crime.[48] The

[46] Another limitation on contractual servitude is that such a contract cannot specify that the bondage is lifelong; at most, it can leave the duration of the bondage unspecified. Either party can sever the relationship by giving notice (§30, Ak 6: 283 / 1996: 432).

[47] Lu-Adler makes a similar point and provides an extremely insightful analysis of this reference to slavery in the West Indies and its relevance (2022a: 274).

[48] Later, Kant makes the same point in a slightly different way: "someone can have as his own an-other *human being* who by his crime has forfeited his personality (become a bondsman)" (Ak 6: 358 / 1996: 494). This fits with what Kant says at the end of the introduction to the *Metaphysics of Morals*, where he refers to slaves (*Leibeigene, Sklaven*) as "human beings without personality" and as "beings that have only duties but no rights" (Ak 6: 241 / 1996: 396). He states that this class has no members, but that does not mean that he believes there are no human beings without personality. Rather, this class is empty simply insofar as he is categorizing different types of relations among persons, or among "subjects between whom a relation of right to duty can be thought of" (Ak 6: 241 / 1996: 396).

enslavement of human beings who have forfeited their personality—penal slavery—is the only form of slavery in the strict sense that Kant accepts as licit within a state (Ak 6: 329–30 / 1996: 471). He mentions one concrete example of penal slavery: a fitting punishment for a thief, "by the principle of retribution," is that the thief loses the right to have property (Ak 6: 333 / 1996: 474). But if thieves cannot own or acquire anything, the state must provide for them. Since the state does not need to provide for such criminals for free, it can reduce them to prison labor and eventually "to the status of a slave [*Sklavenstand*] for a certain time, or permanently" (Ak 6: 333 / 1996: 474).[49] On a more general level, Kant explains in his comments on Gottfried Achenwall's *Juris naturalis pars posterior* that penal slavery is appropriate in cases in which someone has made himself "completely unworthy of freedom by refusing to acknowledge any limits to liberty through laws, and must consequently be subdued through the force and absolute arbitrariness [*Willkühr*] of others" (Ak 19: 557–58). In short, because criminals do not respect the laws that limit liberty in a civil state, they are unworthy of liberty and must be enslaved.[50]

Penal slavery is Kant's only exception to the principle that "no human being in a state can be without any dignity, since he at least has the dignity of a citizen" (Ak 6: 329 / 1996: 471). Importantly, Kant describes penal slaves as the property (*Eigenthum*) of someone else, namely either of the state or of a private citizen (Ak 6: 330 / 1996: 471).[51] This means that Kantian penal slavery can be a form of chattel slavery, that is, a form of slavery in which enslaved people are the private property of the master. He describes penal

---

Beings who lack personality simply do not belong in this typology, but that does not mean that there are no such beings. For a similar interpretation of this passage, see Lu-Adler 2022a: 271.

[49] For a discussion of how odd it is that Kant endorses this kind of slavery, see Schönecker 2021: 613–14.

[50] Kant sometimes describes civil freedom as a freedom that is limited by laws enabling one's own freedom to coexist with that of others. He opposes this to "barbaric freedom," which is a freedom without laws. Human beings who embrace this type of freedom arrogantly value their own liberty over that of others ("Anthropology Mrongovius" [1784–85], Ak 25: 1354–55 / 2012: 455). In his 1791 lectures on anthropology, he furthermore explains that only Europeans or White people have the trait of being "civilized through laws and nevertheless free" (Dohna notes, 1924: 364).

[51] The claim that enslaved people can belong to private citizens contradicts Pascoe's contention that slavery for Kant is always public slavery (2022: 40). Another passage in which Kant appears to acknowledge that penal slaves can be owned by private citizens is from Feyerabend's notes on Kant's lecture course on natural law: "Is it possible to acquire household servants as slaves? It is possible through a crime because he thereby loses his rights" (Ak 27: 1381). Yet another passage is from the *Metaphysics of Morals*: "someone can have as his own another *human being* who by his crime has forfeited his personality (become a bondsman)" (Ak 6: 358 / 1996: 494).

slaves in a very Aristotelian way as "mere tool[s] of another's choice" (Ak 6: 330 / 1996: 471). The master of a penal slave has extensive powers: he can "alienate him [that is, sell him, trade him, or give him away] as a thing, use him as he pleases (only not for shameful purposes) and *dispose of his powers*, though not of his life and members" (Ak 6: 330 / 1996: 471–72). As already seen earlier, this last caveat is weaker than it may initially seem because Kant holds that the right to use the powers of an enslaved person includes the right to use them up, driving the enslaved person to death or despair.[52] This means that while it is impermissible for masters to kill or mutilate their slaves in a direct way, they have the right to do so in an indirect manner, by overworking them. Penal slaves can be treated almost exactly like things.

The way in which Kant discusses penal slavery is important for the question of how universalist Kant's principles are. His description of the status of penal slaves reveals that it is possible for human beings to lack dignity and personality. It is not entirely clear, however, whether penal slaves lack moral dignity and moral personality, or merely civil dignity and civil personality. Let us call the former reading the 'moral personality interpretation' and the latter the 'civil personality interpretation.' For Kant, moral personality is "the freedom of a rational being under moral laws" (Ak 6: 223 / 1996: 378). He does not appear to provide an explicit definition of 'civil personality,' but this term appears to be Kant's way to refer to the rights and obligations that citizens of a state have in virtue of being citizens (see Moran 2021: 116).[53] As we saw earlier, Kant claims at one point that even servants—like all children and women—lack civil personality (Ak 6: 314 / 1996: 458). Yet, since they are passive citizens, they still have some civil obligations and rights (see Moran 2021). In contrast, the penal slave presumably experiences a complete loss of civil personality. This type of slave is, as Kant explains, the only human being in a state who lacks all civil dignity. If the civil personality interpretation is correct, slavery means civil death, or the forfeiture of one's rights as a citizen—quite a traditional understanding of slavery—but enslaved convicts remain persons in the moral sense and thus retain their moral dignity.[54] There is strong textual support for this interpretation, but there are

---

[52] The caveat does mark a difference between the right over enslaved people and the right over vegetables and domestic animals, which an owner can "use, wear out or destroy [*gebrauchen, verbrauchen und verzehren*] (kill)" (Ak 6: 345 / 1996: 483).

[53] Kant acknowledges another type of personality: psychological personality, which is "merely the ability to be conscious of one's identity in different conditions of one's existence" (Ak 6: 223 / 1996: 378).

[54] Schönecker 2021 argues this at length and quite persuasively.

also reasons to think that Kantian penal slaves lose not just their civil personality but their moral personality. While I cannot settle this issue here, I will mention some of the most relevant evidence.

Several of Kant's claims about the penal slave's loss of personality are ambiguous. For instance, in one of the passages from *Metaphysics of Morals* in which Kant rejects voluntary slavery, he states—as seen earlier—that a contract by which one party renounces their freedom completely is self-contradictory because this would entail that this party would "cease to be a person and so would have no duty to keep the contract but would recognize only force" (Ak 6: 283 / 1996: 431). Immediately after this, Kant notes that he is not currently considering ownership rights "with respect to someone who has forfeited his personality by a crime" (Ak 6: 283 / 1996: 431). In these two statements, he is quite clearly referring to a loss of personality in the same sense: criminals forfeit their personality in precisely the sense that would be self-contradictory if it were done through a contract. At first, this may appear to support the moral personality interpretation. After all, it may seem that the loss of personality that is at issue cannot be merely civil, since a loss of civil personality may seem compatible with a duty to keep the contract. Yet this is not as clear as it may seem, since there are good reasons to think that for Kant, rightful contractual obligations can only exist within a civil society (Varden 2008: 19–21), which might mean that it would be contradictory for one party to renounce their civil personality through a contract.

One piece of evidence for the civil personality interpretation is another passage from the *Metaphysics of Morals* in which Kant rejects voluntary slavery. He frames this discussion by claiming—as we saw earlier—that "no human being in a state can be without any dignity, since he at least has the dignity of a citizen," and that the only exceptions are penal slaves (Ak 6: 329 / 1996: 471). This suggests that Kant is interested only in civil dignity and civil personality here, and that this is what penal slaves forfeit. Additional support for the civil personality interpretation is a discussion of the right to punish, which occurs just two pages after the claim about penal slavery that we just examined:

> *Punishment by a court* . . . must always be inflicted upon [the criminal] only *because he has committed a crime*. For a human being can never be treated merely as a means to the purpose of another or be put among the objects of rights to things: his innate personality protects him from this, even though he can be condemned to lose his civil personality. (Ak 6: 331 / 1996: 473)

The claim here appears to be completely general: no human being, even if they have committed a crime, can lose their innate or moral personality; they can at most lose their civil personality. And this is of course in line with the universalist-sounding moral principles that Kant lays out in the *Groundwork* and in the *Metaphysics of Morals*: it is never permissible to treat human beings merely as means, or in a way that is inconsistent with the dignity and personality that all human beings, or all rational beings, innately possess and that distinguish them from things (e.g., Ak 4: 428–29 / 1996: 79–80; Ak 6: 462 / 1996: 579). The passage just quoted appears to state that these principles apply even to criminals; cases in which someone has committed a horrendous crime are not exceptions to these principles. A later passage confirms this: "I cannot deny all respect to even a vicious man as a human being; I cannot withdraw at least the respect that belongs to him in his quality as a human being, even though by his deeds he makes himself unworthy of it" (Ak 6: 463 / 1996: 580). Kant adds that "censure of vice . . . must never break out into complete contempt and denial of any moral worth to a vicious human being" (Ak 6: 463 / 1996: 580). These passages are strong evidence in favor of the civil personality interpretation.

Moreover, as we saw earlier, Kant claims that the master of penal slaves is not allowed to kill or maim them directly (Ak 6: 330 / 1996: 471–72). Indeed, he also claims that "disgraceful punishments that dishonor humanity itself," such as "quartering a man, having him torn by dogs, cutting off his nose and ears," are impermissible (Ak 6: 463 / 1996: 580). This suggests that criminals retain at least a rudimentary form of moral personality and cannot be treated exactly like a thing (Schönecker 2021: 616–17). According to Gottfried Feyerabend's notes on Kant's lecture course on natural law in 1784, Kant claimed explicitly that "the slave [*servus*] cannot be maimed or executed because he has his natural rights. He can never give up [*aufgeben*] his natural rights because otherwise he would stop being a person" (Ak 27: 1381). This is evidence that for Kant no human being—not even the most vicious criminal—can completely lose their moral rights or moral personality.[55] Additional evidence stems from a passage in which Kant defines moral personality and distinguishes persons from things: he explains that nothing can be imputed to a thing, whereas (moral) persons are subjects whose actions can be imputed to them (Ak 6: 223 / 1996: 378). Schönecker argues that this

---

[55] It is possible, of course, that Kant is merely explaining natural law ethics in this passage, rather than endorsing every aspect of it.

means that penal slaves must still be moral persons, because their crimes are imputed to them (2021: 615).

Yet there are also reasons to interpret Kant as holding that enslaved people lose their *moral* personality along with their civil personality. For instance, recall Kant's description of penal slaves as mere tools of their master's choice (Ak 6: 330 / 1996: 471). As he explains in the *Groundwork* when motivating the second formulation of the categorical imperative, persons cannot be used as mere means—or mere tools—because they are ends in themselves. Things, in contrast, can be used as mere means (Ak 4: 428–29 / 1996: 79–80). Thus, if it is permissible to use penal slaves as mere tools, they must be things rather than persons. And it is unclear how to understand this as a mere lack of civil personality: if penal slaves were still moral persons, how could it be permissible for the master to treat them as mere tools? Hence, this suggests that penal slaves have lost their moral personality and need no longer be treated as ends.

Another piece of evidence for the moral personality interpretation is Kant's claim that penal slaves are the property (*Eigenthum*) of their masters (Ak 6: 330 / 1996: 471). Elsewhere, he argues that it is not possible to have another person as one's property because "a human being cannot have property in himself, much less in another person" (Ak 6: 359 / 1996: 494). This entails that penal slaves are not persons—since penal slaves are property, but persons cannot be property—and it seems that the personality at issue in this context is moral rather than civil personality. After all, the reason one cannot have property in oneself appears to be one's moral personhood: as Kant explains earlier in the *Metaphysics of Morals*, a person "cannot be the owner *of himself* (cannot dispose of himself as he pleases) . . . since he is accountable to the humanity in his own person" (Ak 6: 270 / 1996: 421). The obligation to respect humanity in one's own person is clearly tied to moral personality rather than civil personality. This suggests that when Kant says that, for the same reason, one cannot own another person, he is also referring to persons in the moral sense. We cannot own another person because we have an obligation to respect their moral personality. This, in turn, would mean that penal slaves lack moral personality, since they can be someone else's property.

Further support for the moral personality interpretation might be available in Kant's discussion of another form of punishment: the death penalty. Kant accepts capital punishment; he indeed argues that murderers must be executed since "there is no substitute [for the death penalty] that will satisfy justice" in the case of murder (Ak 6: 333 / 1996: 474). As a result, Kant clearly holds that when individuals commit horrendous crimes—such as murder—it is permissible to take away not only their status as a citizen or their civil life but also their biological life. Perhaps this means that they have forfeited their moral personality and need no longer be treated as ends.[56] Kant appears to confirm this in his comments on Gottfried Achenwall's *Juris naturalis pars posterior*, where he claims that murderers must be executed because they cease to have rights and therefore cease to be human (§74, Ak 19: 547). Saying that they cease to be human arguably means that they cease to be persons in the moral sense. It is conceivable that Kant has a similar attitude toward penal slaves. He even suggests this in his comments on Achenwall: an enslaved person does not have a will of his own, or a capacity to choose (*arbitrium*), because he cannot determine his own obligations; he is a thing rather than a person (*servus . . . est res non persona*; §71, Ak 19: 545). Kant adds that slavery degrades humanity; it is the death of the person and the life of the animal and can hence be imposed only in the case of capital crimes (Ak 19: 545).[57] In this text, it is quite clear that Kant describes penal slaves as having lost their moral personality. This text was apparently composed much earlier than the *Metaphysics of Morals*, however, so it is possible that Kant changed his mind on this issue. Nevertheless, he does endorse the death penalty in the *Metaphysics of Morals*, which means that there may be room in Kant's mature moral philosophy for the doctrine that penal slaves are not moral persons.

As our quick examination of the textual evidence has shown, it is far from clear whether the civil personality interpretation or the moral personality interpretation is correct. What is clear is that penal slaves lack personality and dignity at least in the civil sense, if not also in the moral sense. The loss of civil personality, incidentally, is already an enormously significant loss for Kant (Varden 2008; Horn 2014).

Let us now turn to Kant's rejection of hereditary slavery and hereditary servitude. He bases this rejection on the natural law doctrine that all

---

[56] The moral implications of Kant's endorsement of the death penalty are far from straightforward; see Yost 2010 for a helpful discussion. Yost argues that the death penalty is permissible for Kant in part because Kant does not acknowledge an absolute right to life; life has value not as an end in itself, but only "insofar as it serves our moral existence" (2010: 14) or insofar as it is the vehicle for exercising our freedom (2010: 7). Furthermore, Yost contends that executing a criminal does not violate the criminal's moral dignity because an honorable man who deserves death would will his own death, since the stain on that person's honor cannot be removed (2010: 14–16). I am unsure whether this is the correct interpretation. But if it is, the death penalty is not an example in which someone loses their moral dignity.

[57] Kant might here be building on the commonly accepted doctrine that slavery is analogous to death, and that it is permissible to enslave someone in cases in which it would also be permissible to kill them.

human beings are born free, which he discusses in the introduction to the *Metaphysics of Morals*. Freedom, defined as "independence from being constrained by another's choice," is the only "innate right" that human beings possess, or "the only original right belonging to all human beings by virtue of their humanity" (Ak 6: 237 / 1996: 393; translation altered). This right is extremely important. After all, "freedom is a negative condition of all satisfaction of our inclination," and it is "the first good which human beings wish for themselves" ("Anthropology Friedländer" [1775–76], Ak 25: 581–82 / 2012: 135); one cannot be happy without freedom, and "If freedom ceases, the personality of the human being also ceases" ("Anthropology Mrongovius" [1784–85], Ak 25: 1354 / 2012: 455).[58] Kant furthermore claims that the right to freedom includes "innate *equality*, that is, independence from being bound by others to more than one can in turn bind them; hence a human being's quality of being *his own master* (*sui iuris*)" (Ak 6: 237–38 / 1996: 393–94).

This natural right to freedom is clearly incompatible with hereditary slavery, as Kant makes explicit in the context of discussing permissible justifications for bondage: "children (even those of someone who has become a slave [*Sklave*] through a crime) are at all times free" (§30, Ak 6: 283 / 1996: 432). The reason why the children of penal slaves cannot licitly inherit their parents' status is, he explains, that these children have not committed any crimes themselves and hence have not forfeited their natural right to freedom (§30, Ak 6: 283 / 1996: 432).[59] He also refutes an argument that many natural lawyers use to justify hereditary slavery. This is the argument that children who are born to enslaved parents incur a debt to their parents' master, who bears the cost of raising them. Hence, according to this argument, the master has the right to force these children, once they are old enough, to work off this debt as his slaves. Kant objects that there is no such debt because masters have an obligation to raise their slaves' children free of charge. After all, "the slave would have to educate his children if he could,

---

[58] Incidentally, this passage is further evidence for the moral personality interpretation that I discussed earlier: immediately before stating that lacking freedom means lacking personality, Kant notes that lacking freedom entails being a slave and being unhappy (Ak 25: 1354 / 2012: 455). Because the lack of personality at issue appears to be connected to the inability to satisfy one's inclinations, it is plausible that this is a lack of moral rather than civil personality.

[59] He restates this point later in the *Doctrine of Right*: when someone "has become a *personal* subject by his crime, his subjection cannot be *inherited*, because he has incurred it only by his own guilt" (Ak 6: 330 / 1996: 472). Even later, he describes hereditary slavery as "absurd," because "guilt from someone's crime cannot be inherited" (Ak 6: 349 / 1996: 486).

without charging them with the cost of their education, and if he cannot the obligation devolves to his possessor" (Ak 6: 283 / 1996: 432).[60]

In a later section of the *Metaphysics of Morals*, which is devoted to the law of nations, Kant rejects one final type of circumstantial slavery: war slavery, or more specifically, the enslavement of captives in a war among independent states. This rejection builds on the principle that one can only forfeit one's freedom and personality through a crime, that is, that slavery can only be licit when it is a punishment for a crime. Wars among independent states, Kant argues, can never be forms of punishment, since "punishment only occurs in the relation of a superior to those subject to him, and states do not stand in that relation to each other" (Ak 6: 347 / 1996: 485; see also Ak 6: 331 / 1996: 472).[61] This means that it is illicit for the victor in such a war to enslave enemy combatants, "since for this one would have to admit that a war could be punitive" (Ak 6: 348–49 / 1996: 486). Thus, citizens of the defeated state have the right to retain their civil liberty and cannot be enslaved (Ak 6: 348 / 1996: 486).

Does Kant's rejection of all forms of circumstantial slavery—except penal slavery—have implications for the question of how Kant thinks about transatlantic slavery? It would be a mistake, in my opinion, to think that Kant's claims about circumstantial slavery are an explicit—or even implicit—repudiation of transatlantic slavery. In *Metaphysics of Morals*, Kant never examines the moral permissibility of transatlantic slavery explicitly. In fact, at least some of his arguments are specifically about master-slave or master-servant relations among citizens of the same state, or they are about forms of slavery—such as voluntary slavery—that are clearly irrelevant to transatlantic slavery. While Kant does, as we saw, refer to enslaved Black people in the West Indies at one point, he does so merely to illustrate his claim that one cannot voluntarily give someone else the right to use up one's powers. Transatlantic slavery is an example of a type of subjection that cannot licitly originate in a contract. Yet he does not say whether it can licitly originate in something other than a contract. Hence, Kant's rejection of most forms of circumstantial slavery in *Metaphysics of Morals* is not an explicit rejection of transatlantic slavery.

Kant's theoretical points about circumstantial slavery in *Metaphysics of Morals* do not even constitute an implicit repudiation of transatlantic slavery.

---

[60] Kant restates this point in the second part of the *Doctrine of Right* (Ak 6: 330 / 1996: 472).

[61] In this context, it is relevant that Kant also rejects the legitimacy of wars of extermination and wars of subjugation (Ak 6: 347 / 1996: 485).

One reason is that Kant accepts penal slavery, which matters because some early modern writers claimed that many transatlantic slaves are penal slaves. For Kant, the right of punishment is a right that states have against their own citizens, which presumably means that European states or companies do not have a right to punish Africans by enslaving them.[62] Yet he could in principle claim that African governments impose licit penal slavery on their own citizens and then sell these penal slaves to European slave traders.[63] He appears to view that kind of sale as licit because he holds, as we saw earlier, that the master of penal slaves can alienate them against their will. There is no reason to think, as far as I can tell, that he views it as impermissible for a government to sell penal slaves to foreign traders. Thus, Kant's discussion of circumstantial slavery does not imply that transatlantic slavery is illicit. If Kant wanted to argue that transatlantic slavery is not a licit instance of penal slavery, he would have to say more.[64]

There is another, more important reason why Kant's discussion of circumstantial slavery does not imply that he must view transatlantic slavery as illicit. His arguments against various types of circumstantial slavery—even the arguments that he phrases in seemingly universalist ways—could be implicitly restricted to White Europeans, or implicitly exclude some or all Black people. He might hold, for instance, that hereditary slavery and war slavery are permissible with respect to (at least some) Black people, even though they are impermissible with respect to Whites. This could be based, for example, on the doctrine that only White people have a natural right to liberty. Likewise, he might embrace the doctrine of racial natural slavery. Kant could view this doctrine as justifying transatlantic slavery, even if transatlantic slavery is not a licit instance of circumstantial slavery for him. Let us then take a look at the evidence that Kant embraces racial natural slavery as

[62] As I will suggest below, however, he might be able to argue this by using racial natural slavery.

[63] Indeed, Kant describes precisely this practice in his 1782 lectures on physical anthropology: "Negroes enslave their prisoners and sell them to Europeans" (Dönhoff notes, Ak 26: 1080). In the same passage, he claims that Africans often sell their family members into slavery or capture strangers in order to exchange them for alcoholic drinks.

[64] There might be a Kantian doctrine that implies that transatlantic slavery cannot be a licit form of penal slavery: Kant appears to hold that there are no legitimate civil states in Africa because Africans are incapable of self-government (Ak 15: 877–78), which might mean that there are no licit forms of penal slavery within Africa. I thank Huaping Lu-Adler for pointing this out. However, this does not undermine my general point: in order to determine Kant's stance on transatlantic slavery, the theoretical claims about circumstantial slavery from the *Metaphysics of Morals* are not sufficient. They have to be supplemented with Kant's doctrines about race, and even that may not completely settle the question, as we will see.

well as the evidence that his universalist-sounding principles are implicitly restricted to certain racial groups.

5.2.2. Kant on Race, Natural Slavery, and Colonial Slavery

Kant's writings about race are complex and extensive, as is the secondary literature about them. I will here be able to take only a cursory look, concentrating on the claims that are most relevant for determining whether Kant might view transatlantic slavery as justified.[65] The first thing to note is that Kant is a monogenist, since he posits a common ancestral origin or phylum (*Stamm*) for all human beings ("Of the Different Human Races" [1775], §1, Ak 2: 429–30 / 2013: 46). At the same time, however, he argues that there are now important and irreversible differences between racial groups. The ancestral phylum contained the dispositions or "germs" (*Keime*) for traits that would make humans fit for different climates and different ways of life (§3, Ak 2: 434–35 / 2013: 49–50). When humans dispersed across the globe, they gradually acquired these traits. Once that has happened, Kant believes, these traits cannot be changed anymore; they have become "*unfailingly* hereditary," which he views as a necessary condition for racial traits (Ak 8: 99 / 2007: 153).[66]

Kant distinguishes four races, each of which he associates with a color in the 1777 version of "Of the Different Human Races": the northern European race is "Noble blond" (*Hochblonde*), the American Indian race is "Copper red," the African or "Senegambia[n]" race is "Black," and the Asian-Indian race is "Olive-yellow" (§3, Ak 2: 441 / 2013: 69–70; see also Dönhoff notes on physical geography, 1782, Ak 26: 888). He mentions many differences between these racial groups. In addition to physiological traits, he lists several

---

[65] There may be important differences between Kant's views on race in the 1770s and his views from the 1780s onward, which I cannot explore here. For more detailed discussions, see, for instance, Lu-Adler 2023; Sandford 2018; Mensch 2013: 92–109; Harfouch 2018: 105–64.

[66] In the 1775 version of "Of the Different Human Races," Kant makes what appears to be a weaker claim: racial traits are "preserved invariably over many generations [*Zeugungen*], both in all transplantations . . . and in interbreeding" (§1, Ak 2: 430 / 2013: 46). However, he asserts elsewhere that these changes are permanent: "when a race has once established itself . . . no further climatic influences could transform it into another race. . . . This race, . . . when it has once taken root and stifled the other germs, resists all further transformation" (1777, §4, Ak 2: 442 / 2013: 70; similarly, Ak 8: 105 / 2007: 158). Thus—*pace* Justin Smith—there is a sense in which different racial groups for Kant have "separate internal natures" (Smith 2015: 233), even though these natural differences may not count as essential. Incidentally, Kant's theory is a particularly clear illustration of how monogenist theories can be committed to permanent differences.

character traits that he claims are distinctive of each race. He also invokes differences in mental capacities, claiming in one text that the difference between Black and White people "seems to be just as great with regard to the capacities of mind as it is with respect to color" (*On the Feeling of the Beautiful and Sublime* [1764], Ak 2: 253 / 2007: 59). In one infamous passage, he says that being "completely black from head to foot" is "a distinct proof" of stupidity (Ak 2: 255 / 2007: 61). In the same text, he states that Black people "have by nature no feeling that rises above the ridiculous" and then approvingly refers to David Hume's claim that there are no examples of Black people who have "demonstrated talents" or "accomplished something great in art or science or shown any other praiseworthy quality."[67] Kant comments that this shows just how substantial (*wesentlich*) these racial differences are (Ak 2: 253 / 2007: 59).[68] Likewise, in his lectures on anthropology from 1791–92, Kant claims that Africans are "unsuitable for anything that requires understanding [*Verstand*]" (Dohna notes, 1924: 363).

In the 1777 version of "Of the Different Human Races," he moreover describes Black people as "strong, fleshy, and nimble, but, under the ample care of [their] motherland, lazy, soft, and dallying" (1777, §3, Ak 2: 438 / 2013: 67). The reference to laziness is important, as we will see later. Kant appears to view laziness as one of the irreversible traits that this racial group has developed in response to specific environmental conditions, namely, in response to living in a place in which hard work is not necessary (Ak 8: 174n / 2007: 209n). Even more importantly, in his "Sketches for the Lectures on Anthropology" from the 1780s he pronounces the racial group he there calls "Negro" (*Neger*) to be "lively, full of affect and passion, talkative, vain, and given to pleasures," adding that they "acquire the culture of slaves [*Knechte*], but not of freemen, and are incapable of governing themselves. [They resemble] children" (Ak 15: 877).[69] Later in the same text, Kant claims that

---

[67] Kant says something similar in his 1792 lectures on physical geography: "Hume says that among the many thousands of negroes who have been freed over time there is no example of a single one who has distinguished himself through particular skill" (Ak 26: 1132).

[68] Paul Guyer translates *wesentlich* as 'essential' (Kant 2007: 59), but I prefer 'substantial' because Kant does not appear to posit differences that are essential in a strict sense.

[69] Kant makes very similar claims in *Menschenkunde* (1781–82), but without the reference to self-government and the comparison to children (Ak 25: 1187 / 2012: 320). In the passage from *Menschenkunde*, he explains that acquiring the culture of slaves means that "they allow themselves to be trained" (Ak 25: 1187 / 2012: 320). It may also be relevant that Kant claims in his lecture course on anthropology that "Savages have barbaric freedom," that is, they are unwilling to limit their own freedom through laws in order to safeguard the freedom of others. Kant calls this type of freedom "a state of animality" and "unreasonable," and connects it to laziness and arrogance. He contrasts it with civil liberty, which is a liberty limited by laws ("Anthropology Mrongovius" [1784–85], Ak 25: 1354–55 / 2012: 455–56). This suggests that when he describes Black people as incapable of acquiring the

"the Negro can be disciplined and cultivated, but never truly civilized. He automatically lapses into savagery. . . . American Indians and Negroes cannot govern themselves. Suitable only for slavery" (Ak 15: 878).[70] He uses this claim about the incapacity for self-government to support an alarming pre-diction: "All races will be wiped out [*ausgerottet*], except that of the whites" (Ak 15: 878). As he had claimed a few paragraphs earlier, the White race is the only one that "continually progresses in perfection" because it alone is fully capable of culture and civilization (Ak 15: 878). He warns in the same context that miscegenation or racial mixture is "not good" (Ak 15: 878).[71]

These descriptions of alleged racial differences clearly show that Kant views Black people not just as physiologically, characterologically, and men-tally different from White people in several significant respects, but also as inferior. This inferiority, though it originally developed in response to envi-ronmental differences, is a permanent, irreversible, racial trait. Kant's theory of race is hence extremely close to our paradigm of racism.[72]

Some of the differences Kant describes are particularly relevant for deter-mining his attitude toward transatlantic slavery. Most directly relevant are the passages from "Sketches for the Lectures on Anthropology" in which Kant describes Black people as incapable of governing themselves, as child-like, and as suited only for life in slavery. Charles Mills interprets these passages as implying that for Kant, Black people "are natural slaves who may be colonized and enslaved" (2014: 146; similarly Larrimore 1999: 114).[73] Or, to use my terminology, he interprets Kant as endorsing a form of racial nat-ural slavery. Kant holds, after all, that some of the natural differences between Black and White people entail that it is natural for the former to be slaves, and indeed that they are like children, incapable of living freely or independently.

culture of free people, he means that they are incapable of civil freedom and only capable of barbaric freedom.

[70] See also "Anthropology Pillau" (1777–78): "The Negroes . . . are also no longer susceptible of any further civilizing" (Ak 25: 843 / 2012: 276).
[71] Kant says something similar in his 1791 lectures on anthropology: "the races . . . will not fuse, and that would not be desirable. White people would be degraded. For those [other] races do not adopt the customs and habits of Europeans" (Dohna notes, 1924: 364).
[72] While Kant clearly endorses racial hierarchies in several texts, it is helpful to keep in mind that there are also paradigms of racism that do not posit racial hierarchies (Lu-Adler 2022a: 268). Hence, even if Kant abandoned racial hierarchies after composing these texts, as Kleingeld argues (2007: 586–88), this does not mean that he abandoned racist ideas.
[73] As Lu-Adler points out, several of the other traits that Kant ascribes to Black people also suggest that he views them as natural slaves—for instance, physical strength and the ability to be trained (2022a: 279–80). As we will see later, another such trait might be their unique ability to work in Caribbean sugar plantations, of which according to Kant no other racial group is capable.

Further confirmation for this reading comes from Kant's lectures on physical geography (1792), in which he claims that "only Negroes were created for" the type of labor on the Sugar Islands that neither the indigenous people of that region nor Europeans can endure (Dohna Physical Geography 3.3.3, 2005: 241). Likewise, in his lectures on anthropology from 1791–92, Kant claims that Africans "appear to be created for serving others, but never to be civilized" (Dohna notes, 1924: 363). Kant does not explicitly say anywhere, to the best of my knowledge, that this natural suitability makes transatlantic slavery morally permissible. Yet his claim that Black Africans are incapable of freedom and of acquiring any culture higher than that of slaves is very suggestive and appears tailor-made for defenses of transatlantic slavery. Moreover, if Kant held that Black people were "created for" slavery and are naturally suitable for no other way of life, but that it is nevertheless impermissible for Europeans to enslave them, then one would expect him to state the latter in at least some of the places in which he states the former, to avoid being misinterpreted. Thus, Mills's interpretation is very plausible. This, in turn, also suggests that Kant's seemingly universalist moral principles are implicitly restricted to White people, as Mills argues (2014: 146).

The passage in which Kant mentions laziness as a racial trait belonging to Black people is also relevant. In his textbook on anthropology, Kant defines 'laziness' as "the propensity to rest without having first worked," that is, as a propensity for undeserved rest (*Anthropology* §87, Ak 7: 276 / 2007: 376). For him, laziness is not just a character trait but a character vice, and indeed an extremely serious one—more contemptible than cowardice and duplicity (Ak 7: 276 / 2007: 376). The reason why it is such a serious vice is that human beings have a duty to cultivate their capacities through occupations (*Metaphysics of Morals*, Ak 6: 444–45 / 1996: 565). As a result, as Kant explains in his lectures on ethics, "laziness ... is contrary to both the right and the end of humanity in our own person" (Ak 27: 657 / 1997: 393).[74] Hence, describing Black people (and other racial groups) as lazy is a normatively laden judgment. If they cannot overcome their alleged laziness because it is an irreversible racial trait, this also means that they cannot live the way human beings are supposed to live, and they cannot participate in human progress.[75]

---

[74] For in-depth analyses of Kant's views on laziness and its racial dimensions, see Lu-Adler 2022b and Pascoe 2022: 25–33.

[75] For helpful background on Kant's racialized views about human progress and the capacity for civilization, see Lu-Adler 2022b, particularly 2022b: 267–68; see also Larrimore 1999.

It is clear that Kant views laziness as an irreversible racial trait of Black people. For instance, in his essay "On the use of teleological principles in philosophy" (1788), Kant illustrates his doctrine that humans can adapt to different environmental conditions only in "the earliest times" by claiming that Africans who have been taken to northern regions "have never been able to bring about in their progeny . . . a sort that would be fit for farmers or manual laborers" (Ak 8: 173–74 / 2007: 208–9). Their "laziness," in other words, which was originally developed in response to an environment that does not require strenuous labor, has become an irreversible trait and prevents Black people from ever becoming fit for free labor. This, of course, is closely connected to the doctrine of racial natural slavery. It is, after all, a short step from saying that all members of a racial group are incapable of being free laborers to saying that they are fit only for slavery and that it is permissible to force them to work.

Kant elaborates on the point about the unfitness of Black people for free labor in a long footnote, in which he paraphrases a passage from James Tobin's proslavery work *Cursory Remarks*, composed in response to antislavery arguments by James Ramsay.[76] Ramsay, as Kant points out, had advocated employing free Black laborers on West Indian plantations, rather than enslaved people.[77] This, Ramsay argued, would increase their productivity and is hence not just morally required but also "politically profitable" (Ramsay, *Essay* 2.2, 1784: 113–14). Tobin responds that his own experience in the West Indies refutes Ramsay's claim about productivity. Kant appears to take Tobin's side. He calls Tobin "knowledgeable" and then paraphrases Tobin's response as follows:

> among the many thousand freed Negroes which one encounters in America and England he knew no example of someone engaged in a business which one could properly call *labour*; rather that, when they are set free, they soon abandon an easy craft which previously as slaves they had been forced to carry out, and instead become hawkers, wretched innkeepers, lackeys, and

---

[76] Kant paraphrases a passage from Tobin's book (1785: 116), but instead of citing Tobin's book directly, he cites Matthias Christian Sprengel's *Beiträge zur Völker und Länderkunde*, which contains a German translation of excerpts of Tobin's *Cursory Remarks* (Sprengel 1786: 267–92), preceded by a translation of excerpts of Ramsay's *Essay*. The passage that Kant paraphrases is from Sprengel 1786: 286–87.

[77] We explored several of Ramsay's arguments in chapter 2.

people who go fishing and hunting, in a word, tramps [*Umtreiber*]. (Ak
8: 174n / 2007: 209n)[78]

Kant views these purported empirical data as evidence that there are permanent differences between Black and White people that prevent the former
from being productive as free workers, even after having lived for many generations in the same environment as White people. While White people typically have "an immediate drive to activity, . . . which is independent of all
enticement," Black people—like American Indians—lack this inner predis-
position and are unable to acquire it (Ak 8: 174n / 2007: 209n). For Tobin, of
course, this means that it would be a mistake to abolish transatlantic slavery.
Kant does not indicate explicitly whether or not he agrees.[79]

In this context, it is worth noting that for Kant the incapacity for freedom
is sometimes an acquired trait. For example, he warns that when raising
children, one should never "accustom them to renounce all freedom," since
that would make these children insensible to the loss of freedom and in
fact would make them incapable of living without determination by others
("Anthropology Friedländer" [1775–76], Ak 25: 582 / 2012: 136). Slavery
has similar effects, Kant explains elsewhere: it makes enslaved people "im-
mature," that is, renders them unable to use their "own understanding
without guidance from another" ("Anthropology Mrongovius" [1784–85],
Ak 25: 1298–300 / 2012: 412).[80] This acquired immaturity, he adds, can give
slaveowners "the excuse to think [the slaves] could not avail themselves of
their freedom and thus that [the slaveowners] had to make them slaves even
more" (Ak 25: 1299–300 / 2012: 412). He stresses that this excuse is unjustified: if these enslaved people were emancipated, they would learn to live
independently (Ak 25: 1300 / 2012: 412).[81] Kant makes a similar point elsewhere: "one must not always infer that a former slave would misuse [his

---

[78] Kant says something similar in his lectures on anthropology from 1791–92: "The Negroes
(Africans) . . . adopt culture, but either that of a slave or of a tramp. One has never observed any
instances in which a freed Negro has adopted a trade" (Dohna notes, 1924: 363).

[79] Incidentally, Kant's discussion of the disagreement between Tobin and Ramsay shows that he
was well informed about contemporaneous debates about the abolition of slavery. He knew some
of the main arguments for and against abolition, and he knew about the ways in which transatlantic
slaves were treated. That makes it all the more surprising that he does not say more about this issue
and never provides explicit philosophical arguments against transatlantic slavery.

[80] He mentions serfdom as an example of this phenomenon but appears to claim that all forms of
bondage can in principle have this effect.

[81] Later in the same text, Kant also says, "Whoever has been a slave for a long time becomes base
from it; but if one has been free, he will quickly help himself up" (Ak 25: 1354 / 2012: 455).

302 SLAVERY AND RACE

freedom], and for this reason give him no freedom at all. He will surely learn to avail himself well of it," at least eventually ("Anthropology Friedländer," Ak 25: 582 / 2012: 135–36). In other words, Kant argues that the negative effects of slavery are reversible: enslaved people may not know how to live outside of slavery, but they can learn.

It is highly unlikely, however, that Kant has transatlantic slavery in mind when discussing the reversibility of the effects of slavery. In other words, he does not appear to be criticizing the argument that transatlantic slaves cannot be freed because they are incapable of living freely. After all, in one of these texts, Kant mentions the serfs in Courland and Livonia—two early modern Baltic states—as examples of the negative effects of bondage; he does not mention transatlantic slaves (Ak 25: 1300 / 2012: 412). More importantly, if Kant believes—as we saw him state elsewhere—that Black Africans are *naturally* incapable of living freely, rather than as a result of having been enslaved, he must view them as exceptions to the claim that freed slaves can learn how to live independently. Kant's response to the excuse of slaveowners works only for enslaved people whose incapacity for freedom is reversible. For all Kant says here, he might think that the slaveowners' excuse is valid with respect to enslaved Black people since they cannot acquire the capacity for freedom.

Much more direct evidence concerning Kant's attitude toward transatlantic slavery is found in his lectures on physical geography from 1792. There, according to Dohna's notes, Kant argued,

> The trade in Negroes is morally reprehensible [*moralisch verwerflich*], to be sure, but it would take place even if there were no Europeans. And moreover, the people whom they now condemn to slavery used to be executed. Wula . . . on the slave coast is governed by its king with complete despotism; one believes that it is natural that the heads of the people belong to [the kings]. From this one can see that the sale, the fate of Negroes, [is] nevertheless tolerable [*erträglich*]. (Dohna Physical Geography 3.2.4, 2005: 234, trans. based on Kleingeld 2014: 62)[82]

If we consider the first few words of this passage in isolation, it constitutes direct evidence that Kant had moral qualms about the transatlantic slave trade.[83] While he does not say what makes this trade morally problematic, he

---

[82] This passage, except the final sentence, is also included in Ak 26: 1142.
[83] Kant was aware of how brutal transatlantic slavery was; he describes its inhumanity in great detail in his 1782 lectures on physical anthropology (Dönhoff notes, Ak 26: 1080–81).

at least states unequivocally that it is morally problematic.[84] Unfortunately, he does not stop there but instead rehearses two popular proslavery arguments: that many Africans would be enslaved even without European involvement, and that many enslaved Africans would have been executed in Africa if European traders had not purchased them. He also states that the fate of enslaved Black people is "tolerable." One possible interpretation of this latter claim is—which is how Kleingeld reads it—that Kant views slavery as, "on balance, acceptable in the case of blacks" (Kleingeld 2014: 62), because its moral reprehensibility is overbalanced by the alleged fact that Africans would be at least as miserable without the slave trade. That would be quite an astonishing claim for someone like Kant who famously rejects this type of consequentialist calculation. Yet, given the immediate context, a slightly different interpretation seems more likely: the claim could be based on the idea—defended most famously by Montesquieu, as we saw in chapter 4—that slavery is more tolerable for people who live under despotic governments since they are already unfree. Thus, Kant might be claiming merely that Black people can tolerate slavery, not that it is on balance morally acceptable. If that is the correct interpretation, Kant does not tell us in this passage what his overall assessment of the moral permissibility of the slave trade is; he merely states that it is morally reprehensible, and then lists three considerations that allegedly mitigate the badness of this trade. On either reading, this passage is not evidence that Kant categorically opposed transatlantic slavery. Quite to the contrary, it is evidence that he endorsed some of the most popular early modern defenses of slavery, even while admitting that it is morally problematic. Arguably, we can infer from this passage, as well as from the dearth of explicit arguments against transatlantic slavery in Kant's writings, that he did not view transatlantic slavery as a pressing moral issue.[85]

There is one final text that is relevant for determining Kant's attitude toward transatlantic slavery: *Toward Perpetual Peace*, which Kant published in 1795. Some interpreters view this text as evidence that in his later years, Kant was an outspoken critic of racism and colonialism, and that he had come to abandon the racist views he had held in earlier years (Kleingeld 2007 and

---

[84] It is not entirely clear to me what moral reprehensibility entails, for Kant, and more specifically, whether actions resulting in morally reprehensible states of affairs are categorically impermissible. It may be helpful that he also uses this term when discussing the difference between affects and passions in his *Anthropology*: unlike affects, passions are "without exception *evil* . . . [and] not merely *pragmatically* ruinous but also *morally* reprehensible" (Ak 7: 267 / 2007: 368).

[85] This supports Lu-Adler's thesis that Kant never viewed racial slavery "as an urgent *moral* problem to be addressed on its own; by all appearances, he was morally indifferent to it" (2022a: 269).

2014). Yet, as several Kant scholars have pointed out, there are good reasons to think that the implications of this text are far more limited (Lu-Adler 2022a: 280–84; Bernasconi 2011). Let us take a quick look at the relevant passages and then assess their significance. In the second section of *Toward Perpetual Peace*, Kant puts forward three "definite articles" or principles that he claims will enable nations to coexist peacefully. His discussion of colonialism occurs in the context of the third article, which is that "Cosmopolitan right shall be limited to conditions of universal *hospitality*" (Ak 8: 357 / 1996: 328). Cosmopolitan right, as Kant explains earlier in this work, is "the right of citizens of the world," that is, of individuals "regarded as citizens of a universal state of mankind" (Ak 8: 349 / 1996: 322n, italics removed). In the section about the third definite article, Kant argues that cosmopolitan right should include hospitality, or the right not to encounter hostility when visiting foreign lands (Ak 8: 357–58 / 1996: 328–29). He provides some examples of people who violate this right—and, indeed, who violate "natural right"—including the corsairs of the Barbary coast in North Africa, who routinely rob passing ships and enslave foreign sailors (Ak 8: 358 / 1996: 329).

After discussing the rights of visitors, Kant notes that when Europeans visit foreign places, "the injustice they show . . . goes to horrifying length." Indeed, they tend to understand "*visiting*" in a way that is "tantamount to *conquering*" (Ak 8: 358 / 1996: 329). He then mentions several examples—including the colonization of America, "the negro countries," and the West Indies—and accuses European conquerors of acting as if these lands did not previously belong to anyone, that is, of counting "the inhabitants as nothing" (Ak 8: 358 / 1996: 329). After mentioning some other examples, he concludes his discussion of European colonialism as follows:

> The worst of this (or, considered from the standpoint of a moral judge, the best) is that the commercial states do not even profit from this violence; that all these trading companies are on the verge of collapse; that the Sugar Islands, that place of the cruelest and most calculated slavery, yield no true profit but serve only a mediate and indeed not very laudable purpose, namely, training sailors for warships and so, in turn, carrying on wars in Europe. (Ak 8: 359 / 1996: 330)

Several things are noteworthy about Kant's discussion of colonialism in *Toward Perpetual Peace*. First, it is unmistakably a *criticism* of colonialism: Kant claims that European colonial powers have committed, and are still committing, a horrendous injustice. Second, he describes slavery in the West Indies as extremely cruel. Thus, these passages are evidence that in the mid-1790s, Kant was far more critical of the ruthless behavior of White Europeans toward Black and Brown people than his earlier writings suggest.

At the same time, it is important to acknowledge the limitations of Kant's criticism. We can sort Kant's points into two categories: (a) moral criticisms, which include his claim that European colonialism is horrifically unjust, and (b) political and economic criticisms, which include his claim that these colonial endeavors are unprofitable and undermine Europe's prospects for peace. As Kant explicitly tells us, he thinks that the political and economic downsides of colonialism are worse than the moral ones. He adds that this is fortunate from a moral point of view, presumably since it might lead to the termination of practices that are also morally problematic. Yet it is noteworthy that Kant views the political and economic downsides as most significant. This suggests—as several other commentators have argued—that if Kant changed his mind about colonialism, it was not on the basis of a moral epiphany but rather on the basis of pragmatic considerations or changes in geopolitical circumstances. Huaping Lu-Adler argues this particularly persuasively: Kant was willing to tolerate transatlantic slavery as long as he did not see it as standing in the way of the progress of humanity, which for him is the progress of White Europeans. But when Kant started viewing the slave trade as an obstacle to this progress by impeding Europe's prospects for peace and prosperity, he started describing the slave trade more critically. This strengthens the impression that Kant's criticisms were not motivated by a concern for the moral rights and well-being of enslaved Black people (Lu-Adler 2022a: 281–82).

Along similar lines, it is worth noting that the moral criticisms contained in *Toward Perpetual Peace* are quite vague. Kant states that it is wrong to treat the inhabitants of foreign lands as if they were nothing, but he does not say that they have the same moral status as White Europeans. Likewise, he describes West Indian plantation slavery as extremely cruel, but he does not say explicitly that it is morally wrong—much less does he provide an argument for its moral wrongness. Interestingly, in his private notes for *Toward Perpetual Peace*, Kant condemns transatlantic slavery more explicitly: "The trade in negroes, which is already in itself a violation of the hospitality of the people of the Blacks, becomes even more of a violation for Europe through its consequences" (Ak 23: 174). Here, Kant acknowledges that the transatlantic slave trade violates a moral principle—though merely the principle of hospitality. Moreover, he still insists that the negative consequences that this trade has for Europe weigh more heavily than its injustice. It may also be relevant that Kant chose not to include the explicit condemnation of transatlantic slavery in the published version of this essay and that he merely criticizes the transatlantic slave *trade*, not transatlantic slavery more generally.[86] As already seen in earlier chapters, there were many early modern authors who advocated ending the slave trade, but who did not advocate freeing enslaved Black people who were already in the Americas.

Ultimately, what Kant says in *Toward Perpetual Peace* seems perfectly compatible with the racist ideas that he expressed in earlier texts; it is even compatible with the position that at least some forms of colonial slavery are morally justifiable. While Kant claims that it is morally wrong for North African corsairs to enslave shipwrecked foreign sailors, he does not say anything explicit about the moral permissibility of transatlantic slavery, at least in the published version of the text. Nor, indeed, does he say anything in either version that entails a commitment to genuine racial egalitarianism. As a result, this text does not provide sufficient evidence of a principled moral objection to colonial chattel slavery or of a significant change of mind about race and racial natural slavery.

5.2.3. Concluding Thoughts on Kant

One thing that my discussion has shown is that Kant's attitudes toward slavery and race are difficult to pin down. Part of the problem is the intricate interconnectedness and complexity of Kant's system: his views about slavery are connected to his views about moral obligations, many aspects of his political philosophy, his anthropology, his theory of race, and his views about human progress, to name just a few. Kant scholars have made great strides in some of these areas, but a lot of work remains to be done to get a fuller picture. For instance, I hope to have shown that it is worth taking a much closer look at Kant's discussions of circumstantial slavery and carefully examining whether they tell us anything about his views about transatlantic slavery. I have argued, against several other scholars, that Kant's discussions of circumstantial slavery do not have direct implications for transatlantic slavery. And the few places in which he discusses plantation slavery in the West Indies

---

[86] Bernasconi makes both these points (2011: 303).

are far from straightforward. In the end, he does not appear to have viewed it as a pressing moral issue. While he disapproved of the cruel treatment of enslaved people in the West Indies and expressed moral qualms about colonialism and transatlantic slavery in at least one late text, he clearly gave far more moral weight to the political and economic interests of Europeans. This fits well with the racist ideas that Kant expressed in many different texts throughout his career, including his sympathies toward racial natural slavery.

Bibliography

Note on Citation Conventions

For texts that were originally composed in a language other than English, I cite an English translation as well as an edition of the original version whenever possible. When I quote a text and cite an English edition, the translation is from that edition unless I explicitly state otherwise. Whenever I do not cite an English edition, the translation is mine. For primary literature in which there is an edition-independent way to cite—for instance primary works that are divided into short, numbered sections—I include this edition-independent method. In a few cases, I use short titles to refer to primary texts; these are explained in footnotes at the beginning of the section about the author in question.

Primary Literature

Adair, James M. 1790. *Unanswerable Arguments Against the Abolition of the Slave Trade: With a Defense of the Proprietors of the British Sugar Colonies.* London: Bateman.

Adams, John, and Abigail Adams. 1876. *Familiar Letters of John Adams and His Wife Abigail Adams, During the Revolution.* Edited by Charles Francis Adams. New York: Hurd and Houghton.

Adams, Thomas Maxwell. 1788. *A Cool Address to the People of England, on the Slave Trade.* London: Faulder.

Aikin, John, and Anna Laetitia Barbauld. 1796. *Evenings at Home; Or, the Juvenile Budget Opened. Consisting of a Variety of Miscellaneous Pieces for the Instruction and Amusement of Young Persons.* Vol. 6. London: J. Johnson.

Anonymous. 1760. *Two Dialogues on the Man-Trade.* London: Waugh.

Anonymous. 1779. *The Duty and Character of a National Soldier, Represented in a Sermon Preached January 2, 1779 at the High Church in Hull.* London: Johnson.

Anonymous. 1787. "Epilogue to the Padlock: Mungo Speaks." *Gentleman's Magazine and Historical Chronicle* 57: 913–14.

Anonymous. 1795. *Tyrannical Libertymen: A Discourse Upon Negro-Slavery in the United States.* Hanover: Eagle Office.

Anonymous. 1797. *The American in Algiers, or The Patriot of Seventy-Six in Captivity. A Poem, in Two Cantos.* New York: Buel. http://name.umdl.umich.edu/N23981.0001.001.

Anonymous. 1977. "Personal Slavery Established [1773]." In *Am I Not a Man and a Brother: The Antislavery Crusade of Revolutionary America, 1688–1788*, edited by Roger A. Bruns, 245–57. New York: Chelsea House.

Appleton, Nathaniel. 1767. *Considerations on Slavery: In a Letter to a Friend.* Boston: Edes and Gill. http://name.umdl.umich.edu/N08260.0001.001.

Aptheker, Herbert, ed. 1979. *A Documentary History of the Negro People in the United States*. Vol. 1. New York: Carol Publishing Group.

Arbuthnot, John. 1733. *An Essay Concerning the Effects of Air on Human Bodies*. London: J. Tonson.

Aristotle. 1984. "Politics." In *The Complete Works of Aristotle*, edited by Jonathan Barnes, 2:1986–2129. Princeton: Princeton University Press.

Badeau, Nicolas, ed. 1766. *Éphémérides du citoyen ou chronique d'l'esprit national*. Vol. 6. Paris: Delalain et Lacombe.

Basker, James G., ed. 2002. *Amazing Grace: An Anthology of Poems about Slavery, 1660–1810*. New Haven: Yale University Press.

Basker, James G, ed. 2012. *American Antislavery Writings: Colonial Beginnings to Emancipation*. New York: Literary Classics of the United States.

Beattie, James. 1770. *An Essay on the Nature and Immutability of Truth; In Opposition to Sophistry and Scepticism*. Edinburgh: Kincaid and Bell.

Beattie, James. 1793. *Elements of Moral Science*. Vol. 2. Edinburgh: Creech.

Beckford, William. 1788. *Remarks Upon the Situation of Negroes in Jamaica, Impartially Made From a Local Experience of Nearly Thirteen Years in That Island*. London: Egerton.

Belley, Jean-Baptiste. 1794. *Le Bout d'oreille des colons, ou le système de l'hotel de Massiac, mis au jour par Gouli*. Paris: Pain.

Belley, Jean-Baptiste. 2014. "Le Bout d'oreille des colons, ou le système de l'hotel de Massiac [English translation]." In *The Haitian Revolution: A Documentary History*, translated by David Geggus, 112–14. Indianapolis: Hackett.

Benezet, Anthony. 2013. *The Complete Antislavery Writings of Anthony Benezet, 1754–1783: An Annotated Critical Edition*. Edited by David L. Crosby. Baton Rouge: Louisiana State University Press.

Bledsoe, Albert Taylor. 1856. *An Essay on Liberty and Slavery*. Philadelphia: Lippincott.

Bomare, Jacques Christophe Valmont de. 1764. *Dictionnaire raisonné universel d'histoire naturelle*. Paris: Didot.

Bosman, Willem. 1705. *A New and Accurate Description of the Coast of Guinea: Divided Into the Gold, the Slave, and the Ivory Coasts*. London: Knapton.

Bruns, Roger A., ed. 1977. *Am I Not a Man and a Brother: The Antislavery Crusade of Revolutionary America, 1688–1788*. New York: Chelsea House.

Bruslons, Jacques Savary des, and Philemon Louis Savary. 1723. *Dictionnaire universel de commerce: contenant tout ce qui concerne le commerce qui se fait dans les quatre parties du monde*. Vol. 2. Paris: Estienne.

Burgess, Thomas. 1789. *Considerations on the Abolition of Slavery and the Slave Trade, Upon Grounds of Natural, Religious, and Political Duty*. Oxford: Prince and Cooke.

Busbecq, Ogier Ghiselin de. 1771. *Augerii Gislenii Busbequii Omnia quæ extant*. Oxford: Impensis academicis.

Busbecq, Ogier Ghiselin de. 1881. *The Life and Letters of Ogier Ghiselin de Busbecq*. Edited by Charles Thornton Forster and Francis Henry Blackburne Daniell. Vol. 1. London: Kegan Paul.

Capitein, Jacobus Elisa Johannes. 1742. *Dissertatio politico-theologica de servitute, libertati christianae non contraria*. Leiden: Luchtmans.

Capitein, Jacobus Elisa Johannes. 2001. *The Agony of Asar: A Thesis on Slavery by the Former Slave, Jacobus Elisa Johannes Capitein, 1717–1747*. Translated by Grant Richard Parker. Princeton: Markus Wiener.

Carmichael, Gershom. 1718. *S. Puffendorfii de officio hominis et civis, juxta legem naturalem libri duo, Editio nova, aucta Observationibus & Supplementis, Academicæ Institutionis causa adjectis a Gerschomo Carmichael, Philosophiæ in Academia Glasguensi Professore.* Glasgow: Donald Govan.

Carmichael, Gershom. 2002. *Natural Rights on the Threshold of the Scottish Enlightenment: The Writings of Gershom Carmichael.* Edited by James Moore and Michael Silverthorne. Indianapolis: Liberty Fund.

Clarkson, Thomas. 1789. *The Substance of the Evidence of Sundry Persons on the Slave-Trade, Collected in the Course of a Tour Made in the Autumn of the Year 1788.* London: Phillips.

Clarkson, Thomas. 1791. *Letters on the Slave-Trade, and the State of the Natives in Those Parts of Africa, Which Are Contiguous to Fort St. Louis and Goree.* London: Phillips.

Clarkson, Thomas. 2010. "An Essay on the Slavery and Commerce of the Human Species, Particularly the African; Translated from a Latin Dissertation, Which Was Honoured with the First Prize in the University of Cambridge, for the Year 1785." In *Thomas Clarkson and Ottobah Cugoano: Essays on the Slavery and Commerce of the Human Species*, edited by Mary-Antoinette Smith, 57–219. Peterborough: Broadview Press.

Condorcet, Marie Jean Antoine Nicolas de Caritat. 1804. *Oeuvres Complètes de Condorcet.* Vol. 7. Paris: Henrichs.

Condorcet, Marie Jean Antoine Nicolas de Caritat. 2003. *Réflexions sur l'esclavage des nègres et autres textes abolitionnistes.* Edited by David Williams. Paris: Harmattan.

Condorcet, Marie Jean Antoine Nicolas de Caritat. 2012. *Condorcet: Political Writings.* Edited by Steven Lukes and Nadia Urbinati. Cambridge: Cambridge University Press.

Cooper, David. 1772. *A Mite Cast into the Treasury: Or, Observations on Slave-Keeping.* Philadelphia: Crukshank.

Cooper, David. 1783. *A Serious Address to the Rulers of America, on the Inconsistency of Their Conduct Respecting Slavery: Forming a Contrast Between the Encroachments of England on American Liberty, and American Injustice in Tolerating Slavery.* Trenton: n.p.

Cooper, Thomas. 1787. *Letters on the Slave Trade: First Published in Wheeler's Manchester Chronicle; And Since Re-Printed with Additions and Alterations.* Manchester: Wheeler.

Cotton, Rowland. 1778. *Extracts from an Account of the State of British Forts, on the Gold Coast of Africa.* London: J. Bew.

Crawford, Charles. 1784. *Observations Upon Negro-Slavery.* Philadelphia: Crukshank.

Cugoano, Quobna Ottobah. 1999. *Thoughts and Sentiments on the Evil of Slavery.* Edited by Vincent Carretta. New York: Penguin.

Dalrymple, David. 1826. *Decisions of the Lords of Council and Session from 1766–1791.* Vol. 1. Edinburgh: William Tait.

Defoe, Daniel. 1710. *A Word Against a New Election, That the People of England May See the Happy Difference between English Liberty and French Slavery; and Consider Well, Before They Make the Exchange.* London: n.p.

Dexter, Samuel. 1795. "Letter to Jeremy Belknap, 23 February 1795." Massachusetts Historical Society. 1795. http://www.masshist.org/database/577.

Dickson, William. 1789. *Letters on Slavery: To Which Are Added, Addresses to the Whites, and to the Free Negroes of Barbadoes; and Accounts of Some Negroes Eminent for Their Virtues and Abilities.* London: Phillips.

Diderot, Denis, and Jean Le Rond d'Alembert, eds. 1751–65. *Encyclopédie, ou Dictionnaire raisonné des sciences, des arts et des métiers.* 17 vols. Neufchâtel: Faulche.

Diderot, Denis, and Jean Le Rond d'Alembert. 2016. *Encyclopedic Liberty: Political Articles in the Dictionary of Diderot and D'Alembert.* Edited by Henry C. Clark. Indianapolis: Liberty Fund.

Dillwyn, William. 1773. *Brief Considerations on Slavery, and the Expediency of Its Abolition. With Some Hints on the Means Whereby It May Be Gradually Effected.* Burlington: Collins.

Douglass, Frederick. 1882. *The Life and Times of Frederick Douglass: From 1817–1882, Written by Himself.* Edited by John Lobb. London: Christian Age Office.

Du Châtelet, Gabrielle Emilie Le Tonnelier de Breteuil. 2009. *Selected Philosophical and Scientific Writings.* Edited by Judith P. Zinsser. Chicago: University of Chicago Press.

Dubois, Laurent, and John D. Garrigus, eds. 2006. *Slave Revolution in the Caribbean, 1789–1804: A Brief History with Documents.* Boston: Bedford.

Dunbar, James. 1780. *Essays on the History of Mankind in Rude and Cultivated Ages.* London: Strahan.

Edwards, Jonathan, Jr. 1791. *The Injustice and Impolicy of the Slave Trade, and of the Slavery of the Africans: Illustrated in a Sermon Preached Before the Connecticut Society for the Promotion of Freedom, and for the Relief of Persons Unlawfully Holden in Bondage, at Their Annual Meeting in New-Haven, September 15, 1791.* n.p.: Green.

Eliot, Andrew. 1774. *Twenty Sermons on the Following Subjects . . .* Boston: John Boyle.

Elliott, E. N., ed. 1860. *Cotton Is King, and Pro-Slavery Arguments: Comprising the Writings of Hammond, Harper, Christy, Stringfellow, Hodge, Bledsoe, and Cartwright, on This Important Subject.* Augusta: Pritchard, Abbott and Loomis.

Equiano, Olaudah. 2003. *The Interesting Narrative and Other Writings.* Edited by Vincent Carretta. New York: Penguin Books.

Estwick, Samuel. 1773. *Considerations on the Negroe Cause Commonly So Called, Addressed to the Right Honourable Lord Mansfield.* 2nd ed. London: Dodsley.

Felden, Johannes. 1664. *Elelmenta juris universi & in specie Publici Justinianæi.* Frankfurt: Gerlach and Beckenstein.

Ferguson, Adam. 1769. *Institutes of Moral Philosophy: For the Use of Students in the College of Edinburgh.* Edinburgh: Kincaid and Bell.

Ferguson, Adam. 1792. *Principles of Moral and Political Science: Being Chiefly a Retrospect of Lectures Delivered in the College of Edinburgh.* Vol. 2. Edinburgh: Creech.

Fletcher, Andrew. 1698. *Two Discourses Concerning the Affairs of Scotland.* Edinburgh: n.p.

Francklyn, Gilbert. 1789. *Observations, Occasioned by the Attempts Made in England to Effect the Abolition of the Slave Trade; Shewing, the Manner in Which Negroes Are Treated in the British Colonies in the West Indies.* London: Logographic Press.

Franklin, Benjamin. 2005. *The Portable Benjamin Franklin.* Edited by Larzer Ziff. New York: Penguin Classics.

Frossard, Benjamin. 1789. *La cause des esclaves nègres et des habitans de la Guinée, portée au tribunal de la justice, de la religion, de la politique.* Vol. 1. Lyon: Roche.

Fusée-Aublet, Jean-Baptiste-Christophe. 1775. *Histoire des plantes de la Guiane Françoise, rangées suivant la méthode sexuelle.* Vol. 2. Paris: Didot.

Geddes, Alexander. 1792. *An Apology for Slavery; Or, Six Cogent Arguments Against the Immediate Abolition of the Slave-Trade.* London: J. Johnson.

Geggus, David Patrick, ed. 2014. *The Haitian Revolution: A Documentary History.* Indianapolis: Hackett.

Godwyn, Morgan. 1680. *The Negro's & Indians Advocate, Suing for Their Admission to the Church.* London: J.D.

Gouges, Olympe de. 1788. *Zamore et Mirza; ou l'heureux naufrage, drame indien, en trois actes, et en prose*. Paris: Cailleau.

Gouges, Olympe de. 1790. *Les comédiens démasqués ou Madame de Gouges ruinée par la Comédie françoise pour se faire jouer*. Paris: Imprimerie de la Comédie Françoise.

Gouges, Olympe de. 1994. "Translations of Gouges." In *Translating Slavery: Gender and Race in French Women's Writing, 1783–1823*, edited by Doris Y. Kadish and Françoise Massardier-Kenney, translated by Sylvie Molta and Maryann DeJulio, 84–124. Kent: Kent State University Press.

Grotius, Hugo. 2005. *The Rights of War and Peace, Book II*. Edited by Richard Tuck. Indianapolis: Liberty Fund.

Hammon, Jupiter. 1787. *An Address to the Negroes in the State of New-York*. New York: Carroll and Patterson.

Harris, Raymund. 1788. *Scriptural Researches on the Licitness of the Slave-Trade, Shewing Its Conformity with the Principles of Natural and Revealed Religion, Delineated in the Sacred Writings of the Word of God*. London: Stockdale.

Hart, Levi. 1775. *Liberty Described and Recommended; in a Sermon, Preached to the Corporation of Freemen in Farmington, at Their Meeting on Tuesday, September 20, 1774, and Published at Their Desire*. Hartford: Watson.

Haynes, Lemuel. 1990. *Black Preacher to White America: The Collected Writings of Lemuel Haynes, 1774–1833*. Edited by Richard Newman. Brooklyn: Carlson Publishing.

Heineccius, Johann Gottlieb. 2008. *Methodical System of Universal Law: Or, the Laws of Nature and Nations*. Edited by Thomas Ahnert and Peter Schröder. Translated by George Turnbull. Indianapolis: Liberty Fund.

Heinsius, Daniel. 1618. "Georg Richtero S." In *Variarum lectionum libri sex ad Gustavum II*, edited by Jan Rutgers, 318–37. Leiden: ex Officina Elzeviriana.

Helvétius, Claude Adrien. 1758. *De L'esprit*. Paris: Durand.

Hepburn, John. 1715. *The American Defence of the Christian Golden Rule, or an Essay to Prove the Unlawfulness of Making Slaves of Men*. n.p.

Hobbes, Thomas. 1994. *Leviathan: With Selected Variants from the Latin Edition of 1668*. Edited by Edwin Curley. Indianapolis: Hackett.

Hobbes, Thomas. 1998. *On the Citizen*. Edited by Richard Tuck and Michael Silverthorne. New York: Cambridge University Press.

Holmes, George Frederick. 1850. "Observations on a Passage in the Politics of Aristotle Relative to Slavery." *Southern Literary Messenger* 16 (4): 193–205.

Honert, Johan van den. 1736. *Dissertationes apocalypticae exercitiis academicis ventilatae et conscribendo in ipsam Johannis theologi Apocalypsin commentario praemissae*. Leiden: Luchtmans.

Hopkins, Samuel. 1852. *The Works of Samuel Hopkins, D.D.* Vol. 2. Boston: Doctrinal Tract and Book Society.

Hopkins, Samuel. 2002. "'This Whole Country Have Their Hands Full of Blood This Day': Transcription and Introduction of an Antislavery Sermon Manuscript Attributed to the Reverend Samuel Hopkins." Edited by Jonathan D. Sassi. *Proceedings of the American Antiquarian Society* 112: 29–92.

Huber, Ulrik. 1684. *De jure civitatis libri tres: Faciem operis oratio praemissa & argumenta Capitum in calce subjecta exhibent*. Franeker: Johannes Gyselaar.

Hume, David. 1748. *Essays, Moral and Political*. 3rd ed. London: Millar.

Hume, David. 1752. *Political Discourses*. 2nd ed. Edinburgh: Fleming.

Hume, David. 1753. *Essays and Treatises on Several Subjects*. 4th ed. Vol. 1. London: Millar.

Hume, David. 1772. *Essays and Treatises on Several Subjects*. New ed. Vol. 1. London: Cadell.

Hume, David. 1975. *Enquiries concerning Human Understanding and concerning the Principles of Morals*. Edited by P.H. Nidditch and L.A. Selby-Bigge. 3rd ed. Oxford: Oxford University Press.

Hume, David. 1978. *A Treatise of Human Nature*. Edited by L. A. Selby-Bigge and P. H. Nidditch. 2nd ed. Oxford: Clarendon Press.

Hume, David. 1983a. *The History of England from the Invasion of Julius Caesar to the Revolution in 1688*. Vol. 1. Indianapolis: Liberty Classics.

Hume, David. 1983b. *The History of England from the Invasion of Julius Caesar to the Revolution in 1688*. Vol. 5. Indianapolis: Liberty Classics.

Hume, David. 1987. *Essays Moral, Political, and Literary*. Edited by Eugene F. Miller. Indianapolis: Liberty Fund.

Hume, David. 1994. *Political Essays*. Edited by Knud Haakonssen. Cambridge: Cambridge University Press.

Hunt, Lynn, ed. 1996. *The French Revolution and Human Rights: A Brief Documentary History*. Boston: Bedford.

Hutcheson, Francis. 1755. *A System of Moral Philosophy in Three Books*. 2 vols. Glasgow: Foulis.

Hutcheson, Francis. 2007. *Philosophiae Moralis Institutio Compendiaria with A Short Introduction to Moral Philosophy*. Edited by Luigi Turco. Indianapolis: Liberty Fund.

Hutcheson, Francis. 2008. *An Inquiry into the Original of Our Ideas of Beauty and Virtue in Two Treatises*. Edited by Wolfgang Leidhold. Indianapolis: Liberty Fund.

Hutchins, Zachary McLeod, and Cassander L. Smith, eds. 2021. *The Earliest African American Literatures: A Critical Reader*. Chapel Hill: University of North Carolina Press.

Jefferson, Thomas. 1956. *The Papers of Thomas Jefferson*. Vol. 13: *March to 7 October 1788*. Edited by Julian P. Boyd. Princeton: Princeton University Press.

Jefferson, Thomas. 1958. *The Papers of Thomas Jefferson*. Vol. 14: *8 October 1788 to 26 March 1789*. Edited by Julian P. Boyd. Princeton: Princeton University Press.

Jefferson, Thomas. 1984. *Writings*. Edited by Merrill D. Peterson. New York: Literary Classics of the United States.

Jefferson, Thomas. 1986. *The Papers of Thomas Jefferson*. Vol. 22: *6 August to 31 December 1791*. Edited by Charles T. Cullen. Princeton: Princeton University Press.

Jefferson, Thomas. 2004. *The Papers of Thomas Jefferson, Retirement Series*. Vol. 1: *4 March 1809 to 15 November 1809*. Edited by J. Jefferson Looney. Princeton: Princeton University Press.

Jefferson, Thomas. 2014. *The Papers of Thomas Jefferson, Retirement Series*. Vol. 11: *19 January to 31 August 1817*. Edited by J. Jefferson Looney. Princeton: Princeton University Press.

Jones, Absalom, and Richard Allen. 1794. *A Narrative of the Proceedings of the Black People, During the Late Awful Calamity in Philadelphia, in the Year 1793: And a Refutation of Some Censures, Thrown Upon Them in Some Late Publications*. Philadelphia: Woodward.

Kals, Johannes Wilhelm. 1728. *Resp. Disputatio theologica, de natura theologiæ typicæ, ejusdemque explicandæ regulis . . . Præs. J. vanden Honert*. Utrecht: Wilhelm vande Water.

Kant, Immanuel. 1902–. *Gesammelte Schriften*. Berlin: Reimer.

Kant, Immanuel. 1924. *Die philosophischen Hauptvorlesungen Immanuel Kants: Nach den neu aufgefundenen Kolleghefen des Grafen Heinrich zu Dohna-Wundlacken*. Edited by Arnold Kowalewski. Munich: Rösl.

Kant, Immanuel. 1996. *Practical Philosophy*. Edited by Mary J. Gregor. Cambridge: Cambridge University Press.

Kant, Immanuel. 2005. "Vorlesungen über Physische Geographie." Edited by Werner Stark. https://telota-webpublic.bbaw.de/kant/base.htm/geo_base.htm.

Kant, Immanuel. 2007. *Anthropology, History, and Education*. Edited by Robert B. Louden and Günter Zöller. Cambridge: Cambridge University Press.

Kant, Immanuel. 2012. *Lectures on Anthropology*. Edited by Allen W. Wood and Robert B. Louden. Cambridge: Cambridge University Press.

Kant, Immanuel. 2013. *Kant and the Concept of Race: Late Eighteenth-Century Writings*. Translated by Jon M. Mikkelsen. Albany: State University of New York Press.

Kilner, Dorothy. 1786. *The Rotchfords; or, the Friendly Counsellor: Designed for the Instruction and Amusement of the Youth of Both Sexes. In Two Volumes*. Vol. 2. London: John Marshall.

Krise, Thomas W., ed. 1999. *Caribbeana: An Anthology of English Literature of the West Indies, 1657–1777*. Chicago: University of Chicago Press.

Lee, Arthur. 1764. *An Essay in Vindication of the Continental Colonies of America from a Censure of Mr. Adam Smith, in His Theory of Moral Sentiments. With Some Reflections on Slavery in General*. London: n.p.

Leibniz, Gottfried Wilhelm. 1923–. *Sämtliche Schriften und Briefe*. Edited by Deutsche Akademie der Wissenschaften. Berlin: de Gruyter.

Leibniz, Gottfried Wilhelm. 2017. *The New Method of Learning and Teaching Jurisprudence According to the Principles of the Didactic Art Premised in the General Part and in the Light of Experience*. Edited by Carmelo Massimo De Iuliis. Clark: Lawbook Exchange.

Linguet, Simon Nicolas Henri. 1767. *Théorie des loix civiles, ou Principes fondamentaux de la société*. London: n.p.

Locke, John. 1988. *Two Treatises of Government*. Edited by Peter Laslett. Cambridge: Cambridge University Press.

Long, Edward. 1774. *The History of Jamaica. Or, General Survey of the Antient and Modern State of That Island: With Reflections on Its Situation, Settlements, Inhabitants, Climate, Products, Commerce, Laws, and Government*. Vol. 2. London: Lowndes.

Lubert, Howard, Kevin R. Hardwick, and Scott J. Hammond, eds. 2016. *The American Debate over Slavery, 1760–1865: An Anthology of Sources*. Indianapolis: Hackett.

Ludewig, Johann Peter von. 1729. "Neue Schriften / Bücher und Collegia." *Wöchentliche Hallische Frage- und Anzeigungs-Nachrichten* 18 (November): 271–74.

Malouet, Pierre Victor. 1788. *Mémoire sur l'esclavage des Nègres, dans lequel on discute les motifs proposés pour leur affranchissement, ceux qui s'y opposent, & les moyens practicables pour améliorer leur sort*. Neufchatel: n.p.

Mather, Cotton. 1706. *The Negro Christianized: An Essay to Excite and Assist That Good Work, the Instruction of Negro-Servants in Christianity*. Boston: Green.

Mather, Cotton. 1710. *Theopolis Americana: An Essay on the Golden Street of the Holy City: Publishing, a Testimony Against the Corruptions of the Market-Place*. Boston: Green.

Montesquieu, Charles de Secondat. 1878. *The Spirit of the Laws*. Edited by J. V. Prichard. Translated by Thomas Nugent. New ed. Vol. 1. London: George Bell and Sons.

Montesquieu, Charles de Secondat. 1968. *L'esprit des lois*. Edited by Jeannine Kohn. Paris: Club français du livre.

Montesquieu, Charles de Secondat. 1989. *The Spirit of the Laws*. Edited by Basia Carolyn Miller, Harold Samuel Stone, and Anne M. Cohler. Cambridge: Cambridge University Press.

Montesquieu, Charles de Secondat. 2008. *Persian Letters*. Edited by Andrew Kahn. Translated by Margaret Mauldon. Oxford: Oxford University Press.

More, Hannah. 1788. *Slavery, A Poem*. London: Cadell.

Nash, Gary B., ed. 1990. *Race and Revolution*. Madison: Madison House.

Nickolls, Robert Boucher. 1788. *Letter to the Treasurer of the Society Instituted for the Purpose of Effecting the Abolition of the Slave Trade*. London: Phillips.

Nisbet, Richard. 1773. *Slavery Not Forbidden by Scripture: Or, a Defence of the West-India Planters*. Philadelphia: n.p.

Occom, Samson. 2006. *The Collected Writings of Samson Occom, Mohegan: Leadership and Literature in Eighteenth-Century Native America*. Edited by Joanna Brooks. Oxford: Oxford University Press.

Ogé, Vincent. 1789. *Motion faite par M. Vincent Ogé, jeune à l'assemblée des colons, habitans de S.- Domingue, à l'hotel de Massiac, place des Victoires*. Paris: n.p.

Ogé, Vincent. 2014. "Motion faite par M. Vincent Ogé, jeune à l'assemblée des colons [English translation]." In *The Haitian Revolution: A Documentary History*, translated by David Geggus, 48–49. Indianapolis: Hackett.

Otis, James. 2015. *Collected Political Writings of James Otis*. Edited by Richard Samuelson. Indianapolis: Liberty Fund.

Paley, William. 2002. *The Principles of Moral and Political Philosophy*. Indianapolis: Liberty Fund.

Parsons, Theodore, and Eliphalet Pearson. 1773. *A Forensic Dispute on the Legality of Enslaving the Africans, Held at the Public Commencement in Cambridge, New England, July 21st, 1773*. Boston: Boyle.

Porter, Dorothy, ed. 1995. *Early Negro Writing*. Baltimore: Beacon Press.

Potgiesser, Joachim. 1707. *De conditione et statu servorum apud Germanos, tam veteri quam novo, libri tres*. Cologne: Jacob Promper.

Potgiesser, Joachim. 1736. *Commentariorum iuris Germanici de statu servorum veteri perinde atque novo libri quinque*. Lemgo: ex Officina Meieriana.

Pufendorf, Samuel. 1749. *The Law of Nature and Nations: Or, a General System of the Most Important Principles of Morality, Jurisprudence, and Politics*. Translated by Basil Kennet. London: Bonwicke.

Pufendorf, Samuel. 1991. *On the Duty of Man and Citizen According to Natural Law*. Edited by James Tully. Translated by Michael Silverthorne. Cambridge: Cambridge University Press.

Pufendorf, Samuel. 2009. *Two Books of the Elements of Universal Jurisprudence*. Edited by Thomas Behme. Indianapolis: Liberty Fund.

Quincy, Josiah, Jr. 1915. "Journal of Josiah Quincy, Junior, 1773." Edited by Mark Antony De Wolfe Howe. *Proceedings of the Massachusetts Historical Society* 49: 424–81.

Ramsay, James. 1784. *An Essay on the Treatment and Conversion of African Slaves in the British Sugar Colonies*. London: Phillips.

Ramsay, James. 1788. *Objections to the Abolition of the Slave Trade, with Answers*. London: Phillips.

Raymond, Julien. 1791. *Observations sur l'origine et les progrés du préjugé des colons blancs contre les hommes de couleur*. Paris: Belin.

Raynal, Guillaume-Thomas. 1770. *Histoire philosophique et politique des établissemens et du commerce des Européens dans les deux Indes*. Vol. 4. Amsterdam: n.p.

Raynal, Guillaume-Thomas. 2020. *Histoire philosophique et politique des établissemens et du commerce des Européens dans les deux Indes*. Edited by Rigobert Bonne, Anthony Strugnell, and Andrew Brown. Vol. 3. Ferney-Voltaire: Centre international d'étude du XVIIIe siècle.

Rials, Stéphane, ed. 1988. *La déclaration des droits de l'homme et du citoyen*. Paris: Hachette.

Romans, Bernard. 1776. *A Concise Natural History of East and West Florida*. New York: Aitken.

Rousseau, Jean-Jacques. 1964. *Œuvres complètes*. Edited by Marcel Raymond and Bernard Gagnebin. Vol. 3. Paris: Gallimard.

Rousseau, Jean-Jacques. 1997. *Julie, or the New Heloise: Letters of Two Lovers Who Live in a Small Town at the Foot of the Alps*. Edited by Philip Stewart and Jean Vaché. Hanover: University Press of New England.

Rousseau, Jean-Jacques. 2019a. *The Discourses and Other Early Political Writings*. Translated by Victor Gourevitch. 2nd ed. Cambridge: Cambridge University Press.

Rousseau, Jean-Jacques. 2019b. *The Social Contract and Other Later Political Writings*. Translated by Victor Gourevitch. 2nd ed. Cambridge: Cambridge University Press.

Rousselot de Surgy, Jacques-Philibert. 1766. *Mélanges intéresans et curieux, ou abrégé d'histoire naturelle, morale, civile et politique de l'Asie, l'Afrique, l'Amérique, et des terres polaires*. Vol. 10. Paris: Lacombe.

Rowson, Susanna Haswell. 1788. *The Inquisitor; or, Invisible Rambler*. Vol. 2. n.p.: Robinson.

Rowson, Susanna Haswell. 1794. *Slaves in Algiers; or, A Struggle for Freedom: A Play, Interspersed with Songs, in Three Acts*. Philadelphia: Wrigley and Berriman. http://name.umdl.umich.edu/N21056.0001.001.

Rush, Benjamin. 1773a. *An Address to the Inhabitants of the British Settlements, on the Slavery of the Negroes in America*. 2nd ed. Philadelphia: Dunlap.

Rush, Benjamin. 1773b. *Vindication of the Address, to the Inhabitants of the British Settlements, on the Slavery of the Negroes in America*. Philadelphia: Dunlap.

Rush, Benjamin. 1799. "Observations Intended to Favour a Supposition That the Black Color (As It Is Called) of the Negroes Is Derived from the Leprosy." *Transactions of the American Philosophical Society* 4: 289–97.

Rutherforth, Thomas. 1754. *Institutes of Natural Law: Being the Substance of a Course of Lectures on Grotius de Jure Belli et Pacis*. Vol. 1. Cambridge: J. Bentham.

Saffin, John. 1997. "A Brief and Candid Answer." In *The English Literatures of America, 1500–1800*, edited by Myra Jehlen and Michael Warner, 821–25. New York: Routledge.

Sarter, Caesar. 1977. "Essay on Slavery, August 17, 1774." In *Am I Not a Man and a Brother: The Antislavery Crusade of Revolutionary America, 1688–1788*, edited by Roger A. Bruns, 337–40. New York: Chelsea House.

Sarter, Caesar. 1990. "Essay on Slavery." In *Race and Revolution*, edited by Gary B. Nash, 167–70. Madison: Madison House.

Seward, Anna. 1811. *Letters of Anna Seward: Written Between the Years 1784 and 1807*. Vol. 2. Edinburgh: George Ramsay.

Sharp, Granville. 1776. *The Just Limitation of Slavery: In the Laws of God, Compared with the Unbounded Claims of the African Traders and British American Slaveholders*. London: White.

Sidney, Algernon. 1996. *Discourses Concerning Government*. Edited by Thomas G. West. Indianapolis: Liberty Fund.

Smith, Adam. 1976. *The Theory of Moral Sentiments*. Edited by David Daiches Raphael and Alec Lawrence Macfie. Indianapolis: Liberty Fund.

Smith, Adam. 1978. *Lectures on Jurisprudence*. Edited by Ronald L. Meek, David Daiches Raphael, and Peter Stein. Oxford: Clarendon Press.

Smith, Adam. 1986. *The Wealth of Nations*. Edited by Andrew S. Skinner. New York: Penguin Books.

Smith, Charlotte. 1792. *Desmond: A Novel*. Vol. 3. London: Robinson.

Snelgrave, William. 1734. *A New Account of Some Parts of Guinea, and the Slave-Trade*. London: Knapton.

Sonthonax, Léger-Félicité. 1793. *Au nom de la République. Proclamation*. n.p.

Sonthonax, Léger-Félicité. 2014. "Au nom de la République. Proclamation [English translation]." In *The Haitian Revolution: A Documentary History*, translated by David Geggus, 104–9. Indianapolis: Hackett.

Sprengel, Matthias Christian, ed. 1786. *Beiträge zur Völker und Länderkunde: Fünfter Theil*. Leipzig: Weygandsche Buchhandlung.

Stephens, Alexander H. 1866. *Alexander H. Stephens in Public and Private: With Letters and Speeches Before, During, and Since the War*. Edited by Henry Cleveland. Philadelphia: National Publishing Company.

Thompson, Thomas. 1772. *The African Trade for Negro Slaves Shewn to Be Consistent with Principles of Humanity and of Revealed Religion*. Canterbury: Simmons and Kirkby.

Titius, Gottlieb Gerhard. 1709. *Samuelis L.B. de Pufendorf Officio Hominis et Civis Juxta Legem Naturalem Libri Duo. Observationibus Antea Separatim Editis*. Leipzig: n.p.

Tobin, James. 1785. *Cursory Remarks Upon the Reverend Mr. Ramsay's Essay on the Treatment and Conversion of African Slaves in the Sugar Colonies*. London: Wilkie.

Trelawny, Edward. 2018. "An Essay Concerning Slavery (London, 1746)." In *Exploring the Bounds of Liberty: Political Writings of Colonial British America from the Glorius Revolution to the American Revolution*, edited by Jack P. Greene and Craig B. Yirush, 2:1131–64. Indianapolis: Liberty Fund.

Tucker, St. George. 1796. *A Dissertation on Slavery: With a Proposal for the Gradual Abolition of It, in the State of Virginia*. Philadelphia: Carey.

Turnbull, Gordon. 1786. *An Apology for Negro Slavery: Or the West-India Planters Vindicated From the Charge of Inhumanity*. London: Stevenson.

Tyler, Royall. 1802. *The Algerine Captive; Or, the Life and Adventures of Doctor Updike Underhill, Six Years a Prisoner Among the Algerines*. Vol. 1. London: Robinson.

Voltaire. 1968–2022. *The Complete Works of Voltaire*. Edited by Diego Venturino, Nicholas Cronk, N. Elagina, John Renwick, Gérard Laudin, W. H. Barber, Theodore Besterman, Haydn Trevor Mason, and Ulla Kölving. Oxford: Voltaire Foundation.

Voltaire. 1977. *The Portable Voltaire*. Edited by Ben Ray Redman. Harmondsworth: Penguin Books.

Voltaire. 2003. *Candide, or Optimism*. Edited by Gita May and Lauren Walsh. Translated by Henry Morley. New York: Barnes and Noble Classics.

Vultejus, Hermann. 1598. *Institutiones iuris civilis a Iustiniano composita commentarius*. Marburg: Paul Egenolff.

Walker, David. 2011. *Walker's Appeal, in Four Articles: Together with a Preamble, to the Coloured Citizens of the World, but in Particular, and Very Expressly, to Those of the*

United States of America. Chapel Hill: University of North Carolina at Chapel Hill Library.

Wallace, George. 1760. *A System of the Principles of the Law of Scotland*. Vol. 1. Edinburgh: Hamilton and Balfour.

Wesley, John. 1774. *Thoughts Upon Slavery*. London: Hawes.

Wheatley, Phillis. 1966. *The Poems of Phillis Wheatley*. Edited by Julian D. Mason Jr. Chapel Hill: University of North Carolina Press.

Wheatley, Phillis. 2001. *Complete Writings*. Edited by Vincent Carretta. New York: Penguin Books.

Williams, Helen Maria. 1791. *Letters Written in France, in the Summer 1790, to a Friend in England; Containing, Various Anecdotes Relative to the French Revolution*. London: Cadell.

Wollstonecraft, Mary. 1788. "Review of An Essay on the Causes of the Variety of Complexion and Figure in the Human Species . . . By the Rev. Samuel Stanhope Smith." *Analytical Review or History of Literature, Domestic and Foreign* 2 (September–December): 431–39.

Wollstonecraft, Mary. 1789. "Review of The Interesting Narrative of the Life of Olaudah Equiano." *Analytical Review or History of Literature, Domestic and Foreign* 4 (May–August): 27–29.

Wollstonecraft, Mary. 1797. "Review of New Travels into the Interior Parts of Africa . . . Translated from the French of Le Vaillant." *Analytical Review or History of Literature, Domestic and Foreign* 25 (January–June): 464–75.

Wollstonecraft, Mary. 1989. *The Works of Mary Wollstonecraft*. Edited by Janet Todd and Marilyn Butler. Vol. 6. New York: New York University Press.

Wollstonecraft, Mary. 1995. *A Vindication of the Rights of Men and a Vindication of the Rights of Woman and Hints*. Edited by Sylvana Tomaselli. Cambridge: Cambridge University Press.

Woods, Joseph. 1785. *Thoughts on the Slavery of the Negroes*. 2nd ed. London: Phillips.

Woolman, John. 1818. *The Works of John Woolman. In Two Parts*. 5th ed. Philadelphia: Kite.

Woolman, John. 1971. *The Journal and Major Essays of John Woolman*. Edited by Phillips P. Moulton. New York: Oxford University Press.

Secondary Literature

Abanime, Emeka. 1979. "Voltaire antiesclavagiste." *Studies on Voltaire and the Eighteenth Century* 182: 237–51.

Abraham, W. E. 1996. "The Life and Times of Anton Wilhelm Amo, the First African (Black) Philosopher in Europe." In *African Intellectual Heritage: A Book of Sources*, edited by Molefi K. Asante and Abu S. Abarry, 424–40. Philadelphia: Temple University Press.

Acholonu, Catherine Obianuju. 2009. "The Igbo Origins of Olaudah Equiano." In *Olaudah Equiano and the Igbo World: History, Society and Atlantic Diaspora Connections*, edited by Chima J. Korieh, 49–66. Trenton: Africa World Press.

Adiele, Pius Onyemechi. 2017. *The Popes, the Catholic Church and the Transatlantic Enslavement of Black Africans, 1418–1839*. Hildesheim: Olms.

Allais, Lucy. 2016. "Kant's Racism." *Philosophical Papers* 45 (1–2): 1–36.

320 BIBLIOGRAPHY

Amponsah, David Kofi. 2013. "Christian Slavery, Colonialism, and Violence: The Life and Writings of an African Ex-Slave, 1717–1747." *Journal of Africana Religions* 1 (4): 431–57.

Andrews, William. 2001. "Benjamin Banneker's Revision of Thomas Jefferson: Conscience versus Science in the Early American Antislavery Debate." In *Genius in Bondage*, edited by Vincent Carretta and Philip Gould, 218–41. Lexington: University Press of Kentucky.

Anstey, Roger. 1975. *The Atlantic Slave Trade and British Abolition, 1760–1810.* London: Macmillan.

Aravamudan, Srinivas, ed. 1999. *Slavery, Abolition and Emancipation: Writings in the British Romantic Period.* Vol. 6: *Fiction.* London: Pickering & Chatto.

Benot, Yves. 2005. *Les lumières, l'esclavage, la colonisation.* Paris: La Découverte.

Bergès, Sandrine. 2022. *Olympe de Gouges.* Cambridge: Cambridge University Press.

Bernasconi, Robert. 2001. "Who Invented the Concept of Race? Kant's Role in the Enlightenment Construction of Race." In *Race*, edited by Robert Bernasconi, 11–36. Malden: Blackwell.

Bernasconi, Robert. 2002. "Kant as an Unfamiliar Source of Racism." In *Philosophers on Race: Critical Essays*, edited by Julie K. Ward and Tommy L. Lott, 145–66. Oxford: Blackwell.

Bernasconi, Robert. 2011. "Kant's Third Thoughts on Race." In *Reading Kant's Geography*, edited by Stuart Elden and Eduardo Mendieta, 291–318. Albany: State University of New York Press.

Bernasconi, Robert. 2019. "Ottobah Cugoano's Place in the History of Political Philosophy: Slavery and the Philosophical Canon." In *Debating African Philosophy: Perspectives on Identity, Decolonial Ethics and Comparative Philosophy*, edited by George Hull, 25–42. London: Routledge.

Biondi, Carminella. 2015. "L'apport antiesclavagiste de Pechméja et de Diderot à l'*Histoire des deux Indes*." *Outre-Mers* 386–387 (1): 49–64.

Blakely, Allison. 1993. *Blacks in the Dutch World: The Evolution of Racial Imagery in a Modern Society.* Bloomington: Indiana University Press.

Bogin, Ruth. 1983. "'Liberty Further Extended': A 1776 Antislavery Manuscript by Lemuel Haynes." *William and Mary Quarterly* 40 (1): 85–105.

Bogues, Anthony. 2003. *Black Heretics, Black Prophets: Radical Political Intellectuals.* New York: Routledge.

Bok, Hilary. 2018. "Baron de Montesquieu, Charles-Louis de Secondat." In *Stanford Encyclopedia of Philosophy*, edited by Edward N. Zalta, Winter 2018. https://plato.stanford.edu/archives/win2018/entries/montesquieu/.

Boulle, Pierre H. 2007. *Race et esclavage dans la France de l'Ancien régime.* Paris: Perrin.

Boxill, Bernard. 2017. "Kantian Racism and Kantian Teleology." In *The Oxford Handbook of Philosophy and Race*, edited by Naomi Zack, 44–53. Oxford: Oxford University Press.

Brown, Gregory S. 2001. "The Self-Fashionings of Olympe de Gouges, 1784–1789." *Eighteenth-Century Studies* 34 (3): 383–401.

Cairns, John W. 2013. "Maintaining Slavery without a Code Noir: Scotland, 1700–78." In *Lawyers, the Law and History: Irish Legal History Society Discourses and Other Papers, 2005–2011*, edited by Felix M. Larkin and N. M. Dawson, 148–78. Dublin: Four Courts Press.

Cameron, Christopher. 2014. *To Plead Our Own Cause: African Americans in Massachusetts and the Making of the Antislavery Movement.* Kent: Kent State University Press.

Campbell, Mavis. 1974. "Aristotle and Black Slavery: A Study in Race Prejudice." *Race* 15 (3): 283–301.

Carey, Brycchan. 2012. *From Peace to Freedom: Quaker Rhetoric and the Birth of American Antislavery, 1657–1761*. New Haven: Yale University Press.

Carey, Daniel. 1998. "Reconsidering Rousseau: Sociability, Moral Sense and the American Indian from Hutcheson to Bartram." *Journal for Eighteenth-Century Studies* 21 (1): 25–38.

Carretta, Vincent. 1999. "Olaudah Equiano or Gustavus Vassa? New Light on an Eighteenth-Century Question of Identity." *Slavery & Abolition* 20 (3): 96–105.

Carretta, Vincent. 2001. "Introduction." In *Complete Writings*, by Phillis Wheatley, xiii–xxxvii. New York: Penguin Books.

Carretta, Vincent. 2003. "Introduction." In *The Interesting Narrative and Other Writings*, by Olaudah Equiano, ix–xxx. New York: Penguin Books.

Carretta, Vincent. 2005. *Equiano, the African: Biography of a Self-Made Man*. Athens: University of Georgia Press.

Carretta, Vincent. 2016. "Olaudah Equiano and the Forging of an Igbo Identity." In *Igbo in the Atlantic World*, edited by Toyin Falola and Raphael Chijioke Njoku, 188–98. Indianapolis: Indiana University Press.

Clark, Henry C. 2016. "Introduction." In *Encyclopedic Liberty: Political Articles in the Dictionary of Diderot and D'Alembert*, edited by Henry C. Clark, xvii–xxiv. Indianapolis: Liberty Fund.

Coates, Ta-Nehisi. 2012a. "The Myth of Jefferson as 'a Man of His Times.'" *The Atlantic*, 2012. https://www.theatlantic.com/national/archive/2012/12/the-myth-of-jefferson-as-a-man-of-his-times/265816/.

Coates, Ta-Nehisi. 2012b. "Thomas Jefferson Was More Than a Man of His Times." *The Atlantic*, 2012. https://www.theatlantic.com/national/archive/2012/12/thomas-jefferson-was-more-than-a-man-of-his-times/265850/.

Cole, John R. 2011. *Between the Queen and the Cabby: Olympe de Gouges's Rights of Woman*. Montreal: McGill-Queen's University Press.

Countryman, Edward. 2012. *Enjoy the Same Liberty: Black Americans and the Revolutionary Era*. Lanham: Rowman & Littlefield.

Crosby, David L., ed. 2013. *The Complete Antislavery Writings of Anthony Benezet, 1754–1783: An Annotated Critical Edition*. Baton Rouge: Louisiana State University Press.

Curran, Andrew S. 2011. *The Anatomy of Blackness: Science & Slavery in an Age of Enlightenment*. Baltimore: Johns Hopkins University Press.

Dahl, Adam. 2020. "Creolizing Natural Liberty: Transnational Obligation in the Thought of Ottobah Cugoano." *Journal of Politics* 82 (3): 908–20.

Davis, David Brion. 1966. *The Problem of Slavery in Western Culture*. New York: Oxford University Press.

Davis, David Brion. 1971. "New Sidelights on Early Antislavery Radicalism." *William and Mary Quarterly* 28 (4): 585–94.

Davis, David Brion. 1999. *The Problem of Slavery in the Age of Revolution, 1770–1823*. New York: Oxford University Press.

Dillon, Elizabeth Maddock. 2004. "'Slaves in Algiers': Race, Republican Genealogies, and the Global Stage." *American Literary History* 16 (3): 407–36.

Doris, Glen. 2011a. "An Abolitionist Too Late? James Beattie and the Scottish Enlightenment's Lost Chance to Influence the Slave Trade Debate." *Journal of Scottish Thought* 2 (1): 83–97.

Doris, Glen. 2011b. "The Scottish Enlightenment and the Politics of Abolition." PhD dissertation, University of Aberdeen.

Dorsey, Dale. 2021. "Francis Hutcheson." In *The Stanford Encyclopedia of Philosophy*, edited by Edward N. Zalta, Summer 2021. https://plato.stanford.edu/archives/sum2021/entries/hutcheson/.

Drescher, Seymour. 1986. *Capitalism and Antislavery: British Mobilization in Comparative Perspective*. London: Macmillan.

Drescher, Seymour. 2009. *Abolition: A History of Slavery and Antislavery*. Cambridge: Cambridge University Press.

Du Bois, W. E. B. 2007. *The Suppression of the African Slave Trade to the United States of America, 1638–1870*. Oxford: Oxford University Press.

Duchet, Michèle. 1971. *Anthropologie et histoire au siècle des lumières: Buffon, Voltaire, Rousseau, Helvétius, Diderot*. Paris: F. Maspero.

Eberl, Oliver. 2019. "Kant on Race and Barbarism: Towards a More Complex View on Racism and Anti-colonialism in Kant." *Kantian Review* 24 (3): 385–413.

Ehrard, Jean. 2008. *Lumières et esclavage: L'esclavage colonial et l'opinion publique en France au XVIIIe siècle*. Brussels: Versaille éditeur.

Emmer, Pieter C., and Jos J. L. Gommans. 2020. *The Dutch Overseas Empire, 1600–1800*. Cambridge: Cambridge University Press.

Estève, Laurent. 2002. "La théorie des climats ou l'encodage d'une servitude naturelle." In *Déraison, esclavage et droit: Les fondements idéologiques et juridiques de la traite négrière et de l'esclavage*, edited by Isabel de Castro Henriques and Louis Sala-Molins, 59–68. Paris: UNESCO.

Eze, Emmanuel. 1997. "The Color of Reason: The Idea of 'Race' in Kant's Anthropology." In *Postcolonial African Philosophy: A Critical Reader*, edited by Emmanuel Chukwudi Eze, 103–40. Cambridge: Blackwell.

Ferguson, Moira. 1992a. "Mary Wollstonecraft and the Problematic of Slavery." *Feminist Review* 42 (1): 82–102.

Ferguson, Moira. 1992b. *Subject to Others: British Women Writers and Colonial Slavery, 1670–1834*. New York: Routledge.

Fields, Karen E., and Barbara Jeanne Fields. 2012. *Racecraft: The Soul of Inequality in American Life*. London: Verso.

Figal, Sara Eigen, and Mark J. Larrimore, eds. 2006. *The German Invention of Race*. Albany: State University of New York Press.

Fredrickson, George M. 2015. *Racism: A Short History*. Revised ed. Princeton: Princeton University Press.

Galison, Peter. 2019. "21 July 1773: Disputation, Poetry, Slavery." *Critical Inquiry* 45 (2): 351–79.

Garrett, Aaron. 2000. "Hume's Revised Racism Revisited." *Hume Studies* 26 (1): 171–77.

Garrett, Aaron. 2006. "Human Nature." In *The Cambridge History of Eighteenth-Century Philosophy*, edited by Knud Haakonssen, 1:160–233. Cambridge: Cambridge University Press.

Garrett, Aaron. 2023. "Phillis Wheatley and the Limits of the History of Philosophy." In *The Routledge Handbook of Women and Early Modern European Philosophy*, edited by Karen Detlefsen and Lisa Shapiro, 558–70. New York: Routledge.

Gates, Henry Louis, Jr. 1987. *Figures in Black: Words, Signs, and the "Racial" Self*. New York: Oxford University Press.

Gates, Henry Louis, Jr. 1988. *The Signifying Monkey: A Theory of Afro-American Literary Criticism*. New York: Oxford University Press.

Glover, Jeffrey. 2017. "Witnessing African War: Slavery, the Laws of War, and Anglo-American Abolitionism." *William and Mary Quarterly* 74 (3): 503–32.

Goldenberg, David M. 2005. *The Curse of Ham: Race and Slavery in Early Judaism, Christianity, and Islam*. Princeton: Princeton University Press.

Goldenberg, David M. 2017. *Black and Slave: The Origins and History of the Curse of Ham*. Berlin: de Gruyter.

Gregg, Samuel. 2009. "Metaphysics and Modernity: Natural Law and Natural Rights in Gershom Carmichael and Francis Hutcheson." *Journal of Scottish Philosophy* 7 (1): 87–102.

Gunn, Jeffrey. 2010. "Creating a Paradox: Quobna Ottobah Cugoano and the Slave Trade's Violation of the Principles of Christianity, Reason, and Property Ownership." *Journal of World History* 21 (4): 629–56.

Haakonssen, Knud. 1994. "Introduction." In *Political Essays*, by David Hume, xi–xxx. Cambridge: Cambridge University Press.

Haakonssen, Knud. 1996. *Natural Law and Moral Philosophy: From Grotius to the Scottish Enlightenment*. Cambridge: Cambridge University Press.

Hanley, Ryan. 2018. *Beyond Slavery and Abolition: Black British Writing, c. 1770–1830*. Cambridge: Cambridge University Press.

Harfouch, John. 2018. *Another Mind-Body Problem: The History of Racial Non-being*. Albany: State University of New York Press.

Harris, James A. 2015. *Hume: An Intellectual Biography*. New York: Cambridge University Press.

Harvey, David Allen. 2012. *The French Enlightenment and Its Others: The Mandarin, the Savage, and the Invention of the Human Sciences*. New York: Palgrave Macmillan.

Haynes, Stephen R. 2002. *Noah's Curse: The Biblical Justification of American Slavery*. Oxford: Oxford University Press.

Hedrick, Todd. 2008. "Race, Difference, and Anthropology in Kant's Cosmopolitanism." *Journal of the History of Philosophy* 46 (2): 245–68.

Hermans, Theo. 2009. *A Literary History of the Low Countries*. Rochester: Camden House.

Horn, Christoph. 2014. *Nichtideale Normativität: Ein neuer Blick auf Kants politische Philosophie*. Berlin: Suhrkamp.

Howard, Carol. 2004. "Wollstonecraft's Thoughts on Slavery and Corruption." *Eighteenth Century* 45 (1): 61–86.

Hudson, Nicholas. 2001. "'Britons Never Will Be Slaves': National Myth, Conservatism, and the Beginnings of British Antislavery." *Eighteenth-Century Studies* 34 (4): 559–76.

Hunting, Claudine. 1978. "The Philosophes and Black Slavery: 1748–1765." *Journal of the History of Ideas* 39 (3): 405–18.

Immerwahr, John. 1992. "Hume's Revised Racism." *Journal of the History of Ideas* 53 (3): 481–86.

Israel, Jonathan I. 2011. *Democratic Enlightenment: Philosophy, Revolution, and Human Rights 1750–1790*. New York: Oxford University Press.

Jeffers, Chike. 2017. "Rights, Race, and the Beginnings of Modern Africana Philosophy." In *The Routledge Companion to Philosophy of Race*, edited by Paul C. Taylor, Linda Martín Alcoff, and Luvell Anderson, 127–39. New York: Routledge.

Jorati, Julia. 2019. "Leibniz on Slavery and the Ownership of Human Beings." *Journal of Modern Philosophy* 1 (10): 1–18.

Jorati, Julia. Forthcoming. *Slavery and Race: Philosophical Debates in the Sixteenth and Seventeenth Centuries*. New York: Oxford University Press.

Jordan, Winthrop D. 1968. *White over Black: American Attitudes towards the Negro, 1550–1812*. 2nd ed. Chapel Hill: University of North Carolina Press.

Juengel, Scott. 2001. "Countenancing History: Mary Wollstonecraft, Samuel Stanhope Smith, and Enlightenment Racial Science." *ELH* 68 (4): 897–927.

Kaufmann, Matthias. 2019. "Wie Gleich sind Personen—und Menschen? Kant über Geschlechter, Rassen und Kolonisierung." *Jahrbuch für Recht und Ethik* 27: 183–204.

Kendi, Ibram X. 2016. *Stamped from the Beginning: The Definitive History of Racist Ideas in America*. New York: Bold Type Books.

Kirkland, Frank M. 2017. "Kant on Race and Transition." In *The Routledge Companion to Philosophy of Race*, edited by Paul C. Taylor, Linda Martín Alcoff, and Luvell Anderson, 28–42. New York: Routledge.

Klausen, Jimmy Casas. 2014. *Fugitive Rousseau: Slavery, Primitivism, and Political Freedom*. New York: Fordham University Press.

Kleingeld, Pauline. 2007. "Kant's Second Thoughts on Race." *Philosophical Quarterly* 57 (229): 573–92.

Kleingeld, Pauline. 2012. *Kant and Cosmopolitanism: The Philosophical Ideal of World Citizenship*. Cambridge: Cambridge University Press.

Kleingeld, Pauline. 2014. "Kant's Second Thoughts on Colonialism." In *Kant and Colonialism: Historical and Critical Perspectives*, edited by Katrin Flikschuh and Lea Ypi, 43–67. Oxford: Oxford University Press.

Kleingeld, Pauline. 2020. "How to Use Someone 'Merely as a Means.'" *Kantian Review* 25 (3): 389–414.

Kolchin, Peter. 2003. *American Slavery, 1619–1877*. New York: Hill and Wang.

Kpobi, David N. A. 2002. "Free to Be a Slave: Capitein's Theology of Convenient Slavery." In *Merchants, Missionaries, and Migrants: 300 Years of Dutch-Ghanaian Relations*, edited by Ineke van Kessel, 81–87. Amsterdam: KIT Publishers.

Kuitenbrouwer, Maarten. 1995. "The Dutch Case of Antislavery: Late and Élitist Abolitionism." In *Fifty Years Later: Antislavery, Capitalism and Modernity in the Dutch Orbit*, edited by Gert Oostindie, 67–88. Leiden: KITLV Press.

Kurki, Visa A. J. 2019. *A Theory of Legal Personhood*. Oxford: Oxford University Press.

Larrimore, Mark. 1999. "Sublime Waste: Kant on the Destiny of the 'Races.'" *Canadian Journal of Philosophy Supplementary Volume* 25: 99–125.

Larrimore, Mark. 2008. "Antinomies of Race: Diversity and Destiny in Kant." *Patterns of Prejudice* 42 (5): 341–63.

Le Hir, Marie-Pierre. 1994. "Feminism, Theater, Race: *L'esclavage des noirs*." In *Translating Slavery: Gender and Race in French Women's Writing, 1783–1823*, edited by Doris Y. Kadish and Françoise Massardier-Kenney, 65–83. Kent: Kent State University Press.

Levecq, Christine. 2008. *Slavery and Sentiment: The Politics of Feeling in Black Atlantic Antislavery Writing, 1770–1850*. Durham: University of New Hampshire Press.

Levecq, Christine. 2013. "Jacobus Capitein: Dutch Calvinist and Black Cosmopolitan." *Research in African Literatures* 44 (4): 145–66.

Levecq, Christine. 2019. *Black Cosmopolitans: Race, Religion, and Republicanism in an Age of Revolution*. Charlottesville: University of Virginia Press.

Lewis, Dwight Kenneth, Jr. 2019. "Anton Wilhelm Amo's Philosophy and Reception: From the Origins through the *Encyclopédie*." PhD dissertation, University of South Florida.

Lovejoy, Paul E. 2016. "Olaudah Equiano or Gustavus Vassa: What's in a Name?" In *Igbo in the Atlantic World*, edited by Toyin Falola and Raphael Chijioke Njoku, 199–217. Indianapolis: Indiana University Press.

Lu-Adler, Huaping. 2022a. "Kant and Slavery—Or Why He Never Became a Racial Egalitarian." *Critical Philosophy of Race* 10 (2): 263–94.

Lu-Adler, Huaping. 2022b. "Kant on Lazy Savagery, Racialized." *Journal of History of Philosophy* 60 (2): 253–75.

Lu-Adler, Huaping. 2023. *Kant, Race, and Racism: Views from Somewhere*. Oxford: Oxford University Press.

MacLam, Helen. 1990. "Black Puritan on the Northern Frontier: The Vermont Ministry of Lemuel Haynes." In *Black Preacher to White America: The Collected Writings of Lemuel Haynes, 1774–1833*, edited by Richard Newman, xix–xxxviii. Brooklyn: Carlson Publishing.

McClish, Glen. 2007. "A Man of Feeling, a Man of Colour: James Forten and the Rise of African American Deliberative Rhetoric." *Rhetorica: A Journal of the History of Rhetoric* 25 (3): 297–328.

Menn, Stephen, and Justin E. H. Smith. 2020. "Introduction." In *Philosophical Dissertations on Mind and Body*, by Anton Wilhelm Amo, 1–147. Oxford: Oxford University Press.

Mensch, Jennifer. 2013. *Kant's Organicism: Epigenesis and the Development of Critical Philosophy*. Chicago: University of Chicago Press.

Miller, Christopher L. 2008. *The French Atlantic Triangle: Literature and Culture of the Slave Trade*. Durham: Duke University Press.

Mills, Charles W. 1997. *The Racial Contract*. Ithaca: Cornell University Press.

Mills, Charles W. 1998. *Blackness Visible: Essays on Philosophy and Race*. Ithaca: Cornell University Press.

Mills, Charles W. 2005. "Kant's Untermenschen." In *Race and Racism in Modern Philosophy*, edited by Andrew Valls, 169–93. Ithaca: Cornell University Press.

Mills, Charles W. 2006. "Modernity, Persons, and Subpersons." In *Race and the Foundations of Knowledge: Cultural Amnesia in the Academy*, edited by Joseph Young and Jana Evans Braziel, 211–51. Urbana: University of Illinois Press.

Mills, Charles W. 2007a. "Reply to Critics." In *Contract and Domination*, edited by Carole Pateman and Charles W. Mills, 230–66. Cambridge: Polity.

Mills, Charles W. 2007b. "The Domination Contract." In *Contract and Domination*, edited by Carole Pateman and Charles W. Mills, 79–105. Cambridge: Polity.

Mills, Charles W. 2014. "Kant and Race, Redux." *Graduate Faculty Philosophy Journal* 35 (1/2): 125–57.

Mills, Charles W. 2021. "Locke on Slavery." In *The Lockean Mind*, edited by Jessica Gordon-Roth and Shelley Weinberg, 487–97. London: Routledge.

Minkema, Kenneth P. 2002. "Jonathan Edwards's Defense of Slavery." *Massachusetts Historical Review* 4: 23–59.

Monoson, S. Sara. 2011. "Recollecting Aristotle: Pro-slavery Thought in Antebellum America and the Argument of *Politics* Book I." In *Ancient Slavery and Abolition: From Hobbes to Hollywood*, edited by Richard Alston, Edith Hall, and Justine McConnell, 247–77. Oxford: Oxford University Press.

Montgomery, Benilde. 1994. "White Captives, African Slaves: A Drama of Abolition." *Eighteenth-Century Studies* 27 (4): 615–30.

Moore, James, and Michael Silverthorne, eds. 2002. *Natural Rights on the Threshold of the Scottish Enlightenment: The Writings of Gershom Carmichael*. Indianapolis: Liberty Fund.

Moran, Kate A. 2021. "Kant on Traveling Blacksmiths and Passive Citizenship." *Kant-Studien* 112 (1): 105–26.

Mori, Naohito. 2021. "Civility and Slavery: The Problematic Basis of Civilized Society in Hume's History of England." In *The Scottish Enlightenment: Human Nature, Social Theory and Moral Philosophy: Essays in Honour of Christopher J. Berry*, edited by R. J. W. Mills and Craig Smith, 173–98. Edinburgh: Edinburgh University Press.

Mullen, Stephen. 2022. "Centring Transatlantic Slavery in Scottish Historiography." *History Compass* 20 (1): 1–14.

Murphy, Mark. 2019. "The Natural Law Tradition in Ethics." In *Stanford Encyclopedia of Philosophy*, edited by Edward N. Zalta, Summer 2019. https://plato.stanford.edu/archives/sum2019/entries/natural-law-ethics/.

Muthu, Sankar. 2003. *Enlightenment against Empire*. Princeton: Princeton University Press.

Nash, Gary B., ed. 1990. *Race and Revolution*. Madison: Madison House.

Newman, Richard. 1990. "The Paradox of Lemuel Haynes." In *Black Preacher to White America: The Collected Writings of Lemuel Haynes, 1774–1833*, edited by Richard Newman, xi–xvii. Brooklyn: Carlson Publishing.

Oldfield, John R. 2013. *Transatlantic Abolitionism in the Age of Revolution: An International History of Anti-slavery, c. 1787–1820*. Cambridge: Cambridge University Press.

Orrù, Elisa. 2020. "Olympe de Gouges on Slavery." *Diacronìa* 2 (2): 95–121.

Parker, Grant Richard. 2001. "An Introduction to the Life and Work of Capitein." In *The Agony of Asar: A Thesis on Slavery by the Former Slave, Jacobus Elisa Johannes Capitein, 1717–1747*, by Jacobus Elisa Johannes Capitein, 3–78. Princeton: Markus Wiener.

Pascoe, Jordan. 2022. *Kant's Theory of Labour*. Cambridge: Cambridge University Press.

Peabody, Sue. 1996. *"There Are No Slaves in France": The Political Culture of Race and Slavery in the Ancien Régime*. New York: Oxford University Press.

Peters, Tacuma. 2017. "The Anti-imperialism of Ottobah Cugoano: Slavery, Abolition, and Colonialism in Thoughts and Sentiments on the Evil of Slavery." *CLR James Journal* 23 (1–2): 61–82.

Pluchon, Pierre. 1984. *Nègres et juifs au XVIIIe siècle: Le racisme au siècle des lumières*. Paris: Tallandier.

Popkin, Richard H. 1992. *The Third Force in Seventeenth-Century Thought*. Leiden: Brill.

Prah, Kwesi Kwaa. 1992. *Jacobus Eliza Johannes Capitein, 1717–1747: A Critical Study of an Eighteenth Century African*. Trenton: Africa World Press.

Raphael-Hernandez, Heike, and Pia Wiegmink. 2017. "German Entanglements in Transatlantic Slavery: An Introduction." *Atlantic Studies* 14 (4): 419–35.

Rickman, Moi. 2005. "'Tied to Their Species by the Strongest of All Relations': Mary Wollstonecraft and the Rewriting of Race as Sensibility." In *British Women's Writing in the Long Eighteenth Century: Authorship, Politics and History*, edited by Jennie Batchelor and Cora Kaplan, 140–57. London: Palgrave Macmillan.

Roberts, Rodney. 2020. "American Indian Inferiority in Hume's Second Enquiry." *Journal of Scottish Philosophy* 18 (1): 57–66.

Rosenthal, Bernard. 1973. "Puritan Conscience and New England Slavery." *New England Quarterly* 46 (1): 62–81.

Saillant, John. 2003. *Black Puritan, Black Republican: The Life and Thought of Lemuel Haynes, 1753–1833*. Oxford: Oxford University Press.

Sala-Molins, Louis. 2006. *Dark Side of the Light: Slavery and the French Enlightenment*. Minneapolis: University of Minnesota Press.

Sandford, Stella. 2018. "Kant, Race, and Natural History." *Philosophy & Social Criticism* 44 (9): 950–77.

Schaub, Diana J. 2005. "Montesquieu on Slavery." *Perspectives on Political Science* 34 (2): 70–78.

Schönecker, Dieter. 2021. "Verlieren Verbrecher ihre Würde? Zur Analyse einer brisanten Stelle in Kants Rechtslehre (RL 329–30)." *Journal of the History of Philosophy* 59 (4): 607–28.

Sebastiani, Silvia. 2013. *The Scottish Enlightenment: Race, Gender, and the Limits of Progress*. New York: Palgrave Macmillan.

Seeber, Edward Derbyshire. 1937. *Anti-slavery Opinion in France during the Second Half of the Eighteenth Century*. Baltimore: Johns Hopkins Press.

Sens, Angelie. 1995. "Dutch Antislavery Attitudes in a Decline-Ridden Society, 1750–1815." In *Fifty Years Later: Antislavery, Capitalism and Modernity in the Dutch Orbit*, edited by Gert Oostindie, 89–104. Leiden: KITLV Press.

Smedley, Audrey. 1993. *Race in North America: Origin and Evolution of a Worldview*. Boulder: Westview Press.

Smith, Justin E. H. 2015. *Nature, Human Nature, and Human Difference: Race in Early Modern Philosophy*. Princeton: Princeton University Press.

Smith, Mary-Antoinette. 2010. "Introduction." In *Thomas Clarkson and Ottobah Cugoano: Essays on the Slavery and Commerce of the Human Species*, edited by Mary-Antoinette Smith, 9–47. Peterborough: Broadview Press.

Stannard, David E. 1992. *American Holocaust: Columbus and the Conquest of the New World*. New York: Oxford University Press.

Sypher, Wylie. 1939. "Hutcheson and the 'Classical' Theory of Slavery." *Journal of Negro History* 24 (3): 263–80.

Terjanian, Anoush Fraser. 2013. *Commerce and Its Discontents in Eighteenth-Century French Political Thought*. Cambridge: Cambridge University Press.

Tessman, Lisa. 2005. *Burdened Virtues: Virtue Ethics for Liberatory Struggles*. New York: Oxford University Press.

Thomas, Hugh. 1997. *The Slave Trade: The Story of the Atlantic Slave Trade, 1440–1870*. New York: Simon & Schuster.

Thomson, Ann. 2017. "Colonialism, Race and Slavery in Raynal's Histoire des deux Indes." *Global Intellectual History* 2 (3): 251–67.

Tomaselli, Sylvana. 2021. *Wollstonecraft: Philosophy, Passion, and Politics*. Princeton: Princeton University Press.

Ukaegbu, Dorothy C. 2009. "Status in Eighteenth-Century Igboland: Perspectives from Olaudah Equiano's Interesting Narrative." In *Olaudah Equiano and the Igbo World: History, Society and Atlantic Diaspora Connections*, edited by Chima J. Korieh, 94–116. Trenton: Africa World Press.

Valdez, Inés. 2017. "It's Not about Race: Good Wars, Bad Wars, and the Origins of Kant's Anti-colonialism." *American Political Science Review* 111 (4): 819.

Valls, Andrew. 2005. "'A Lousy Empirical Scientist': Reconsidering Hume's Racism." In *Race and Racism in Modern Philosophy*, edited by Andrew Valls, 127–49. Ithaca: Cornell University Press.

Vanpée, Janie. 2014. "Reconfiguring Family Legitimacy: Olympe de Gouge's *L'Esclavage des Noirs*." *Women in French Studies* 2014 (1): 106–16.

Varden, Helga. 2008. "Kant's Non-voluntarist Conception of Political Obligations: Why Justice Is Impossible in the State of Nature." *Kantian Review* 13 (2): 1–45.

Varden, Helga. 2017. "Kant and Women." *Pacific Philosophical Quarterly* 98 (4): 653–94.

Watkins, Margaret. 2013. "A Cruel but Ancient Subjugation? Understanding Hume's Attack on Slavery." *Hume Studies* 39 (1): 103–21.

Watkins, Margaret. 2017. "'Slaves among Us': The Climate and Character of Eighteenth-Century Philosophical Discussions of Slavery." *Philosophy Compass* 12 (1): 1–11.

Wheeler, Roxann. 2001. "'Betrayed by Some of My Own Complexion': Cugoano, Abolition, and the Contemporary Language of Racialism." In *Genius in Bondage*, edited by Vincent Carretta and Philip Gould, 17–38. Lexington: University Press of Kentucky.

Wheelock, Stefan M. 2016. *Barbaric Culture and Black Critique: Black Antislavery Writers, Religion, and the Slaveholding Atlantic*. Charlottesville: University of Virginia Press.

Whitford, David M. 2009. *The Curse of Ham in the Early Modern Era: The Bible and the Justifications for Slavery*. London: Routledge.

Whyte, Iain. 2006. *Scotland and the Abolition of Black Slavery, 1756–1838*. Edinburgh: Edinburgh University Press.

Wiencek, Henry. 2012. *Master of the Mountain: Thomas Jefferson and His Slaves*. New York: Farrar, Straus and Giroux.

Willis, Andre C. 2018. "Hume's Legacy Regarding Race." In *The Humean Mind*, edited by Angela M. Coventry and Alex Sager, 497–510. New York: Routledge.

Wolpe, Hans. 1957. *Raynal et sa machine de guerre: L'Histoire des deux Indes et ses perfectionnements*. Stanford: Stanford University Press.

Yost, Benjamin S. 2010. "Kant's Justification of the Death Penalty Reconsidered." *Kantian Review* 15 (2): 1–27.

Zack, Naomi. 2002. *Philosophy of Science and Race*. New York: Routledge.

Index

For the benefit of digital users, indexed terms that span two pages (e.g., 52–53) may, on occasion, appear on only one of those pages.

Printed in Great Britain
by Amazon

63104368R00199